Henryk Grossman

and the Recovery of Marxism

Henryk Grossman and the Recovery of Marxism

RICK KUHN

UNIVERSITY OF ILLINOIS PRESS

Urbana and Chicago

Frontispiece: Portrait of Henryk Grossman from Henryk Großmann, VdN-Akte 13630, Bezirksrat Leipzig 20237, Sächsisches Staatsarchiv Leipzig; reproduction by Sächsisches Staatsarchiv Leipzig.

Library of Congress Cataloging-in-Publication Data
Kuhn, Rick, 1955–
Henryk Grossman and the recovery of Marxism / Rick Kuhn.
p.   cm.
Includes bibliographical references and index.
ISBN-13: 978-0-252-03107-6 (cloth : alk. paper)
ISBN-10: 0-252-03107-5 (cloth : alk. paper)
ISBN-13: 978-0-252-07352-6 (pbk. : alk. paper)
ISBN-10: 0-252-07352-5 (pbk. : alk. paper)
1. Grossman, Henryk, 1881–1950.   2. Economists—Germany—Biography.
3. Socialists—Germany—Biography.   4. Economists—Poland—Biography.
5. Socialists—Poland—Biography.   6. Marxian economics—History—20th
century.   I. Title.
HB107.G76K85   2007
335.4092—dc22[B]   2006019429

Contents

Preface

While conducting the research for Henryk Grossman's biography, I often gave people three reasons for the project. The first was that it involved a search for my own roots. I meant this metaphorically. This book investigates the history of the labor movement, Marxist theory, and working-class struggles for socialism. These are institutions, ideas, and actions that I regard as part of my heritage as a socialist.

There was also a more concrete sense in which the research examined my own background. As kids my parents, Gerda and Kurt Kuhn, fled Nazi-controlled territory with their parents in 1938 and 1939, because they were Jewish. My own politics have been shaped by an early identification with oppressed Jews, like most of those in this story.

My parents came to Australia from Vienna: their background was central rather than eastern European Jewry. But, using skills developed in the Grossman research, I discovered that my mother's mother, Klara Pisko, née Margulies, was a Polish Jew. This was news to my mum too. Klara was born in Podhajce in 1904, several years before the family moved to Vienna. In fact, much of central European Jewry during the early twentieth century had eastern European roots. Podhajce was a small Jewish town in eastern Galicia. It's now in the Ukraine and known as Pidhaitsi. While Klara was a little girl there, workers in the town set up a branch of the Jewish Social Democratic Party of Galicia, the organization Henryk Grossman led.

My second reason for poking into Henryk Grossman's life was more mercenary. Most of my research until I began the project, around 1993, had been focused on Australia: Australian politics, the history of the Australian labor movement, and Australian political economy. This provided very little justification for overseas travel.

I started to learn German, which I had heard my parents speak with my grandparents when I was a child, again in 1989. Three years of German in high school, under the tuition of an old bloke with a smoker's cough, who had no apparent vocation for teaching and seemed to be a relic of the Holy Roman Empire, hadn't got me far. The quality of German instruction at the Australian National University was vastly superior. No doubt my own motivation was also a factor. In 1991, my partner, Mary Gorman, our three-year-old daughter, Alyx, and I spent most of my first period of academic study leave from the Australian National University in Germany.

For two months we lived in an apartment on Straußberger Platz. When it was a construction site, the building we lived in, or one of its seven-story neighbors for kilometers along both sides of Frankfurter Allee, had been the detonation point of the 1953 workers' uprising in east Berlin. Mary and I studied at the Goethe Institut, in west Berlin.

We did manage to get Alyx admitted to a kindergarten near home. The accessible system of free childcare, which was one of Stalinist east Germany's few positive features, had not yet been dismantled. But, hardly surprising, no one at the *Kita* spoke any English. Although I spent a couple of days there with her, Alyx was not happy. So Mary would study German during the morning session at the Institut. I would look after Alyx and then take her across Berlin to Mary and stay to participate in the afternoon session. At this time, the direct subway link between east and west Berlin, destroyed at the end of the war, had not yet been restored. So the trip across town was an adventure in itself. Especially the task of schlepping Alyx in a stroller up and down the stairs between the subway and the mainly elevated railway.

We gave up on the Goethe Institut before the end of the course. But the tuition there was excellent and, reinforced by the need to cope with everyday life and political activity in the small Sozialistische Arbeiter Gruppe (Socialist Workers Group), led to a rapid improvement in my German.

After my sabbatical, I did some teaching and writing on German politics.

But Henryk Grossman provided me with an excuse for further, extensive overseas travel. He had written his best-known works in German and I was now equipped to tackle them and related literature. German was also a stepping stone to learning Yiddish, which was vital to understanding Grossman's early political engagement.

In pursuit of Henryk, I visited archives and libraries from Berkeley to Kraków, from Tellow (in Mecklenberg-Vorpommern) to New York and from Warsaw to Sydney. Thanks to Rakesh Bhandari, I discovered that the most important source for what Grossman was like as a person was the Christina Stead Collection, in the National Library of Australia in my hometown, Canberra.

Grossman's theory of economic crisis was the third reason for looking at him in detail. Anwar Shaikh's brief but excellent survey of the history of Marxist crisis theory provided a sympathetic account of Grossman's position. It indicated that he was the first person to insist that the tendency of the rate of profit to fall lay at the heart of Marx's understanding of capitalism's inability to maintain growth without periods of sharp economic contraction.[1] I was persuaded.

An abridged translation of Grossman's book on crisis theory was published in 1992. Some of his work had originally appeared in English. But most of his writings had not been translated and information about Grossman himself was very thin on the ground. Henryk and his ideas warranted further investigation.

This book examines Grossman's experiences, his ideas, and the connections between them. In places, especially parts of chapter 5, the discussion of his economic theory is quite technical. The truncated but signposted account of basic Marxist economics in earlier chapters should make that discussion easier to grasp. The technical passages can, however, be skipped without losing track of Grossman's story or the evidence for my argument that his work remains important.

My research soon convinced me, and I hope to persuade you, that the standard criticism of Grossman's theory of economic crises—that it predicted the "automatic" collapse of capitalism—was wrong. Under the influence of the international class struggles during the period of the Russian revolution, he had restored fundamental elements of Marx's economic theory and developed them. That was a major contribution to the recovery of Marxism as the theory and practice of working-class self-emancipation.

Acknowledgments

The kindness, encouragement, assistance, tolerance, and help in various forms provided by many people and several institutions made the research embodied in this book possible.

Gerda Kuhn and Tom O'Lincoln read through and made valuable suggestions about drafts of the entire book. Rakesh Bandhari and Sam Pietsch gave me important pointers and advice. I also benefited from the aid, among others, of Irena Bal, Jairus Banaji, Gideon Freudenthal, Aleksandra Witczak Haugstad, Jürgen Hensel, Makoto Itoh, Jack Jacobs, Mario Keßler, Bob Kuhn, Wolfgang Maderthaner, Christoph Matschie, Peter McLaughlin, the late Walentyna Najdus, Bertell Ollman, Antony Polonsky, Alejandro Ramos, John Rosenthal, Hazel Rowley, Jürgen Scheele, Peter Schöttler, Michał Sliwa, Stefan Toth, Feliks Tych, and Paul Zarembka.

Chimen Abramsky, William Ash, Tadeusz Kowalik, Karl Heinz Lange, Ilse Mattick, Eva Müller, Gerhard Müller, and Halina Woyke knew Henryk Grossman or others in this story and generously shared their memories with me.

For permission to use materials or for particular assistance in their use I am grateful to Michael Maaser and the Archiv der Johann-Wolfgang-Goethe-Universität Frankfurt am Main; the Archiwum Akt Nowych, Warsaw; Jadwiga Szyposz and the Archiwum Panstwowe, Kraków; Alicja Kulecka, Hanna Krajewska and the late Julian Bugejski and the Archiwum Polskiej Akademii Nauk, Warsaw; the Bundesarchiv Stiftungarchiv, Berlin; Ron Geering, Margaret Harris, and the Christina Stead Collection of the National Library of Australia, Canberra; the Friedrich-Ebert-Stiftung, Bonn; Rolf Bartz and the Johann-Heinrich von Thünen-Museum, Tellow; the late Bono Wiener and the Kadimah Jewish Cultural Centre and National Library, Melbourne; Peter-Erwin Jansen, Susanne

Löwenthal, and the Leo-Löwenthal-Archiv, Frankfurt am Main; Gunzelin Schmid Noerr, Jochen Stollberg, and the Max-Horkheimer-Archiv, Frankfurt am Main; Mrs. H. Weiss and the Metrikelamt, Israelitsche Kultusgemeinde, Vienna; the Sächsisches Staatsarchiv, Leipzig; the Universitätsarchiv Leipzig; Leo Greenbaum and the YIVO Archive, New York.

I benefited from translations of important sources by Eugene Bajkowski, Dominika Balwin, Shirad Galmor, Magda Iwasiw, Floris Kalman, Zbiszek Polak, Vlasta Vlaicevic, and Halina Zobel.

The Deutsche Akademische Austauschdienst and the Faculty of Arts, Australian National University provided financial support for the research, while an ANU subsidy in February 2005 contributed to the publication of this book at a more affordable price.

Discussions and activity with other Marxists since the mid-1970s, in recent years with comrades in Socialist Alternative, shaped the understanding of the world and the project of working-class self-emancipation that underpins my account of Henryk Grossman's life.

My parents, Gerda and Kurt Kuhn, my partner Mary Gorman, and our daughter Alyx Kuhn Gorman, not only tolerated my relationship with Henryk Grossman for well over a decade, but also gave the emotional, intellectual, and practical support without which my efforts would have been impossible.

Abbreviations

APAN	"Henryk Grossman," III-155, Archiwum Polskiej Akademii Nauk, Warsaw
APK	Archiwum Panstwowe w Krakowie, Kraków
Archiv	(Grünbergs) *Archiv für die Geschichte des Sozialismus und der Arbeiterbewegung*
Arplan	Arbeitsgemeinschaft zum Studium sowjet-russischer Planwirtschaft, Working Group for the Study of the Soviet Russian Planned Economy
AUJ	Archiwum Uniwersytetu Jagiellonskiego, Kraków
Beer Collection	Nachlaß Max Beer Box 1, Archiv der sozialen Demokratie der Friedrich-Ebert-Stiftung
Braeuer Collection	Braeuer Nachlaß, Johann-Heinrich von Thünen Museum, Tellow
Bund	Algemeyner Yidisher Arbeter Bund in Lite, Poyln un Rusland, General Jewish Workers Union of Lithuania, Poland, and Russia
Bund Archive	Bund Archive, Yidisher visnshaftlikher institut/Institute for Jewish Research Archive, New York
Comintern	Communist International
DDR	Deutsche Democratische Republik, German Democratic Republic
ECCI	Executive Committee of the Communist International
FBI	Federal Bureau of Investigation
FBI file	Henryk Grossman file, Federal Bureau of Investigations, Washington
General Party	Sozialdemokratische Arbeiterpartei Österreichs, General Social Democratic Workers' Party of Austria

GPSD — Galicyjska Partia Socjaldemokratyczna, Social Democratic Party of Galicia

GUS — "Akta osobowe Henryka Grossmana," Glowny Urzad Statystyczny, Centralna Biblioteka Statystyczna, Warsaw

HUAC — U.S. House of Representatives Committee on Un-American Activities

IfS — Institut für Sozialforschung, Institute for Social Research

IISG — Mattick Collection, Internationaal Instituut voor Sociale Geschiedenis, Amsterdam

JSDP — Jewish Social Democratic Party of Galicia

JüSDP — Jüdische sozial-demokratische Partei in Galizien, Jewish Social Democratic Party of Galicia

KPD — Kommunistische Partei Deutschlands, German Communist Party

KPRP — Kommunistyczna Partia Robotnicza Polski, Communist Workers Party of Poland

LLA — Leo-Löwenthal-Archiv Universitäts- und Stadtarchiv Frankfurt am Main

MHA — Max-Horkheimer-Archiv, Universitäts- und Stadtarchiv Frankfurt am Main

MHGS — Max Horkheimer's *Gesammelte Schiften*

ÖSK — Österreichisches Staatsarchiv, Kriegsarchiv

POUM — Partido Obrero de Unificación Marxista, Workers' Party of Marxist Unification

PPS — Polska Partia Socjalistyczna, Polish Socialist Party

PPS (Left) — Polska Partia Socjalistyczna (Lewica), Polish Socialist Party (Left)

PPSD — Polska Partia Socjalno-Demokratyczna Galicji i Śląska, Polish Social Democratic Party of Galicia and Silesia

PU — Uniwersytet ludowy, People's University

PZ — Poale Zion, Zionist Labor Party

RSDLP — Rossiyskaya Sotsial'demokraticheskaya Rabottskaya Partiya, Russian Social Democratic Labor Party

RSG — Rote Studentengruppe, Red Student Group

Schreiner Collection — Albert Schreiner Nachlaß, NY 4198/70, p. 124, Stiftung Archiv der Parteien und Massenorganisationen der DDR, Bundesarchiv Berlin

SDKPiL — Socjaldemokracja Królestwa Polskiego i Litwy, Social Democracy of the Kingdom of Poland and Lithuania

SED — Sozialistische Einheitspartei Deutschlands, Socialist Unity Party of Germany

SFIO   Section Française de l'Internationale Ouvrière, French Section of the Workers' International

SPD   Sozialdemokratische Partei Deutschlands, German Social Democratic Party

Sprawa Grossmana   Sprawa Grossmana, 305/V/11 podt. 3, Zespol akt PPS, Archiwum Akt Nowych

SPSL   Society for the Protection of Science and Learning/Academic Assistance Council Files, Department of Western Manuscripts, Bodleian Library

SSAL   VdN-Akte von Henryk Großmann 13630, Bezirksrat Leipzig 20237, Sächsisches Staatsarchiv Leipzig

Stead Collection   Christina Stead Collection MS4967, National Library of Australia

Taubenschlag Collection   Rafał Taubenschlag, III-98 j. 80, Archiwum Polskiei Akademii Nauk, Warsaw

UAL   "Henryk Grossmann," PA 40, Universitätsarchiv Leipzig

UFM   "Grossmann, Heinrich," Akten der WiSo Fakultät," Sig 452 Abt 150 Nr 376, Archiv der Johann Wolfgang Goethe Universität, Frankfurt am Main

USSR   Union of the Soviet Socialist Republics

USDP   Ukrains'ka Sotsial-Demokratychna Partiya, Ukrainian Social Democratic Party

WWP   Wolna Wrzechnica Polska, Free University of Poland

ZfS   Zeitschrift für Sozialforschung

ŻPS   *Żydowska Partia Socjalistyczna,* Jewish Socialist Party (Jewish Social Democratic Party of Galicia)

ŻPSD   *Żydowska Partia Socjalno-Demokratyzna,* Jewish Social Democratic Party of Galicia

Henryk Grossman
and the Recovery of Marxism

1

Growing Up in Galicia

Herz Grossman and Sara Kurz moved up and out of Tarnów, a modest-sized Galician town, to the city of Kraków. Sara's brothers and other members of the Kurz clan also left Tarnów for Kraków and Vienna in the 1870s.

Sara lived with Herz. His commercial activities were very successful. In Tarnów, he had pursued the traditional Jewish occupation of running a bar. In Kraków, he became a businessman—more specifically, a small industrialist and a mine owner.[1] Sara and Herz were Jewish, but increasingly assimilated to the Polish high culture of Galician government, big business, and art.

Constitutional reform in 1867 had given a large degree of control over the Austro-Hungarian Empire's Polish province, Galicia, to a thoroughly undemocratic Sejm (parliament). The administration of the province, based in Lwów (Lemberg in Yiddish, L'viv in Ukrainian) was exercised by the thin layer of fabulously wealthy landed magnates, at the top of the *szlachta*, the numerous Polish nobility. The government of Galicia sustained the oppression of Jews, as well as the Ukrainian peasants who made up a majority of the population in the east of the province. Jews and Ukrainians, the Yiddish and Ukrainian languages were discriminated against in the interests of the *szlachta*.[2]

Kraków was the cultural capital of partitioned Poland. Its prestigious university, theaters, performances of classical music, the Academy of Fine Arts, and the Academy of Sciences made the city a focal point for modern Polish national culture, intellectual innovations, and artistic movements. No doubt of particular interest to Herz and Sara when they moved, the city was also the administrative center and commercial hub of western Galicia, which was far more economically developed than the east of the province.

Herz and Sara had five children in Kraków. Taube, named for one of Sara's sisters, was born in 1876, when Herz was thirty-four and Sara twenty-two. Then came Jakob in 1877. He died after three years. Rebeka was born in 1879.[3] Chaskel, named after his grandfather, was born on April 14, 1881. But, a sign of the growing influence of Polish culture on his parents, young Chaskel was known, like his father, as Henryk Grossman, just as his mother was Salome rather than Sara.[4] In 1884 Bernard was not given a Yiddish name at all. At home the family spoke Polish and, possibly, French.[5] But the assimilation had limits. Young Henryk and Bernard were both circumcised and, by 1900, were registered members of the Jewish community.[6]

The prosperity of the Grossman family buffered it from the consequences of social prejudices, political currents, and laws that discriminated against Jews. The Grossmans' home was a symbol of their social situation. They lived in a substantial building at Ulica Starowislna 27, in a well-to-do area between the Kazimierz, the Jewish quarter, and the ancient inner city.[7] In one respect, however, Herz/Henryk and Sara/Salome had a thoroughly unconventional relationship. Perhaps because Henryk senior was someone else's husband when he and Sara started living together, they were only married in 1887, three years after the birth of their last child.[8]

Young Chaskel/Henryk did not have a traditional Jewish education. From the age of eleven he attended the Święty Jacka Gimnazjum (St. James academic high school) where the language of instruction was Polish. For eight years Henryk traveled three kilometers to the school, which lay on the other side of the inner city from home. A privileged social background was normally essential to enter a *gimnazjum*, which was the only route to university. But, unlike the only older secondary school in Kraków, set up for young aristocrats, St. James was a bourgeois institution, open to talent (so long as it was backed by cash). Nine of the forty-six other boys in Henryk's class were also Jewish.

The school provided a liberal education with a strong emphasis on languages. Young Grossman's overall academic performance was above average, but not outstanding. In French, however, which he studied in his third to sixth years, his work was consistently excellent. Chaskel also did well in his (Jewish) religion classes.[9] On June 15, 1896, at the age of fifty-four, his father died.[10] This clearly affected the fifteen-year-old. His only unsatisfactory grade at school was in mathematics during the following semester, the sole semester for which Henryk's overall result was second- rather than first-class. But his academic performance soon recovered and, on June 12, 1900, he graduated from the *gimnazjum*.

After the death of Henryk senior, the Grossman family's financial situation changed, but its circumstances were still very comfortable. In 1897, Salome and her children moved to Ulica Święty Sebastiana 36, another impressive building a couple blocks away, just inside the Kazimierz. Salome transferred her assets from business into real estate—she owned the apartment block in which they lived—and could also fall back on the prosperous Kurz clan.[11] Her relatives became an even more important part of Henryk's life after his father's death. Salome's younger cousin, Markus Binem Kurz, a businessman, lived around the corner. There was regular contact too with her older brother, Israel, in Vienna. His son Oskar had been born there four years after Henryk. The boys became lifelong friends.[12]

Henryk had great confidence in his own abilities. This was not only a consequence of his well-off and supportive family and academic achievements. He was good looking—1.64 meters (5 feet, 5 inches) tall, with regular features, curly blond hair, and blue eyes[13] and he had absorbed the sense of self-worth and personal honor, typical of the *szlachta* and emulated by members of other Galician elites. In 1944, his friend Christina Stead wrote: "Grossman is going to take me to the movies again of course, Saturday. He is *very grudgingly* going on Alf's ticket to the theatre: but how he hates it! What? He? A Pole? On another man's ticket! Only a long tradition of unmitigated gallantry permits him to do it."[14]

He enjoyed the theater, the masterpieces of Polish literature, art exhibitions, and especially classical music. During the 1890s, Polish artists and intellectuals discovered the rugged mountains, south of Kraków. Henryk shared their fashionable, slightly bohemian enthusiasm for skiing, mountain air, and rambling in the Tatras.[15] Yet he was not simply a Pole. The Jewish workers, artisans, petty traders, and small businesspeople, crowded nearby in the run-down and impoverished tenements of the Kazimierz, were familiar to him from an early age. The bigotry of Polish society meant that, as a Jew, he shared something with them, even if he did not grow up speaking Yiddish.

While at St. James, Henryk had engaged in a program of self-education well beyond the curriculum. His very wide reading included "thousands" of cheap Reclam editions in German of classic literature.[16] Involvement in the socialist movement also started while Henryk was still at school.[17] Christina Stead noted

How he became a socialist. At 15. It was May First. He was living in his father's house, a wealthy town house. Troops were in the courtyard and in the courtyards of other houses near and concealed elsewhere in the street. Every one jittery; servant girl quite pale and chambermaid upset—what will happen to us, what will they do. By they meant workers. Down street was meeting hall (socialist) for workers and great Polish socialist (apparently later not so reliable) was to address them. Cordon of police drawn across street etc. He looked out window, saw workmen arriving. He eventually went to hall, (I crawled between their legs, "I so small, they so tall") (whose legs? probably soldiers and in meeting hall) and saw about 500 workmen unarmed, and this man addressing them. He heard the arguments of socialism and was impressed and moved; what harm were they doing and soldiers going against them. After that he read "brochures" and became socialist. He was angry indignant this very day because he saw the fear and injustice of his own people, they even got in supplies [of] water and candles and rumor was that socialists (workmen) were going to cut off gas, water and food on May First. When he had seen them he could not believe but was indignant. He said to them at home "Of what are you afraid?"[18]

This interest in the socialist movement and its challenge to the established order emerged around the time that the crucial and intimate enforcer of social constraints on him, his father, died. After Henryk's first encounter with socialists, "he rapidly mastered all the Marxist literature." Nor was the young Grossman's new commitment purely intellectual. He also became involved with other radical secondary students—working late into the night on socialist politics, helping with the production of a socialist magazine,[19] probably the Lwów-based student monthly, *Promień* (The Ray), which appeared from 1899. It campaigned against the servility promoted by the Galician school and university systems, exposed malpractices by bureaucrats and teachers, and published articles on a very wide range of subjects. Through the magazine, Grossman developed contacts beyond Kraków. By the end of the decade, he had taken on leaders of the Galician social democratic movement in theoretical terms at a socialist conference in the Lwów opera house.[20]

The socialist movement Henryk Grossman joined was a recent development. Galicia's working class was small and inexperienced. The province was one of the least industrialized territories of the Austro-Hungarian Empire.[21] In 1900, when the population was 7,316,000, three-quarters of the workforce was still engaged in largely semi-feudal agriculture.[22] But socialist groups had managed to form a party in Galicia a decade earlier, in the wake of the establishment of the Social Democratic Workers' Party of Austria, mainly by German-Austrian and Czech socialists, and unprecedented May Day demonstrations in the Polish province. The Galician Workers' Party, renamed the Social Democratic Party of Galicia (GPSD) at its first Congress in 1892, involved Polish, Ukrainian, and Jewish workers.[23]

Although the party was formally Marxist, left-wing Polish nationalists who favored the GPSD's reconstitution as a Polish organization came to dominate it. Among them were not only the preeminent Ignacy Daszyński, a Pole, but also a layer of assimilated Jews, including Herman Diamand, Emil Haecker, and Max Zetterbaum. These men played vital roles in the party's organizational, publishing, and parliamentary activity.[24]

The theoretical level of Galician social democracy was never high. Later, "Ignacy Daszyński, our famous member of parliament, a pioneer of socialism, an orator . . . admitted that he too found *Das Kapital* too hard a nut. 'I have not read it,' he almost boasted, 'but Karl Kautsky has read it and has written a popular summary of it. I have not read Kautsky either; but Kelles-Krauz, our party theorist, has read him and he summarized Kautsky's book. I have not read Kelles-Krauz either, but that clever Jew, Herman Diamand, our financial expert, has read Kelles-Krauz, and has told me all about it.'"[25]

In the course of the 1890s, the Galician socialists were able to build the first small workers' education and mutual assistance associations into the beginnings of a trade union movement in the larger cities. They set up similar organizations in new towns, supported workers' struggles, and established a party press. Affiliated workers' associations and unions were the party's basic units: a portion of their members' subscriptions went to fund its activities.

One of the GPSD's most important breakthroughs was the victory two of its candidates achieved in the 1897 elections to the Austrian parliament, the Reichsrat. The Austrian government had just generously bestowed on men without any property qualifications—the vast majority of the male population—the right to elect a small minority of the parliament.

Daszyński won a seat in Kraków. Jewish workers made up a significant component of his majority.[26] Neither the father of Austrian social democracy, Victor Adler, nor any other prominent German-Austrian leader was successful in the elections, and there were equal numbers of German and Czech social democratic representatives in the Reichsrat. Extremely competent, particularly as a public speaker, and having the advantage of being neither a German nor a Czech, Daszyński now became a significant figure in the General Austrian Social Democratic Workers Party—not only in the Galician organization, but as the leader of the whole social democratic fraction.[27]

Daszyński had, however, already had international exposure at congresses of the Second International, that is, of the international socialist movement. From their initial appearance at the Second Congress in 1891, the Galician social democrats were part of a Polish contingent, alongside representatives from parties in the other territories of occupied Poland, rather than the Austrian delegation.

Particularly after Friedrich Engels died in 1895, the dominant orthodoxy of the International tended to focus on organization—personified in the deeds of social democratic parliamentarians, trade union officials, and party leaders—as an end in itself, rather than on class struggle as a means of transforming mass consciousness and society. This became apparent in the work of the most prominent theorist in the German Social Democratic Party (Sozialdemokratische

Partei Deutschlands, or SPD) and the International, Karl Kautsky. He eventually regarded revolution and socialism as less the result of creative acts of self-liberation by the working class than the products of inexorable historical processes.[28]

This orthodox Marxism of the International obscured crucial elements of Marx's critique of capitalism. The fetishism of commodities, the way capitalism conceals its own fundamental mechanisms, had been central to both his economic analysis and revolutionary politics. Marx had insisted that capitalism could not maintain workers' living standards because it was inherently crisis prone and he had concluded that it would be necessary to smash rather than simply take over the institutions of the capitalist state.[29] The International and many of its affiliates played down these aspects of Marxism, but their verbal radicalism allowed them to conceal their practical accommodation to the status quo and the national priorities of the states in which they operated.

The relationships between the Polish and German-Austrian social democratic leaders paralleled those between the Polish ruling class and the imperial Austrian state. From the early 1890s, there was an alliance between the dominant currents in German-Austrian and Galician/Polish social democracy, personified by the ties between their most prominent figures, Victor Adler and Daszyński.

In the course of the decade, the internal structure of Austrian social democracy became increasingly federal. At its Vienna Congress in 1897, the party transformed itself into a federation, sometimes known as the "little International," of the German(-Austrian), Czech, Polish, Italian, and South-Slav parties.[30] The change was an attempt to deal with national tensions in Austria and the socialist movement itself by making concessions to nationalism within the party, rather than by systematically opposing all forms of national oppression.[31]

The alliance between the German-Austrian and Galician sections now became even more important. In return for its positive attitude to Polish independence and financial support, which kept the GPSD's most important newspaper *Naprzód* (Forward) afloat,[32] the German-Austrian party gained the assistance of the Poles in determining the policy of the federal General Party. This reduced the influence, in particular, of the Czech organization, after the German-Austrian section the largest in Austrian social democracy.

In 1899, the predominantly nationalist leaders of Galician social democracy were able to achieve a long-awaited change, already foreshadowed in 1897. The establishment of the new, small, and weak Ukrainian Social Democratic Party (USDP) allowed them to transform their organization into an explicitly national party: the *Polish* Social Democratic Party (PPSD). The General Party's Brünn Congress, in September 1899, admitted the USDP as a component party just a week after its formation.[33]

At the same Congress, the General Party adopted a nationality program. Having made concessions to nationalism in its own internal structure, the party now demanded that the empire be transformed into a federation of (not necessarily contiguous) territories made up of members of particular nationalities. The resolution did not deal specifically with the pressing and contentious issue of language rights at all. It simply stated that the rights of minorities would be protected in the national, self-administered territories that made up the future federation.[34]

Austrian social democracy did little to disarm the appeal of nationalism to workers by clearly opposing the national oppression experienced by many of them at the hands of the German ruling class in the Austrian Empire as a whole or the Polish ruling class in Galicia. No current within the Austrian movement differentiated between the nationalism of oppressor and oppressed groups.

A Student Revolutionary

Henryk Grossman went straight from school to study in the law and philosophy faculties of Kraków's ancient Jagiellonian University. He must have relished the greater freedom of a university student's life. There was less supervision of political activity and much more time for nonacademic pursuits than at school.

In his classes, Grossman met students from all over partitioned Poland, including the Congress Kingdom of Poland, under Russian rule, and the Polish districts of the German Kingdom of Prussia. The Austrian Empire was less repressive, or less efficient in its police state methods, than the German and Russian empires and the only universities where Polish was the language of instruction were in Kraków and Lwów.

While most of his subjects were legal ones, he took other courses that brought him into contact with influential intellectual currents in Poland and Europe. One of Grossman's political economy professors was Włodzimierz Czerkawski (1866–1913), the leading Polish exponent of the Austrian school of Karl Menger and Eugen Böhm-Bawerk—a variant of what, in English-speaking universities, is now called neoclassical economics or simply economics.[35] Stefan Pawlicki, a Catholic priest, taught Henryk philosophy. The young Jewish socialist enjoyed Father Pawlicki's courses; he took six of them.

Grossman attended Michał Bobrzyński's class on "Public administration and Austrian administrative law."[36] Bobrzyński was a prominent figure in the Kraków school of Polish historiography. Hostile to the institutions of the prepartition Polish state, the school's perspectives provided a rationale for Austrian rule over Galicia. This was particularly the case for Bobrzyński, who combined his chair in legal history with long-term membership of the Galician Sejm and was appointed governor of the province in 1908.

His studies, especially in law, immersed Grossman in some of the most important and systematic justifications for the existing social order. Already the product of key bourgeois institutions, a privileged family, and an elite school, he rounded out his training as a traditional intellectual, prepared to provide ideological support for the established order, in the Law Faculty of the Jagiellonian University.[37] Although far from an infallible recipe for conservatism, the conventional content of courses and the hidden curriculum of deference to professorial authority were reinforced by the exclusive nature of the university, with its small enrollment and generally wealthy students. The prospect of comfortable careers also helped persuade most of the few whose parents were poor to embrace the status quo. Henryk had absorbed some ruling-class tastes and even personality traits. Once he came of age at twenty-one, however, he did not, to his mother's disappointment, take on major responsibilities in the family's business enterprises.[38] *For him, capitalism was not a means to personal well-being but a system based on the exploitation of workers that oppressed, among others, Ukrainians and Jews.*

While he took university courses, Grossman should have been in classes an average of about twenty hours a week.[39] But, given his other activities, it seems unlikely that he turned up at every lecture and seminar. From the late 1890s, parallel to his preparation to be a traditional intellectual, Henryk went through experiences that shaped him as an "organic intellectual of the working class," who identified with and articulated workers' interests.[40] This began at school, with involvement in the Galician socialist movement.

Comrade Grossman was not, however, an orthodox member of the PPSD. An early indication was the dash under "Nationality" on the enrollment form for his second semester of university studies.[41] He had initially described himself as being Jewish by religion and Polish by nationality. The previous generation of university-educated, Jewish socialists in Galicia, like Herman Diamand, regarded themselves as "Poles of the Mosaic faith." But for many Jewish socialists of Henryk's generation, the emergence of political anti-Semitism in the 1890s made the odds that Polish nationalism, socialism, and Jewish rights could be reconciled seem slim.

When Grossman was first a university student, his primary political attachment was to Ruch (Movement), the main organization of radical and socialist university students in Kraków. Ruch was, however, a common vehicle for students associated with several socialist currents—not only the PPSD but also two sizable socialist parties active in the Kingdom of Poland. Both had been set up in 1893. One was the Social Democracy of the Kingdom of Poland and

Lithuania (SDKPiL), led by Rosa Luxemburg and Leo Jogiches; the other, the Polish Socialist Party (PPS), whose most prominent figure was Józef Piłsudski.[42] Grossman identified with the Marxist SDKPiL rather than the nationalist PPS.

At university, he continued to support rebellious school students. During the 1901 summer break and under the auspices of Ruch, Grossman co-convened a Galician-wide conference of graduating secondary school students in Kraków, backed by *Promień*. His collaborator in the project was Zygmunt Żuławski, a third-year university student and member of the Ruch Executive. The right-wing press went crazy over the 1,500 invitations they issued. But the gathering was a success: two hundred students attended. At the conference, Henryk not only gave a talk on "What the senior secondary school gives us" but also on "Anti-Semitism."[43]

Outside the Russian Empire, the Jewish population of Galicia (812,000 in 1900) was the largest in the world. Jews were particularly concentrated in the more backward, eastern part of the province, a majority living in small Jewish villages (*shtetlekh*, singular *shtetl*).[44] During the late nineteenth century, capitalist penetration of the Galician countryside changed and then undermined traditional Jewish social roles as intermediaries between the peasants, the Polish landowning aristocracy, and urban markets.[45] Old positions in the administration of feudal estates, as licensees of the nobility's privileges (notably the sale of alcohol) and, above all, in commerce were progressively undermined.

Improved means of communications, the expanded scale of market-oriented production, modern credit arrangements, larger commercial concerns reliant on waged rather than family labor, and the foundation of state-supported cooperatives squeezed many Jews out of the countryside and traditional jobs. The emergence of modern, political anti-Semitism in Poland during the 1890s, with boycotts of Jewish businesses, accelerated the process.[46] In 1898, anti-Semitic agitation by Father Stanisław Stojałowski, the leader of a populist peasant movement, provoked widespread rural pogroms in western Galicia.[47]

Austrian law defined Jews as a religious group.[48] After 1867 they were equal to non-Jews as far as the legal system was concerned. Almost. If you had money, life as an assimilated Jew could be very comfortable. But if, like the vast majority of Jews in Galicia, you were poor and your first language was Yiddish, you were at a disadvantage even compared to poor Poles. Yiddish was not recognized as a language in the education system or by other public authorities. Contracts written in Yiddish were not legally enforceable; the courts did not accept testimony in Yiddish.[49] Jews also suffered from entrenched, if unofficial, discrimination. They were dramatically underrepresented in appointments to the public service, judiciary, and universities.[50]

When it came to the question of oppression, Ruch was not only concerned with the treatment of Jews. Again with Zygmunt Żuławski, Grossman petitioned the rector of the Jagiellonian University for permission to hold a general meeting of students on the demands of Ukrainian students for a Ukrainian university in Lwów.

Colleague Grossman opened the large meeting in the ancient Collegium Novum on November 27. It did not immediately consider the issue of a Ukrainian university in Lwów. In a clever maneuver by the socialists who had convened the gathering or a lucky spontaneous move from the floor, an urgent issue took priority. The meeting heard a lengthy report on the persecution of Polish-speaking children and their parents in Prussia's Polish territories. The authorities were punishing them for campaigning against the conduct of education entirely in German. The motion condemning this was carried by acclamation.

A very favorable climate was thus established for the discussion of the Ukrainian students' fight against repression in Galicia. The meeting overwhelmingly carried a motion supporting the Ukrainian demand and expressing hope for unity in the struggles of the Ukrainian and Polish people.[51]

His fellow student radicals trusted comrade Grossman. In November 1902, Władysław Gumplowicz was elected president of Ruch with Henryk Grossman as vice-president. A year later these positions were taken over by Rudolf Moszoro, a member of the SDKPiL, and Karol Sobelson, who later as Karl Radek became an important figure in that party and then the Russian Communist Party, while Grossman was elected secretary. When, in 1904, there was a controversy about Radek's personal behavior—another member of the organization, Antoni Zembaty, alleged that Radek, then the group's secretary and organizer, had stolen some books from him—Ruch resolved the issue through formal arbitration.[52] Moszoro and Grossman conducted an inquiry and the arbitration court, of which they were members, unanimously exonerated Radek, without implying criticism of Zembaty, who accepted the decision.[53]

The membership of Ruch was never large. In 1900 there were 36 members, growing rapidly to 68 in 1902 and peaking at 110 in 1903. Numbers dropped to 57 in 1904, although the group's final meeting in October was attended by 80 people, including Grossman.[54] Ruch was very active among workers as well as students. Zygmunt Żuławski was heavily involved in helping Polish workers to build trade unions; Henryk Grossman concentrated on organizing Yiddish-speaking workers.[55] His activities also included contributing material to *Promień*. He became the publication's Kraków distribution agent and headed its branch editorial office.[56]

Ruch organized lectures and debates. Between October 1903 and February 1904, the topics of eight lectures ranged from the general strike, through "art and life," to the law of the conservation of energy.[57] A lecture in late 1904 was given by Bronisław Grosser. He was a student from Warsaw and an excellent speaker. Grosser's address dealt with his party, the General Jewish Workers Union of Lithuania, Poland, and Russia (known as the Bund)—then easily the largest Marxist organization in the Russian Empire. He attracted the attention of the left in Kraków. Participants in the subsequent discussion included Emil Haecker, the chief editor of the PPSD's *Naprzód;* Maksymilian Horwitz of the PPS, later a leader of the PPS (Left) and a founder of the Polish Communist Workers Party; SDKPiL member Feliks Dzierżyński, who from the end of January 1903 guided the organization in Congress Poland from Kraków and later became a senior member of the Russian Communist Party; and Grossman.[58]

Grosser also brought the latest news of the revival of political activity in Russia, prompted by the deeply unpopular Russo-Japanese War. The conflict had begun in February 1904 and the Tsar's forces suffered a string of military and naval disasters. Many political refugees, fleeing persecution and conscription, slipped across the border into Galicia. There they gained political and material support from local socialists. Students, among others, held meetings on the situation in Russia. At one general student assembly, in June, Grossman cosponsored a motion condemning the Russian state and those Poles in the Congress Kingdom who supported it.[59]

The traffic between Russia and Austria-Hungary was not all one-way: opponents of Tsarism sent literature or infiltrated into Russia through Galicia to agitate against the war and the regime. Members of Ruch, including Radek and Grossman, played an important role in smuggling SDKPiL material into the Kingdom of Poland. In February 1904, Grossman also joined the Kraków branch of the Fund for the Assistance of Political Prisoners and Exiles, an organization of SDKPiL members and sympathizers.[60] His house was a hub for the flow of information into and out of Russia and was on the route of political refugees fleeing the autocracy.[61]

As struggles in the Congress Kingdom heated up, there was a surge in the energy and activity of the Galician left and the level of social conflict rose across Austria-Hungary. This was not only a matter of solidarity actions, but also the growth of class conflicts and workers' organizations. As Grossman had completed the coursework requirements of his degree by the summer of 1904, he was now available for full-time political activity. The polarization taking place within the left, on both sides of the Russian frontier, provided one of the main contexts for this work.

For the dominant current in the PPS and its Galician allies in the PPSD, Polish independence was the fundamental priority: the political crisis in Russia opened up new opportunities for the Polish nation. This perspective had organizational implications. It was necessary, in particular, to strengthen relations among the nationalist sections of the Polish socialist movement on the territory of the three partitioning powers. Already in 1902, Daszyński had justified the decision by the Prussian PPS to split from the SPD in the interests of the struggle for national self-determination. In doing so he had enthused about the spiritual unity of the national community.[62]

On the other hand, the SDKPiL, Bund, left-wing sections of the PPS, and groups that had split from it, together with the left of the PPSD, not to mention the Russian social democrats, saw new possibilities for bringing down the Tsarist autocracy. They stressed the importance of united working-class struggle across national lines. Many of the activists in Ruch became increasingly hostile to the PPSD leadership.

The depth of divisions in the PPSD was apparent at the Ninth Party Congress, from October 30 to November 1, 1904. Conflicts already broke out during the discussion of standing orders. Later, Żuławski, concerned about the party's neglect of the trade unions, moved a vote of no confidence in the Executive for its "absolute lack of interest and disregard for workers' affairs." According to a police report, "if it had not been for the terrorism of the presidium, Żuławski's motion would have been adopted."[63] Daszyński and his allies also fended off a challenge over their attitude to Jewish workers. Grossman took part in that debate. With greater success, he also moved a resolution calling on local party committees to promote the organization of young workers.[64]

The main controversy at the Congress was over a proposal that the PPSD formalize the intimate relationship between the leadership around Daszyński and the PPS in Prussia and the Kingdom of Poland, by entering into a fraternal alliance (*sojusz bratni*) with them. The arrangement was designed, in particular, to preclude cooperation with other socialist parties in the Kingdom of Poland.[65]

The District Committee in Stanisławów, in eastern Galicia, offered an alternative resolution, moved by Anzelm Mosler, a Jewish lawyer and extremely talented socialist organizer, with a mass following among Ukrainian agricultural workers. It rejected the idea of an exclusive relationship with the PPS and called on "the Executive Committee to propagate social democratic literature without reference to the organization which published it." As the PPS was not a social democratic, that is, Marxist, party the motion implied a preference for its rivals.[66]

Żuławski also spoke against the official resolution. But Daszyński's proposal for a formal alliance with the PPS was carried by a vote of 52 to 26.[67]

Promień, the main organ of socialist students in Poland, was under the influence of the PPS. A bunch of its adherents, whose sympathies lay with the SDKPiL, Bund, and Proletariat (a small socialist group) in the Kingdom of

Poland, split from *Promień* to establish a new journal.[68] With his background of running *Promień*'s activities in Kraków, it was logical that Grossman should become the responsible editor and publisher of *Zjednoczenie* (Unification).

On January 2, 1905, the main Russian naval base in the Far East, Port Arthur, surrendered to the Japanese. Revolution broke out in St. Petersburg and a series of other industrial cities, after the massacre of peaceful demonstrators on "Bloody Sunday," January 22, 1905. The working class was the decisive force in the campaign for social change, crucially in crescendos of mutually reinforcing strikes over economic and political demands, but also in demonstrations and protests. The movement spread across the Russian Empire and was particularly strong in Congress Poland. The organizers of *Zjednoczenie* found a confirmation of their revolutionary working-class politics in events over the border.

There were some parallels in Galicia, where economic recovery had already led to increasing levels of strike action by workers. The membership of social democratic unions more than doubled between the end of 1900 and the end of 1904.[69] The veteran leaders of the PPS, however, now regarded class conflict as a diversion from the fight to liberate Poland. They and the PPSD leadership rejected cooperation with Marxists—Polish or Russian—in the struggle against the Tsarist state.

The first, forty-page issue of *Zjednoczenie* appeared in mid February 1905. Its editorial promised that the journal would pursue a more open-minded approach than *Promień*, which boycotted material from parties other than the PPS. The statement mentioned another question that was consuming a great deal of Grossman's time: the rights of nations other than the Poles: "So we won't just tolerate Ruthenians [Ukrainians] or deny Jews the right to self-determination. People who regard themselves as a nation are a nation. This is the only rational argument."[70]

In order to clarify political differences, the journal began a series of articles on "The socialist and opposition movements under the Tsar"; the first dealt with the Russian Social Democratic Labor Party (RSDLP). It quoted at length from a 1903 essay by RSDLP leader Vladimir Ilych Lenin on the national question, including his negative assessment of the PPS.[71]

The first issue also carried an article on the Russian revolution from the Committee for Support of the Revolution on the Territory of the Russian State, immediately followed by a three-line call from the editors for donations, which could be sent to the "relevant Committee" through the *Zjednoczenie* office.[72]

Having recently formalized its own relationship with the PPS, the PPSD leadership was less than impressed by the split from *Promień*, particularly when it was led by a PPSD member. Even before the first issue of *Zjednoczenie* had appeared, with its sustained criticisms of the PPS and side-swipes at leaders of the PPSD and Austrian General Party, *Naprzód* launched an attack on the new journal and initiated the "Grossman affair."

In a short announcement, the PPSD's newspaper cautioned readers against people raising funds "for *Zjednoczenie,* which will be founded by a comedian and political swindler who has attacked our party for years with vile slanders," under the pretext of collecting for the party. That was on Friday, February 2. There was a further brief warning in the Sunday issue. It noted that *Zjednoczenie* was designed to combat *Promień,* which had good relations with the party.[73]

Henryk Grossman approached the editor of *Naprzód,* Emil Haecker, to clear up the situation and ask that a correction be published. The allegations of fraud were simply a fabrication. Haecker was not persuaded and threatened Grossman, Janek Bross (known in Yiddish as Jakob Bros), and Maksymilian Rose (another Jewish university student close to Grossman) with expulsion from the party. Far from being intimidated by this party heavyweight and confident about his own position and rights, Grossman wrote to the PPSD Executive Committee on the 15th asking it to take action on the unwarranted attacks.[74] But further assaults on *Zjednoczenie* and Grossman appeared in *Naprzód.*[75] For readers, the message was clear: Grossman and others associated with *Zjednoczenie* were wreckers, parasites on the workers' movement, and their fundraising activity was fraudulent.

Immediately after the latest allegations in *Naprzód,* Grossman, outraged, sent a curt note to the party Executive Committee demanding an arbitration court to hear the charges he now leveled "against the editor in chief of *Naprzód,* or against the author of the note which insults me as the editor in chief of *Zjednoczenie.*"[76] As the complicity of the PPSD Executive in the campaign against Grossman and *Zjednoczenie* became apparent, his allies started to organize too. *Zjednoczenie* published a pamphlet, already written on February 18, *"Naprzód" on "Zjednoczenie" (A Contribution on the Characteristics of the Galician Swamp).* Going through all of the relevant items in *Naprzód,* point by point, it defended both *Zjednoczenie* and Grossman. The pamphlet also pointed out how Grossman had worked successfully to build the workers' movement and had recently been mentioned on the front page of *Naprzód* itself.[77]

Not only radical students, but also sections of the PPSD's own organization mobilized in Grossman's support. Radicals opposed to the party leadership still dominated the Stanisławów District Committee, whose secretary was Józef Mosler, Anzelm's cousin. On February 19, the Stanisławów Committee called on the party's Executive to condemn *Naprzód*'s behavior and guarantee members' right to criticize.[78] The District Committee in Przemyśl, where Henryk Grossman's collaborator on *Zjednoczenie,* Arnold Gahlberg, lived, condemned the tactics of the Grossman group, but objected to the methods the party was using to combat it.[79]

After these and other protests, the PPSD leadership, on Tuesday, the 21st, adopted a dual strategy to deal with Grossman and *Zjednoczenie*. It held a meeting to consider the issues and invited Grossman to attend. According to the police informant who was present, Grossman objected to being treated like a thief because he was collecting funds for the student Committee for Support of the Russian Revolution in Geneva.[80] The Executive presented him with an ultimatum: resign from the editorship of *Zjednoczenie* within forty-eight hours or be expelled.[81] During the meeting Henryk lost his temper at the way the Executive was using *Zjednoczenie* as an excuse to silence its critics and at the continuing slurs on his integrity. The following day he reaffirmed his refusal to obey the party directive. "Respected comrades," he wrote—the highly formal salutation expressing both irony and, perhaps, chagrin at his own volatile behavior at the meeting—"Having considered the matter today, this time calmly, I would like to confirm to you all that I said yesterday while present at the Committee meeting. I await your sentence, however, I declare that I will not give up my position as editor of *Zjednoczenie* as this would be contrary to my perception of my rights as a member of the Party."[82]

Another aspect of the Executive's strategy was a token concession. In response to Grossman's protests and in order to give the impression of fairness, *Naprzód* on February 21, published a mealy-mouthed elaboration of its statements about the fraudulent collection of funds. It was far from being a retraction, let alone an apology.[83]

Neither the Executive's threats nor its sham of conciliation were effective. Grossman's stance found support at a gathering of two hundred people—mainly university students—in the Hotel Klein on Wednesday, the 22nd. After Moszoro opened the meeting, Maksymilian Horwitz and Władysław Gumplowicz moved that, as the party Executive had dealt with the matter, the discussion should end. When the meeting's hostile attitude to this proposal became clear, about sixty supporters of the PPSD leadership departed. Those remaining then unanimously passed resolutions against *Naprzód*'s polemics. Another motion, which condemned the policy of the PPSD Executive as a "moral inquisition directed against free socialist criticism which is an absolutely necessary condition for the development of the spirit and idea of socialism," was eventually carried 60 to 22.[84]

The Executive formally expelled Grossman from the party on Sunday, February 26.[85] But some PPSD leaders were increasingly uneasy about the level of support Grossman was finding.

Then the secretary of the Kraków Jewish Agitation Committee, Maurycy Papier, informed the party Executive that it would be convening a special meeting on Saturday, March 4, to discuss the Grossman affair. He invited the Executive to attend.[86] That meeting was a turning point. Grossman repudiated his association with *Zjednoczenie*. Less than two weeks later, the Executive readmitted him to the PPSD.

The Grossman affair was a complicated and hectic succession of *Naprzód* editorial decisions and sessions of the PPSD Executive on the one hand; protests from Grossman, District Committees, mass meetings of students, and rank-and-file party members, on the other. It began as an attempt by party leaders to expose, discredit, isolate, and suppress what they perceived as a small group of undisciplined student wreckers, led by Grossman.

The way the affair ended can only be understood in the context of the history of the Jewish labor movement in Galicia from the early 1890s, its recent rapid growth, and Grossman's efforts, over several years, to combine Jewish workers' resistance against their own oppression with the general proletarian struggle against capitalism.

Ups and Downs in Jewish Workers' Organizations

Galician Jews were disproportionately concentrated in increasingly uncompetitive small businesses. They were, nevertheless, only slightly underrepresented among wage earners.[87] Working conditions were generally appalling. In 1900 miners, printers, and machine builders worked a mere nine hours a day, six days a week. Employees in small workshops might labor for up to sixteen hours a day. Real wage levels in Galicia were generally lower than in other provinces of the Austro-Hungarian Empire. The hours and incomes of many of the self-employed were even worse.[88]

From very modest beginnings during the early 1890s, in Lemberg and Stanislawów, Jewish workers began to build associations that were affiliated to the GPSD. These groups performed educational, cultural, and union functions. At this stage, Daszyński argued that Jews were a nation and rejected assimilationism: the idea that Yiddish-speaking Jewish workers should and inevitably would adopt the Polish language and "higher" Polish culture. A short-lived attempt to set up a Jewish social democratic organization and newspaper independent of the Galician party failed. The GPSD subsequently published, if somewhat sporadically, newspapers in Yiddish.[89]

A network of general associations of Jewish workers, often called Briderlekhkeyt (Brotherhood), spread across the larger towns in Galicia. Their educational and organizing activities included combating Zionist influence in the Jewish working class.

From the end of the 1890s, however, the Jewish workers' associations in Galicia suffered a severe decline; "sparks still continued to flicker, but gradually all the organizations began to die out." The situation was worst for the Briderlekhkeyt organizations in western Galicia.[90] In 1901 the association in Kraków collapsed "and within three months so did the entire [social democratic] work amongst the Jewish proletariat" in that city.[91] Two factors that affected the organization of the Galician working class in general were responsible for the problems faced by Jewish workers: continued state repression of social democratic activity following the pogroms in 1898 and, most important, the ebbing of working-class self-confidence, as reflected in falling numbers of workers taking strike action, even before the deep recession of 1899–1902.

There was a third factor that undermined the Jewish organizations in particular: the opportunist attitude of the PPSD's own leaders, including Daszyński and most of his Jewish comrades. Grossman later argued that this involved an accommodation to Jewish clericalism by making appeals to religious solidarity.[92] But the party's increasing nationalism and assimilationist attitude to the Yiddish-speaking population was even more damaging. For example, its Yiddish newspaper was not published regularly during the late 1890s. It only resurfaced briefly during election campaigns.[93] Given the GPSD's limited publication program in Yiddish, an unofficial committee of Jewish members in Lemberg made use of material from the Bund and America.[94] Nor did the party do anything else to coordinate or concentrate the resources of the Jewish socialist associations across the province, which could have helped them deal with repression and the effects of the economic slump.

From 1902, at the latest, Grossman ignited new sparks of Jewish workers' organizations in Kraków and fanned them into healthy flames.[95] Already concerned about anti-Semitism, he developed an interest in the national question as it related to the Jewish working class. The issue was literally before his eyes in the Kazimierz. If Kraków was a conglomerate monument to Polish history, the Kazimierz was a museum of a different kind, its old and decrepit buildings, narrow lanes and synagogues documenting a history of poverty and oppression.

Grossman learned Yiddish, so he could agitate among Jewish workers.[96] This was not a straightforward activity. To start with, as a middle-class and fashion-conscious student who was not an orthodox Jew, he didn't look at all like the workers he was trying to reach. The differences were even more obvious once he opened his mouth, because of his accent. This was even before he started to talk politics. It would be counterproductive to pretend to be something that he was not. In any case, doing so was beneath Grossman's dignity. How then to take the first steps, not just to winning some arguments with Jewish workers, but also their trust? "Where were the Jews? In a Zionist café or more than one. What could he do? He went to café, sat at a table, talked to one or another, weaned away to Socialism, one then another, two or three, began to form movement this way."[97] Just twelve members established a new general

Jewish workers association, Postęp (Progress), on December 20, 1902, with Henryk Grossman as its secretary. This activity was time-consuming, but Henryk's class load during his second year at university was light.[98]

One of Postęp's early breakthroughs was among Jewish bakers.[99] But the group was open to all Jewish workers. Its regular meetings and lectures provided a forum for discussions about organizing at work, politics, literature, and science.

As the association grew, it rented its own rooms in the Kazimierz[100] and became a seedbed for other, more specialized organizations, including Jewish/Yiddish (the terms are the same in the Yiddish language) cultural groups and branches of the central social democratic unions, based in Vienna. Grossman was pivotal in this activity. A sympathetic account of the conflicts over *Zjednoczenie* noted that he had "recruited at least half of the membership of the Jewish proletarian organization" in Kraków.[101]

PPSD leaders were happy about the reestablishment of Jewish workers' associations affiliated to the party, although they were largely oblivious to the early stages of this process and did little to support it. Ruch, with its workers' affairs committee, however, promoted this activity. The efforts of a layer of Jewish university students, led by Grossman and Bros in Kraków, were a decisive factor in the reemergence of socialist organizations among Jewish workers. Another student, Karol Eyneygler, alongside several veteran worker militants, played an important role in the growth of such associations in Lemberg, where they had never entirely collapsed.[102]

The revival of the PPSD's Jewish membership was conditioned by economic growth, after severe recession gave way to Austria's "spectacular boom stretching from roughly 1903 to 1907."[103] The working class grew rapidly. In 1902 there were 181,500 workers (narrowly defined) in Galician industry, mining, and trade and transport; by 1912 there were 301,500. Kraków's population grew by more than half, from 91,800 in 1900 to 152,000 in 1910.

By 1903, when Grossman was the secretary of both Ruch and Postęp, the membership of the student group reached its peak of 110 members, while the Jewish workers' organization had 130 adherents and was still growing rapidly.[104]

Grossman and the other socialist students building workers' associations, together with the young workers they had drawn into politics, were undergoing a political transformation. Their sustained engagement with the workers' movement turned them all into organic intellectuals of the working class. Both activists with proletarian backgrounds—like the sign painter Moyshe/Maurycy Papier, one of Henryk's first recruits, and the boot makers Yonah Blum and Peysekh Dembitser—and apprentice traditional intellectuals—like Grossman,

Bros, and Rose—were learning how to articulate workers' demands systematically and to lead struggles around working-class demands.[105]

At the PPSD's Eighth Congress in January 1903, leaders like Diamand reaffirmed their assimilationist outlook. The party's Yiddish organ having ceased
to appear regularly, he encouraged Jewish workers to absorb superior Polish
culture and read either Polish or Ukrainian social democratic newspapers.[106]
But Daszyński, an experienced tactician, quickly recognized that many Jewish
members were dissatisfied with the PPSD's approach and that this could
increase support for an independent Jewish organization, as proposed by dissidents in the Lemberg Briderlekhkeyt. He undertook to convene a special conference of Jewish members to clarify the issues.[107]

Thirty-six of the forty-one delegates at the conference in Lemberg on May
9–10, 1903, came as supporters of an independent Jewish party.[108] But the leaders of the PPSD, particularly Diamand, engaged in a concerted campaign
against the proposal. They invoked the authority of Victor Adler and called for
unity in the face of the recent Kishinev pogrom in the Russian Empire.[109]

All but two of those present voted for Diamand's motion. One person
abstained, from a position hostile to the idea of an independent Jewish organization, which the PPSD leaders called "separatism." Even though he was, for
the moment, entirely isolated, Henryk Grossman abstained for the opposite
reason: he had not been convinced to give up his support for a Jewish party.[110]
On the basis of the practical experience of building Postęp, he argued that the
PPSD was not capable of simultaneously advancing the international proletarian struggle against capitalism and Jewish workers' efforts to throw off their
specific oppression. Only a Jewish party could combine these tasks.[111]

The supporters of an autonomous Jewish organization had been compre-
hensively outmaneuvered. Many of the activists in Jewish unions and educational associations linked to the PPSD soon became convinced that
Grossman's stance at the conference had been correct. Furthermore, the conference consolidated links between the Jewish activists in Lemberg and the
generally younger militants in Kraków.[112]

Buoyant economic conditions continued to underpin the growth of working-class self-confidence, cross-national solidarity, and socialist influence in
Galicia. In 1904 Anzelm Mosler led a May Day demonstration of six thousand in
the small town of Buczacz. Hundreds of Jewish workers marched alongside
thousands of Ukrainian peasants. In June, the PPSD mobilized ten thousand
workers for a march to the graves of two Jewish youths murdered by the authorities during the long strike in Lwów's construction industry two years earlier.[113]
The trade union movement and hence PPSD membership was expanding. The

Jewish proletariat too was organizing on an unprecedented scale, especially in Lemberg, with the largest concentration of workers in Galicia and a group of experienced working-class Jewish activists, and Kraków.[114]

The young militants around Henryk Grossman and Postęp helped commercial workers set up a separate union, just as they assisted women workers and young workers to establish their own associations. By 1905, painters, tilers, tailors, bakers, metal workers, and suitcase makers were organizing their union activity within Postęp itself.[115]

A Provincial Jewish Agitation Committee, set up as a sop to the Jewish activists at the May 1903 conference, was a dead letter. But its local equivalent in Kraków came under the control of the leaders of Postęp and was very active. In August 1904, the Kraków Committee's report on the previous six months stated that it had met thirteen times. Before May Day it had convened twelve public assemblies and one closed gathering using Yiddish. In addition to the activities of other groups of Jewish workers, the report noted that women hairdressers had established their own association. It also highlighted problems arising from the lack of a Yiddish-speaking party agitator. Twenty-two Jewish associations were now affiliated to the PPSD in Kraków.[116]

Although many Jewish workers were rapidly moving toward socialist politics in Galicia's largest cities, the situation elsewhere in the province was more uneven. Despite the potential for recruiting Jewish workers to the movement, the inactivity of the Provincial Jewish Agitation Committee meant that resources were not coordinated and deployed across Galicia to build Yiddish-speaking groups in places with few or inexperienced, local activists. The demise of the PPSD's Yiddish newspaper and the party's ban on the distribution of literature from the Bund were further obstacles to effective organizing.[117]

The issue was not just a *slow* rate of building around socialist politics. Even as the fighting spirit of the Austrian proletariat revived, competition from Labor Zionism challenged the ability of social democrats to organize Jewish workers at all. The first Labor Zionist association in Galicia, a union of commercial workers, was established in June 1903. Austrian unions with a Zionist orientation held a congress in Kraków in May 1904 and founded the Austrian Poale Zion (Labor Zionist) Party.[118] In the autumn, the Poale Zionist newspaper, *Yidisher arbeyter,* which had earlier been written in German, started appearing in Yiddish. One of its main targets was Jewish workers in the PPSD.[119]

Poale Zion (PZ) offered an escapist response to the oppression experienced by Jewish workers in Europe. It promoted both the ultimate goal of a Zionist state and the practical path of emigrating to Palestine, though this was trod by only a minority of the movement's supporters. While social democrats mobilized workers to struggle against despotism and for democracy and socialism,

Zionism held out the prospect of a Jewish homeland achieved by means of colonialism, diplomatic deals, and collaboration with emperors.

To the socialist activists building Jewish workers associations in Galicia, the PPSD leadership seemed too relaxed about the growth of rival Labor Zionist groups. On August 16, 1904, Grossman reported on agitation among Jewish workers at a meeting of the Union of Workers' Associations (the peak body of the social democratic union movement in Kraków). The rise of Zionism in the Jewish community was obvious, he said, while socialist agitation was weak. It was essential to find agitators who could speak Yiddish and to build a Jewish socialist organization that had greater autonomy from the party.[120]

Soon after, on August 28–29, eighteen Jewish activists gathered for a secret meeting in Przemyśl. Delegates from Lemberg, Kraków (including Grossman), Przemyśl, Jarosław, Tarnów, Stanisławów, Kolomea, and Vienna participated.[121] The majority decided that it would be premature to set up an independent Jewish social democratic organization immediately. But the conference made two important decisions. One was to move a motion of no confidence in the Provincial Jewish Agitation Committee at the PPSD's Ninth Congress in October. The other was to establish a secret Committee of Jewish Workers in Galicia, to prepare the way for an autonomous Jewish socialist party. Ruben Birnbaum was elected the committee's chairperson and Karol Eyneygler its secretary. Both lived in Lemberg.[122] But Eyneygler later recalled, "It already became clear to us all on the first day [of the meeting] who would take over the leadership of the Party. There was already not a shred of doubt that the leading role would fall to the extremely talented Kraków comrades."[123]

The PPSD leadership soon got wind of these developments. Daszyński charged that "the Bund was forming a branch in Galicia and had held a secret meeting in Przemyśl together with our Jewish comrades." The fact that the Kraków militants had organized a commemoration of the execution, on May 28, 1902, of the Bundist hero Hirsh Lekert was, he said, further evidence of this plot.[124] A shoemaker, Lekert had attempted to assassinate the governor of Vilna (the capital of the Russian province of Lithuania), who had ordered the flogging of Jewish workers arrested for demonstrating on May Day, 1902.[125]

Daszyński was partly right. There was a connection with the Bund, though it was not playing an active role in Galicia. Links between the Bund and Jewish activists in Lemberg went back years. The Lemberg militants had been using material in Yiddish from the Bund's Foreign Committee for ages, because such publications were not being produced by the PPSD.[126]

During 1904, the "Bundist worldview" of a small circle of leading activists in Kraków, also "took hold and crystallized in discussions" with Sinai Jakobi. Through him they gained access to the literature of this organization of Jewish

Marxists in Russia for the first time. Jakobi, a typesetter, had been a member of Bund committees in Warsaw and Łódź.[127] Bronisław Grosser's visit, later in the year, consolidated this influence on Grossman, Bros, and Rose, and opened up contact with the top leadership of the Bund.[128] Grossman became involved in smuggling its literature into the Russian Empire, as he did SDKPiL material.[129]

The advocates of an independent Jewish social democratic party in Galicia campaigned for their position at the PPSD's Ninth Congress in October–November 1904. There was an intimate connection between their involvement in debates over the proposed fraternal alliance between the PPSD and the PPS and the organization of Jewish workers. In both cases the Jewish militants were fighting the Polish nationalism of Daszyński and other party leaders. That alliance directly threatened the relationship between the Galician socialists building Jewish workers organizations and the Bund.

The august chamber of the Kraków City Council, where the Congress took place, lent a grand atmosphere to the Congress.[130] But even before the proceedings were fully underway, party officials sought to undermine the credibility of the Jewish militants, questioning their credentials. Objections were raised against Eyneygler's mandate from the Lemberg cabinet-makers; Bros's from the Kraków Jewish Agitation Committee; and Grossman's from a student organization. The Credentials Committee gave them the benefit of the doubt, "to avoid the impression that it wanted to prevent free expression and their defense of their own position."[131]

In the discussion of the party Executive's report, Grossman, as the secretary of Postęp, pointed out that it mentioned neither the activity of the Jewish workers organizations nor the *in*activity of the Provincial Jewish Agitation Committee. As agreed in Przemyśl, he moved a motion of no confidence in the Jewish Agitation Committee. It was defeated, with fifteen delegates, only one of whom was not Jewish, voting for and fifty-eight against.[132] While they had allies on the issue of the relationship between the party and the PPS, on the question of organizing Jewish workers the Jewish militants were pretty much on their own.

Later the Congress discussed alternative motions on the organization of Jewish workers, from Herman Diamand, for the PPSD Executive, and Karol Eyneygler. Diamand's motion regarded "a separate class organization of the Jewish proletariat as harmful for the proletariat as a whole. A separate organization of the Jewish proletariat is in the interest of the ruling class of exploiters, Zionist and anti-Semitic demagogues and all kinds of chauvinists."[133] After twenty comrades had contributed to the debate, the level of support for the Jewish activists' position remained the same: fifteen delegates opposed the Executive's resolution, while sixty-four supported it.[134]

Two weeks after the Congress, the party Executive dissolved the local Jewish Agitation Committee in Lemberg. It did not take the same action against the local committee in Kraków, perhaps because it regarded the generally older and more experienced separatist leaders in Lemberg as a greater threat than the pesky students in Kraków. Daszyński had praised the oratorical talents of Grossman, Rose, and Bross at the Congress, while emphasizing their inexperience, and patronizingly offered them better outlets for their energies.[135] This proved to be a serious mistake. Kraków was not only the hotbed of opposition to the party leadership among students, soon expressed through *Zjednoczenie,* but also among Jewish workers' associations and unions affiliated to the PPSD.

The Proletariat and the Jewish Question

The supporters of a Jewish party decided to publish a private magazine, *Der yidisher sotsial-demokrat* (Jewish Social Democrat), edited by Yehusha Neker in Lemberg.[136] While working to bring out the first issue of *Zjednoczenie,* Grossman also wrote a pamphlet in Polish, expounding the position of the secret Committee of Jewish Workers in Galicia. *The Proletariat and the Jewish Question,* published in January 1905, was dedicated to Henryk's close friend Janek Bross. Studded with quotes from Schopenhauer, Machiavelli, Francis Bacon, classical Polish writers, and others, the pamphlet argued for a Jewish socialist party in sometimes melodramatic language. Despite his stylistic excesses, derived from romantic Polish literature, Grossman made a clear case that such a party was the only means by which Jewish workers in Galicia could effectively organize and join the ranks of the class-conscious, international proletariat. The establishment of a Jewish social democratic party was the solution to the Jewish question *within the labor movement.* The pamphlet is Grossman's first identifiable publication.

Against the Polish nationalist legend of Jewish backwardness and cultural inferiority, Grossman sustained an essentially Bundist position, taking issue with both Zionists and assimilationist Polish socialists. The Bund's success demonstrated how Jewish workers could be involved in the class struggle side by side with workers of other nationalities. In less than a single decade, the Bund had "rapidly clos[ed] the chasm of decades which until recently separated the Jewish proletariat from its non-Jewish surroundings."[137]

In pre-capitalist societies, Jews suffered a common oppression. Under capitalism this oppression was transformed. Now, Grossman maintained, there was no Jewish question in general. There was, rather, one Jewish question for the Jewish bourgeoisie and another for the Jewish proletariat. Drawing on Helvetius's description of the contradictions between two hostile nations, rulers and ruled, concealed in the appearance of national unity, he pointed out that "in a capitalist society there *is no uniform national consciousness*."[138] It was therefore entirely false to argue, as the PPSD did, that "the solution to the Jewish question is a *fair organization of relations* between Christian and Jewish communities."[139] The bourgeois Jewish question, the oppression of the Jews in general "despite its specific anti-Jewish form, is only a part of a general campaign in a class society, and the oppression of Jews is a part of a general oppression. For the *proletariat*, the Jewish question in this sense has ceased to be an issue."[140] Class-conscious workers knew that it was necessary to overturn capitalism and the various forms of oppression it sustained. The struggle against the oppression of the Jews had to be taken up today, but would only be resolved under socialism: "The oppression of the Jewish proletariat as Jews will disappear when class society, of which it is a manifestation, also disappears. The victorious proletariat, having destroyed the class form of society, will abolish every oppression, as it removes the need for oppression and its tools!"[141]

The immediate issue was how to mobilize Jewish workers, so "the Jewish question can only be considered as a *question about the choice of the most effective means* for attaining the goal of proletarian power."[142] The answer depended on whether capitalism was undermining or developing the Jewish working class's national consciousness as a collective actor.[143] Grossman argued that, rather than catechistically repeating Marx's comments in 1843 on the Jewish question, contemporary Marxists should apply his method to current circumstances.[144] It was clear that the Jewish masses had not been assimilated, contrary to Marx's prediction. As for the future, Grossman attacked the positions of both the PPS theorist Kelles-Krauz and the Bundist Vladimir Medem. Against them, he maintained that the survival of a distinctive Jewish national identity over the longer term was not an open question.[145]

In order to provoke discussion, Grossman put his own argument about assimilation in an extreme form and explicitly left out of the account "counter-tendencies operating in the opposite direction." This was because "for many years, in the discussion of polonization, factors that were really or apparently leading to assimilation were misapprehended and overemphasized, while counterposed factors were disregarded. It would be redundant to address the former again here. My task has been to point out *new* phenomena, not to reiterate old pronouncements."[146] He engaged, in other words, in the risky, but sometimes necessary political practice of stick bending: the accepted position of the party on an issue was distorted, so it was necessary to make exaggerated arguments in the opposite direction in order to bend the line straight.[147]

Grossman argued that Jewish workers would remain a distinctive group as the growth of large-scale industry would reduce their need to learn Polish, because Jewish and non-Jewish workers in larger enterprises would remain segregated. The assimilationist position of the PPSD was therefore out of touch with current social developments.[148]

Capitalist development, Grossman nevertheless acknowledged, gave rise to general tendencies toward assimilation that had implications for "whether any independent nations would exist in the future."[149] This point accorded with Marx and Engels' insight that capitalism tends to homogenize conditions of life across the world and to diminish national differences.[150] Unlike the leading theorists of the PPS/PPSD, the Bund (Medem),[151] and the Austrian Social Democratic Party (Karl Renner and later Otto Bauer), Grossman did not therefore regard nations as permanent social phenomena.

From his observations about the obstacles to assimilation, Grossman, at this stage, only drew conclusions for social democratic organization rather than for the fight against the oppression of Jews in capitalist society.[152] The solution to the Jewish proletariat's Jewish question was the establishment of a Jewish social democratic party within the framework of the Austrian General Party. Far from being a return to the ghetto, as the polonizers argued, such a party would contribute to the dissolution of the ghetto.[153] Opposition to a Jewish party was opportunism, "capitulation in the face of prejudice and patriotic traditions. Capitulation even before the struggle has begun."[154]

Ghettoized in a corner of the party of a different nationality, the Jewish proletariat could not effectively participate in the struggle for socialism. The task was impossible within the framework of the PPSD, whose leaders specifically designated their organization as a Polish national party and failed to satisfy Jewish workers' needs for agitators, literature, and especially central coordination. Grossman believed that to sustain, let alone expand the Jewish workers' unions, associations, and activities in Galicia, an independent Jewish workers' organization was essential.[155]

Consciously or unconsciously, Grossman's pamphlet made the same fundamental points as Yulii Martov's 1895 May Day speech in Vilna, which marked an important step in the formation of the Bund.[156] Its focus on organizational questions also reflected the preoccupations of orthodox Second International Marxism.

The activities of Jewish militants in Kraków, preparing for a new party, were as important as *Zjednoczenie* in explaining the wild and apparently confusing events that made up the Grossman affair.

He and his friends had decided in August 1904 that it would be premature to depart from the PPSD immediately. They must have anticipated their defeat at the party Congress but seen its debates as a means to publicize their arguments and thus build support for the establishment of a new party some way down the track.

Soon Grossman was leading the wider internationalist Marxist current in Galicia by taking on responsibility for *Zjednoczenie*. This did not seem counterposed to the project of establishing a Jewish party. On the contrary, the stronger the left of the socialist movement was in Galicia, both inside and outside the PPSD, the more sympathy, he thought, the Jewish working class's demand for an independent party would win in the wider socialist movement.

Meanwhile, Daszyński wanted to consolidate his victories at the 1904 party Congress. The fraternal alliance with the PPS had been formalized in the face of opposition from the party's left wing, while the increasingly worrisome Bundists had been defeated on the question of organizing Jewish workers. During the Grossman affair, both men discovered that achieving their goals was going to be more complicated than they had expected.

By attacking Grossman as the editor of *Zjednoczenie,* the leadership of the PPSD engaged in a test of strength with its opponents. But it had not anticipated the response of many workers, party units, and students. Organized Jewish workers, in particular, had a keen understanding of the significance of the campaign against Grossman and *Zjednoczenie.*[157]

Henryk Grossman was not prepared to accept *Naprzód*'s libels against him and *Zjednoczenie* meekly. But he was worried that expulsion from the party would cut him off from the organized Jewish workers in union branches and associations like Postęp, which were affiliated to the PPSD. That would make his efforts to create a new party much more difficult, if not impossible.

The PPSD's leaders soon became aware of just how much support Grossman had among both Jewish and Polish workers. The pamphlet that defended *Zjednoczenie* stressed comrade Grossman's contribution to organizing Jewish workers, high school students, and commercial employees. His name was "known to every conscious Jewish proletarian in Kraków."[158] The PPSD Executive could, perhaps, dismiss this assertion because it stemmed from Grossman's student partisans. Similar comments in a letter from the party's Jewish Agitation Committee in Kraków, signed by its chairperson, Bros, and secretary, Papier, on February 21, should have been taken more seriously.

Bros and Papier wrote on the insistence of meetings of Jewish workers, which had expressed outrage at the accusations against comrade Grossman. They started by pointing out that "Grossman earned his Party credentials by dedicating himself to organizational and agitational work for years." In conclusion, they wrote that "The Jewish Agitation Committee, after meticulous analysis of arguments about the matter and the impression created by the article and warning in *Naprzód* . . . draws attention to the current division in the associations and expects a judgment which will hopefully soften relations and establish conditions for undisturbed work in the future."[159]

The Executive may have regarded the letter as a bluff. It expelled Grossman on February 26. But the same day Majzels, an activist in Postęp, warned a closed party meeting of 150 members, including Daszyński and Haecker, that Grossman had engaged in "superb" activity and large numbers of workers were prepared to defend him. Grossman confirmed this. The PPSD leaders, taken aback, were critical of the ineffectiveness of the Kraków District Committee's supervision of the Jewish associations.[160]

At the meeting convened by the Jewish Agitation Committee on March 4, Daszyński realized that the reports of Grossman's popularity among Jewish workers were not exaggerated. Three hundred party members turned up to hear the editors of *Naprzód*, Haecker, and *Zjednoczenie*, Grossman. Large numbers of Jewish workers—located in Daszyński's own Reichsrat constituency, some of them also voters in the small traders curia that he represented on the Kraków town council—supported this disruptive university student. The discussion, chaired by Bros, went on for six hours. Having grasped the situation, Daszyński was keen to avoid alienating large numbers of workers from the party and undermining his own electoral base. He opened the way to Grossman's reinstatement as a PPSD member.

Grossman, Daszyński suggested, could be readmitted to the party if those present convinced him to resign from *Zjednoczenie*. The "misunderstanding" that had led *Naprzód* to question Grossman's integrity could easily be cleared up with the publication of a statement in the newspaper. A worker moved a motion to this effect. It was carried unanimously.[161] Daszyński's compromise forced Grossman to make a choice between the goals of building the Jewish socialist movement and a radical, cross-national opposition to the PPSD leadership.

Jewish Socialists and the National Question in Galicia

Grossman's support for an independent Jewish social democratic party in Galicia was theoretically compatible with the approaches to the national question *within the socialist movement* of both the General Austrian Social Democratic Party and the Bund. Their positions on how to resolve the national question *at the level of state institutions* were also broadly compatible, favoring federal rather than unitary structures for both social democratic movements and the imperial Austrian and Russian states.[162]

Although the General Austrian Social Democratic Party formally supported the transformation of the Austrian Empire into a federation of nationalities, its

German-Austrian component had taken up Karl Renner's idea of resolving the national question by constituting the empire's nations as voluntary national cultural institutions whose activities were not confined to any particular territory.[163] It loudly proclaimed its commitment to internationalism and the right of peoples to self-determination but in practice supported a policy that left *"the decisive positions of state power in the hands of the German minority."*[164] Like the PPSD, moreover, the General and the German-Austrian parties dramatically underplayed the political significance and social consequences of anti-Semitism. The Bund, however, favored the demand for national cultural autonomy *for Jews* in the Russian Empire.

Grossman was also familiar with other approaches to the Jewish question in eastern European social democracy. He had had close contact with the SDKPiL. The Polish social democrats in Russian Poland took a hard line against all forms of nationalism and, on paper, favored a centralized rather than federal structure for the RSDLP. But, in practice, the SDKPiL had not joined the RSDLP when it re-formed in 1903 because it was too soft on Polish nationalism and therefore the PPS.

The position of the RSDLP on the national question had been articulated by Lenin, in a document that the first issue of *Zjednoczenie* had quoted.[165] At the party's 1903 Congress, a majority decided that the RSDLP should have a unified rather than a federal structure. Lenin regarded the autonomy accorded to constituent organizations of the Russian party in its 1898 rules as "providing the Jewish working class movement with all it needs: propaganda and agitation in Yiddish, its own literature and congresses, the right to advance separate demands to supplement a single general Social Democratic program and to satisfy local needs and requirements arising out of the special features of Jewish life."[166]

It was precisely these means of organizing that the PPSD leadership denied the Jewish workers in Galicia. Lenin's Bolsheviks also supported the right of oppressed nationalities to self-determination, that is, to break away from existing states. Leon Trotsky later put his finger on the fundamental distinction between the Austrian and the Bolshevik positions on the national question: "despite all the thorough investigations undertaken at the beginning of the Century, the [Austrian] Party never made the distinction between oppressed and oppressing nations, which was the key to Bolshevik nationality policies."[167]

The Bund, Lenin maintained, substituted the fig leaf of federalism *within* the party, which would undermine the capacity of the Russian Empire's working class to struggle against the Tsarist autocracy, for the policy of supporting the right of oppressed nations to break up existing states.[168] Both before and after the 1903 Congress, Lenin also stressed the importance of the entire party defending the rights of oppressed groups—Jews, women, Christian sects, students, and subordinate nationalities: "working class consciousness cannot be genuine political consciousness unless the workers are trained to respond to *all* cases of tyranny, oppression, violence, and abuse, no matter *what class* is affected."[169]

At the meeting of Jewish workers on March 4, Grossman declared that he accepted Daszyński's deal and would leave *Zjednoczenie*'s editorial board. He traded off involvement in *Zjednoczenie* against a way back into the party, with his honor intact. His statement was greeted with "a massive salvo of applause" and the meeting closed with the singing the "Red Flag" and "The Song of Labor."[170]

With this step, building a new Jewish party became Grossman's absolute political priority. The best opportunity before World War I to build a cross-national current in Galicia with a commitment to struggle and positions on the Jewish and national questions like those of the RSDLP disappeared. Daszyński's maneuver in breaking Henryk Grossman from *Zjednoczenie* did not succeed in retaining the most significant Jewish working-class organizations in the PPSD. But it prevented them from forming the core of a rival revolutionary party that sought to recruit Polish, Jewish, and Ukrainian workers to its ranks. The potential for doing so was soon apparent: once it was formed, even the new *exclusively Jewish party* was able to organize Polish workers into social democratic unions and win them to its militant politics.

Comrade Grossman quickly confirmed his departure from *Zjednoczenie* in writing. The following Sunday, *Naprzód* published his response to the charges of fraud and noted that *Zjednoczenie* had explained that the "relevant Committee" to which it was sending funds for the Russian revolution was indeed the student "Committee for Support of the Revolution on the Territory of the Russian State." On March 16, eighteen days after expelling him, the PPSD Executive readmitted Grossman to the party.[171] The Grossman affair seemed to end with concessions on both sides.

The logic of Grossman's choice is not difficult to see. First, opposition to the opportunist politics of the PPSD leaders among organized Polish workers was limited. Second, although the Bolsheviks, unlike the PPSD, took the struggle against oppression seriously, Lenin had rejected the idea that Jews were a nation and argued that the alternatives facing the Jews were isolation and assimilation.[172] This sounded worryingly similar to the PPSD's formal position of fighting for Jewish equality, while its assimilationist practice created obstacles to mobilizing Jewish workers. The situation of the Jewish working class in Galicia, the federal structure of the Austrian General Party, and the prestige of the Bund, made the project of establishing a new Jewish social democratic party, within the Austrian social democratic federation, seem more realistic than that of challenging the PPSD for the leadership of the entire Galician working class.

Toward a Jewish Social Democratic Party

The spirit of reconciliation embodied in Grossman's departure from *Zjednoczenie* and readmission to the party quickly evaporated. With a minor exception, the PPSD Executive soon endorsed the content of all *Naprzód*'s articles against *Zjednoczenie*.[173] It also explicitly forbade party members from participating in organizations or editorial committees hostile to the positions of the PPSD or other parties in the fraternal alliance.[174]

In retrospect, party leaders could now fit events at the PPSD's 1904 Congress, the appearance of *The Proletariat and the Jewish Question,* and then *Zjednoczenie* into a pattern, rather than dismiss them separately as the actions of over-excited students. In moving that the PPSD Executive readmit Grossman to the party, Daszyński pointed out that the editor of *Zjednoczenie* "had all the Jewish members behind him and that any split from the body of the Party would be a disaster." He reiterated that "the Executive had made a major error in neglecting to supervise Grossman's activities and those of other Jewish agitators who were around him, in forming a strong faction."[175] Daszyński and his comrades took steps to make up for this neglect.

Zygmunt Żuławski, formerly Grossman's comrade in Ruch and less than six months earlier an ally in the struggle against Daszyński's politics at the Ninth PPSD Congress, was a key figure in this development. The PPSD Executive successfully divided their opponents in the party by co-opting him, while going in hard against *Zjednoczenie* and then against the dissident Jewish activists. The third Galician Trade Union Conference of March 26–27, 1905, elected Żuławski, now a supporter of Daszyński, as secretary of the Galician Trade Union Federation,[176] with prime responsibility for carrying out its policies. The gathering's most important policy decision was to reorganize the province's union movement.

Against the background of the economic boom and the revolution in Russia, union activity and recruitment had begun to skyrocket in 1905. To reinforce this trend, the Conference decided that provincial trade unions would be replaced by branches of the central social democratic unions, based in Vienna. Branches of the central unions were more robust because they could draw on the considerable resources, including sickness, unemployment, and strike funds, of the much larger all-Austrian organizations.

Another change, with a quite different logic, was bundled together with the plans for the provincial trade unions: general educational associations and unions, like the Briderlekhkeyts in Lemberg and Przemyśl and Postęp in Kraków, would be wound up by the end of the year.[177] The decision was inspired by the PPSD and had already been foreshadowed at the party's Eighth Congress in 1903.[178] Daszyński welcomed the liquidation of the local associations because it would soon eliminate "Bundist daydreams" and "nests of sedition."[179] While the Polish general workers' associations were moribund, their Jewish counterparts were thriving.[180]

Daszyński wanted to inoculate Jewish workers against dissidents and integrate them into bodies whose leaders were loyal to the PPSD. Hence the PPSD began to publish a new Yiddish weekly newspaper, the *Yidishe arbeyter-tseytung* (Jewish Workers' Newspaper) at precisely this time. Together these steps were intended to consolidate an important component of the PPSD's electorate, especially in the Kraków and Lwów constituencies, which already elected or might elect party members to the Reichsrat. It would be unfortunate for the PPSD if some members, resenting the destruction of the Yiddish-speaking associations they had built, did not join unions and union branches that conducted their affairs in Polish. Yet, from the perspective of the PPSD leadership, such collateral damage was far better than standing by while whole associations slipped beyond the party's control.

But the Jewish workers' associations and their leaders were in no mood to await their own destruction passively, like cattle in a meat works stockyard. The outcome of the Grossman affair had increased the morale of those advocating a Jewish social democratic party in Galicia. So had the prominent role of the Bund in the revolutionary movement in Russia. Marxist organizations there were growing explosively and the Bund was still the largest of them.[181]

The political and industrial climate during the winter of 1904–5 was hot: the general associations of Jewish workers achieved major organizing successes and were actually *creating* new branches of the central unions. Briderlekhkeyt in Lemberg had set up a cabinet-makers' union, embracing all Jewish workers in the trade, after a successful strike. It had also established a branch of the central bakers' union with 150 members, a 45-strong branch of the central shoe makers' union, a tailor's union, and a youth organization of 230, including 80 women. There were about 80 recently unionized Jewish workers around Briderlekhkeyt in Przemyśl.[182] By May Postęp in Kraków included a number of strong industry groups: 40 painters, 60 makers of shoe uppers, 60 tailors, 30 bakers, 30 metal workers, 20 luggage-makers, and 150 commercial workers. A women workers' association with 120 members, 300 adherents of the Vienna-based socialist youth association, and another 80 individuals were also organized in Postęp.[183]

Even before the move against the general workers' associations, Jewish activists in Lemberg, already outraged by the dissolution of their local Jewish

Agitation Committee, were impatient to leave the PPSD.[184] Bros and Grossman had to visit Lemberg repeatedly to calm down comrades there, in order to avoid premature action that might undermine years of work. Recently engaged in the hectic series of political moves and countermoves which revolved around *Zjednoczenie* and the struggle over PPSD's nationalist commitment to the PPS, the Jewish dissidents in the Kraków party now started to organize even more feverishly. Blum, Papier, Bros, and Grossman came from Kraków to attend a second meeting of the secret Lemberg-based Committee of Jewish Workers in Galicia, formed in August 1904 to prepare for a Jewish social democratic party.[185]

With the Jewish proletariat's capacity for political and social activity under threat, its leaders felt compelled to act quickly. Organized along similar lines to the Bund, why couldn't Jewish workers in Galicia also move into the front ranks of working-class struggle?

The circumstances of the hastily convened meeting in Lemberg indicated the contrast between the organizing abilities of the activists from Kraków, who had recently forced the PPSD to readmit Grossman to the party, and their Lemberg comrades: "The meeting took place in Winitz's little room by the light of a small petroleum lamp. When the petroleum ran out, we continued our discussions by candle light. Soon this went out too and the discussions had to be postponed. The final decisions were taken on the street."[186] The committee decided to shift its base of operations to Kraków, where Henryk Grossman would take over as secretary and it would set a date for the split.[187]

A closed meeting of forty activists then took place in Kraków. Grossman, having been readmitted to the party two weeks before, argued that "being a member of the PPSD did not serve anyone's interests. So it was necessary to establish a separate party to look after the exclusive interests of the Jews." To do this it was necessary to agitate and collect funds across Galicia. The gathering adopted a motion to split from the PPSD.[188]

At a further meeting in the Postęp hall, a few days later, 140 activists discussed when to form the new Jewish Social Democratic Party. They chose May Day.

Grossman explained the situation in a letter to the Bund. "Although the socio-political conditions in which we fight are not the same, our struggle is based on the same, common theoretical foundations: the Jewish proletariat must have an organization adapted to the environment of the Jewish masses. We know that only such an organization can transform, as you already have, today's backward, impoverished Jewish workers, oppressed by poverty, into a conscious and courageous revolutionary vanguard! Thus you are and will be the model for a whole new generation of Jewish workers and intellectuals."

He also sought help, in the form of literature in Yiddish, a pamphlet on Zionism in particular, and articles, especially on Russian developments, for the *Yidisher sotsial-demokrat*. Referring to his own situation and that of other student activists, he noted that, "as we lack strength in writing in Yiddish, every article written in Yiddish is an immense help."[189]

The committee prepared the apparatus of the new party in advance with impressive efficiency. It established a secretariat, Galician Executive, and local committees, wrote proclamations, and schooled agitators. Henryk Schreiber, one of the conspirators, described the preparations for the split.

> The most difficult part of this work was that it had to be done in secrecy so as not to alarm the PPS[D]. In the [Jewish workers'] associations we worked in a normal way. Until 10 pm we had to be activists of the old Jewish sections of the PPS[D]. Later hours we devoted to the fulfillment of all the difficult tasks that historical necessity had placed on our then very young shoulders.
>
> The spring of 1905 was exceptionally beautiful and warm. Every day around 10 pm, the agitators we had selected and instructed would disappear from the [rooms of] our associations with a different group of workers determined in advance. The often very difficult process of enthusing the still bewildered Jewish workers took place under the starry sky of a spring evening, amongst trees covered with new leaves in Kraków's old Planty [the park around the inner city].
>
> In a period of a few weeks over 400 members of the Kraków organizations were won over in this way as loyal Jewish social democrats.
>
> Around April 1905 we were already able to call larger meetings of our supporters. They took place on the stage of an amateur dramatics group of the Culture Association, in the Union Hotel on Getroygas. That is where most of the meetings of the organizing committee and the agitators, who received specific instructions every day, happened.
>
> This sometimes led to comical interludes. For example, on one occasion an uninvited guest, a Jewish PPS[D]er who was a member of the Culture Association turned up. We had to immediately conduct a discussion evening about art. The comrade also participated in the discussion which went very well. But we lost a whole hour of our very limited time.[190]

The entire Jewish Agitation Committee of the PPSD in Kraków endorsed the formation of a new party.[191] By early April, the leading activists in Kraków and Lemberg had won over Jewish workers' associations, not only in their own towns but also in Tarnów and Przemyśl where the Kraków group had contacts among Jewish students.[192] In Lemberg a series of meetings on the significance of May Day was used to ready wider circles of workers for the split.[193]

The PPSD leadership was certainly aware that the separatists were up to something. In April 1905, Emil Haecker invited Victor Adler to state publicly, in

Kraków, that a Jewish party would not be recognized by the Austrian social democratic federation. This would, he wrote, 'have an enormous significance [in the struggle] against the Zionist endeavors'.[194] Haecker hoped that Adler's authority would again be enough to quell the Jewish militants, as in May 1903. Unlike the police, who were receiving very detailed reports of developments,[195] he can't have had much idea of how extensive preparations for the split were.

2

Leading the Jewish
Social Democratic Party

A New Party

On Monday, May 1, 1905, Jewish workers rallied early, at 8:00 a.m., in Kraków, Lemberg, Przemyśl, and Tarnów.[1] May Day was no public holiday, so they were on strike. Militants distributed the new party's founding manifesto, "What do we want?",[2] Grossman's pamphlet on the proletariat and the Jewish Question, the new magazine *Der yidisher sotsial democrat,* and the Bund anthem, "Di shvue" (The oath).[3] In Kraków, the mass meeting heard Yonah Blum speak on the eight-hour day and Maks Rose on the demand for universal suffrage. Jakob Bros explained the nature of workers' solidarity and proclaimed the formation of the Jewish Social Democratic Party of Galicia (JSDP), "a party arising *not against* the Polish or Ruthenian parties, but *alongside them.*" Then

> After a choir sang the Marseillaise a huge, demonstrative procession of Jewish workers formed up to join the Polish comrades at the riding school and rally together with them. All Jewish unions joined the ranks. Fifteen red placards, with slogans in Yiddish and Polish . . . , were carried above the tightly packed crowd. This impressive procession, in fours and eights, sparkled with red. Everyone was decorated with red carnations—the symbol of this year's May Day. Satisfaction and happiness radiated from all faces: everyone was beaming. Three hundred young people with their banner were for the first time taking part in this festive procession beside old, grey-headed proletarians—perhaps their fathers—all concerned with one thought, with one and the same sentiment.
>
> Hearts beat with happiness in response to the events of the day: at the sight of hundreds of demonstrating Jewish workers; at the thought that the sublime idea of socialism had reached even these, the most disenfranchised of people; and at

the thought that the Jewish proletariat had now straightened its hunched form, lifted its head bravely and come to *self-awareness*. This wonderful procession, having passed through the Jewish district, grew like a wave, swelled. The closer it came to the riding school, the larger it became. The number of demonstrators amounted to over 2,000 Jewish workers.[4]

Joining the PPSD's May Day demonstrations, which began at 10:00 a.m., was a powerful display of the new party's commitment to international working class solidarity, confirmed by collections JSDP members made for the PPSD's *Naprzód*.[5]

The JSDP's manifesto was signed by twenty-four activists and dated April 30. Two signatories, Franciszka Fargel and Helene Metsger, were women. The core of the new organization consisted of artisans living in the Yiddish milieu, like Blum, Papier, Poch, and Neker, and university students (or recent graduates), like Grossman, Bros, Rose, and Eyneygler, who already had years of experience in organizing Jewish workers. The mass of Jewish workers organized in unions and educational associations supported the JSDP.[6]

Grossman was the principal author of *What Do We Want?*[7] There were, it argued, significant obstacles to mobilizing Jewish workers, not only because of Galicia's backwardness, but because they were a distinctive group with a specific history, social environment, and characteristics. "It is necessary not only to speak to Jewish workers in a different language, one must also understand their psychology. One must be able to speak to their souls, fire them up, revolutionize and seize them!"[8] Drawing on arguments in *The Proletariat and the Jewish Question*, the manifesto identified how the Polish socialists' approach to agitation among Jewish workers, premised on the assumption that they were assimilating, amounted to a policy of polonization. "An alien, Polish ideology, which could neither win them over nor fire them up, was forced upon the Jewish masses and . . . the psychology of suffering was drummed into Jewish workers. Instead of arousing a sense of their own power and health, and a sense of their worth as Jews, they were mournfully told: Jew, you're doomed; you will disappear. Instead of awakening their dignity everything was done to shake and weaken their dignity. People like Hirsh Lekert do not emerge from such an atmosphere!"[9]

What Do We Want? provided a brief history of Jewish socialist organizations in Galicia and their recent relations with the Polish party, which had culminated in the formation of the JSDP. An independent Jewish party was the only organization that, "suited to the needs and life of the Jewish masses and to their ways of thinking, is able to spread socialist ideas amongst them, to produce the press it needs, to educate agitators."[10] As a part of international social democracy, the new party insisted on its hostility to Zionism, which it understood as a bourgeois, nationalist movement.[11]

Thanks to the split, the Polish party had lost a substantial proportion of its membership, probably more than a quarter. PPSD leaders now opportunistically brandished the slogan of "proletarian solidarity," in an attempt to recover influence in the Jewish working class.[12] They had no success. PPSD members labeled adherents of the new party "the separatists." Friendlier commentators sometimes referred to the JSDP as the Galician Bund or ŻPS (from its initials in Polish).

The final meeting of the PPSD's Kraków Jewish Agitation Committee took place on May 2, the day Daszyński denounced the JSDP in *Naprzód.*[13] Only accredited delegates of Jewish organizations were admitted, but "more than 400 workers, in spite of high temperatures and the tense atmosphere stayed until the end, providing evidence of enormous interest in our affairs and of enormous participation in the independent Jewish organization. The meeting lasted 6 hours."

The first speaker in the discussion of whether to wind up the Committee in favor of the JSDP was Henryk Grossman, whose time for the next years was mainly taken up by his work as the leader of the new party, and in responding to attacks on it from bosses, the state, Zionists, and the PPSD. The following debate involved three PPSD loyalists, as well as Blum, Dembitser, Bros, and Rose. The vote to dissolve the Committee was carried, with four hundred votes in favor and twelve against.[14]

Despite her hostility to the PPSD, Rosa Luxemburg of the Social Democratic Party of the Kingdom of Poland and Lithuania also criticized the establishment of the JSDP, days after the split, in an aside to a polemic against the PPS, whose nationalism she had long criticized. She noted that the PPSD's support for the nationalist and separatist policies of the PPS organizations in the Russian and German empires had come back to haunt it, in the form of the JSDP's declaration of independence.[15] This was a cheap shot: she never bothered to explore either the PPSD's relationship with Jewish workers or the radical differences between the comradely attitude of the JSDP to both the PPSD and the Austrian General Party, and the hostility of the PPS to German and Russian social democracy.

The JSDP expected a hostile response from the PPSD, but hoped for friendlier relations with the General Austrian Social Democratic Party. Henryk Grossman and seven other members of the Organizing Committee for the new party had written to the secretary of the Austrian General Party, on April 30, announcing their decision to found the JSDP on May 1 and seeking its admission to the Austrian social democratic federation.[16] They were soon disappointed. According to the *Arbeiter-Zeitung*, the newspaper of the German-Austrian party, a separate organization of Jewish workers in Galicia was "thoroughly harmful."[17]

Grossman was, however, able to address a special meeting of the Executive of the General Party in Vienna, that considered the JSDP Organizing Committee's letter and the formation of the Jewish party.[18] Grossman was no babe in the Vienna woods. He was already familiar with the city, thanks to earlier visits, particularly to the Vienna branch of the Kurz clan. When he took the train to the imperial capital, he was also psychologically prepared for a confrontation with the Executive of the General Party. His writing style in the early documents of the JSDP already demonstrated greater maturity and control than his pamphlet on the Jewish question, published a few months before. Grossman had lost his temper in discussions with the PPSD Executive when presented with the ultimatum to leave *Zjednoczenie*. That he regretted. But the experience was useful. It now helped him to channel his emotions more effectively while explaining the circumstances that had made the establishment of the JSDP necessary. When challenged about its attitude to the authority of the General Party, he made it clear that, while "the decisions of the Executive of the General Party had great moral authority," no resolution of the General Executive would lead the new party to dissolve itself. But the Executive resolved unanimously not to recognize the JSDP, because it supposedly "contradicted the Brünn program and the organization of our Party."[19]

That was not the end of the matter. Just as Grossman had appealed his expulsion by the PPSD Executive to the Polish party's Congress, the JSDP appealed the decision of the General Party's Executive to the next General Party Congress, to be held in October 1905.

In the meantime, the JSDP defended itself against criticisms, slanders, and violence. The PPSD supplemented polemics against the JSDP, which for a period appeared daily in *Naprzód*, with physical attacks. PPSD thugs brutally assaulted the gray-haired Yitskhok Blind, despite his years of service to the Polish party, and disrupted the new party's meetings.[20] But, by the end of May, the JSDP had acquired correspondents in a series of additional eastern Galician towns.[21]

To counteract the PPSD's attacks, the JSDP appealed directly to Polish workers. Five thousand copies of the JSDP manifesto were issued in Polish, in addition to the six thousand published in Yiddish. The party's pre-Congress bulletin, *Before the Congress*, also appeared in both languages.[22] Unfortunately, and this was the fundamental weakness of the strategy of setting up the JSDP rather than a new, cross-national party, there was no effective radical socialist current around which Polish workers and activists could cohere in Galicia in order to combat the nationalism and reformism of the PPSD.

The new party's pre-Congress bulletin began with a "Reply to the Social Democratic Party of Galicia," probably written by Grossman,[23] in the light of his encounter with the General Party Executive. He began by demolishing the accusation that a conspiracy had ambushed the PPSD with the split. This was absurd, after three years of conflict within the Polish party over the organization of Jewish workers. It was hard to repress a smile at the sight of comrade Daszyński—just when the majority of Jewish workers had left the Polish party—chasing after them shouting: "Wait! It's a conspiracy. We didn't expect this, we didn't know that this is what you really think!"

In 1902, Grossman pointed out, Daszyński himself had argued the case for the equality of national social democratic organizations, in comments on the conflict between the PPS (in Prussia) and the Social Democratic Party of Germany. The PPS, moreover, had demanded independence from the overall German party, while the JSDP sought only independence *within* the Austrian General Party. Surely, Grossman suggested, there was a contradiction between Daszyński's position on the PPS and the JSDP. Based on a detailed examination of the records of General Party congresses, Grossman demonstrated that nothing in the policies or statutes of Austrian social democracy stood in the way of the JSDP's affiliation.[24]

The JSDP's own founding Congress took place in Lemberg on Friday 9 (the anniversary of Hirsh Lerkert's execution) and Saturday, June 10. The decision to meet on the Sabbath was in line with the antireligious traditions of the Jewish socialist movement.

"A well trained male choir giving a beautiful rendition of 'Di Shvue,'" the Bund's anthem, opened the Congress.[25] The ballroom of Dank's Hotel was decorated with red banners carrying socialist and revolutionary slogans. Portraits of Marx, Lassalle, and, between them, Lerkert, decorated the platform. There were fifty-two delegates, including three women, from eight urban centers in Galicia, and 350 guests. In a letter to the Bund, Grossman claimed that representatives of "about 2,000 organized workers, that is nearly a third of all those in Galicia who are organized!" attended the Congress.[26]

Having provided a theoretical justification for the foundation of the JSDP during the first session of the founding Congress, Grossman later introduced the discussion of agitation and tactics and proposed a resolution on relations with the PPSD and the General Party. This confirmed the efforts of the interim Organizing Committee to put pressure on the PPSD by entering into a dialogue with rank-and-file Polish socialists. The Congress unanimously adopted the General Party program of 1901, its 1899 nationality program and Grossman's motion that the JSDP considered itself a component of the General Party.[27]

The most heated debate was over the question of what made the party distinctive. Comrade Mandel, from Przemyśl, asked why the JSDP didn't raise Jewish national demands—precisely the question raised, with more hostile intent, by the PPSD. A series of leading figures in the party responded: Rose,

Grossman, Bros, and Eyneygler explained that the Jewish party was not set up for nationalist reasons but as a necessary means to agitate effectively among Jewish workers.[28] This argument underpinned the JSDP's manifesto and the "Reply to the Social Democratic Party of Galicia." The dominant position in the Jewish party, it filled the rhetoric of the Austrian General Party with a sometimes explicitly Bundist content and disingenuously omitted to mention that most leaders of both the Bund and JSDP supported the demand for Jewish national cultural autonomy.

There was, however, a different, theoretically incompatible argument that contradicted the Bund's perspective but was persuasive in its pragmatism. First, the PPSD was nationalist and incapable of relating to Jewish workers. Second, the General Party was organized on a federal basis. So, while a militant, internationalist organization of the entire Galician proletariat was desirable, the only means currently available for the social democratic organization of the Jewish proletariat was an independent Jewish party, which could hope to gain affiliation to the General Party. Anzelm Mosler summed up this position very clearly, in the best received speech at the JSDP's founding Congress:

> I personally believe that the best form of organization would indeed be territorial. That is, instead of Polish, Ruthenian and Jewish parties on Galician territory we should have a single party, a Galician one. However, if the Germans, the Czechs, the Poles, etc. each have their own organizations; if a different principle is applied to the question of organization, then I don't see any reason why Jewish workers should not have the same rights as all the others.
>
> Is it really written down somewhere that there shall only be *six* national organizations (the German, Czech, Polish, Italian, Slovenian and Ruthenian) and not, God forbid, seven?! We see, actually, that the number of national organizations is not fixed. Initially we had three organizations, the German, the Czech and the Polish. After 1897 there were, in addition, the Italian and the Slovenian and, finally, in 1899, the Ruthenian. So we see that the number of organizations is not fixed. From three it leapt to six and now, without any magic, the seventh, Jewish Party appears.[29]

This position paralleled the preference for a single centralized social democratic organization in Russia expressed by the SDKPiL and, more consistently, the Bolsheviks. For Mosler, it was the PPSD's nationalism, rather than any principle of Jewish organizational independence, that ruled out such an organization in Galicia.

The Congress decided that, in view of the acknowledged theoretical weakness of the Lemberg organization, the JSDP's Executive would sit in Kraków, where seven of its members lived. The other three would have to travel from Lemberg. At the age of twenty-four, Grossman, the secretary of the Organizing

Committee and already the new party's most prominent leader, became the secretary of the JSDP.[30] After he, Eyneygler, and Poch had made addresses to conclude the Congress formally, the delegates and guests partied until late at night in the Saxon Gardens, with speeches and socialist and revolutionary songs. A photographic postcard of the delegates to the Congress, reproduced on the following page, commemorated the event. Grossman is the second from the right in the front row, reclining against Janek Bross.[31]

Mass Struggle

Although the mutiny on the battleship *Potemkin* started on June 27, the revolutionary movement in Russia ebbed for several months after May 1905. But in Austria it was a hot and militant summer. Vast new segments of the Galician population—Poles, Ukrainians, and Jews—were politicized for the first time. In Kraków and Lemberg, the JSDP was involved in a series of strikes and led previously ununionized Jewish and even Polish workers into the socialist movement. Experienced militants from the two capitals, in particular, made successful expeditions to smaller towns, where Zionist influence was strong. By the end of October, there were already local committees or individual delegates in eleven other towns from the far western to the eastern borders of Galicia.[32] One of the new party's first priorities was to organize schools for agitators, to train members in spreading the social democratic message to rallies, meetings, and individual workers.[33]

Developments in Russia raised expectations in the Austro-Hungarian Empire. Austrian workers fought not only to improve their economic conditions but also over political demands. Among Jewish workers there was a surge in demand for radical literature, which the Bund, quickly responding to Grossman's request, helped satisfy.[34] The relationship was, however, reciprocal: he continued to organize the smuggling of material into and out of Russia and even the printing of literature for the Bund.[35]

In September, the Austrian General Party began a campaign of meetings, rallies, and marches across the empire around the demand for universal suffrage. The JSDP joined in the agitation. In Kraków, the Jewish party convened a public discussion on Saturday, October 14. Of those wanting to attend, only 1,500 could cram into the functions room at the Hotel Klein.

Comrade Grossman opened the meeting with a short speech: he drew attention to the importance of the political movement in Austria; the great tasks before the Austrian proletariat in general and the Jewish proletariat in particular. "The Jewish workers in Kraków and Galicia are conducting an independent struggle against political injustice for the first time. The electoral system has

The placard reads "The first Congress of the Jewish Social Democratic Party of Galicia held in Lemberg on June 9–10, 1905." Henryk Grossman is second from the right in the front row. From the Archives of the YIVO Institute for Jewish Research, New York.

given them no rights at all, or no true rights, where the burdens and taxes which oppress the proletariat are determined. In an Austria which already totters like a sick old man, whose filthy body stands on broken feet, in such an Austria, Prime Minister F. Gautsch has denied the people their rights."[36]

Union activity and organization developed rapidly in Lemberg and Kraków. For example, Jewish house painters in Kraków, under the JSDP leadership of Maurycy Papier, prepared a campaign over wages and conditions at weekly meetings from March and also held joint meetings with Polish workers in the trade. Forty-one struck for a week from July 2. The PPSD's *Yidishe arbeter-tseytung* and Żuławski, criticized the action, which the PPSD labeled "foolish." But they won a wage rise of more than 15 percent, a reduction in the working day from eleven or twelve to ten hours, the May Day holiday, a closed shop, and, if there were two holidays in a week, pay for one of them. These gains were typical of the dramatic increases in Galician wages during 1905, in both absolute and relative terms.[37]

As in Russia, the political demonstrations and mass strikes of October and November 1905 prompted higher levels of struggle over wages, hours, and conditions. Even excluding the vast numbers of participants in the massive political strikes of October 23 in Lwów and November 28 across the whole province (and Austria), the number of Galician workers who struck over economic demands rose 35 percent between 1904 and 1905, to 11,589.[38]

At the founding Congress of the JSDP Franciszka Fargel had moved a successful motion that more attention should be paid to organizing and agitating among women workers. Her efforts among women workers in Kraków were soon emulated elsewhere in Galicia. In most places where the party existed, it recruited women. In Lemberg, Tarnów, and Podgórze, applications were made for the official registration of women workers' associations, like the one in Kraków.[39]

Outside the large cities, the main political obstacle to winning Jewish workers over to social democracy was Zionism. A JSDP meeting in Podgórze, just across the bridge over the Vistula from Kraków, turned into a debate with local Zionists. In his contribution, Grossman "showed how false the Zionist 'love' of the Jewish people was. With sharp words and quotations from the Zionist press, he demonstrated what a swindle these people's position on the revolution in Russia was. Further, the speaker gave a popular explanation of the meaning of socialism, how enormously significant and vital it was for the working class. Finally, he proved that a workers' organization in general and the JSDP in particular was a necessity."[40]

The JSDP recruited rapidly. In a letter to the Foreign Committee of the Bund in late July, Grossman claimed the party had grown from two thousand members, at its foundation, to about three thousand. This was probably an overestimate, made to support his request that the Bund send a comrade to edit the new weekly newspaper planned by the party.[41] But in late October, the JSDP's report to the Austrian General Party Congress claimed that 2,500 was a conservative assessment of the number of workers belonging to its affiliated associations and unions. Given that PPSD delegates were in a position to ridicule unrealistic membership claims at the Congress, the figure is very plausible. It represented growth of 25 percent in less than six months.[42]

To sustain this expansion and educate its members, the JSDP needed a more regular organ. From October 6, 1905, the weekly *Der sotsial-demokrat* (Social Democrat) became a key element of the party's activity. The newspaper was based in Kraków. The Bund was unable to provide an experienced editor so, when the first issue appeared, the job was done by Jakover, a pharmacist, while Grossman was the publisher and legally responsible for the publication.[43] The establishment and regular appearance of the *Social Democrat*, despite financial difficulties and censorship, was a strong indicator of the party's growth and health. Such a publication was a huge task for a small organization, overwhelmingly made up of impoverished workers. What is more, a number of the intellectuals who worked on the *Social Democrat*, including Grossman, could not write in Yiddish.

The General Party Congress

In early September 1905, the JSDP formally appealed to the General Party Congress, scheduled for the end of October, against the decision of the General Party Executive not to recognize it.[44] There was no reply. So, on October 23, the day of the political strike in Lwów, Grossman wrote to Victor Adler personally. He was not about to let the General Executive or its most prominent member get away with ignoring this embarrassing question. His note was abrupt.[45] But it had the desired effect. The issue was placed on the agenda of the forthcoming Congress.

Grossman prepared two broadsheets, in German, for distribution among delegates to the Congress. One was an address, "To the social democrats in Austria"; the other, a report on the conditions of Jewish workers in Galicia and the activities of the JSDP.[46]

The address explained why the Jewish party should be recognized as a component of the General Party. The case began with a long extract from the Bund's message to the JSDP's founding Congress. It had two functions. On the one hand, it indicated that the new Galician party was not an appendage of the Bund, which "limits its activities to the interests of the Jewish proletariat in Russia." The message, on the other hand, made it clear that the largest social democratic organization in the Russian Empire regarded the emergence of the JSDP as entirely justified.[47]

Grossman went on to outline the orthodoxy of the JSDP's politics. There was, however, a distinctive Jewish proletariat, with its own language and cultural-social milieu in Galicia. Like the working classes of other nations in Austria, the Jewish workers therefore needed their own autonomous, national party to organize the struggle against the Jewish bourgeoisie. Given the JSDP's adherence to the program and tactics of the General Party, "the current conflict is purely organizational."[48]

While the address provided a theoretical case for recognition of the JSDP its activity to this point outlined in the report was "the best proof that we not only have a right to our organization . . . but that it is also viable and justified."[49] The report's account of the effects of economic developments on Jewish workers in Galicia extended the analysis in Grossman's pamphlet on the Jewish question into a brief but impressive Marxist account of the contradictions of capital accumulation in the Province. "With the extension of the railway and roads and the emergence of many markets, the artisanal products of small masters are more and more undermined. They no longer work on orders from individuals. In the larger towns production is for large department stores, intermediaries or exporters. Here the small masters increasingly become dependent wage workers producing shoddy goods for the local market. . . . Increasingly the figure of the merchant, the dealer (exporter) steps between the direct producer and consumer. This anticipates the emergence of capitalist factory owners and a higher stage of capitalist development." In the process, a modern working class, represented by the labor movement was emerging. "To the extent that this movement demands better conditions of work and wages, it leads to the concentration and capitalization of production, which can better afford these higher expenses. The transition to industrialism and to factory production, however, encounters from the start its most significant obstacle: the lack of any protection for outworkers."

The General Party's campaign to regulate outwork was therefore very important for Jewish workers. It would limit their exploitation by employers and "call a halt to the swindle of the Jewish 'philanthropists,' who want to give many Jewish families the opportunity to exist by extending out-work," and accelerate the process of industrialization. "We know that the proletarian labor movement can only develop through and against capitalism."[50]

The bulk of the broadsheet, describing the JSDP's political and organizational work and achievements, embodied a single, powerful argument for recognition by the General Party: that it was effective in involving Jewish workers in the socialist movement.[51]

Given the balance of forces in the General Party, dominated by the alliance between the German-Austrian and Polish organizations, it was unlikely that the Congress would recognize the JSDP. As it turned out, an extremely favorable development prevented the JSDP delegates from testing their strength in a vote at the Congress. Workers in Russia had begun to set up councils, *soviets*, to coordinate the strike movement. Soon these revolutionary institutions began to function as alternative governments, challenging the authority of the Tsarist state.

The day the General Party Congress opened, Monday, October 30, Tsar Nikolai II finally responded to the pressure of the revolutionary strike movement with his October Manifesto. He promised a constitution including a broad suffrage and a parliament (Duma) with control over the budget.

After receiving this news, the Congress focused almost exclusively on the escalating Austrian movement for universal suffrage. A massive social democratic demonstration filled Vienna's Ringstrasse that evening. Large demonstrations took to the streets in cities and towns across the empire during the following days. The three JSDP delegates, "Abraham Poch and Lennel Blum and Heinrich Großmann [sic], secretary," agreed that discussion of their appeal should be postponed and issued a declaration, which concluded that "just as the Jewish proletariat has shed its blood together with the proletariat of Poland and Russia in the streets of Warsaw, Łódź and all over Russia for the common cause, we also want to demonstrate that the Jewish proletariat in Galicia will do its duty too in the struggles which the Austrian proletariat undertakes. Long live international social democracy."[52]

The General Party's demands for which the JSDP's concerns were sacrificed were very moderate. Where the Russian social democrats rejected the Tsar's concessions, calling for a republic or a constituent assembly, Austrian social democracy confined its campaign to the demand for universal, equal suffrage, conducted through secret ballots. It construed even this in a way that left more than half of the adult population without a vote. Adelheid Popp, a leader of the Austrian social democratic women's movement, announced to the Congress that women would renounce their demand for the franchise in the current campaign, in the interests of a more effective struggle.[53]

The Austrian campaign for universal suffrage accelerated. There were clashes between marchers and police in Vienna on November 2.[54] After troops fired on protestors in Wenceslas Square on November 4, radical groups in Prague began to build street barricades.[55]

The JSDP, like the officially recognized sections of the General Party, threw itself into the campaign. Grossman and Blum reported on the Congress and the movement for electoral reform to a party meeting in Kraków on Saturday

November 4, helping to build a rally the next day. Around twenty thousand people turned out for the protest.[56] The following weeks saw hundreds of meetings and demonstrations in favor of universal suffrage across the Austrian Empire. Police attacked rallies in Lemberg and Tarnopol (now Ternopil in the Ukraine).[57]

On Sunday, the 5th, there was a public meeting on electoral reform and the elections to the Kraków *kehile* (local Jewish administration with authority, under Austrian law, over Jews in religious and related matters), organized by the Party of the Independent Jews, also known as the Jewish Democrats. Attempting to broaden the influence of the JSDP, Grossman participated in the discussion. He appealed to democratic sections of the Jewish bourgeoisie to support the proletariat's struggle for universal suffrage and attacked the Zionists, who had demanded that the meeting be called off because Jewish blood was being shed in Russia; they encouraged people "not to struggle, but to weep."[58]

The high point of the movement was a general strike on Saturday, November 28. The JSDP, with Grossman in the forefront, put huge efforts into building the stoppage. On Monday, November 13, he was in Tarnów speaking to party members on the importance of general strike action and political organization. Then, after leading a discussion about Zionism and the pogroms in Russia at the Forverts hall in Kraków on Friday, he was back in Tarnów on Saturday, the 17th, to talk at a public meeting on the general strike and universal suffrage.[59] On Sunday evening there was a discussion of the general strike in the hall of the JSDP-led commercial workers' union in Kraków. Grossman was one of the main participants. During the following week, the party in Kraków held three public meetings: two in Kraków itself and one in Podgórze, which Grossman addressed.

On the day of the strike, business stopped across the empire and there were enormous workers' rallies and processions. In Vienna alone, a quarter of a million people joined the strikers' march. One hundred and fifty thousand demonstrated in Prague.[60]

In Kraków, four thousand people were already in the square off Ulica Święty Sebastiana, down the road from Grossman's home, at 9:00 a.m. By 10:00 a.m. the square was overflowing with people who wanted to hear the JSDP's speakers. Grossman, in the longest speech, argued that in fighting for universal suffrage Jewish workers should not forget the national question. But the Zionists' argument that proportional representation would solve the national question was false. It would not prevent the smaller nationalities from being minorities in parliament. "If we want a fundamental solution to the national question in Austria, we have to demand national autonomy, so that it will no longer be possible for the larger nations to overpower the smaller nations." He also proposed a motion, which expressed this analysis and was adopted unanimously. This address was interrupted by the arrival of eight hundred to a thousand young workers with their own banner. Grossman briefly broke off his address to welcome them.

By the end of the JSDP's rally, six to eight thousand people were present. They marched to the Polish socialists' assembly point. On the way, a group of Polish comrades, who had been waiting for them, joined their procession. When the mass of Jewish demonstrators joined the Polish strikers, there was a spontaneous meeting addressed by Józef Drobner of the PPSD and Bros of the JSDP, who ended with the cry "Long live the Polish and Jewish Parties!"

The combined demonstration—fifty thousand people according to the socialist press—marched to and filled the large Rynek Głowny (central market square) in the largest demonstration in Kraków's history.[61]

After the success of the general strike, the Czech social democrats wanted to call a further general strike for early December. But Adler and other leaders of the General Party were committed to the parliamentary process and afraid that the movement might get out of hand. They accepted the government's endorsement of electoral reform at face value, overruled the Czech social democrats, and curtailed a movement that had the potential to win far more than universal suffrage, to bring down the government or even the empire. As a consequence, even the introduction of universal suffrage was delayed. Bogged down in parliamentary haggling, the new electoral procedures only became law on January 26, 1907.[62]

* * *

Although the General Party Congress had not recognized the JSDP, the Jewish party was not entirely isolated in the social democratic movement. It adhered to the General Party's program and participated in the mass struggles of 1905–6 alongside members of the parties affiliated to the Austrian social democratic federation. In these revolutionary conditions, the lack of a formal relationship between the JSDP and General Party was not only of secondary importance, but could also appear a temporary problem. From the start, the JSDP had friends in the Bund and among Jewish socialists in the neighboring Austrian province of Bukovina. In early 1906, the theoretical organ of the Czech party, *Akademie: Socialistickă Revue,* published a justification for the formation of the JSDP by Henryk Grossman.[63]

The article repackaged the arguments in earlier JSDP documents for a new audience. Grossman compared the struggle of Galician Jews against the PPSD leadership for national rights inside the social democratic movement to relations between the Czech and German-Austrian parties. In doing so he stimulated a very sensitive Czech nerve. Similarly, increasingly influential dissidents in the USDP, who wanted to terminate their party's client relationship with the PPSD, were sympathetic to the JSDP.[64]

Consolidating the Party

Tsarist troops broke up the St. Petersburg Soviet on December 16 and arrested its leaders. By the end of the month, an insurrection initiated by the Moscow Soviet had been put down after days of street fighting. It was not, however, until mid-1907 that the Tsar was finally able to reassert his autocratic power. In Austria, the organized labor movement continued to grow rapidly during 1906 and 1907, while the economic boom lasted.[65]

Meanwhile, the campaign for electoral reform remained at the center of social democratic agitation for more than a year. At the same time, the JSDP continued to lead Jewish workers' struggles for wages, better working conditions, and union recognition. Nor did the JSDP neglect the theoretical education of its members. Grossman, for example, spoke on Karl Marx when, in early March 1906, the Forverts association in Kraków celebrated the twenty-third anniversary of his death. In July 1907, the *Sotsial-demokrat* marked the fortieth anniversary of the publication of the first volume of Marx's *Capital*. The article provided a conventional account of the relationship between the labor theory of value, social classes and the inevitability of socialism, the foundations of Marxist economics, and Grossman's understanding of society.[66]

The exchange value of commodities (the ratios in which they are exchanged) is ultimately determined by the amount of socially necessary labor (the normal amount of labor under current, average conditions of production) that goes into making them and the machinery, equipment, and raw material consumed in their creation. That labor is performed by workers who sell their ability to work (labor power) to employers.

The value of labor power is determined in the same way as other commodities, by the amount of labor that goes into ensuring that workers return to work day after day and can create the next generation of workers. But workers are capable of more work in a day than is necessary to simply reproduce themselves. This surplus labor gives rise to surplus value in the commodities they make. That is the source of employers' profits. With the application of technology, the productivity of labor increases and with it the amount of surplus value. Capitalist competition leads to the concentration and centralization of production: as smaller capitalists go under, the scale of production increases. Workers are concentrated in larger and larger factories, promoting a greater awareness of their own power.

Meanwhile, with electoral reform held up by reactionaries in the Reichsrat,[67] the JSDP's Executive planned to use the JSDP's Congress, at the end of May 1906, to prepare party members for a renewed period of mass struggle. The Executive also linked the issue of universal suffrage to the fight against the national oppression of Jewish workers by raising the demand for national cultural autonomy.

Grossman's contribution to the discussion on the party's activity over the past year, during the first session of the Congress, was greeted by applause lasting several minutes. It was not only the remarks he had just made that were being acclaimed, but also Henryk Grossman as the founding secretary and preeminent leader of the JSDP. Members recognized that the party was, to a large extent, his creation.[68]

The JSDP now had more than 2,800 members and had extended its presence into a series of new towns.[69] One of its main achievements was the creation of a layer of organic intellectuals of the working class, with both middle- and working-class backgrounds, capable of leading Jewish workers' struggles.[70]

The party secretary delivered a long report on electoral reform, the current political situation, and the national question, opening the most important discussion at the Congress. He justified the party's internationalism and militant tactics by placing the issue of universal suffrage in the context of the proletariat's broader struggle. Political intrigues, he pointed out, had blocked legislation for universal suffrage. The time was approaching when "the proletariat had to take the final step along the path of legal means of struggle and this step will be the general mass strike." In contrast to the right wing of the social democratic movement, Grossman emphasized the limits of the Marxist commitment to bourgeois legality:

> [Working class] power is used in different ways. There were times when the proletariat fought, weapons in hand, on the barricades. Then weapons gave way to voting slips. Now we are preparing for a mass strike which is the start of an active revolutionary struggle . . .
>
> So we are not supporters of revolution for its own sake—but nor are we supporters of legality for its own sake. We regard barricades and voting slips as good in the same way. They are only means to our goal, to achieve rights for the oppressed working class . . . The time is coming when we will again shake things up with the old revolutionary enthusiasm. The mass strike, the last step on the legal path is the first step of the revolution![71]

It might be objected that Galicia was too backward and agrarian to sustain a general strike, Grossman acknowledged. In reply, "we will point on the one hand to Russia. And we will ask: where are the large industries there? Where in Russia are there important trade unions. And yet Russia is the classic land of the mass strike! And on the other hand we will point to the *mood* of our masses and we will say: that is our power, that is the guarantee for the mass strike. It will help us to fulfill our duty, as a party and as a working class."[72]

Grossman's analysis of the relationship between periods of revolution and quieter political development and his attitude to the mass strike expressed the views of the center and left of European social democracy.[73]

The center, which included Adler, Bauer, and Kautsky, while more willing than the right to discuss revolution, was no more prepared to initiate one. In Vienna, the leadership of the German-Austrian party only began to actively prepare the working class for a mass strike over the introduction of universal suffrage, on Sunday June 10, a few days before its scheduled start. There was no public discussion of the revolutionary implications of the mass strike tactic in the German-Austrian party like the one Grossman initiated in the JSDP. The General Party leaders' announcement of the strike demonstrated their concern that it should not slip out of their control and threaten the established order: there would be a three-day stoppage in Vienna "and *only* in Vienna."[74]

But there was no general strike. The Electoral Reform Committee of the Reichsrat's House of Representatives resumed its consideration of the issues and the General Party called off its action. The JSDP had to go along with this decision. Once they had decided to build a specifically Jewish party within the General Party, rather than a revolutionary current involving workers of all nationalities in Galicia (or the empire), Grossman and his comrades were hostages to the flawed reformist tactics of Austrian social democracy. The German-Austrian leaders repeated their error of November 1905, again accepting government assurances and calling a halt to militant action. So the shape and timing of electoral reform were determined in a vastly less favorable political forum than the factories and streets: the Reichsrat. There the debates revolved around nationalist concerns and promoted nationalist ideas, including in the labor movement.

The final deals done to get the legislation through both houses of the Reichsrat meant that it fell a long way short of universal and equal suffrage, let alone democratic government. Women, everyone younger than twenty-four, and recipients of public charity could not vote. In eastern Galicia special two-member seats were established, to make sure that the Polish minority was overrepresented. The power of the unelected House of Lords was actually increased.[75]

After outlining how the working class could win universal suffrage, Grossman went on, at the JSDP's 1906 Congress, to criticize voting systems counterposed to the one based on single member constituencies with the same number of voters in each, proposed by the government and supported by the General Party. He rejected claims by the government, the Zionists, and supporters of proportional representation that the electoral reforms they supported could resolve the national question. His conclusion on this point was convincing: "electoral systems, even the best of them, won't end national struggles."[76] But he and the JSDP Congress believed that, in national cultural autonomy, *they* had a solution to the national question.[77]

The Proletariat and the Jewish Question had focused on the Jewish question *within* the social democratic movement, rather than the way to combat anti-Semitism and national oppression in the outside world. JSDP publications and pronouncements during the first year of the party's existence had consistently affirmed the party's adherence to the program of the Austrian party, including its national program. Circumstances had changed. The leaders of the *Jewish* Social Democratic Party now thought it was time to include a strategy for combating the oppression of Jews in the party's program.

After the general social democratic Congress in 1905, the immediate need for the strictest programmatic orthodoxy in order to impress the General Party had passed. The JSDP's Executive knew that leading figures in the German-Austrian party favored Renner's proposal for national cultural autonomy. It was no secret. Grossman's speech at the JSDP's first public meeting in Przemyśl, on Sunday, December 31, 1905, had dealt with the topic.[78]

Recent developments in Russia also encouraged the Jewish Marxists in Galicia to change their official position on the national question. The Sixth Congress of the Bund, in October 1905, formally incorporated the demand for national cultural autonomy into its minimum program. This had not proved to be an obstacle to unity when the Bund rejoined the RSDLP at a unification Congress in April–May 1906, less than a month before the JSDP's Congress.[79]

What is more, the JSDP was not entirely isolated, even though it remained formally outside the General Party. Programmatic orthodoxy no longer seemed essential in order to maintain friendly relations with the Czech, Ukrainian, and Bukovinian social democratic parties. A representative of the Bund, one of its founders, "Lonu" (Shmuel Gozhansky), even addressed the second JSDP Congress.[80]

The motion on the national question that Grossman proposed to the Congress drew on the approaches of Renner and the Bund. Once democratized, through the introduction of universal suffrage, parliament's competence in the area of national cultural affairs—essentially educational matters—should be passed to democratic national cultural institutions. "However far this idea is from being realized," he asserted, reproducing the General Party's positive attitude to the empire, "everyone knows it has to be realized if Austria is not to fall apart." Grossman also thought that, "freed from national conflict, the central parliament will become a field of utterly unobscured class struggle."[81]

It was certainly true that education was a key issue in national conflicts in Austria and that the absence of state-funded instruction in Yiddish was an important question for the Jewish working class. The idea that national cultural autonomy would remove the national question from the political and economic agenda was, however, utopian. The national question cannot be reduced to educational and linguistic matters.[82] Grossman's own mention, in passing, of the 1906 controversy over the Hungarian demand for an autonomous tariff was an excellent demonstration of the inextricable links among national, economic, and political issues. When people think in nationalist categories, there are no questions that are not national questions.[83] Grossman's resolution calling for national cultural autonomy for the different nations in Austria was, nevertheless, adopted unanimously.[84]

The Congress returned Grossman to the party Executive. But, now that the party was firmly established, Henryk Schreiber/Shrayber, a young law student and participant in the party's theatrical activities, with a bourgeois background like Grossman's, took over the increasingly routine job of party secretary.[85] Until late October 1906, Grossman continued to hold the posts of the publisher and responsible editor the *Sotsial-demokrat.* They required little work, but did involve considerable legal vulnerability.[86]

Debating Tactics

After the JSDP's Congress, the impressive growth in the breadth and depth of the network of unions and workers' associations affiliated with the party continued. Sixteen Jewish and three Polish butchers in Przemyśl, for example, organized themselves into a union for the first time, with the encouragement of the Jewish party.[87]

During the second half of 1906, there was a major controversy within the party over strategy. Grossman was very ambitious about the JSDP's potential to increase its influence by embracing "a new phase in our movement." *Sotsial-demokrat* published his two-part article "On Our Agitation and Propaganda" which opened a discussion of the party's perspectives.

During the first phase of its development, Grossman argued, the party had for the first time pursued the task of systematically organizing Jewish workers in the smaller towns and *shtetlekh* of Galicia. The PPSD's failure to do so had led to the repeated collapse of Jewish workers' organizations. The backwardness of the Galician economy made efforts to organize workers very difficult. But to the extent that socialists succeeded in building trade unions in the smaller towns and villages, they could improve the lives of workers in remote areas. Extending his analysis in the report to the General Austrian Social

Democratic Congress in October 1905, Grossman explained that "the modern workers' movement ... is a factor that has a revolutionary influence on the economic evolution of the periphery of Galicia and *drives* the general evolution of the Province. In a province where the *szlachta*'s agrarian interests lead it to use all the means at its disposal to limit the development of industry, its sole counterweight is the workers' movement which even revolutionizes the most distant parts of the periphery."[88]

In doing so the labor movement expanded the scope for political activity in the cities. The persistence of starvation wages and sixteen to twenty hours of labor a day in the villages put continuous pressure on working conditions in the larger urban centers. The problem of internal migration was compounded by emigration: "How many intelligent workers have left Galicia in the last 10 years! It is not hard to work out the consequences of this for organizations in the larger cities."[89]

In the second part of his essay, Grossman argued that the party could dramatically increase its influence if it adopted the right policies. Its influence among the Jewish masses was no longer threatened by the PPSD. Now the JSDP could achieve political hegemony among Galician Jews, by becoming a popular movement with an appeal that extended beyond the working class to small businesspeople and professionals, and even to some democratic elements in the Jewish bourgeoisie who could also contribute additional funds to the party. But the JSDP and the *Sotsial-demokrat* were neglecting issues that could attract middle-class supporters, as opposed to what he saw as the current overemphasis on trade union matters and its own internal affairs. "Nothing is written or practically nothing is written about the general economic or political relations in a particular town, about the local councils, about the *kehile,* about the local Polish or Ukrainian politicians, about their policies in the Sejm or the [Reichsrat]."[90]

Building trade unionism, Grossman argued, would still be the starting point for work outside the larger towns. But in the urban areas the party would have to participate in much wider political activities. In the first elections to the Reichsrat under universal suffrage, the JSDP might stand candidates in Kraków and Lemberg. The Executive also wanted to start publishing a Polish periodical, in order to expand the party's influence. This perspective could only be achieved if members made more money available for the tasks facing the party; Grossman concluded his article with an appeal for funds.[91] Many comrades were reluctant and tardy in paying their party dues.

All this assumed that the social climate of the previous year and a half would continue, that there would be high levels of popular unrest and working-class struggle. Such conditions would make the Jewish working class a stronger pole of political attraction for the Jewish petty bourgeoisie, particularly if the JSDP continued to grow rapidly and coordinate the activities of the Jewish proletariat.

Karol Eyneygler was more in touch with conditions in the murky pool of Galician politics. He poured cold water on Grossman's analysis. In the *Sotsial-demokrat*, he pointed out that, even in the unions, the JSDP was still vulnerable to the PPSD. Żuławski and Weisberg, a second Galician trade union organizer paid for by the central unions, worked politically for the PPSD and against the JSDP.

In a more concrete discussion than Grossman's, Eyneygler conceded that it might be necessary to stand candidates for Reichsrat seats in Kraków and Lemberg so that Jewish social democrats did not have to choose between voting for petty bourgeois Zionists or the representatives of the Jewish big bourgeoisie. But "our involvement in electoral activity won't have the significance for our Party that it had for the PPSD."[92] He held no hope that a JSDP candidate might be elected. On the question of funds Eyneygler was also more sober: "I must confess that comrade Grossman cannot be our Party's 'finance minister.' His plan to get money from the petty bourgeoisie is inadequate." To attract support from the petty bourgeoisie, the JSDP would, first, have to become a much more significant force in society. Agitation among the Jewish intelligentsia, perhaps, would achieve better results.[93]

Eyneygler's analysis of the political situation proved to be more accurate than Grossman's. Reactionaries across Europe were recovering their self-confidence, as the Tsarist regime increasingly reasserted its power in Russia during 1906. The economic boom that had begun around 1903 in Austria was sustained until 1907 and Austrian trade unions continued to recruit during 1906, though at a slower rate than during the previous two years.[94] But, now that the huge mobilizations and the strike movement of 1905 had subsided, Austria's rulers were probing for ways to reassert their power and turn the clock back. Employers, too, were becoming more confident and it was harder for workers to win industrial disputes.

Grossman himself had recently experienced the aggressive mood of Jewish reactionaries in small towns and *shtetlekh*.[95] Building a socialist organization in such places could be physically dangerous. A new Jewish workers' group in Chrzanów, for example, faced fierce hostility from Jewish bosses.[96]

The population of Chrzanów, about forty-five kilometers to the west of Kraków, was less than six thousand and more than half the inhabitants were Jewish.[97] Most of the bosses were Khasids, members of fanatical Jewish sects, each focused on its own "wise man." They dominated their underpaid employees not only at work, but through control over the kehile and municipal council. Such community leaders did not welcome outside agitators who disrupted this paternalistic and (for employers) profitable order, with its fifteen-hour working day. The mayor expelled two JSDP members from the town in early June 1906, after local Zionists had denounced them.[98] The small-time autocrats soon decided to tackle the problem of socialist influence more forcefully.

Outsiders, especially well-dressed gentlemen among traditionally bearded, hatted, and clothed inhabitants, were not difficult to pick out. When Henryk Grossman came to speak at a meeting, on June 23, 1906, the Khasidic zealots incited a large crowd to beat him up and trash the premises of the recently established Forverts (Forwards) Association.[99] In Christina Stead's short story, based on the incident, the police eventually escorted him to the station. On arriving back in Kraków, "he found an excited crowd of workers at the station and in front of them was his sister, Mrs Rock, very pale, almost white, looking terribly anxious . . . the news had got around that he had been killed."[100]

The money lenders and capitalists of Chrzanów had defamed Jewish socialists as wanting to organize pogroms, as in Russia. But "who took the Jew's side in Russia and who defended them, if not the socialists?" asked 1,500 JSDP leaflets distributed after the attack.

Seeking to neutralize the local workers' religious beliefs while emphasizing their class interests, the leaflet pointed out that socialists regarded religion as a private matter. "We only want to improve the situation of the workers, to make them aware and to educate them." On the other hand, the local bosses, despite their piety, attacked the socialist association on the Sabbath just like the hooligans who attacked Jewish shops during the recent Białystok pogrom, in the Russia Empire.[101]

The supporters of the JSDP in the small towns were, however, far from defenseless. They had a party behind them and Grossman also had the advantages and connections of a middle-class law student. He initiated legal action against the holy dignatories who ran Chrzanów. The party warned that it would "answer violence with violence. We will see who is stronger, hundreds and thousands of organized workers or a band of cheats and money lenders."

When the matter finally came up in court, eleven months later, Grossman accused the pious, parochial despots, motivated by their wallets, of using religion to incite the assault. By winning his case before the magistrate in Chrzanów, he turned the affair into a victory for the JSDP and a publicity coup.[102]

The experience of a prolonged lockout in the Lemberg clothing industry during September and October, even though the employers did not win the dispute,[103] must have suggested that the balance of class forces had begun to shift in favor of the bosses. By the middle of October, Grossman realized that his recent conclusion—that there would soon be a very rapid and qualitative increase in the JSDP's influence—had been wrong. The challenges facing the party were turning out to be of a more defensive kind than he had expected. On this basis, he was confident that the JSDP could manage without him for a while.

Quite suddenly, he "departed for Vienna to pursue important affairs there for a long period." Having handed over the position of party secretary earlier in the year, he also passed on some residual responsibilities to Shrayber and his post as publisher and legally responsible editor of the *Sotsial-demokrat* to Adolf Shpanlang.[104]

Whether romance, family, and/or business matters also prompted his presence in Vienna, it is clear that Grossman devoted much of his time there to academic studies. During winter semester 1906–7, he worked in the seminar of Dr Carl Grünberg, the most prominent socialist university teacher in Austria.[105] Although he had published a series of studies in economic history and the history of socialist thought, Grünberg was still a junior professor (*Extraordinarius*).

Grossman's priorities were changing. He began to plan an academic career. That meant completing his degree at the Jagiellonian University and undertaking a higher doctorate (*Habilitation*), the prerequisite for a university appointment. For two years, after completing his undergraduate coursework, Grossman had been a professional revolutionary, supported by his very well-to-do family. Now the progress of his friends' studies and the slowing of the pace of political events led him to think that he might not remain a full-time political activist forever. Without giving up his political outlook, he began to consider the merits of adopting the guise of a traditional intellectual, at least in terms of having a normal profession and a conventional livelihood. It was a path that friends and other socialist activists had taken.

Rafał Taubenschlag was such a friend. Not a political activist, he graduated in Kraków much more rapidly than Grossman, after studying law and then philosophy. Taubenschlag won a scholarship to the University of Leipzig to work on the history of law in the ancient world.[106]

Janek Bross had begun his university studies two years after Grossman. Together they had built the JSDP in Kraków and Galicia as a whole. But, without a wealthy family behind him, Bross adopted a more urgent approach to his academic work, taking out his law degree in mid-1907, and looked forward to a career as an attorney.[107]

Legal practice was less attractive for Grossman. Certainly, it might provide something to fall back on. Coming from a more modest background, Grünberg had made a living during the 1890s as an attorney and then a judicial official. But Grossman's financial situation was very comfortable. Involvement in Grünberg's seminars was a first step in a more direct path to an academic post.

An analysis of the political economy of the Jewish working class had underpinned Grossman's justification for the establishment of an independent Jewish social democratic party. He had made original arguments about the development of the Jewish proletariat and Galician economic conditions, in his pamphlet on the Jewish question, the JSDP's report to the 1905 Congress of the General Austrian Social Democratic Party, and his recent discussion of agitation and propaganda in the *Sotsial-demokrat*.[108] There was an overlap between this area of interest, driven by immediate political concerns, and Grünberg's scholarly research on Austria's economic history during the eighteenth and nineteenth centuries.

Grossman's love life may also have prompted him to take the pursuit of a traditional career more seriously. The relationship between his parents had been unconventional, at least until their marriage when he was six years old. In sexual matters, what was important for him, too, was love rather than legality or respectable morals, although he had conventional views about monogamy. One of his love affairs, according to Christina Stead, took him into Russia, following "a beautiful and brave girl" to Kiev. "She was eighteen, and a gun-runner for the revs." Customs officials did not trouble this young high society woman, carrying guns in her silk underwear.[109] There is no trace of Grossman's other romances, until he fell for Janina Reicher.

Janina was eighteen months younger than Henryk.[110] Her father, Edward, was a very successful businessman, from Alexandrowo (now Aleksandrów Kujawski) in the Congress Kingdom. Aleksandrów, just over the border from Thorn (Toruń) in Germany's Polish province of West Prussia, was an excellent location for a commercial entrepreneur. Henryk and Janina had similar social backgrounds. It is possible that they met as a result of business contacts between the Kurz and Reicher families. On the other hand, she may have come to Kraków to attend one of the city's private art academies and encountered Henryk in the world of Kraków's high culture, at the theater, concerts, art exhibitions, or through friends.[111] She was beautiful: slim, pale-eyed, with a delicate mouth and nose. Wearing her dark hair up highlighted her long neck. But Janka, as Henryk called her, put truth before vanity in a self-portrait. She depicted the crooked ring finger on her slender right hand.[112]

Edward had taste and expressed his assimilation to Polish culture through his interest in art. He invested a proportion of his very substantial profits in paintings and drawings by Polish artists. An emphasis on self-portraits gave particular distinction to Reicher's large and representative collection. Its catalogue included many of the stars in the constellation of nineteenth- and early twentieth-century Polish painting, such as Matejko, Grottger, and Norwid.[113]

Janina grew up in an environment lit by the work of these artists. Her father's tastes also ran to the work of the Young Poland movement, centered in Kraków.

Janina decided to become an artist herself and began to paint in Aleksandrów. As a young woman, she moved to Kraków. The nationalist traditions of Polish art had some influence on her work, though the intent of a romantic portrait of handsome, young Henryk in the traditional costume of a Polish nobleman was, no doubt, more whimsical than patriotic, given his detestation of the *szlachta*.[114] He kept a photograph of it until the end of his life. Janka also became a gifted miniaturist.[115] In 1908, the bans for their marriage were issued in Kraków.

The Election Campaign

Trotsky observed that from 1907–8 there was an international ebb-tide in the workers' movement following the flood-tide, whose high point had been the 1905 revolution in Russia.[116] In Austria, however, mass activity among workers and peasants revived during the campaign for the Reichsrat election in May 1907. This movement took a strictly legal form, focused on change through parliament, rather than self-activity. It proved to be the last major wave in the Austrian upsurge, although trade union membership in Galicia did not subside until 1908.[117]

After unsuccessful negotiations with the PPSD, the JSDP decided not to contest the elections but rather to support Polish and Ukrainian social democratic candidates, while nevertheless using the election campaign to promote the party's own program.[118] Ensuring that progressive rather than Zionist or conservative, bourgeois Jewish candidates would win in the urban electorates where many of the voters were Jewish was a priority for Grossman and his party, now committed to a sensible assessment of the resources at their disposal and the possibilities presented by elections.[119] Grossman set out the party's strategy for the election campaign at a closed meeting on Saturday, March 23, 1907.[120] He then led the JSDP's electoral work in Kraków, which included a voter registration drive, its own public meetings, and interventions into those of other parties.[121]

In Kraków, the Jewish Marxists' most significant activity in the election campaign was to organize a public meeting on "Who should the Kazimierz electorate vote for?"[122] The two candidates for the seat were invited to participate. The event took place on a Sunday evening, in order to draw in people some distance from the social democratic movement, religious as well as nonobservant Jews. It succeeded: the large functions room of the Hotel Klein was full. While the Jewish Democrat Dr. Adolf Gross, the candidate favored by the JSDP and PPSD, accepted the invitation to attend Józef Sare, the conservative candidate of the *kehile*, did not.

The main speaker at the meeting was Grossman. He offered a critique of right-wing Jews, like Sare, "who don't want autonomy for the [Jewish] people. What they have in mind is the autonomy of the current *kehile* bosses."[123]

Although they were not standing in the Kazimierz electorate, Grossman also attacked the Zionists, who were contesting seats elsewhere in Galicia. Their electoral campaign did not raise the issue of Palestine, their preoccupation for fifteen years. Instead their program consisted of the demand for more Jews in the Reichsrat. In practice, therefore, the Zionists were promoting clericalism among the Jews and therefore among the Poles. For socialists, on the other hand, religion was a private matter.[124]

Grossman spelled out the JSDP's demands on all candidates: they should not join the Polish or Jewish, that is Zionist, clubs in the Reichsrat; they should vote with the social democratic fraction in matters affecting workers; and they should support the principle of national cultural autonomy for all peoples. In relation to the Jews, national cultural autonomy included recognition of Yiddish in the craft tribunals and by craft inspectors; state-run evening and primary schools with Yiddish as the language of instruction; and official acceptance of Saturday as the day of rest for Jews.[125]

May Day 1907 fell in the middle of the election campaign. The JSDP rally of two thousand people in Kraków's Edison Circus began with the Workers' Choir singing of "Di shvue." The first speaker on the platform was comrade Antman. He declared that, having conquered universal suffrage for elections to the Reichsrat, the working class's next task was to reform the franchise for the Sejm, local government, and corporate bodies. Not only for men, but for women too!

Decked out with a red carnation, like the other comrades, Grossman argued that in the impending elections, voters could advance the cause of legislation protecting conditions at work. Henryk Shrayber called for peace between nations and denounced militarism. The police inspector in attendance repeatedly interrupted the speeches and threatened to close down the assembly. But the rally ran its full course, ending with the "Internationale."[126]

Social democratic candidates received over a million votes and won eighty-nine seats in the 1907 Reichsrat elections. Until the German clericals and Christian Socials united, the socialists were the largest parliamentary bloc.

The agitational work of talented young Jewish social democrats contributed to the success of six PPSD and two USDP candidates. Their efforts were important in seats where Jewish votes were decisive. But the contributions of JSDP activists could take peculiar forms. One of them, Feliks Gutman, recalled that "at an election meeting in Nowy Sącz, the chairperson introduced me to the audience with the following words: 'and now the son of our beloved leader Ignacy will present a talk—comrade Feliks Daszyński.' This announcement was greeted with thunderous applause."[127]

Herman Diamand's victory in a largely Jewish Lwów constituency, in particular, owed much to the JSDP, which counteracted Poale Zionist efforts to direct working-class support to the Zionist candidate. Grossman later estimated that the JSDP had contributed eight hundred to a thousand votes to Diamand's majority.[128] During and for a while after the election campaign, PPSD hostility to the JSDP eased a little, a pattern repeated in the lead-up to subsequent elections.

Recognizing the Downturn

After the Reichstag election, Trotsky pointed out, "in Austria the thread of achievements started by the working class broke off, social insurance legislation rotted in the government offices, nationalist conflicts began again with renewed vigor in the arena of universal suffrage, weakening and dividing the Social Democracy."[129] The leadership of the JSDP now came to understand the full extent of the shift in the balance of forces away from the working class and, on August 3–4, 1907, held a conference to reorient its work. It seems that Grossman was not present.

His personal plans paralleled the party's growing grasp of the deteriorating political situation. Having worked with Grünberg in Vienna during the winter semester 1906–7, he prepared for the first of the three final examinations he had to pass before being awarded a doctorate in law and politics by the Jagiellonian University. His performance in this legal studies exam, on July 24, was less than outstanding. Edmund Krzymuski, professor of criminal law, assessed it "insufficient." But the other three examiners regarded his grasp of the law as "sufficient" and he passed.[130]

Soon Grossman was devoting a great deal of time to a major project that was a transition between the practical politics involved in leading the JSDP and the kind of concentrated academic research he was planning to pursue in Vienna. Initially a serial in the *Sotsial-demokrat,* from September to November 1907, *Der Bundizm in Galitsien* (Bundism in Galicia) appeared as a pamphlet early in 1908.[131] It was the most substantial justification for the existence of the JSDP ever published, a major advance on Grossman's *The Proletariat and the Jewish Question* and his other writings in defense of the party in 1905 and 1906.

A couple of months before the appearance of *Bundism in Galicia*, the German-Austrian social democratic party published Otto Bauer's influential *The Question of Nationalities and Social democracy,* with its explicit attacks on the Jewish separatists. Bauer's work may well have been a factor in Grossman's decision to reexamine the origins and development of Jewish workers' organizations in Galicia during the 1890s.

There were serious flaws in Bauer's understanding of the relationship between nations and class. His theory was grounded in what we today label social Darwinism. Thus he argued that nations were both natural (racial) and cultural communities.[132] His theory that biological evolution played a role in recent human history was a hostage to the vulgar Darwinist assumption that race was fundamental in explaining contemporary society. This was radically different from Marx's approach.

Bauer made a special effort, in the section following his own outline and justification of "the personality principle," that is, national cultural autonomy, to quarantine the Jewish question from his general conclusions.[133] Lenin later pointed out that "this proves more conclusively than lengthy speeches how inconsistent Otto Bauer is and how little he believes in his own idea, for he excludes the *only* extra-territorial . . . nation from his plan for extra-territorial national autonomy."[134] Bauer's attitude toward the Jewish separatists in Galicia was a product of a different, opportunist consistency—in accommodating to the established order. This practical consistency gave rise to theoretical incoherence when theories that justified it in one area were an obstacle in another.

The immediate target of *Bundism in Galicia* was not, however, Bauer's high theory but misleading Zionist and PPSD explanations of the JSDP. Grossman demonstrated that his party was far from being the product of Zionist influence on the Jewish working class. By outlining developments during the 1890s, his study documented the social forces that consistently drove Jewish workers toward forming an independent political organization and created a receptive environment in Galicia for the example and ideas of the Bund in Russia.[135] Grossman offered a sophisticated and dialectical analysis of the relationships among political organization and consciousness, national oppression, and the routine struggles of the Jewish working class, quite different from Bauer's questionable amalgam of social Darwinism and historical materialism.

The causes and characteristics of national consciousness among Jewish workers and the Jewish middle class were very different, according to Grossman. He had already explained, in his earlier pamphlet on the Jewish question, the economic circumstances that gave rise to Jewish national awareness among Jewish workers. Quite different forces shaped the outlook of the Jewish bourgeoisie and intelligentsia. The development of their worldview followed a pattern found in other nations.[136]

When Galicia achieved provincial autonomy, many jobs in the public service, previously occupied by Germans and German speakers, were opened to Poles. This attracted Ukrainian and later Jewish intellectuals to Polish culture. But by the end of the 1880s there were more intellectuals than jobs. Ethnic Poles were now privileged in public appointments over Jews and Ukrainians. Jewish intellectuals turned to nationalism.[137] The "Jewish question" now emerged and so did two answers to it: one corresponding to the interests of the bourgeoisie and intelligentsia, the other to the interests of the working class.[138]

Jewish bourgeois nationalism in the form of Zionism, like Polish nationalism, demanded an independent territorial state. It had, however, no practical program and, Grossman maintained, refused to fight for democracy here and now, let alone the immediate interests of the working class. "It is absolutely clear that even the greatest reactionary can demand a people's or even a 'socialist' republic in Palestine and as a result fail to take advantage of the existing constitution or to *struggle* for the democratization of a given country. This indirectly bolsters the absolutism of the clerical and warmongering Austrian bureaucracy. This reactionary standpoint found its best expression in the formula that Zionism, as a *general-nationalist* movement, cannot limit itself to any particular class or group; on the contrary it must include people from all social strata and from the most diverse political camps, uniting east, west, north and south."[139]

The first sign of a working-class response to the Jewish question was the attempt to set up an independent Jewish socialist party in 1892. Its initiators wanted to establish a federal relationship with the Austrian social democratic movement. Despite its rapid collapse, due to the economic backwardness of Galicia and the limited development of the proletariat, between 1892 and 1897 Jewish workers built their own associations within the framework of the GPSD.[140] But, while sponsoring these associations, the GPSD made concessions to Jewish clericalism and devoted few resources to their development. They were therefore vulnerable to Zionist competition.[141]

The Austrian General Party's adoption of a federal structure in 1897 was a turning point for Jewish workers' organizations in Galicia, as Grossman had pointed out before.[142] He endorsed the General Party's opportunist affirmation that "Austria exists and *constitutes the area* in which social democracy must conduct its activity, so its struggle against the state is at the same time a struggle to maintain this state," by eliminating national conflict.[143]

The leaders of the GPSD, however, regarded the new party structure as a license to implement their nationalist perspectives and prepared to turn their organization into a Polish national party. They pragmatically gave up their internationalist objections to the establishment of a Jewish social democratic party, which would compete with the GPSD/PPSD for members, and opposed such a development on assimilationist grounds instead.[144]

The PPSD was, Grossman noted, progressive in its anti-Zionism and identification of the common interests of the Jewish proletariat and the proletariats of other nations in Austria, that is, in its commitment to general Marxist principles. But the version of socialism the Polish party presented to Jewish workers was too abstract. It did not address their immediate problems as both an oppressed and an exploited group; it offered no guidelines for contemporary political practice or struggles. The Jewish question, it was asserted, would be resolved under socialism. In this way the PPSD promoted passivity among the Jewish masses.[145]

So there was a basic similarity between the PPSD and Zionist positions. By invoking a solution in the distant future, whether in Palestine or under socialism, they "*cut themselves off* from the real context in which a solution to this question is necessary." "Both make a mockery of historical circumstances of time and place."[146] "By removing themselves from the real circumstances, which form the *basis* of the Jewish question, both tendencies have unequivocally shown that *the organic connection between the Jewish question* (like any other social issue) and *the given socio-political system of a state,* is a mystery to them. So too is the corollary that the Jewish question which has arisen on a particular socio-political basis cannot be solved separately from that basis and its circumstances. This can only occur *through a struggle on the basis of these social circumstances and against them.*"[147]

No wonder that, over the period between 1897 and 1899, the Jewish social democratic workers' current in Galicia disappeared and "through its material neglect of the Jewish workers' movement, the PPSD helped to deliver the Jewish working class to the swindle of Zionist ideology."[148] It had "turned the class struggle of the Jewish proletariat into a chauvinist fight between *two nationalisms.*"

Grossman made the dynamics and the damaging consequences of the nationalism of the dominant groups in Austrian social democracy very clear in his critique of the PPSD's capitulation to bourgeois ideology, that is, Polish nationalism. Bauer, by way of contrast, blamed the working classes of the oppressed nations for the nationalism of the workers of the dominant nations in Austria.

The organizational and programmatic model provided by the Bund, Grossman pointed out, was attractive to Jewish workers who were not prepared to wait for the ultimate victory of socialism or a state in Palestine before taking up the struggle against social and national oppression:[149] "Socialism acquires strength in a given country or people only *when it applies its theory to the specific development and problems of that country or people.*"[150] The "analysis of *all the practical interests* of the Jewish workers' movement and all the important phenomena of Jewish social life" was a precondition for making socialism relevant to Jewish workers and winning them from rival ideologies.[151]

Only a Jewish working-class party, Grossman reiterated, could do these things. In *Bundism in Galicia,* however, he developed a more dialectical explanation of why this was the case than in *The Proletariat and the Jewish Question.* His earlier argument had the focus on objective historical processes and political organization that was characteristic of the orthodox Marxism of the Second International. He now dealt seriously, if briefly, with the relationships among class interest, struggle, consciousness, and the nature of revolutionary politics. This paralleled Lenin's approach and anticipated Lukács's and Gramsci's postwar discussions of the role of the party in the development of class consciousness.[152]

> Recognition, based on scientific socialism, that all forms of social consciousness are to be explained in terms of *class* and group interests is of great practical significance in the assessment of a proletarian party, i.e. social democracy. This is also significant to the extent that it is true *in reverse,* that is, the class interests of the proletariat find their expression in party consciousness (in the form of a program); party consciousness is the multi-faceted expression of the proletariat's class interests and the most far-reaching interpretation of conclusions drawn from the objective trends of real social development. Workers' parties do not always fulfill this requirement (as evidenced by the PPSD). Both the character and the content of collective party thought remain *directly dependent on the particular party's adjustment to the very working class* whose expression it should be.
> . . . The closest possible adaptation of the party organization to the historical forms of the Jewish proletariat's condition . . . could only be achieved through the mutual organic growth of the party organization and the workers' movement itself, just as the latter has grown out of capitalist society.[153]

In contrast to Lenin, however, Grossman regarded the federal structure of Austrian social democracy as a principle. Hence Grossman's failure in the favorable circumstances of early 1905 to persist with the construction of a political alternative to the PPSD in Galicia (and therefore to the leadership of the Austrian General Party) that took the fight against national oppression as seriously as the RSDLP/Bolsheviks did. Such an organization could have mobilized Jewish, Polish, and Ukrainian workers together more effectively against national oppression and over economic and broader political issues than separate, national social democratic parties.

Paralleling *Bundism in Galicia*'s case for an independent Jewish social democratic party were its arguments for the pursuit of national cultural autonomy by an independent Jewish social democratic party. But most of them could just as easily have provided a rationale for a consistent struggle for Jewish civil rights, including language rights, by a centralized party. Perhaps only in the area of education policy would this alternative to national cultural autonomy have resulted in substantially different demands.

In contrast to the PPSD's position that there was no need for Jewish workers to take up the Jewish question, as their distinctive problems would be solved with the victory of socialism, Grossman invoked Marx's fundamental and distinctive conception of socialism: "The words of the *Communist Manifesto* that '. . . the emancipation of the workers must be the act of the working class itself . . .' mean, as far as the Jews are concerned, that their emancipation can only be the product of their own political struggle. And really, equal national rights for the Jewish proletariat are not at all an exotic blossom, ripening somewhere outside the sphere of the day-to-day struggle, that will somehow bring the Jews good fortune on the victory of socialism. Equal rights can only be *the result* of an inner development which includes both a *subjective* factor, i.e. the Jewish working class, and an *objective* factor, i.e. the rest of the capitalist society."[154] A few years earlier, on the other side of the Continent, James Connolly had expressed ideas about the liberation of Irish workers in remarkably similar terms.[155]

The Jewish working class, organized through its own party, was faced with a paradox, wrote Grossman. The mass of the working class needed national cultural institutions in order to become politically conscious. But such institutions could only be the result of the mobilization of a class-conscious working class.

> The resolution of this apparent contradiction will be achieved through *the very class struggle* of the Jewish proletariat itself. Through its political struggle the Jewish proletariat achieves its national and cultural requirements in the state and also becomes both class and nationally conscious. To the extent that it becomes nationally conscious and develops itself, by achieving class consciousness through political struggle, the Jewish proletariat forces its opponents to make concessions and thus both transforms its environment, capitalist society, and prepares that environment to take its national cultural needs into account.
>
> The above-mentioned, subjective and objective conditions for achieving equal national rights for Jews are bound together and influence each other. The means for realizing this struggle and the whole evolutionary process is precisely the independent organization of the Jewish working class.[156]

In *Bundism in Galicia,* Grossman synthesized the lessons of his political experiences in the Jewish workers' movement. The pamphlet had weaknesses. It generalized the organizational forms of Austrian social democracy into a principle. As a corollary, it accepted the illusion, current in both the Bund and the German-Austrian party, that national cultural autonomy could resolve the national question within the framework of the Austrian Empire. Grossman's argument that socialism and national liberation were fundamentally about the mutual transformation of the working class and its circumstances through class struggle, however, was an important reclamation of Marx and Engels' revolutionary conception of working-class self-emancipation, expressed in the second section of the *Communist Manifesto* on proletarians and Communists.

It cut through the mechanical orthodoxies of the Second International and anticipated the theory and practice of the October 1917 revolution in Russia and the early Communist International. In particular, Grossman's analysis of a specific, oppressed working class and its adoption of Bundist perspectives reached the same conclusion that György Lukács was to draw for the working class in general more than fifteen years later. The working class was a unique subject/object of history; while it was the result of historical processes, through its own party the working class could also consciously shape history. Published in Yiddish, Grossman's insight had no impact on the wider socialist movement although it did inform his own work when he next engaged with questions of socialist strategy, years later. For the time being, Grossman was cutting back his level of political activity.

Just as a reactionary period followed the defeat of the 1905 revolution in Russia, a much longer conservative phase in European politics set in after the 1848 revolutions. During the 1850s Marx, to the extent that his finances permitted, devoted his time to research on the logic of capital accumulation. Working in the library of the British Museum he assembled raw data for this analysis. Following his stint in Vienna with Grünberg and his law examination in mid-1907, *Bundism in Galicia* was a further step into the anteroom of Grossman's own British Museum.

In late July 1908, Grossman took another pace in this direction, his politics exam. Three of his four examiners were involved in politics themselves. Professors Estreicher and Jaworski were supporters of the reactionary *szlachta* regime in Galicia. Professor Czerkawski was a representative of the Polish People's Centre, an antisocialist organization set up under the patronage of the Catholic clergy and active among workers and peasants.[157] His inquisitors could hardly applaud Henryk Grossman's political views but at least they unanimously pronounced his performance in the examination "sufficient."[158]

The JSDP's Place in the Political Landscape

Bundism in Galicia was Henryk Grossman's last major theoretical contribution to the JSDP. His final practical activities in the party were in campaigns against political and industrial maneuvers by the PPSD, and his role at the JSPD's Third Congress.

The PPSD had set up a "Jewish Section" in the wake of the split that had established the JSDP. This attempt to woo Jewish workers was a failure. By the end of September 1907, the JSDP had more than five times the membership of the Jewish Section.[159]

At the PPSD's Eleventh Congress, on June 8, 1908, in Kraków, some delegates, including Jędrzej Moraczewski, a member of the Reichsrat, and two other members of the PPSD Executive, as well as the secretary of the Jewish Section, Nathan Korkes, supported Daniel Gross's motion accepting that Jewish workers were entitled to their own separate party. The delegates from four towns in eastern Galicia were even mandated to vote for outright recognition of the JSDP.

Keen to observe the events himself and to stir up the conflict in the PPSD, Grossman, as a member of the public, attended the Congress debate on the question of Jewish organization. His provocation worked. Emil Bobrowski, who was even skeptical about the need for a Jewish Section in the PPSD, suggested that "among [JSDP] leaders there is a drive to join our Party under certain conditions." This claim gave Grossman the opportunity to pass a note up to the chairperson. Later in the debate, Samuel Shorr argued that the Jewish Social Democratic Party "does not constitute a political organization. It is more of a trade union organization and a bad one at that. For those who want a separate organization he pointed to the leadership of H. Grossman, who never asked for any advice and in his hubris split from the PPSD and set up a separate party."

With delegates under heavy pressure from Daszyński, Diamand and Tadeusz Reger (the PPSD leader in Austrian Silesia), the majority at the Congress rejected Gross's proposal and confirmed the rebadging of the Jewish Section as the Jewish Social Democracy (JSD). Once the vote was out of the way, the chairperson read out Grossman's note facetiously denying that he had given any indication that he wanted to join the PPSD. Then the Congress made the subordination of the JSD to the PPSD absolutely clear by *appointing* its leadership.[160]

The JSDP immediately started campaigning to ensure that no one would be taken in by the repackaging of the Jewish Section. In doing so, it took advantage of the reemergence of serious divisions over the Jewish question inside the PPSD to consolidate its position among Jewish workers, particularly in several eastern Galician towns that had been the Jewish Section's strongholds. Articles in the *Sotsial-demokrat*, meetings of organizations affiliated to the JSDP, its own mass meetings in Kraków and Lemberg, and interventions in public meetings called by the PPSD hammered home the message.[161] As the party's preeminent, founding leader; as a witness to the events at the PPSD congress, his status bolstered by Shorr's denunciation; and as the JSDP expert on relations between the PPSD and the Jewish working class, reaffirmed by the publication of *Bundism in Galicia*, Grossman was the key speaker at the mass meetings.

On the sweltering night of Wednesday, June 17, the functions room at the Klein hotel was packed for the Kraków meeting. Grossman highlighted the contradiction between Diamand's words at the PPSD Congress—that no one had the right to interfere in the Jewish proletariat's determination of its own form of self-organization—and the Polish party's practice. "Tonight's meeting should be a heated protest," he declaimed, "against the way the 11th Congress of the PPSD appropriated the right to decide on the question of the organization of the Jewish proletariat." The PPSD leaders were "Talmudists in their reasoning on the Jewish question."[162]

The following Saturday afternoon, Grossman and Anselm Mosler addressed the JSDP's meeting in Lemberg. Although it was again stiflingly hot, five hundred people turned up, including eighty Sectionists. In the discussion, a Poale Zionist and another nationalist Jewish socialist accused the JSDP of demanding too little and lacking national spirit. In his reply, Grossman conceded some of their case. "That you are nationalists, we don't want to dispute with you. That is, actually, the difference between you and us. We are Jewish social democrats and you Jewish nationalists. We lead the class struggles of the Jewish proletariat. We fight for equality. We want the Jewish nation to be equal to all other nations. Cultivating nationalism with its accompanying chauvinism, you want to capture the Jewish proletariat in the net of chauvinism, under the mask of your peculiar socialism."[163]

The cosmetic changes to the Jewish Section achieved little for the PPSD. Organized Jewish workers, that is, mainly those already aligned with the JSDP, were singularly unimpressed. A PPSD meeting in Stryj (now Stryi in the Ukraine), to which JSDP members were invited, voted overwhelmingly to call on Jewish workers to join the JSDP.[164] Under the impact of the controversy and the JSDP's campaign, other Jewish PPSD members went over to the Jewish party too.[165]

Before its Third Congress, in October 1908, the JSDP had about 3,500 members, and a presence in 36 towns.[166] Around this time, a mere 320 Jews, in 4 towns, were members of the PPSD through the JSD. There were another 340 Jews in the party who were not associated with its Jewish Section.[167] Overall, the PPSD had no more than 13,000 members, in Galicia and the highly industrialized districts of Austrian Silesia.[168] The JSDP was, moreover, significantly larger than the Galician Section of the Labor Zionist movement.[169]

The bludgeon of the PPSD's influence in the Galician trade union movement was a more effective weapon in its campaign against the JSDP than the Jewish Section and the JSD. The secretary of the Austrian Trade Union Commission had reassured Henryk Grossman, when he was in Vienna in December 1906, "that we are entirely satisfied with you. I say that openly. Jewish branches keep good accounts. They are not outside the central unions." But Daszyński and Żuławski, the leader of the social democratic union movement in Galicia, insisted on the social-democratic character of the trade unions, that is, that they should be under PPSD leadership.[170]

Three-quarters of Galician tailors were Jewish and a majority of delegates to the Galician Conference of the Tailors' Union were from JSDP-led branches. The union nevertheless issued publications in Polish but not Yiddish.[171] During the summer of 1908 union leaders tried to turn Jews into second-class members by depriving them of payments when they were unemployed. The maneuver was designed to pressure Jewish tailors out of branches affiliated to the JSDP and into branches associated with the Polish party.[172]

The Jewish branches of the union protested and party comrades with legal training put together a carefully argued address, in German, to the Tailors'

Union Executive in Vienna from the five hundred Jewish members of the union in Galicia.[173] The JSDP mobilized the entire organized Jewish working class in their support.

The Kraków Committee of the party, for example, held a very well-attended public meeting. Despite high summer temperatures, people could not all fit into the Forverts hall and the adjoining courtyard to hear a three-hour explanation and discussion of the issues. Moyshe Papier moved a motion condemning the PPSD for its anti-Semitic tactic of smearing the entire Jewish working class as swindlers. In seconding the motion, Grossman said that there had always been anti-Semitic individuals in the PPSD and explained why. One could be indignant about the anti-Semitic behavior of individuals. But one has to engage in the fiercest struggle against the *anti-Semitic tactics* the Polish party had now adopted in its attack on Jewish workers. It was necessary, he argued, to stir up public opinion against the PPSD's "exceptional laws" for Jewish workers and to involve not only workers but all progressive elements.[174]

The campaign in support of the tailors was successful. The union's Executive in Vienna backed off and reinstated the rights of Jewish unionists in Galicia. Its fingers burned by this experience, it eventually conceded that they would have their own newspaper and that the union statutes would be published in Yiddish. Despite the PPSD's efforts, "there was a spirit of cooperation between Jewish and Polish branches [of the union] as wages struggles were conducted jointly."[175]

At the JSDP's Third Congress on October 17–18, 1908, everyone knew that Grossman would soon be leaving Kraków to live in Vienna. But this did not prevent him from making a series of major contributions, as he had at the party's previous two congresses. Nor did it undermine his authority.

On the morning of the first day of the Congress, Grossman introduced the recommendations of the Finance Committee and spoke in the discussion about the party press. In the afternoon he introduced a controversial proposal to transfer the party Executive from Kraków to Lemberg and, shortly after that, the item on the JSDP's relationship with other parties.[176]

"The seat of the Executive should really have been in Lemberg from the start," Grossman argued. "That it has not been there was only a consequence of the fact that, three years ago, the Lemberg comrades were not politically developed enough. The situation, however, has changed. Our program has been decided on and is now well known. Our Lemberg comrades, who earlier saw the distinctiveness of our Party in Jewish pedigrees, today understand and are in a position to defend our political and economic program."[177] What is more, Grossman explained, "Kraków is too far from the centre of Jewish proletarian life. This centre is Lemberg . . . Only in eastern Galicia, can one place a hand on the pulse of Jewish proletarian life. Only there can you quickly orient yourself to the situation." What is more, if the Executive moved to Lemberg, the local organization in Lemberg would also be strengthened.

It was not the case, Grossman thought, that there were fewer comrades capable of undertaking responsible party work in Lemberg than in Kraków. But several speakers, including leading figures like Ruben Birnbaum, himself from Lemberg, and Anzelm Mosler seriously doubted the ability of the Lemberg comrades to lead the whole party. The skeptical comrades were probably right, even though the party's expert on trade union affairs and former *Sotsial-demokrat* editor, Papier, had already moved from Kraków to Lemberg and Grossman was about to leave Kraków too. In supporting the transfer, Michał Shuldenfrey from Kraków, argued that "if it doesn't matter where the Executive is located, then wouldn't it all be the same if it sat in Vienna, considering that comrade Grossman will now be living there?"[178]

Lemberg, however, lacked not only Grossman but also the wide layer of talented young intellectuals, current or recent university students as well as workers, who had been the core of the JSDP's leadership in Kraków from the party's foundation.[179] The proposal to reduce the role of these experienced leaders was particularly risky during a deep recession that sapped the already waning vitality of the labor movement and reduced the resources available to the party. But the motion to transfer the Executive was carried by 30 to 24. Immediately after the vote, the Congress selected the new party Executive. Grossman, despite his imminent departure for Vienna, was reelected.

Then the galleries filled up, as the Congress was reopened to the public for the next item on the agenda: Grossman's report on "Our relations with the political parties in the province." Maintaining sensible relations with other political currents, particularly the PPSD, required a cool head. During the discussion of the report on party activity, on the first day of the Congress, comrade Gleyzner had accused the Executive of inconsistency in relations with the PPSD-dominated Provincial Trade Union Commission. Given that the commission was undermining the activities of the Jewish party, he argued, union branches under JSDP leadership should pull out of it. Comrade Grossman had felt forced to respond. "We should not withdraw from the mighty tribune constituted by the Provincial Trade Union Congress. That is where we come into contact with Polish comrades, who have the struggle against us imposed on them. These comrades, workers, convince themselves at the Trade Union Congress that we are not 'separatists,' but members of the same organization as they are. They learn how to assess the campaign conducted against us by their leaders."[180] If anything, he thought, the party had failed to make sufficient use of the commission and to publicize its abuses enough. The point was to combine a hard critique of the

PPSD with activity, especially continued involvement in the mainstream of the union movement, that undermined its attacks on the JSDP in practice. After World War I, Lenin and the Communist International advocated this kind of approach under the label of "the united front tactic."[181]

Now, in his outline of the main forces in Galician politics since the transformation brought about by the introduction of universal suffrage for the Reichsrat elections, Grossman pulled no punches in his assessment of the politics of the PPSD leadership. He also analyzed the other parties operating in Galicia.[182] The resolution that summed up his perspectives emphasized the need for self-reliance and, in tacit acknowledgment of the degeneration of the General Party, failed to mention the wider Austrian social democratic movement. "The Jewish Social Democratic Party of Galicia regards itself as isolated in the political and social struggle for the emancipation of the Jewish working class. Both the Polish and the so-called Jewish parties are hostile to this struggle."[183] The motion was carried with unanimous support.

The Congress over, Grossman had just over a month to prepare for his final examination, in history, on November 25. The panel of examiners included Professor Stanisław Estreicher and the dean of the Law Faculty, Władysław Jaworski. Both were politically active conservatives and Jaworski was a member of the Sejm. All four examiners found Grossman's performance "sufficient." There had been enough delays, which had nothing to do with the Jagiellonian University, in his academic progress and the university authorities seemed keen to terminate their relationship with him. A doctorate in law was awarded to "Henricus Grossmann" on the day of the examination.[184]

Shortly after, Grossman left Kraków for the imperial capital. There he and Janina Reicher married.[185] Grossman asked comrades not to send telegrams to the wedding. Instead Papier, Vasserman, and Krants, all Lemberg members of the JSDP Executive, announced in the *Sotsial-demokrat* their congratulations and their contributions, in honor of the occasion, to the party's press fund.[186]

3

Respectable Careers

In late 1908, Henryk Grossman left Kraków and seemed to be starting a new life in Vienna, the capital of the Austro-Hungarian Empire. He was pursuing goals that could easily conflict with political engagement: domestic happiness and a conventional career. According to some Jewish reference works, this was a sharp break, as he "left the workers' movement," "settled in Vienna and withdrew from Jewish life in general."[1] Grossman's departure from Kraków certainly coincided with a slump in the struggles of the eastern European labor movement and he was less politically active for a while. But he remained a Marxist.

Grossman was already familiar with Vienna. He had family there, including his cousin Oskar Kurz, four years younger and about to graduate as a medical doctor. Oskar was a close friend and also involved in the social democratic movement.[2] For Grossman's fiancée Janka, keen to broaden her horizons and develop her talents a painter, Vienna and Paris were logical destinations after her move from Congress Poland to Kraków.[3] In the period before World War I, Vienna was the site of intellectual and cultural ferment and revolt. With the demise of liberalism as a political force, a section of the Viennese bourgeoisie and particularly the assimilated Jewish middle class increasingly had to find its creative outlets in personal development and art, or at least its appreciation.[4]

On December 1, 1908, Henryk and Janina were married. Twenty-seven and twenty-five years old, they were a stunning couple. Her father Edward and uncle Stanisław were official witnesses at the ceremony in the Vienna City Synagogue.[5] Grossman now embarked on a double career path in the law and academia. Both promised a public profile and economic security.

The complexities of Austria-Hungary's capitalist development generated the artistic creativity of fin de siècle and early twentieth-century Vienna. They also produced other intellectual phenomena, including the rise of the Austrian school of economics, on the one hand, and sophisticated Marxist explorations of contemporary society, on the other. Carl Grünberg, the first professor with Marxist inclinations to lecture at a German-speaking university, and the archives of the imperial capital were for Grossman the main attraction in Vienna. Grünberg was Grossman's academic patron and became a close friend. With Grünberg's support and guidance, Grossman began to work on a major piece of research that would be the basis for a higher doctorate (*Habilitation*) and hence a university post.[6]

Grossman was, like Grünberg, a bright, fatherless Jewish lad from the outer reaches of the empire. Despite his much more secure financial situation, he had in Kraków already begun to follow Grünberg's career strategy.[7] Legal practice could provide a comfortable income and lifestyle while Grossman developed a scholarly profile and sought a university post. But his doctorate in law could only be translated into a money-making resource after a seven-year legal apprenticeship. This he started in Vienna, later describing his status during this period as "assistant attorney and private scholar."[8] In 1914, after sitting out his probation, he set up a legal practice at the Landesgericht (provincial court) in Vienna.[9]

Perhaps the only fruit of Grossman's fall-back profession in the law was the final demise of the neglected given name on his birth certificate. Chaskel became Henryk for legal purposes in early 1915.[10] Even the execution of this convoluted procedure, however, may have been entrusted to someone more seriously committed to the practice of Austrian law.

Legal training placed few demands on his time. Although not enrolled as a student, Grossman attended seminars at the University of Vienna, not only Grünberg's but also those of Eugen von Böhm-Bawerk. A leading representative of the Austrian school of economics founded by Karl Menger, Böhm-Bawerk had written an influential critique of Marxist economics in 1896.[11] At some stage before World War I Grossman also studied in Berlin.[12]

After leaving Kraków, Grossman's main academic activity, however, was archival research as part of Grünberg's long-term project, "on which he worked with his students: comprehending Austria's great epoch of reform [in the eighteenth century] from all sides, with perspectives from agrarian, industry and trade history."[13] His task was to examine the impact of the trade policy that the reforming Habsburg monarchs, Maria Theresia and her son Josef II, implemented in Galicia between 1772 and 1790. The primary sources were in the archives of Vienna, Paris, Kraków, and Lwów.[14] Through this research, Grossman not only gleaned material for his thesis but also developed expertise in statistical methods, became an expert on the history of statistics in Austria, and made a series of professional contacts. During visits to Lwów and Kraków, he maintained personal and political relationships in Galicia. The most important materials for his inquiries, however, were in the imperial capital.[15]

Unlike Carl Grünberg, Grossman never formally repudiated the Jewish religion. Given his materialist outlook, spiritual beliefs were hardly a factor in this stance (nor were they in Grünberg's case). Austria-Hungary was not a secular state. If a Marxist had to be affiliated with a religion, then the choice could be a matter of making a political statement, personal convenience, or sentimental attachment. Far from there being a sharp break with Jewish life when he went to Vienna, after years of involvement in the struggles of Jewish workers against both exploitation and their oppression as Jews, Grossman continued his formal affiliation to the Jewish community. For official purposes, this remained the case for the next forty years.[16]

In any case, for Grossman, as he moved from Kraków to Vienna, Jewish life and Jewish identity was more the JSDP and its milieu than the Jewish religion. He certainly did not cut all his ties to the party, let alone give up on socialist politics, for he remained a member of the JSDP's Executive. From Vienna it would have been difficult to play a prominent role in the organization, especially as his time was now mainly taken up with other concerns. But on visits to Lemberg, he could occasionally participate in executive meetings.

Grossman also had contact with the small JSDP organization in Vienna, the Ferdinand Lassalle Club. In February 1910, for example, he combined his political and academic pursuits by delivering a lecture to club members on the economic history of the Jews in Galicia.[17] Continuing membership of the JSDP and reservations about the leadership of German-Austrian social democracy meant that he did not join any other party.

Paris and Politics

Within eighteen months of their marriage, Henryk and Janka began a long stay in Paris. Their son Jean Henri was born there, on October 16, 1910.[18] Janka explored the Parisian art scene. Vienna might have been a center for cultural innovation, but Paris offered the world's most creative milieu for painters. The Salon d'Automne in 1912 and 1913 included the first public exhibitions of Janka's work in Paris. Among the paintings she displayed in 1912 were two portraits of a baby, probably her son.[19]

Given the limited extent of the archival materials in Paris relevant to his research, there was plenty of time for Grossman to enjoy the city. He gained firsthand experience of politics in a more thoroughly parliamentary state than Galicia under the *szlachta* or Austria under Emperor Franz Josef. Parliamentary democracy did not mean that class conflicts were less intense in France. The Briand government smashed a railway strike in October 1910, by arresting its leaders, conscripting the workers, and threatening those who continued to strike with court martials. Nor were the imperialist concerns of the bourgeois Republic any less obvious than those of the Dual Monarchy.

The French socialist Jean Jaurès greatly impressed Grossman, as he had Rosa Luxemburg.[20] While Jaurès belonged to the possibilist (reformist) wing of the French socialist movement, he understood that socialism did not consist of tenets in a book. Unlike the pious orthodox Marxist Jules Guesde, from the late 1890s Jaurés had actively campaigned against the reactionary, anti-Semitic frame-up of Captain Alfred Dreyfus, a Jewish army officer convicted of spying for Germany. After repudiating the idea of socialists taking ministerial posts in bourgeois governments, Jaurès was the main architect of the unification of the fractured French socialist movement into the SFIO (Section Française de l'Internationale Ouvrière, French Section of the Workers' International) in 1905. He was assassinated in July 1914 because of his consistent opposition to militarism and war, even though, as Grossman mentioned much later to Christina Stead, he "did not really understand the capitalist roots of imperialism."[21] In a 1932 article on Jaurès, Grossman applauded the French socialist leader's oratorical talents, engagement with political events, and "capacity to turn the feelings that gripped the masses into convincing formulations." Jaurès displayed precisely these characteristics during the railway strike. As French workers became more radical—particularly during the period when Henryk and Janka were in Paris—Jaurès, "theoretically a reformist, but under the pressure of the masses, supported the class struggle and put greater and greater stress on the role of the proletariat in the historical process. Shortly before his death he was inclined to centrist and leftist views. Meanwhile, the orthodox Marxist Guesde evolved in the opposite direction and, in practice, stood on the right wing of the Party."[22] If Jean Henri Grossman reflected his parents' first names in his own, he also bore that of Jaurès.

The archive of the Ministry of Foreign Affairs was the site of most of Grossman's research work in Paris. There he came across some eighteenth-century espionage. The French ambassador to the Habsburg Court had sent home the summary table of a population census conducted in Vienna in 1777. This had little to do with Austrian trade policy in Galicia. But it was the first detailed census of Vienna that had come to light. So Grossman sent the ambassador's report, the table, and a few paragraphs of notes to the *Statistische Monatschrift*, the journal of the Austrian Central Statistical Commission. This, his first academic publication, provided a corrective to statements about Vienna's population in the standard literature.[23]

Despite the distractions of parenthood, academic work, and all that Paris had to offer politically and culturally, Grossman maintained his political connections with the Jewish working class in Galicia. He could not attend the JSDP's Fourth Congress in October 1910. But the party was far from dissatisfied with him. His telegraphed greeting was acknowledged after messages from the Bund and German Social Democratic Party were read out and before those from the Jewish social democrats in Bukovina. The Congress returned him to the Executive.[24]

Only in October 1911, three years after he left Krakow, did the party elect an Executive without Grossman. The Fifth Congress confirmed the fusion of the JSDP and the PPSD's small Jewish Social Democracy. Space had to be found on the new Executive to accommodate representatives from both organizations. In the unification process, the JSDP made concessions to the increasingly nationalist perspectives of the Austrian social democratic movement and the PPSD and dropped the demand for Jewish cultural national autonomy.[25]

Following his departure from the JSDP Executive, there was hardly any sign of political activity by Grossman for a decade and few indications of his political views. There are two reasons for this. First, a lack of sources, apart from some hints in his published work. Second, Grossman was politically isolated.

The breakup of the General Austrian Social Democratic Party along national lines, in the period after the 1907 elections to the Reichsrat, resulted from and intensified the opportunist and nationalist tendencies in the movement. By 1910, there was an opposition, the "Reichenberg left," in the German-Austrian Social Democratic Party. This current rejected the leadership's compromises with the Austro-Hungarian state, especially on questions of militarism and German nationalism. It was, however, mainly confined to northern Bohemia (Reichenberg is now Liberec in the Czech Republic).[26]

For Grossman, joining the German-Austrian party once he had decided to remain in Vienna would have been a betrayal of principles. He had the self-confidence to stick to his political views without being active in a party that espoused them. Accusations against Karl Radek led him to take a public stand on a political conflict in the international socialist movement. This related to his role as chairperson of the 1904 inquiry by socialist students into accusations that Radek had stolen books from a comrade. The commission had exonerated Radek.

In 1912, the SDKPiL split over the ineffective and authoritarian leadership of its Executive, dominated by Leo Jogiches. Most of the membership of the party inside the Kingdom of Poland and a large proportion of those in exile joined the "Splitters." In response, Jogiches began a campaign to smear and expel his opponents, including Radek, who now lived in Germany. Jogiches resurrected old charges against Radek—that he had stolen books and a suit, shat a bed, ripped off a union, and lied—and expelled him from the divided SDKPiL on August 21, 1912.

The left-wing SPD organization in Bremen, where Radek had been a journalist for the local socialist newspaper, immediately organized its own commission of inquiry.[27] Grossman learned of it from the SPD's flagship newspaper, the Berlin *Vorwärts,* and was aware of Jogiches's campaign inside the SDKPiL. He quickly wrote a statement for the Bremen investigators, outlining the results of the Kraków inquiry, which had "unanimously pronounced the accused *Radek not guilty on all counts* . . . The affair of the theft of books in 1904 has been dead for 8 years and it should finally disappear from the world."[28] In signing his declaration, Grossman described himself as a writer rather than a legal practitioner, but his education in the law was obviously useful in formulating the statement.[29]

Despite the favorable outcome of the Bremen commission, the right wing of German social democracy used the pretext of his expulsion from the SDKPiL to exclude Radek from the SPD. He fared better in the Russian party, where the Bolsheviks supported him and the Splitters, in a three-way struggle against Jogiches and the Mensheviks, for control of the Russian social democratic movement, of which the SDKPiL was a component. In February 1914, a commission of inquiry in Paris, set up by the Russian movement, rehabilitated Radek. By calling the revival of the accusations against Radek "malicious," Grossman had lined up with the Bolsheviks in the conflict within the SDKPiL, Russian social democracy, and the International.

The implications of the fight between left and right in the social democratic movement, which was a factor driving the Radek affair in Germany, became dazzlingly clear on the outbreak of World War I. Despite their formal opposition to war, a large majority of the parties affiliated to the Socialist International supported the military efforts of their own states and ruling classes. This was true of the French, German, and German-Austrian parties, the PPSD, USDP, and, more ambiguously, the JSDP. The collapse of the Second International was detailed in a collection of documents published by Carl Grünberg in his journal, *Das Archiv für die Geschichte des Sozialismus und der Arbeiterbewegung* in 1916. Grossman contributed to this project by translating three statements by the PPSD in August 1914 into German.[30]

Building an Academic Career

After returning from Paris in 1911, Grossman settled down in Vienna to complete his research. For a while the family lived in an elegant house with large rooms at St. Veitgasse 20 in Hietzing, the 13th District, on the western edge of the grounds of the Schönbrunn palace. But, in 1912, the Grossmans moved into a first-floor apartment in a newer and larger building nearby, at Neue Weltgasse 19. The wooded hills of the Lainzer Tiergarten, part of the Wiener Wald, still adorn the landscape to the west along the main street, Hietzinger Hauptstraße, with its shops and street car line to the city center. Other rail links were also within walking distance. The Unter St. Veit area of Hietzing was and still is a leafy villa suburb of large houses, accommodating professionals and the well to do. The Grossmans' building was decorated in a late Secession style, with simple geometric and textural elements, reminiscent of the work of the prominent Secession architect Josef Hoffmann. The small Hügel Park, commemorating the founder of the Austrian Horticultural Society and ideal for little children, is a couple of minutes' walk away.[31]

From Vienna, Grossman submitted a six-page research note in Polish to the most prestigious journal of Polish history. Appearing in 1911, this became his second academic article and the first published fruit of his main research project. It dealt with estimates of the size of the Polish territory occupied by Austria during the eighteenth century. As in the shorter note on the Viennese census, Grossman outlined the analyses in the relevant literature and their flaws, before describing his own, superior calculations.[32]

He presented a much more substantial paper, published in January 1912, to the 5th Conference of Polish Economists, in Lwów, drawing his project to the attention of a Polish public, which was the main audience for both its academic and political conclusions. The paper on Galician industrial and commercial policy, under Empress Maria Theresia and Emperor Josef II, dealt with issues that were particularly sensitive for the Polish national movement in all its colorations: from Russophile conservatives to the PPSD. Contrary to the nationalist orthodoxy, Grossman argued that early Habsburg policies in Galicia had not been designed to prevent economic development and turn the province into a colonial market for goods from the heartlands of the empire. On the contrary, the enlightened absolutist monarchs pursued mercantilist policies designed to promote Galicia's trade and industry. Their regime contrasted favorably with the feudal order of the Polish Republic, which had hindered the expansion of industry and urban life for decades.

By arguing that the main flaw in the Austrian economic policy for Galicia during this period was discrimination against the Jews, Grossman made a further attack on Polish national prejudices. Jews had been a large proportion of the urban population and, as merchants, had pioneered industrialization by promoting the putting-out system in textile production and other industries. The large fiscal burdens imposed on them impoverished an economically dynamic element in the province. This hindered industrialization. Over a hundred years later, the backwardness of Galicia and the disadvantage of the Jewish population were still apparent.[33]

The period of economic progress under Josef was brief. "With the death of the great monarch, the epoch of industrialization in Austria and Galicia came to a halt. At the time of the French revolution, into the Napoleonic period and for many years to come, feudal, agrarian, conservative reaction, in Austria as well as Galicia, choked embryonic industry. Fear of revolution, fear of big capital, which supported the First Consul [Napoleon], fear of the spirit of unrest which began to develop in industrial centers (unemployment!) led to an unceasing fight against industry, especially big industry in Austria in the period to 1835.... That 'Austria should remain an agrarian country' became the only aim of economic policy during this period."[34]

Overall, Grossman concluded that "during the 18th Century there was no conflict of economic interests between Galicia and Austria, as has been so far asserted in the literature on this subject." His perspective undermined the conventional nationalist view that the Polish nobility had been a progressive force, embodying the spirit of Polish independence. Grossman's argument could draw on the work of the scholarly, if apologetic Kraków school of historiography, associated with his former teacher Michał Bobrzyński.[35] The school supported Austrian rule in Galicia. Grossman, however, pointed out that "on the surface there were some conflicts, but in reality the industrial interests of Galicia were strictly tied to Austrian industrial development. So long as the dominant trends in Austria were progressive, in the period of reforms and industrialization, the same trends were apparent in Galicia. The moment that Austrian industry started to tremble, industrial development in Galicia was choked off. Both were victims of feudal, agrarian, conservative reaction not the industry of other countries!"[36]

In the *Sotsial-demokrat,* six years before, Grossman had already argued that the *szlachta* was the main obstacle to the industrialization of Galicia.[37] His scholarly elaboration of this argument retained its original, Bundist shape. Conducted in terms of conflicting material class interests, his study made Polish chauvinism, a reactionary imperial state, and the persecution of the Jews responsible for Galicia's backwardness. Despite its polemical intent, this work, or one closely related to it, won the Julius Wawelberg prize of the University of Lwów's Philosophy Faculty.[38]

The *Statistische Monatschrift* published a further report, on Galicia's foreign trade under Maria Theresia and Josef II, drawn from Grossman's main research project in 1913.[39] Its empirical core was a meticulous account of the available statistics on Galicia's trade balance. Warning that, given the unreliability of the statistics, their absolute size was of less significance than trends over time, Grossman displayed considerable ingenuity, using the available figures and information about the value of trade, levels of tariffs, and tariff income to estimate the value of total imports and exports.[40] Like the short piece on the Vienna census, the article demonstrated Grossman's statistical skills and interest in the history of Austrian statistics to professionals in the public service, as well as academics.

The political message of this essay was similar to that of his broader account of Galician economic development. Grossman identified Maria Theresia and Josef II's efforts to develop the Galician economy, in the face of Prussia's blockage of the trade route down the Vistula.[41] Then, rather than highlighting the reactionary influence of the Polish nobility—a key issue in Polish debates—he directed his argument against apologists for the Habsburgs, noting that "the ossification of state administration that began with Kaiser Josef's death was also apparent in the area of statistics."[42] The article also explained the close relationship between the efforts of the absolutist state to control society and its need for more reliable statistics.[43]

In September 1913, Henryk Grossmann finished writing *Austria's Trade Policy with Regard to Galicia during the Reform Period of 1772–1790*, which presented the results of his main project. Dedicated to "my wife Janka," the book of more than five hundred pages was published as the tenth volume in Grünberg's Studies on Social Economic and Administrative History series, days before the outbreak of World War I.[44] It incorporated the material and arguments of his earlier publications on Galicia but made its case in much greater detail and with full references. Grossman announced that the book was part of a larger study of the transition from feudalism to capitalism, to be completed in a second volume, some of whose conclusions had been aired in "The Industrial and Commercial Policy of the Theresian-Josephine Regime."[45]

The structure of the book's argument recalled Grossman's method in *The Proletariat and the Jewish Question:* he adopted, "quite consciously, in a certain sense, a devil's advocate" approach against another nationalist legend. This was the Polish nationalist argument that Austrian occupation held back Galicia's economic development. The lack of critical historical work in this area, the scale of the subject matter, and limited space meant that the text "on the one hand is overburdened with details and on the other is nevertheless often only able to offer overviews."[46] Subsequent researchers have benefited from these details, as Grossman had made extensive use of sources destroyed during World War II.

Drawing on complementary analyses by his contemporary Franciszek Bujak, Grossman rejected any romanticization of the old Polish Republic. "The principal cause of the lack of industrial development and city life in Poland is the same as the reason for the tragic downfall of Polish state life in general: 200 years of short-sighted economic policy dictated by the class interests of the Polish nobility!"[47] So, after the first partition of Poland in 1772, the Austrian authorities in Galicia were confronted with a very backward province, cut off from its previous markets. The policies of Maria Theresia and Josef II were designed to sustain the economy of their new Galician possession and increase its value. They promoted production for the local market, attempted to secure new markets for the province's exports, and eliminated the tax-free status of enterprises run by the *szlachta*. Their "reforms were . . . unavoidable for Galicia and beneficial for the majority of the population. The Polish nobility was in the mass still too backward and spiritually decadent to understand, still less to accommodate itself to the work of reform."[48]

One of the first reviews of the book was in the theoretical journal of German-Austrian social democracy.[49] It was by Jakob Pistiner, a leader of the social democratic movement in Bukovina and, from 1913, the representative of its Jewish Section on the Executive of the JSDP.[50] His complaint that "the Kaiser's good will" was Grossman's explanation for Austrian policies in Galicia, "and not the deeper economic connections and necessities," had no foundation.[51] Nor did Pistiner's warning that the book "has to be read critically, because it is not based on the materialist conception of history."[52] His unfriendly comments suggest that a considerable gap had emerged between Grossman's politics and those of both the JSDP and, particularly, mainstream German-Austrian social democracy with its pro-Austrian policies.

Much later, Grossman claimed that his study of Austrian trade policy in Galicia was "written from the standpoint of historical materialism." "I show how Emperor Joseph II pursued the same goal as the French Revolution did later on, namely the transition from a decentralized feudal state to a centralized capitalist regime. As the bourgeoisie was strong in France, the revolution was driven from below and the bourgeoisie achieved its goal. It was different in Austria. As the bourgeoisie was still weak, undeveloped, the goal which Joseph II pursued could only be achieved from above, with the help of the bureaucracy. This also explains why the project failed."[53]

Although the book did not refer to Marx or any other Marxists, Grossman's claim was justified. The language of the preface and its outline of the book's argument about "the transition from the traditional to the modern mode of production," clearly expressed a Marxist framework, as did the materialist and class analysis in the main text. Grossman's concluding statement was very much in the spirit of long-term historical materialist analysis: "The Austrian bureaucracy of that time, so unpleasant for many, was thus for Galicia the instrument of an objectively unavoidable historical process. An unprejudiced assessment must concede that the mercantilist economic policy of the Austrian regime in the newly won territory, taken as a whole and apart from mistakes which are of lesser significance, was historically unavoidable and therefore justified."[54] Roman Rosdolsky drew on and endorsed Grossman's account in an explicitly Marxist work on eighteenth-century economic reform in Galicia, published in 1962. While the second volume of Grossman's study never appeared, Rosdolsky's book undertook some of the analysis that the preface to *Austria's Trade Policy* had promised.[55]

The absence of references to Marxists in the book was no accident. In addition to being a contribution to the historical materialist understanding of the transition to capitalism in eastern Europe, it also had a more prosaic function, as Grossman's *Habilitationsschrift:* to demonstrate his professional competence to academic and state authorities overwhelmingly hostile to Marxism. The rubric he used for *Austria's Trade Policy,* "characterizing an entire historical epoch economically means understanding it as a link in a greater process of economic development," was taken from Gustav Schmoller, the founder of the younger historical school of economics. But it expressed a perspective that was also integral to Marxism. Grossman inherited the meticulous research methods of the historical school from Grünberg, but for him this tradition was less a stepping stone to historical materialism, as it had been for his teacher, and more a cover for his preexisting Marxist convictions.

The attention *Austria's Trade Policy* received must have been gratifying. In five mainstream journals, the work was praised for its scholarship, including by members of the historical and Austrian schools of economics.[56]

By completing the book, Grossman freed up time for his family. Janina had given birth to their second son, named Stanislaus Eugen after his mother's uncle, on May Day 1914.[57]

Grossman at War:
Politics and Professional Development by Other Means

Grossman did not share the patriotic fervor of July–August 1914. He only entered the army in February 1915 when he was conscripted into the 5th Field Artillery Regiment.[58] As an educated man, "Heinrich Großmann" was designated a "volunteer for the duration of the war," destined for an officer's commission. During the first stages of his army career, he stated that he was an apprentice legal attorney, a profession that would indicate a more definite status to military bureaucrats than *writer.*[59] After basic training, he spent a period as a noncommissioned officer and, by September, was a sergeant.

The nature of his activities well into 1916 is unclear. Given that a volunteer for the duration of the war would normally have become a junior officer in well under a year, having spent at least two months in the field, it seems likely that Grossman was, for a quite a time, engaged in administrative work, with considerable scope to pursue his nonmilitary interests.[60] This is confirmed by the publication of his study of the origins of official statistics in Austria in mid-1916 and a defense of it against criticism some months later.[61]

Grossman only spent a short time in the field, initially as a noncommissioned training officer, then fighting with his unit in the region of Volhynia (now in the Ukraine). It was flat, forested country, dotted with swamps. Early on the morning of June 4, 1916, the Russian forces began a heavy artillery barrage, the first stage in an offensive, commanded by General Brusilov. A first minor victory against the Brusilov offensive occurred on June 10. Grossman was involved in heavy fighting near the small town of Kołki when Russian troops were pushed back from swampy and wooded ground on the northern side across the Styr River. The Austrian and German forces were nevertheless forced into further retreats. Overall, the Russian campaign cost the Austro-Hungarian forces over a million troops, more than either side lost during that by-word for senseless slaughter on the Western Front, the first battle of the Somme.[62]

The war was bad for the businesses that underpinned the incomes of both Henryk's and Janina's families. Army pay was no substitute. Janina had, however, already demonstrated her competence as an artist: her work had been exhibited in Paris and, in 1914, a *Portrait of Professor Karol Grünberg* and *Portrait of Dr AG* [sic], was shown in Kraków.[63] Portraiture, particularly as loved ones depart in wartime, can be a good source of funds. So she set out to earn money as a painter[64] and the Grossmans were able to maintain their establishment in Neue Weltgasse throughout the war.

The focus of Grossman's research shifted after he finished *Austria's Trade Policy*; there is no evidence that he went far in preparing the promised sequel. He did, however, develop one aspect of his earlier research. The history of official Austrian statistical collections now became the topic of a substantial article, "The Origins and Historical Development of Official Statistics in Austria." In preparing this social and class history, Grossman was the first to disturb the dust on extensive primary materials, noting that "treasures still slumber in the lap of our archives, which only await a researcher who understands how to use them." Following the destruction of many of the original documents, his monograph now provides contemporary researchers with their only access to some of these statistical gems.[65]

The study was of major interest to the Central Statistical Commission and appeared in the *Statistische Monatschrift*. Grossman acknowledged the friendly support of Professor Karl Pribram in the use of the commission's archive.[66] Pribram, both a colleague of Grünberg's at the university and a senior official at the Austrian Central Statistical Commission, also wrote a favorable review of *Austria's Trade Policy* around this time.[67]

Citing Grünberg, Pribram and *Austria's Trade Policy*, Grossman's study explained efforts to unify the Habsburg Empire administratively and commercially as a response to external pressures that followed Maria Theresia's accession to the throne. The transition from the state structure of the "feudal-estate constitution of the Middle Ages to the constitution of the specific Theresian-Josephine welfare state" was a precondition for, and accelerated by, the collection of official statistics.[68] "Only to the extent that the state, bit by bit, eliminated the privileged position of the nobility and clergy and supported itself on the much wider base of the peasant and bourgeois estates, did the mass of the population win significance as a factor in the state's power. In this way the need also arose to understand this mass, which was extensive and difficult to assess, numerically."[69]

The conduct of the first censuses was in the hands of the clergy and the nobility. But it was against their own interests to do the job properly. Subsequently, census collection was entrusted to the army. Grossman promised a presentation of this reform in a second part of his study which, like the sequel to *Austria's Trade Policy*, never appeared.[70]

As in *Austria's Trade Policy*, few Marxists inhabited the extensive references and footnotes of this work. But Grossman's later claim that it too was written from a historical materialist perspective was warranted.[71] Thus he explained the purpose of the essay, in terms as compatible with historical materialism as the methods of the historical school, by quoting from Karl Theodore von Inama-Sternegg, one of the fathers of modern official statistics in Austria: "Every situation is only to a small extent a direct product of the relations which at the time surround it; most significantly it is an expression of the life and effects of the social forces of an earlier period."[72]

Grossman also cited Karl Renner, then the leader of the pro-war right wing of Austrian social democracy, who had made the same viewpoint more epigrammatically: "every land and people carries within itself the ruins of its history for decades and centuries; states and nations also suffer from inherited diseases [*sind erblich belastet*]."[73] In this way, Grossman expressed a well-crafted ambiguity: patriotism and/or profound skepticism about the Austrian state. The final words of a further quotation, from the enlightened statesman and advisor to Maria Theresia, Baron von Borié, which concluded his study were similarly ambiguous: "Austria above all, if only it wants this."[74]

In part, Grossman couched his work on the history of Austrian statistics as a critique of a sloppy book on Austrian censuses by Alfred Gürtler, professor of statistics at the University of Graz. Gürtler had ignored basic primary sources and made fundamental factual errors. His whole approach, moreover, was "an unforgivable collapse back into the mistakes of the transcendental Hegelian approach to history, in which history does not simply pass, but is revealed as a process in which Reason gradually asserts itself."[75] Gürtler's reply opened with his strongest argument, that the title of Grossman's study was "un-German." In response Grossman restated his criticisms even more starkly, and reinforced them with evidence contained in Gürtler's own, inept self-defense.[76]

Twenty years later Grossman recalled this controversy. Even though he had a very high regard for his own abilities, his observations were, at least in part, ironic. "My book on the establishment of the Austrian census was . . . directed against Professor Gürtler in Graz (I was at that time an unknown young doctor). My book had the honor of being published by the Central Statistical Commission of Austria. My critique was shattering for Gürtler. He could not demonstrate that a single one of my sentences was false—and was thus finished as an academic. He turned to politics—and became an Austrian minister!"[77]

Grossman's capacity for economic research was a more important asset for the Austrian military authorities than his strictly martial skills. Military priorities imposed elements of a command economy on all the belligerents during World War I. Governments increasingly subordinated or suppressed domestic markets for both material commodities and labor power in order to maximize their chances of success in what was now the most important form of economic competition, the armed conflict. There were few people in the Austrian public service and military with the skills and knowledge necessary to exercise state control over a war economy. University graduates with the necessary competence were in short supply. But conscription meant that they could be easily mobilized for economic management, once the scale of the task was recognized and the necessary institutions were established.

As a statistician, an economist, and a historian, who could speak German and Polish fluently and had a smattering of Russian too, Grossman was particularly well suited to prepare information about economic conditions in and the resources of the Kingdom of Poland for policy makers in Vienna. In September 1916, the recently established Scientific Committee for the War Economy of the War Ministry appointed him from the field to be its representative to the General Government in Lublin, the administrative center of the Austrian-occupied sector of the Kingdom of Poland. This territory was important not only for its agricultural resources but particularly because of the coal and metallurgical industries of Dąbrowa.[78]

The Scientific Committee argued that, as he had taken the officer examination and "will be responsible, through contact with military and civil authorities, for the collection of material on the war economy and the preparation of reports, it is in the interests of the service that he be promoted to Ensign."[79] Only an officer could get a serious hearing from the officials and army officers who ran the Economic Section of the General Government. Four months later he was promoted to lieutenant.

Grossman was now part of a high-powered military think tank that was soon incorporated into Division 10 of the War Ministry, the institution that unified the previously uncoordinated management of the war economy.[80] The staff of the division included the cream of the younger generation of professional economists, from across the theoretical spectrum.

In addition to economic and statistical studies, during 1916–17 Grossman also seems to have taken an interest in the social history of physics, particularly Descartes' understanding of mathematics as a means to reduce human labor.[81] But from his assignment to Lublin onward, he was able to increase his profile and pursue a career as a professional economist and statistician, not simply through spare time research, but also in his official capacity. The war had not stopped his research work and 1917, in particular, was a very productive year for him.

In February 1917, Grossman wrote a critical report on economic statistics produced by the Statistical Office of the General Government. By applying Karl Pribram's insights about the ratios between different elements in agricultural production, he derived estimates of the value of industrial assets and used these in a calculation of the total wealth of the Kingdom of Poland before the war. Pribram, in turn, assessed the report and endorsed it enthusiastically. In the winter of 1917–18, Grossman gave a lecture on the theory behind his estimates, "A Method for Calculating Social Wealth," at the Academy of Sciences in Kraków, a prestigious body whose archives he had used in researching *Austria's Trade Policy*.[82]

*   *   *

Both his official research and work liaising between the General Government in Lublin and the Scientific Committee ensured that Grossman spent considerable time in Vienna.[83] So "Dr. Henryk Großmann in Wien" was well placed to contribute an account of the organization of credit in the Kingdom of Poland to a collection of lectures from a course on the Kingdom of Poland before the war, published after June 1917 by the Viennese Free Association for Further Education in Political Science. The scheduled speaker on "Banks and the Cooperative System" was not able to participate in the lecture course in March; Grossman's comprehensive essay was included to ensure that the same gap did not occur in the publication.

On November 5, 1916, the German and Austrian governments had granted the Kingdom of Poland a sham independence, hoping to win some popular support there for their war against Russia. Conditions in the Kingdom of Poland had become a matter of urgent interest in Vienna, for both the Austrian government and Polish nationalists. Grossman's essay provided not only a systematic account of the development of credit institutions and arrangements in the Kingdom, but also a diagnosis of their weaknesses and a series of policy recommendations.[84]

The analysis was politically circumscribed by its appearance during the war, in a book surveying the Kingdom of Poland from the viewpoint of conventional public policy. Yet Grossman was still able to introduce some obliquely revolutionary elements into his discussion. His mention of the merits of land reform in Ireland for overcoming the problem of dwarf holdings, also typical of the peasantry in the Congress Kingdom (and, he did not need to mention, Galicia), challenged the interests of the Polish aristocracy and could be expected to trigger associations with the Easter Rising in Dublin the previous year. An outline of Polish financial institutions' solidity in crisis situations, in a later section, included a loving description of how effective workers' action had been at the high point of the 1905 revolution: "The strike movement in 1905 halted the entire economic life of the country; trade and exchange faltered, horrendous amounts of goods spoilt in transit, payments could not be made and various firms collapsed."[85]

While Grossman was stationed in Lublin, a new Russian revolution dramatically changed the situation on the eastern front. The essentially spontaneous insurrection by working women and men in Petrograd in March, supported by rank-and-file soldiers and sailors showed that even during (*indeed,* because of) the war, ordinary people could topple repressive governments. Workers, soldiers, and peasants created institutions of radical mass democracy, the *soviets* (councils). Through the soviets, workers exerted control over production, troops limited the power of their officers, and peasants started sharing out the land. Public authority, including over the allocation of resources, notably food, was divided between the embryonic new state of the soviets and the old state, headed by a provisional government that promised but did not initiate democratic elections, laws on land redistribution, and an end to food shortages. This dual power situation was extremely unstable.

From September, the Bolsheviks began to win majorities in the soviets of a series of cities. In November (October according to the old Russian calendar), they had a majority in the Second All-Russian Congress of Soviets. The insurrection they organized overturned the provisional government, and handed full political authority to the new workers' state, with its distinctive soviet institutions.

The initial popular enthusiasm for the war, even in the German provinces of the Austro-Hungarian Empire, had declined as in Russia, with the mounting injuries and deaths of friends and relatives, martial law, and more and more severe rationing. The Russian revolution provided an example of workers deposing an emperor and taking power into their own hands. To Grossman, as to millions of workers and socialists, the Bolshevik revolution demonstrated that radical working-class politics could be practical and successful.[86]

The new soviet government in Russia arranged a cease-fire on December 15 and entered into peace negotiations with the Central Powers. For the rulers of Austria-Hungary—the weakest of the great powers, weakened further by the war—a treaty with Russia was a much more serious priority than the administration of the Kingdom of Poland. In early December 1917 Grossman, his competence in the Russian language improved by practice in Lublin, was recalled to the War Ministry in Vienna. He became a consultant (*Referent*) on economic aspects of the peace negotiations, in the War Economy Section of the War Ministry.[87]

The urgency of the peace negotiations on the Austrian side was reinforced by developments a long way from the front. The first hunger riot in Vienna had taken place on May 16, 1916. A strike wave, eventually involving 700,000 workers, enveloped the industrial centers of the empire in January 1918. The strikers called for improved food rations and changes in factory discipline. They also raised "Bolshevik" demands for peace, political rights, solidarity with the Russian revolution, and against capitalism. In addition, the movement triggered protests against national oppression.

A combination of military repression and empty promises, sold to the workers by the leadership of the Social Democratic Party, eventually terminated the strike wave in the German-Austrian provinces.[88] The party wanted anything but a repeat of the October Revolution in Russia and even played the anti-Semitic card in its efforts to discredit the left radicals who wanted to take the struggles forward.

The Austro-Hungarian regime became increasingly desperate to negotiate its way out of the war. Building on techniques he had used in his research on the economic history of Galicia, Grossman had developed a talent for dealing with "statistical and economic tasks, especially in matters where, due to the lack of adequate materials, the method chosen was conjectural."[89] Thanks to his skill, Lieutenant Grossman now had close contact with senior public officials. "On the instructions of Count Czernin," the Foreign Minister until April 1918, he "calculated the expenditure of the Austro-Hungarian Empire on maintaining Russian, Romanian and Italian prisoners of war, estimated expenditure by relevant countries in maintaining Austro-Hungarian prisoners of war, and the balance of these accounts."[90] So Grossman helped prepare briefs for Czernin, who faced Leon Trotsky and Karl Radek during the peace negotiations with Russia, in Brest Litovsk.[91]

In June 1918, the month of the final agreement with Russia on the repatriation of prisoners of war, Grossman returned to the Scientific Committee for the War Economy. Now that his particular capacities had been recognized, he described his civilian occupation as "writer (economics and statistics)" rather than "lawyer."[92] He was appointed as a consultant on social policy,[93] an area of increasing military concern as unrest among workers grew. Among other tasks Grossman's responsibilities in Vienna included calculations of production, imports, and exports for the occupied Kingdom of Poland and later a similar analysis for the whole empire, while the regulations of the War Production Law (Kriegsleistungsgesetz) were in effect.[94] Well placed to intensify his links and relations with a group of rising academics, his post was a prime jumping off point for a civilian career.

During the war, Janka's work as an artist did not stand still either. In 1917, her *Portrait of a Child* was included in the Annual Salon of the Society for the Encouragement of the Fine Arts in Warsaw. After the expulsion of the Russians from Poland, she had extensive contact with her family in the Kingdom of Poland. Her father published, in Vienna, a catalogue of his outstanding art collection. It featured four of her oil paintings and her miniature of Edward Reicher himself, beside the work of Poland's most gifted artists over the previous hundred years.[95] She continued to advertise her services as an artist in the business section of the Vienna *Address Book* until 1919. "Großman, Janina academic painter," rather than Henryk, was then identified as the occupant of Neue Weltgasse 19. She remained listed at this address until 1924.[96]

Revolution Undermined

In early November 1918, the revolutionary actions of soldiers, sailors, workers, and, in Austria-Hungary, nationalist mobilizations ended the war and the German and Austro-Hungarian monarchies. At this point Grossman seemed to have excellent prospects in peacetime Vienna. An appointment to a senior post (*Hofsekretär*) in the Austrian Central Statistical Commission was "long prepared for and imminent." Grossman's connections with the commission and Karl Pribram, in particular, were paying off. After the acceptance of *Austria's Trade Policy* as his *Habilitation* thesis, which Grünberg was organizing at the Viennese Faculty of Law and Politics,[97] such a post could be combined with academic pursuits and university teaching. As Pribram's career showed, it provided a well-paid path to securing a professorial chair.[98]

Despite the hopes of the masses whose actions brought down both Kaisers, the revolutions in Germany and Austria-Hungary did not result in peace, democracy, or social justice. The new parliamentary regimes maintained the old class relations, inequalities of wealth, and much of the old state machinery in their police and armed forces, public services, and judiciaries.

In Germany, where the industrial proletariat was a particularly powerful force, the social democratic government entered into an alliance with the army leadership and the reactionary, paramilitary *Freikorps* to suppress the revolutionary movement. In January 1919, they put down the Spartakist (communist) uprising in Berlin and murdered the communist leaders Karl Liebknecht and Rosa Luxemburg.

The incompleteness of the revolution in Austria, too, meant that Grossman could not pursue his career plans in Vienna. On November 11, 1918, Kaiser Karl, the last Austrian emperor, abdicated. The Austrian Republic was declared the following day. Its first chancellor, the right wing social democrat Karl Renner, presided over an all-party coalition government, in which Otto Bauer was the foreign minister. The last thing this government, including its social democratic members, wanted was for workers to take power.[99] Bauer, Friedrich Adler, and other leaders of the party's mainstream left played a particularly important role in bridling the revolutionary enthusiasm of the Austrian working class, coordinating social democratic control over soldiers' and workers' councils, and subordinating them to the government.[100] The left radical opposition transformed itself into the Communist Party of Austria in November 1918. It was tiny, with no serious roots in the working class and little experience as an organization to draw on. In the face of the Social Democratic Party with a loyal left wing that was shaping its rhetoric, though not its practice, the Austrian Communists had little impact on national politics.

To create a sense of loyalty to the new state, the coalition government appealed to and reinforced prejudices against "foreigners." The Social Democratic Party's leaders were not prepared to place a basic commitment to civil equality before the stability of bourgeois democracy in the Austrian Republic. The government moved to weaken the working-class identity that the workers' councils embodied. It declared that only people who had been formally registered as residents on its territory *before the war* were citizens of the rump state of German-Austria. People from Dalmatia, Istria, or Galicia who officially registered later were denied citizenship. This provision was primarily designed to prevent roughly 35,000 Galician Jews, most of them refugees, from staying in Vienna.[101] All parties in the provisional National Assembly "agreed that rules had to be found to make it impossible for Jewish refugees who were in German-Austria to become citizens."[102]

Renner argued successfully that the Law on German-Austrian Citizenship should not stipulate that people would have to express their adherence to the German nation before being recognized as citizens. But in doing so he pandered to anti-Semitism. "The entire press of the world, particularly in the west, is dominated by journalists who are in a majority Jewish and the foreign press are extremely sensitive about the question of the treatment of the Jews as citizens."[103]

As the official history of the Austrian Statistical Commission notes in coy terms, the government subjected the Austrian public service to a nationalist purge.[104] Grossman had begun to live permanently in Vienna by 1910, at the latest. But he had not changed his official registration of residency from Kraków, where his widowed mother still lived.[105] He was no longer eligible for a post in the Commission. As Grünberg later put it, Grossman "experienced the blow of being designated a Pole."[106]

He departed for Poland several months later. There is no evidence that he was politically active during the Austrian revolution. In Warsaw, however, he not only pursued his professional career but also returned to active politics, as a Communist.

4

A Communist Academic

When Henryk Grossman moved to Poland in 1919, the new state with its capital in Warsaw was still being constructed. The Russian, German, and Austrian revolutions of 1917 and 1918 had broken up the old empires and opened the way to a reunited, independent Poland. Józef Piłsudski, the former PPS leader, became president and remained in power until 1922.

A fractured Polish Republic emerged under circumstances of economic collapse and intense national and class conflicts. Its territories were only loosely linked together, with distinct traditions of administration and law, and economies oriented to the markets of the old imperial capitals and heartlands. There was no direct rail link between Warsaw and Kraków, for example. Under the second Republic economic activity in Poland never recovered to the levels of production in 1913.

Before he began a career as a public servant in Warsaw, Grossman returned to Kraków.[1] Apart from visiting family and friends, he delivered a lecture on the theory of economic crisis to the Academy of Sciences on June 16, 1919. In the winter of 1917–18, when he had first addressed the Academy, he had presented a thoroughly professional paper that demonstrated his technical virtuosity as a statistician. Since then the political climate had changed radically. During late 1918, workers in industrial centers across central and eastern Europe had created councils, like the soviets in Russia. Further socialist revolutions were real possibilities. Grossman's 1919 paper took sides in the continuing class struggles, insisting that capitalism was inherently crisis prone. On the basis of the labor theory of value, it began a process of recovering Marx's insights into the nature of capitalist economies, obscured by the leading theorists of the Second International, including both the orthodox Karl Kautsky and the revisionist Eduard Bernstein.

The paper outlined Grossman's understanding of Marx's method. As in physics, it argued, "naïve empiricism must be abandoned and—experiments being out of the question—logical constructions must be attempted . . . The question of whether crises result from the essence of the economic mechanism under consideration can only be explained when we make this mechanism independent in our thought of the disturbing influences of foreign markets and investigate it as existing for itself, as if in a vacuum."[2]

Grossman rejected Rosa Luxemburg's underconsumptionist argument that capitalism is incapable of consuming its whole output and tends to break down as non-capitalist territories, whose markets can absorb excess capitalist output, become economically developed.

For years after her murder in January 1919, Luxemburg's views continued to influence the left of the international socialist movement, especially in Germany and Poland. Her 1913 study, *The Accumulation of Capital,* was a very important reference point for Grossman's work in economics. Luxemburg and Grossman were both committed to a fundamentally revolutionary, Marxist perspective. But their views about Marx's method and the contradictory logic of capital accumulation were at odds, as their positions on the tactical questions involved in the formation of the JSDP and the Radek affair had been. Grossman argued that a tendency to break down already arose in a very simple model of capitalist production, even before the presence or absence of foreign markets was taken into account.

Before the war, Otto Bauer, one of Grossman's opponents in the Austrian social democratic movement, following the Russian economist Tugan-Baranovsky, had demonstrated against Luxemburg that capitalism would not break down, so long as the right proportions were maintained between the values of the output of different departments of production (producing means of production—machinery and equipment—and means of consumption, the food, clothing, etc., that workers require to reproduce their labor power). Crises result, Bauer maintained, from the disproportion among the values of the output of these departments.[3] Each industry has to produce just the right amount of products of the correct exchange value to match other sectors' demands and capacities to purchase them. In general, disproportion in the value of commodities produced by different departments means that it will not be possible to sell everything that has been made.

Although Bauer's argument was the starting point for his own analysis, Grossman offered a supplementary explanation of how disproportion arises. In doing so, he stressed an issue that had been neglected after Marx: the contradiction between commodities as items with specific uses (use values) and commodities as embodiments of specific quantities of labor, produced for profit (values, which take the form of their exchange values, see page 49, above).[4] Proportionality in production has to be maintained not only among the values of different commodities but also among the use values created: the physical amounts produced have to match the material (use value) requirements of purchasers of specific means of production and consumption. If, for example, too many cars are made, compared to the number of tires, some of them will be useless and unsaleable.

While Rudolf Hilferding had made a similar point in 1910 as an aside,[5] Grossman placed it and a much broader appreciation of the distinction between use value and value at the center of his understanding of capitalism. At this stage, he used it to radicalize the argument that disproportionality caused economic crises. Even more important, the recovery of Marx's account of the production process as at once a labor process, creating use values, and a valorization process creating values, enabled him to identify production as the site of capitalism's fundamental economic contradictions. As he later pointed out, the distinction between use value and value is at the heart of Marx's account of the exploitation of wage labor.[6] Grossman's emphasis on this point returned the working class and exploitation to the center of Marxist economics.

Other Marxist economists, whether highlighting underconsumption or disproportion as the cause of crises, had accepted the surface appearance of capitalism by focusing on market relations. Their accommodation to the prejudices of common sense and bourgeois economics was another aspect of the reformist tendencies of Second International Marxism. The leaders of the largest parties of the International had increasingly looked to parliamentary processes, rather than the actions of the working class itself, as the means to achieve socialism. Lenin's theoretical work, *State and Revolution,* soon confirmed by the October Revolution in Russia, had recovered Marx's conclusion that only through its own revolutionary activity could the working class take power by destroying the machinery of the capitalist state.[7] Grossman expanded this recovery into the area of Marxist economics. His own experiences in the labor movement and long-standing commitment to the fundamental Marxist premise that the emancipation of the working class had to be the act of the working class itself were preconditions for this achievement. Of equal importance in making his work possible were Lenin's pamphlet and the Russian revolution.

György Lukács was at the same time extending this renewal of Marxism to philosophy. In his discussion of reification (the way that, under capitalism, social relationships between people appear to be immutable objects) and the fetishistic nature of bourgeois economics, published several years after Grossman's lecture on economic crisis, Lukács himself identified the importance of Hilferding's aside about use value.[8]

The sophistication of the short paper Grossman delivered in 1919 was the result of years of systematic reading and thought about Marxist economics. A few months later, he indicated "that in the near future I will publish a major theoretical study whose completion was put on hold because of the war and my military service."[9]

Resuming a Career and Political Activity

The topic of Grossman's first address to the Academy of Sciences in Kraków, as opposed to his exploration of Marxist theory, made him attractive as a potential senior public servant. The government of independent Poland now had an urgent need for detailed information about the territories, peoples, and economic resources it presided over. Galicia provided disproportionate numbers of experienced officials for the new Polish state. While the most backward province of partitioned Poland, Galicia was the only one run by a Polish-speaking administration. The founding head of the Polish Central Statistical Office (GUS) in 1919, Józef Buzek, had been the president of the Austrian Statistical Bureau for Galicia. Although himself a member of the middle-of-the-road Piast peasant party, under Buzek GUS was a refuge for leftists.[10]

Familiar with Grossman's work, at the very least because both had contributed chapters to the 1917 book on the Kingdom of Poland before the war,[11] Buzek appointed his co-contributor to a senior position at GUS in December 1919. Grossman resumed the career, blocked by the racism of rump Austria's coalition government, in independent Poland.

Initially, Grossman was a senior specialist (*Referent*) on the sixth salary grade, at 600 marks a month. Given the high level of inflation, this was augmented by 400 marks for war service and an indexed supplement of 320 marks. In March 1920 he was promoted to ministerial councilor, retrospectively from the beginning of February.[12] Buzek put Grossman in charge of preparations for Poland's first population census, an area where veterans of the Statistical Bureau in Lwów had limited expertise. The census was a huge operation, employing around sixty thousand census collectors alone. What is more, it was to be undertaken during the autumn of 1920, after only a few months of preparations, whereas planning for the 1921 English census had already begun in 1919.[13]

In the first volume of the GUS journal, *Referent* Grossman outlined the significance and tasks of the Polish census, using census results and commentaries from Austria, Germany, France, Britain, the Philippines, and Switzerland (among others). He specified the key features of the census: its legislative basis; its timing and frequency; the relationship between forms and individuals; and the use of data collectors. Given the urgent need for a wide range of information, the census collected statistics not only about population but also employ-ment and industry.

In formulating the census question on language, Grossman expressed polit-ical concerns that dated back at least to the JSDP's campaign over discrimina-tion against Yiddish in the Austrian census of 1910. "The census totally rejects the Prussian and Austrian traditions and opts for an objective analysis. The Austrian instructions for census collectors . . . read: 'For each Austrian citizen the language that he/she uses daily should be reported. However, only one lan-guage should be stated from those listed below . . .' This census does not restrict answers but aims at discovering the truth."[14] Grossman's political engagement was, however, now expanding well beyond the expression of views like these, which many liberals and reformist socialists shared.

During the closing months of 1918, workers' councils spread from Lublin to all major industrial centers in Poland. The Polish Socialist Party (PPS), formed through the fusion of the PPSD and the faction of the PPS formerly led by Piłsudski, was the dominant force in the councils. With Ignacy Daszyński at its head, the PPS sought to defuse the revolutionary situation and, in July 1919, the government suppressed the councils. The idea that they could be the embryo of a workers' state had as little appeal to the PPS as to the Austrian social democrats. Polish social democracy, however, faced much more serious com-petition from the left than its Austrian counterpart.

Two organizations with deep roots in the industrial working class of the Kingdom of Poland, the SDKPiL and PPS (Left), fused to form the Communist Workers Party of Poland (Kommunistyczna Partia Robotnicza Polski, KPRP), at the end of 1918. The KPRP had five to ten thousand members, concentrated in industrial centers by mid-1919, when the PPS had a more dispersed membership of around 24,000.[15] The new Communist Party could also draw on widespread working-class sympathy for the Russian revolution. The final issue of the JSDP's newspaper before the Jewish Social Democrats in Galicia fused with the Polish Bund in 1920, for example, expressed solidarity with the revolution in Russia and denounced Polish military intervention against the Soviet state.[16]

Membership of the KPRP was risky. Never legally registered, the party led, at best, a semi-clandestine existence. Becoming a Communist was hardly a sensi-ble course for anyone preoccupied with building a successful career or with respectability. Confident and passionate about his views, Grossman regarded it as below him to be intimidated out of political activity. The dominance of revi-sionism in Galicia and Vienna had limited the scope of his involvement in the socialist movement before the war. Now the Russian revolution had dramati-cally reshaped left-wing politics in Europe and was opening up new possibili-ties for engagement, which he embraced.

In 1920, Grossman joined the KPRP, as many other former members of the JSDP and especially the Bund did between 1919 and 1923.[17] In practice, he had revised his decision in 1905 to pursue a Bundist path and abandon the project of building a cross-national radical socialist current in Galicia around *Zjednoczenie*. On the model of the Bolsheviks and unlike the Bund, the Polish Communist Party united workers of all nationalities in a democratic and centralist organization, to fight for working-class interests and to extend the civil rights (rather than to establish the cultural autonomy) of national minorities.

The issue of communism was at the center of Polish politics in 1920. In April, Piłsudski ordered the invasion of the Soviet Ukraine. The Polish army took the Ukrainian capital, Kiev, in May.

To secure its home front, the Polish regime rounded up large numbers of left activists. By May, two thousand Communists were in prison. The repression intensified in June, as Soviet troops mounted a successful counteroffensive. Communists could no longer engage in any legal or even semi-legal activity. In many areas outside its strongholds in Warsaw, Łódź and the Dąbrowa Basin, the KPRP disintegrated for a period.[18] Grossman had no sympathy with his government's foreign or domestic policy. Despite the intensely nationalist atmosphere, when approached to buy war bonds he offered to make a donation to a fund for starving babies.[19]

The Red Army liberated Kiev, then the rest of the Ukraine, and moved on to undisputedly Polish territory, approaching Warsaw, Toruń, and Lwów by early August.[20] Poles of military age were conscripted. As a former artillery officer, Grossman was posted to the Artillery School in Toruń.[21]

The town was threatened by Red Cavalry on August 15. But the crisis was soon over. The Polish army under Piłsudski started a successful thrust from the south on August 16. This maneuver outflanked the Russian forces concentrating on Warsaw and decisively defeated the Red Army. Hostilities ceased in October, but Grossman's superiors in the army had already terminated his military responsibilities. He "was relieved of his command because of suspicious behavior and [was] thereafter under police surveillance." While there was suspicion about him, there was, apparently, no proof. He later told Christina Stead that he had assisted the Soviet forces; there was a railway "engine within range of [the] Russians, no one could run it, he could [and] therefore ran it to the Russians."[22]

Railways also played a role in Grossman's domestic and professional life after the Polish-Soviet War. In October, the Ministry of Finance approved payment for the transfer of the Grossmans' household goods by rail from Vienna to Warsaw. There was, however, some delay before the Grossmans had their own furniture at home, in apartment 3, on the desirable floor one up from street level at Ulica Żórawia 24a, in the center of Warsaw. The chaos on the Polish rail network meant that the wagon containing their furniture was held up at both the Vienna and Warsaw ends, increasing costs already blown out by inflation to 90,000 marks, compared to the 56,000 marks allocated for transport expenses.[23] Despite the move, the Grossmans retained their apartment in Vienna. Given that she only started exhibiting in Warsaw in 1925, Janka may have spent a considerable amount of time during the early 1920s outside the Polish capital.[24]

While still responsible for preparing the census, postponed because of the Polish-Soviet War, Grossman wrote a report on rail freight statistics, which was published in the GUS journal. It assessed contemporary practices in other countries and how they could be improved and applied to Poland. In the solid tradition of promoting the imperial interests of one's own public service department, Ministerial Councilor Grossman proposed that responsibility for the task should be transferred to GUS.[25]

In his work at the Statistical Office, Grossman was formulating policies and directing tasks that were crucial for the conduct of government business in Poland. Then, suddenly, on June 30, 1921, he gave one month's notice of his resignation. He later explained this in delicate terms: "certain difficulties which arose from my conception of my scientific responsibilities as the leader of the population census led me to leave my position in order devote myself, henceforth, to research and teaching." Carl Grünberg's account was blunter. Grossman departed from GUS "because he was not prepared to accept the fudging [Frisierung] of the census results in favor of the Polish majority and against the interests of the minorities."[26]

Thirty to 40 percent of Poland's population was not ethnically Polish. In several eastern provinces, Ukrainians and Belorussians were in the majority. Polish chauvinist parties and the governments in which they participated did not want to acknowledge these facts. How could a man of honor, a veteran of struggles against the national oppression of the Jewish working class by the Austrian and Galician authorities, be expected to look the other way when the Polish state used similar tactics?[27]

At GUS there was sympathy for Grossman's stance. Thus, after he had resigned, the agency's journal published his 1917 study of the wealth of the Kingdom of Poland, following inquiries from both the deputy minister for labor and Professor Corrado Gini, an Italian consultant to the League of Nations. Gini used Grossman's results in his own calculations of the wealth of the whole territory of independent Poland.[28]

Then, three years later, GUS published a substantial monograph by its former employee. It dealt with the 1808 and 1810 censuses in the Duchy of Warsaw, making their main results available to the public for the first time. Napoleon had established the Duchy, in 1807, out of territories Prussia had gained in the second and third partitions of Poland. This partial and brief reconstitution of Poland was a foundation for the widespread sympathy for France, French culture, and the French language in the partitioned country, which had been a feature of Grossman's own upbringing.

His study was based on extensive archival research, in both Warsaw and Kraków. He tracked down the original census forms as well as statistical and descriptive reports. The monograph compared the methodology that underpinned the censuses to procedures used during that era in other countries; drew conclusions about the demographic and economic structure of the Duchy; examined the relationship between evidence drawn from the censuses and other literature on Polish economic history; and assessed the condition of statistical science in the Polish state set up by Napoleon. The monograph was Grossman's last work in the areas of the history of public statistics and Polish economic history.[29]

The Free University and the People's University

From GUS, Grossman went to the Free University of Poland (Wolna Wrzechnica Polska, WWP). He was appointed to a full professorship in economic policy there in 1922. The WWP emerged in 1918 from Warsaw's Association for Scientific Courses. Set up as a private body in 1906, during the Russian revolution, the association was the first university-level institution in the Russian Empire to offer courses in Polish since the Tsarist crackdown after the uprising of 1863. Many of the WWP's staff were on the left and its offerings expanded quickly after the war, to include the social sciences. Five new chairs in the Faculty of Political and Social Sciences, including Grossman's, were created in 1921–22. Around this time, there were about 1,500 students formally enrolled at the WWP and almost nine hundred more attending classes.[30]

Among Grossman's colleagues was Zofja Daszyńska-Golińska and, later, the anthropologist Władysław Gumplowicz, members of a somewhat older generation of former PPSD intellectuals. Adam Pragier, the professor of finance, was a leading figure in the PPS. The professor of sociology Ludwik Krzywicki had been one of the first popularizers of Marxism in Poland, as early as the 1880s. Adam Ettinger, who became the professor of criminology and retained his links with the radical left, had been delegated by the Bund to join and help rebuild Polish social democracy in the late 1890s, after it had been broken up by arrests.[31]

Grossman's teaching load at the WWP was not heavy, three to six hours a week. His core course was on trade policy. He also offered occasional classes on economic statistics, the struggle for international markets, and the economic history of western Europe.

It seems Grossman had the confidence of most of his colleagues, not just the Marxist minority, as he was the secretary of the Faculty of Political and Social Sciences in 1924–25. Respect for his professional competence found expression outside the WWP too. An active participant in the discussions of the Warsaw Association of Economists and Statisticians, he was elected to the society's Central Council in 1924. Through the association, a friendship developed between Grossman and Roman Jabłonowski, a founding member of the Warsaw Committee of the KPRP and, from April 1922 to early 1925, a member of the party's Central Committee.[32]

Grossman's relatively light teaching responsibilities at the WWP meant that he had a lot of time for research and politics. As repression eased somewhat after the Polish-Soviet War, the scope for radical political activity expanded. The KPRP had already begun to rebuild its influence in the autumn of 1920. Rising support for the party during 1921 resulted in the election of Communists to lead a series of trade unions.[33]

Given that the party was still subject to police harassment, cultural and educational front organizations provided an important means to engage in legal activity. They could bring a range of militants—workers from different sectors, students, intellectuals, peasants—together under party auspices, in a way that trade unions, for example, could not. The largest such organization was the People's University (PU), set up in 1915. Communists and PPS members were involved in the institution after the war but, in the course of 1921, paralleling the advances the party made in the union movement, communist influence became predominant. The People's University offered popular and specialist courses and collaborated with the trade unions' Workers' School, a communist initiative that offered a three-year academic secondary school program for adults.

At the very least through comrades who had played a prominent role in the Adam Mickiewicz People's University in Kraków before the war, and possibly as an active contributor to its activities, Grossman was familiar with this kind of operation. At the start of 1922, the chairperson of the PU in Warsaw was Ester Golde-Strozecka; the deputy chairperson, Zygmunt Heryng; and the secretary, Henryk Grossman. The communist philosopher Stefan Rudniański was on the governing board. Later Grossman took over the chair and continued in this role until 1925.[34]

The scale of the PU's activities was substantial: it had its own premises, including a cinema, and hired additional venues as needed. It organized about forty lectures a month, each attended by fifty to three hundred people, and programs of talks for trade unions. Among the lecturers were Communists on the staff of the WWP, like Grossman, Ettinger, and Zygmunt Heryng; high school teachers; Rudniański; and Jerzy Heryng, Zygmunt's son. While working full-time for the party, Jerzy Heryng was on the PU payroll. For a time, Bolesław Bierut, then a party activist in his late twenties, from 1948 Communist Poland's Stalinist chief, was employed by the People's University as a bookkeeper.[35]

Through his involvement with Jewish workers in the PPSD and then the JSDP, Grossman already had extensive experience of cultural and education activity as a means of building a political party. The political nature of his involvement with the PU was particularly apparent in the subject of a talk he gave to its Socio-economic Discussion Group, in which he participated as a representative of the university's administration: "Issues in Marxism and Goals for the Work of the Group in the Current Period."[36]

Young members of the party looked up to Grossman. There were few intellectuals, still less professors, who not only identified themselves as Marxists but also risked political persecution through activity in the KPRP. A sketch in a theatrical review put on by party members labeled him "one of the three 'wise men' (Rudniański, Ettinger, Grossman), about whom it was sung: 'Each of us is famous for his wisdom, who is the wisest?' "[37]

While at the WWP, Grossman continued the tradition, observed by the JSDP from 1906, of celebrating the date of Marx's death.[38] He made a triple contribution to mark the fortieth anniversary. During the winter semester 1922–23, he taught a course on "The economic system of Karl Marx and its position in economic theory (in the course of the 40 years since his death)."[39] Stanisław Tołwiński, a young radical whom Grossman and leftist colleagues helped get up to speed in social and statistical theory for his job at GUS, was intrigued by the way his professor presented Marxist theory.[40]

Grossman's second anniversary activity was to organize the publication, in Polish, of several important, but previously untranslated texts by Marx. He annotated, introduced, and translated Marx's letters to Kugelmann and the *Critique of the Gotha Program*. The short book was issued by the legal, but communist-controlled publishing house, Książka (Book), which had close links with the PU and its staff.[41] Grossman was also involved in another Book project, the preparation of a new translation of *Capital*.[42]

The introduction to the collection offered a pioneering exploration of the initial reception of Marx's work in Poland, well before a Marxist current emerged.[43] Grossman pointed out that, as early as 1874, a Catholic priest had written the first Polish study of socialism and Marx, which was, moreover, a serious and sympathetic account!

Stefan Pawlicki, "from his conservative position, discovered the bankruptcy of official liberal economics, in comparison to scientific socialism" because he, too, was critical of capitalism, though on a backward-looking basis. But this was precisely on the condition that "the immediate threat of a workers' movement did not exist and the issue of socialism arose not from local economic experience but came from the outside world, as a reflection of distant conflicts. That was the golden age of scientific discussion about socialism in Poland . . . He advanced an objective view typical of those scholars who, while opposed to the socialist movement and regarding it as a threat to their own class, could nevertheless see that the movement embodied a truth or partial truth. Instead of blindly condemning it as an abomination, they wanted to 'understand it well and completely.' "[44] The Jewish Communist clearly had a soft spot for this priest: as an undergraduate, Grossman had taken six of Father Pawlicki's philosophy courses. Grossman's introduction went on to explain the context and significance of the *Critique of the Gotha Program.*

A short article on "The Economic System of Karl Marx" in *Kultura Robotnicza* (Workers' Culture) was Grossman's third contribution to the Marx anniversary. The journal, edited by Jan Hempel and Jerzy Heryng, both senior Communists, was the organ of the Workers' Culture Association and the PU. The association, set up in September 1920, coordinated the expanding cultural activities of left-wing unions, cooperatives, and literary and social groups. As most of the KPRP's press was underground, *Workers' Culture,* a legal periodical with a circulation of over four thousand, was particularly important for the party.[45]

Like the introduction to his translations of Marx, this piece began with the bourgeois reception of Marx. It provided a good description of the degeneration of mainstream economics, from its achievements in the early nineteenth century to the rise of the neoclassical school, which still dominates the discipline today. Neoclassical economics was "a system more subtle than that of the medieval schoolmen. Economic laws could even be constructed, so long as they were not the laws of the real world. Thus a new bourgeois theoretical school emerged. Having previously escaped into the realms of history and ethics, it now escaped into *psychology.* This led from the surface of economic facts into the sphere of individual, inner psychological life, describing objective and accessible facts in terms of invisible psychological facts, inaccessible to research."[46] The main focus of Grossman's essay was, however, on the way the workers' movement regarded and used *Capital.* Drawing on Lenin's explanation of the degeneration of German social democracy, it argued that,

> in the course of the everyday *practical* struggle, an elite labor bureaucracy and labor aristocracy, which accepted the capitalist system and did not see any reason to abolish it, emerged from the proletariat. So, in the *theoretical* battle, the elite of the proletariat's educated leaders agreed with the current system, and

employed their talents to glorify it. In the second volume of *Capital*, Marx gives some consideration to the possibility of production and consumption within the capitalist system becoming permanently *stable*. Hilferding, Kautsky and O. Bauer rushed to answer: such equilibrium is not only possible, but the mechanisms of capitalism are such that they automatically tend to restore equilibrium in production if it is temporarily disrupted.[47]

This approach diminished Marxism "to the level of pre-Marxist theory (i.e. J. B. Say, Bastiat and Carey)." Grossman's criticisms indicated that he regarded the topic of his 1919 paper, the theory of economic crises, as a central issue for revolutionary politics. "Marxian economics *is the only scientific theory*, which predicted processes that are now under way, analyzed them and formulated the laws of their historical development, *the process of the breakdown and collapse of the capitalist system*. The opportunist literary attempts to distort Marxist theory, still being undertaken, must always fail when confronted with reality."[48]

Grossman also observed that the posthumous publication of the third volume of *Capital* in 1894 was a turning point for the understanding of Marx's work. It was, however, a turning point that Marxists such as Kautsky had not identified, failing to see any connection between Marx's discussion of the tendency for the rate of profit to fall and his theory of economic crises.[49] The intersection between revolutionary politics and this explanation of crises became the core of Grossman's major theoretical project in economics. The capitalist production process, grasped as a contradictory unity of use value and value, and Marx's method were important themes in the project, as they had been in his paper to the Academy of Sciences. By December 1924 Grossman had identified the internal contradictions of Otto Bauer's model of proportional capitalist reproduction as a means to explain the logic of accumulation in a manuscript study.[50] Later he titled it "Developmental Tendencies of Contemporary Capitalism" and then, to stress his views about Marx's method, "The Development Tendencies of 'Pure' and Empirical Capitalism."[51] He claimed the work was

1. the first attempt to reconstruct the method which underlies Marx's economics
2. ... an analysis, with a critique of previous presentations of specific parts of Marx's economic system, in particular his account of the reproduction process, at whose centre point stands *Marx's account of economic collapse*, reconstructed here for the first time.[52]

In December 1923, Grossman used another anniversary to explore theories of economic crisis before Marx. He lectured on Simonde de Sismondi to the

Economists' Society a little late, as Sismondi was born on May 9, 1773, near Geneva. The paper appeared in French the following year, as a seventy-seven-page monograph in the Free University Library series.[53] Its publication, "with the cooperation of the Institute," was an early link between Grossman and the Institute for Social Research in Frankfurt, where Carl Grünberg had become the first director in 1923.[54]

In the monograph, Grossman contrasted his own assessment of Sismondi with those of Charles Rist and Rosa Luxemburg. Rist, one of France's leading economists, was the author of a standard reference work on the history of economic thought.[55] Although Grossman rejected many of Rist's conclusions about Sismondi,[56] the French professor later complemented his Polish colleague on the study.[57] Rosa Luxemburg had undertaken an extensive treatment of Sismondi in *The Accumulation of Capital*, emphasizing the distance between him and Marx.

Grossman drew radically different conclusions. For a start, Sismondi employed precisely the Marxist method Grossman had described in 1919, abstracting from less important aspects of concrete reality in order to identify the core features of capitalism. The Swiss economist considered, in particular, the possibility of equilibrium between production and consumption in a country isolated from foreign trade and lacking pre-capitalist formations. "Karl Marx adopted the same methodological foundations forty years later in his *Capital*."[58] By way of contrast, Luxemburg regarded foreign trade and remnants of previous modes of production as necessary conditions for capitalist growth.

The method of abstraction has, however, to be applied judiciously. Sismondi's critique of *classical* economics, as described by Grossman, applies even more forcefully to *neoclassical* economics, which dominates the profession today. "Sismondi rejects this abstraction [of the classical school] not because it is abstract but because it is an abstraction which does not correspond with reality, because it *does not take account of essential* characteristics of the capitalist system. The simplification of reality should have its limits. 'The abstraction proposed ... is much too violent; it is not a *simplification*, it is a *distortion* which removes from our view all the operations ... in which we can distinguish truth from error' ... Sismondi is thus not opposed to abstraction in general, but solely to abstraction which leaves to one side the essential elements of reality."[59]

Grossman identified the distinction between use value (the way commodities satisfy specific concrete needs) and value (the amount of abstract social labor embodied in commodities) as a crucial feature of Sismondi's analysis.

Capital, Sismondi contended, is itself the most abstract form of value. In a system based on exchange, the goal of production is profit.[60] He regarded capitalism "not as a system producing *real goods* for the satisfaction of needs but as the production and accumulation of *abstract exchange value*. It was therefore fair to regard Sismondi as the first economist who scientifically discovered capitalism."[61]

Sismondi also expressed "the germ of the doctrine later developed by Marx, which he called *economic fetishism*, according to which the capitalist system has an objective tendency to obscure its real character, its institutions and the real source of its wealth."[62]

The recovery and application of the theory of fetishism, which Lukács called reification, was the source of some of the most powerful insights in the essays that made up the Hungarian Communist's *History and Class Consciousness*, published in 1923. It is possible that Grossman was influenced by Lukács in highlighting the importance of the concept.[63] In his 1919 essay Grossman had, on the other hand, already identified the fundamental nature of Marx's distinction between use value and (exchange) value, which provided a basis for criticizing the illusions arising from an exclusive focus on value. Nor did Grossman now refer to Lukács's treatment of Sismondi and failure to identify Sismondi's insights into commodity fetishism.[64]

For Sismondi, the contradiction between use and exchange value meant that a disproportion arises between the scale of production and people's needs for specific commodities as use values. Because production is regulated by profit and not need, a part of the social output remains unsold and does not contribute to the growth of wealth (in the form of use or exchange values).[65]

The classical economists argued that market forces result in harmonious equilibrium. In their model, declining prices, which result from insufficient demand compared with supply, will lead to falls in the level of production. Sismondi disagreed. Many producers will *increase* production in the face of falling prices, as they try to maintain their incomes. Grossman had already endorsed this observation in his 1919 presentation. So, under capitalism, crisis is not a passing episode but "a phenomenon that is renewed without cease, periodically and necessarily to the point that its regular repetition can be predicted."[66]

Although he had criticisms of Sismondi, Grossman explained that Marx took over several of his predecessor's insights, particularly that it was *socially necessary* labor time (see page 49, above) which underpinned exchange value; that labor was the source of profit, rent, and interest; and that the contradiction between use and exchange value gave rise to economic crises.[67]

In political terms, according to Grossman, Sismondi implicitly advocated a minimum and a maximum program. His reform program was designed to improve the immediate situation of the working class, although he did not have any illusions about the state as a neutral institution. Grossman adopted a controversial characterization of Sismondi as a socialist. Here, as with the issue of fetishism, Grossman may have drawn on Lukács, in pointing out that Sismondi had not only diagnosed capitalism's crisis tendencies but also saw the necessity of a superior system of production beyond capitalism in which free competition was superseded "by an administrative system."

Unlike the utopian socialists, Sismondi grasped that conflict between capital and labor was inevitable. He favored the abolition of abstract exchange value, the market and money, and the transformation of capitalist production in the interests of the working class. But Sismondi did not recognize that the abolition of exchange value implied the elimination of private ownership of the means of production, the usual standard for socialist politics. Hence Marx's conclusion that "he forcefully *criticizes* the contradictions of bourgeois production, but he does not *understand* them."[68] Grossman elaborated on this point. Sismondi grasped how the current economic system, based on abstract exchange value, is riven by a fundamental contradiction that leads to insoluble problems. "It is on this point that Sismondi's doctrine constitutes one of the most important sources for the genesis of the scientific economic theory of Karl Marx."[69]

Beyond Sismondi, through eighteenth-century physiocracy and mercantilism, Grossman's interest in the history of political economy extended back to the fifteenth century and even antiquity. He collected materials on the economic ideas of Copernicus, whose statue near the main university buildings in Kraków was unveiled when he was a student, and shared them with Jan Dmochowski. A Polish edition of Copernicus's treatise on money and other economic texts, prepared by Dmochowski, was published in 1923.[70] Dmochowski presented his benefactor with a signed copy of the book dedicated to "esteemed Prof. Dr. Henryk Grossman." It was also while in Warsaw, if not earlier, that Grossman began to investigate the history of slavery in Christendom.[71]

Persecution and Exile

Grossman conducted his academic and political work after leaving the GUS in the context of major social conflicts. The new Polish state had established its authority in 1919, but the political situation in Poland remained extremely volatile until the end of 1923. Two factors were involved. The first was the economic and political fragility of the new republic. Particularly after September 1921, governments were short-lived and lacked reliable parliamentary majorities.[72] The second factor was the continued combativeness of the working class.

During 1923 in Poland, as in Germany, economic conditions deteriorated sharply. Governments turned high inflation into hyperinflation by printing money to fund budget deficits. The level of class struggle and social discontent rose. Early in the year workers participated in widespread strikes over economic demands. In response hundreds of Communists and militant unionists were again arrested and several trade unions closed down by General Sikorski's "Cabinet of pacification."[73] Soon the authorities banned Workers' Culture and its journal, although it was quickly succeeded by another publication, *Nowa Kultura* (New Culture), with the same editorial team.[74]

As workers tried to keep wages in line with soaring prices, the level of strike activity rose from July. Union membership expanded to 1,200,000. On July 6, a clash between troops and strikers at a demonstration in Kraków, where the KPRP had a minor presence, ended with workers spontaneously taking control of the city center. Frightened by the prospect of civil war, the PPS rapidly negotiated an end to the strike movement.[75]

Changes in policy during 1922–23 nevertheless increased the Communist Party's ability to relate to workers' struggles and those of oppressed groups. The KPRP was a part of the Moscow-based Communist International (Comintern) and adopted its united front tactic of seeking to mobilize reformist alongside revolutionary workers, by seeking joint action with social democratic parties and trade unions. The Comintern also prompted the KPRP to revise other aspects of the sectarian heritage of the SDKPiL. The party adopted a more sympathetic attitude to the struggles of oppressed nationalities. It stopped calling for the collective operation of large rural estates and took up the demand that land be redistributed to the peasantry. As a consequence, KPRP influence rose significantly, not only among ethnically Polish workers but also in wider circles of Jews, White Russians, Ukrainians and Germans, and peasants.[76]

The efforts of Polish governments to maintain social control continued to include the harassment of Communists. In November and December, the authorities even closed Book's retail operation. The political police's campaign against communism targeted Grossman among other party members and sympathizers. From 1922 to 1925 he was arrested and imprisoned five times, for "hostility to the state." "My educational activity was increasingly persecuted," he later wrote, "searches were made at my institution, during which police agents also planted forged documents, and I was in police custody for two, four, even eight months." Given these disruptions, the extent of Grossman's publications, particularly the substantial monographs on Sismondi and the censuses of the Duchy of Warsaw, was impressive. Despite the fact that he was never convicted, during the periods in jail—the shortest lasted eight days—he was suspended from his post at the WWP and received no income.[77]

The KPRP was not able to take full advantage of the Polish crisis in 1923. This was not only a matter of the party's limited resources, reduced further by arrests. The Executive Committee of the Communist International (ECCI) undermined the potential of the united front tactic by overestimating the willingness of social democratic leaders to pursue workers' demands. Unrealistic expectations about the PPS and the left wing of the German Social Democratic Party disoriented the Polish and German Communist Parties, precisely when social conflicts were most intense. The Communist Parties failed to take advantage of revolutionary opportunities when hyperinflation and class struggles peaked in October (in Germany) and November (in Poland). The resolution of the Polish and German crises in favor of the established order closed the postwar period of deep political instability and revolutionary potential in Europe.

In Poland, a new nonparty government of the right, under the financial expert Władisław Grabski was able to control inflation and presided over a series of conservative and reactionary measures. These included religious education in state schools by teachers appointed by the Catholic Church, state payments to Catholic priests, and the closure of most schools that taught in Ukrainian and Belorussian, majority languages in provinces on the eastern borders of Poland.[78] Attacks on the Communist Party intensified as the ruling class regained self-confidence.

The premises of the People's University were sealed in the middle of July 1924. On the evening of August 6, the political police raided apartment 9 at Ulica Królewska 31 in central Warsaw. It was rented in Grossman's name and used by the Secretariat of the Communist Party's Central Committee. Four people were arrested on the spot. The police picked up ten more, among them "big fish" in the party, during the night.

Members of the Central Editorial Group of the party including Jerzy Heryng, the editor of New Culture, were also caught in the roundup of Communists that followed the raid. Grossman was taken into custody and held in the notorious Pawiak prison. Altogether, the police arrested almost 11,000 suspected Communists in Poland between 1919 and 1926. A large proportion, after the mid-1920s certainly a majority, were never convicted. Grossman's experience was typical. "Communists who avoided arrest were rather an exception and most of them were held in detention many times."[79]

The KPRP did not overcome the shortcomings of its policies or deal with police harassment by adopting a measured response to Grabski's policies. Instead, even though the circumstances were now much *less* favorable, the party behaved as though revolution was on the immediate agenda. While factors internal to the party and the Polish situation were involved, this was largely a consequence of developments in Russia.

Isolated by the failure of the revolution to spread to central or western Europe, the Russian workers' state had begun to degenerate. Different sections of the Russian Communist Party expressed the interests of different social forces. On the left, Trotsky focused on the working class inside and outside Russia; Bukharin, on the right, emphasized the importance of the peasantry's contribution to Russian economic growth; Stalin, the general secretary of the Russian Communist Party, promoted the interests of the intertwined bureaucracies of the party and state.[80]

After illness removed Lenin from the political scene in early 1923, conflict over the leadership and direction of the party broke into the open. As the bureaucracy became an increasingly coherent, distinct, and self-aware layer in society, Stalin's power increased. His faction was able to dominate the party, the Russian state, and the Comintern, initially through alliances, first with a section of the left, led by Grigorii Zinoviev and Lev Kamenev, then with the right. By the end of the 1920s, Stalin had defeated his factional rivals in the CPSU and eliminated the last vestiges of the workers' state created by the revolution in 1917.

In December 1923, the KPRP's Central Committee offered a critique of the Comintern's tactics in Germany and warned against the current campaign against Trotsky in the Russian party. Under pressure from the Communist International and Stalin in particular, the Polish party quickly backed off on the issue of conflicts in the Russian party, but not its assessment of developments in Germany. Given that many members of the Polish Central Committee lived in Russia, the KPRP was particularly vulnerable to manipulation by the Russian party. The ECCI tipped out the old Polish leadership and installed a new group, with substantial but only minority support among the rank and file.[81]

There is no surviving evidence of Grossman's attitude toward the faction fights in the KPRP, CPSU, and Comintern, while he was in Poland. But Communists around the world, whether explicitly or implicitly, eventually had to adopt an attitude toward Stalinism. Most, at least initially, accepted it as an expression of Marxism. A small proportion resisted it, in the name of Marxism and working-class revolution, from inside or outside the official movement. More abandoned both communist politics and the idea of working-class self-emancipation.

The new Polish leaders implemented the Comintern's recent sharp turn to the left, despite the stabilization of European capitalism.[82] Far from promoting any cooperation with social democratic parties, Communists now encouraged insurrections and proclaimed that social democrats were "social fascists." In Poland and many other countries the membership and the credibility of the communist movement among workers declined.

In line with an international pattern, the new leadership of the Polish party carried out Comintern directives to "Bolshevize" its organization. A campaign against the Luxemburgist heritage in the party was an important aspect of this process. The fundamental issue was not the status of Luxemburg's contributions to Marxist theories of the national or land questions, the class struggle, or capitalist economic dynamics. The vilification of Luxemburgism was designed to ensure that members of the Polish party would uncritically accept every political turn made by the Comintern leadership and capitalist local representatives. There was a parallel development in Germany, where the leftists Ruth Fischer and Arkadi Maslow took over the leadership of the party in 1924, with the blessing of the Communist International. Fischer described Luxemburg's influence as "a syphilis bacillus."[83]

In Poland, the faction fighting in the Communist Party coincided with a period of severe repression. Soon after Grossman's arrest, in August 1924, *New Culture* was banned and the People's University permanently shut down.[84] While the prospects for reviving the journal or the PU were poor, there was a well publicized campaign for the more limited goal of freeing Grossman. This involved legal proceedings and personal approaches to members of the government.

Eventually, Grossman was released on bail after prominent scholars intervened on his behalf with Prime Minister Władysław Grabski. Grossman seems to have eventually made an unofficial deal with the Polish authorities, for a kind of qualified exile. He would leave the country but could return for two weeks a year, so long as he only saw his family and did not engage in political activity. On November 4, 1925, he arrived in Frankfurt am Main from Warsaw. His mentor, Carl Grünberg, had arranged a post for him at the Institute for Social Research.[85]

Even before leaving Poland, Henryk and Janka's marriage had broken down. Although they eventually divorced, they apparently remained friends.[86] A key issue in the separation seems to have been his political activity and imprisonment. In semi-fictional notes based on Henryk, Christina Stead wrote that Janka left him as a result of family pressure while he was in jail.[87] Stead's factual report of a conversation with Grossman about Grünberg's wife may well have reflected his sympathy for Janka when their marriage was stressed. He maintained that "no wife should sacrifice for anyone." "He cries indignantly 'It is better to be selfish, it is protection: it is better for everyone.' Weird little darling! Some more: 'He could have been a great romantic, he is very romantic at heart, but he suppressed it.' "[88] Christina Stead's notes also indicate that while he was subject to persecution he left many of his papers and letters with his mother, "who destroyed them for fear of police visits . . . thus the documentation of a generation was lost."[89]

5

Marxist Economics
and the Institute
for Social Research

Bert Brecht grasped the contradictory nature of the Institute for Social Research (Institut für Sozialforschung, IfS), if not the details of its foundation, in notes for a novel about socialist intellectuals isolated from the working class: "a rich old man (weil, the speculator in wheat) dies, disturbed at the poverty in the world. In his will he leaves a large sum to set up an institute that will do research on the source of this poverty, which is, of course, himself."[1]

This was the unique organization Henryk Grossman joined in November 1925. It was very well funded to conduct scholarly Marxist research. The staff and students of the institute, on generous salaries and scholarships, were housed in a new building, had access to its specialist library and archive, and had links with innovative Marxist thinkers across Germany and the world.

The IfS was the product of the German revolution and its failure. The institute brought together a group of brilliant Marxists, not in an organization dedicated to the overthrow of capitalism but in one integrated into the conservative and elitist German university system and financed by profits from international grain dealing, the meat trade, and property speculation.

The slaughter of World War I and the suffering it inflicted on the majority of the German population, the Russian revolution of 1917 and the revolutionary upheavals of 1918 across Europe, followed by a period of profound economic and political instability until late 1923 radicalized a large section of the German working class, the biggest and best organized in Europe. The German Communist Party (Kommunistische Partei Deutschlands, KPD) had only a few thousand members when it was set up at the very end of 1918. By October 1920, it had become a mass organization with over 400,000 members.

Along with tens and hundreds of thousands of workers, these events radicalized a layer of young intellectuals from other social classes. The German revolution in November 1918 ended World War I, overturned the *Kaiserreich*, generated workers' and soldiers' councils across Germany, and threatened the capitalist order. It also inspired Felix Weil (son of the multimillionaire businessman and grain trader Hermann Weil), who "put himself, in full uniform, at the disposal of the Frankfurt Workers' and Soldiers' Council during the November Revolution of 1918, along with his personal cadet from the student fraternity." Two other university students, Max Horkheimer and Friedrich Pollock, the sons of wealthy Jewish industrialists in southern Germany, witnessed the Soviet Republic in Munich "from a rather dignified distance."[2] They too were attracted by Marxism.

Although Weil, Horkheimer, and Pollock responded to the real possibility of socialist revolution in Germany, they never joined the Communist Party. Where Grossman was an organic intellectual of the working class—his outlook and politics had been shaped by direct involvement in workers' struggles—they can be understood as traditional intellectuals ideologically conquered by the working class, at least for a time. But, "looked at from the standpoint of the active labor movement, they were always outsiders."[3]

During the early 1920s, Felix Weil was close to the KPD and financed a number of left-wing causes. He became a major shareholder, for example, in Wieland Herzfelde's radical Berlin publishing house, Malik, which issued Georg Grosz's savage cartoon portfolios and György Lukács's *History and Class Consciousness*.[4]

In the summer of 1923, Weil funded a Marxist Study Week organized by the communist activist and philosopher Karl Korsch. Lukács and Pollock also attended. Lukács and Korsch were the most influential Marxist philosophers of the 1920s. The successful Bolshevik revolution in Russia and the formation of the Communist International were the most important practical expressions of the recovery of Marxist politics, formulated particularly in Lenin's writings on the nature and tasks of the revolutionary party and in *State and Revolution*. Korsch and Lukács extended this alternative to the orthodox Marxism of the Second International into philosophy.[5]

Lukács's book expressed Marx's dialectical conception of revolution in Hegelian terms. The working class was an object of history, created by the process of capital accumulation. The experience of the class struggle, which was also a consequence of capitalist relations of production, meant that the proletariat could also become the subject of history, conscious that its interests could only be realized through socialist revolution.[6]

Felix Weil's most ambitious project for the promotion of revolutionary ideas was to create a body, endowed by his father and attached to the University of Frankfurt am Main, that would engage in Marxist research and employ some of his radical friends. In a period of constrained public finances, but expanding student numbers, the Faculty of Economics and Social Science at the university was especially attracted by the offer of free accommodation on the ground floor of the institute's building and money for the professorial chair its director would occupy. Other institute staff with the necessary qualifications would also be available to teach at the university.

Frankfurt am Main was in Prussia, by far the largest state in the federal Weimar Republic. The state's government was dominated by the Sozialdemokratische Partei Deutschlands (Social Democratic Party of Germany, SPD) until 1932, and was well disposed to the idea of a Marxist institute under its authority. After all, the SPD was both concerned about its respectability and still, nominally, Marxist. The IfS seemed to combine both elements.[7]

The institute formally opened in 1924, after the period of social upheaval from 1918 to 1923 had already closed. Its first director, Grossman's close friend and mentor Carl Grünberg, had moved from Vienna to Frankfurt am Main to take up the post in 1923. He brought to the new institute his abilities as a researcher and organizer, his considerable academic reputation as an authority on the history of socialism and the labor movement, and his *Archiv,* the most prestigious scholarly journal in the world devoted to these topics. Many prominent European social democrats had contributed to the *Archiv* and Grünberg remained on friendly terms with leaders of the Austrian party, several of whom had studied under him. Under him the IfS had a close relationship with the Marx-Engels-Institute in Moscow, whose head, David Riazanov, was another former student.[8]

Grünberg provided Grossman with a means to avoid political persecution in Poland by becoming a semi-exile, at the age of forty-four, and research associate of the institute in Frankfurt. Grossman replaced Richard Sorge, who for some years had been using his academic career as a cover for clandestine communist organizational tasks. In 1924 Sorge departed for Moscow and a career as a Soviet spy. When Grossman arrived in Frankfurt the other associates were Pollock, who was also an economist, and the sinologist Karl Wittfogel.[9] Wittfogel was an active KPD member, involved in workers' education. He had joined the institute earlier in 1925. These two new employees, with strong communist associations, got on well and conducted a lively correspondence when Wittfogel was out of town.[10] Many of the students who took up institute scholarships to conduct doctoral research under Grünberg were Communists.[11]

The IfS provided Grossman with a very favorable milieu for intensive research, insulated from the pressures of employment in a more conventional bourgeois institution.[12] A foreigner, he was not legally permitted to belong to a political party; the institute and its members were already under surveillance; and prominent political engagement in Frankfurt might have jeopardized his ability to return to or even visit Poland.[13] So he never joined the German Communist Party, although he was a close sympathizer. As a consequence, his situation in Germany also ensured that he was not subject to the full blast of Stalinization, as the counter-revolution in Russia imposed centralized bureaucratic structures and doctrines concocted in Moscow on the international communist movement.

The alliance between the SPD and representatives of the old imperial order that had defeated the socialist revolution in Germany meant that the army, judiciary, and public service were still dominated by reactionaries, hostile to the Weimar Republic. The political atmosphere in Germany was nevertheless more open than in Poland. There was a vastly larger audience for left-wing ideas and Marxist theory, now the main focus of Grossman's research, publications, and teaching. In Frankfurt, the Communist Party had a significant presence. Eight KPD members were elected, in May 1924, to the City Council, which was dominated by the SPD and its bourgeois allies.[14]

Meanwhile, the situation for the labor movement in Poland deteriorated further. In May 1926, Jozef Piłsudski's military coup, supported by the Polish Socialist Party and, initially, the Communist Party, restricted public debate and criticism even more. The coup made returning to Poland even less attractive. But Grossman had family ties there. Janka, his wife and sons lived in Warsaw. His brother, Bernard, and his mother were in Poland too. She continued to live at their old home in Kraków.

But political developments are always difficult to predict. Conditions might improve in Poland or deteriorate in Germany. Grossman did not have a tenured university job in Frankfurt: for the time being he kept his options open and did not resign from the WWP.[15]

It was not only political and financial circumstances at the institute that were favorable. Grossman was very comfortable there at a personal level too. He had plenty of time to pursue his own research projects and got on well not only with Carl Grünberg but also Felix Weil, Fritz Pollock, and Max Horkheimer, who succeeded Grünberg as director. By 1929 Henryk referred to them publicly not simply as colleagues, but as "my friends."[16] The constraints associated with working at the institute were hardly disagreeable. Grünberg sometimes interrupted, "tapping on ceiling with cane and yelling . . . stop working come to movies."[17]

Movies weren't the only distraction Frankfurt had to offer and Grossman did not confine his social life to colleagues at the institute. He enjoyed the extensive cultural life—concerts, theatrical performances, and exhibitions— the wealthy city supported. In its numerous bookshops, he indulged in biblio- phile pleasures. He kept his large library, including "a beautiful edition of Francis Bacon's *Opera omnia* of 1665, and many other philosophical and art books," in his office at the institute.[18]

Grossman lived close to work: around 1931 at Feuerbachstrasse and in 1933 at Leerbachstrasse, north of the Old Opera House, a lively part of Frankfurt near cafés and cinemas.[19] He knew Ernst Schoen, the cultural director of the Süd- westdeutscher Rundfunk (South West German Radio) and the Hungarian composer, conductor, and cellist Mátyás Seiber who taught at Hoch's Conser- vatory.[20] The young actor, Dorothea Wieck, was a friend. She was a member of the company at Frankfurt's principal theater, the Schauspielhaus, between 1929 and 1931. Grossman later claimed that he had advised her on tactics for secur- ing a favorable film contract in Berlin.[21] In 1931 Wieck starred in Leontine Sagan's radical *Girls in Uniform,* with its sensitive treatment of relationships in a repressive girls' boarding school.

Grossman also associated with Hermynia Zur Mühlen, an early member of the KPD in Frankfurt. Her background was the rarefied upper reaches of the Austro-Hungarian aristocracy. Zur Mühlen was well known as the author of proletarian children's stories, including a collaboration with Georg Grosz, and as the translator of the Malik editions of Upton Sinclair's novels.[22]

Academic Formalities

Apart from research, recreation, and following political developments, Gross- man also devoted time to what should have been formalities to expand the scope of his academic activities. As previously agreed with Grünberg, he took steps to gain a higher doctorate soon after his arrival in Frankfurt, so that he could teach at the university as an unsalaried lecturer (*Privatdozent*). Both the institute's director and his new assistant expected that the Faculty of Econom- ics and Social Sciences and the Prussian minister for science, culture, and edu- cation would approve the degree.

The Prussian police and provincial authorities, however, still had unrecon- structed, reactionary, pre-war mindsets, hardly touched by the democratic values of the Weimar Constitution. They could no longer exclude all social democrats from university teaching, as they had before the war, but these bureaucrats tried to maintain a vestige of the old political standards by draw- ing the line at Communists.[23]

Grossman's efforts to gain permission to apply for an *Habilitation* provided the police with an opportunity to shake the red rattle. They intervened in the process, objecting that Grossman was—on the basis of his association with Grünberg!—a dangerous left radical. They did not mention his activities in Poland. Friction over borders and the treatment of the German minority in Poland, apparently, subverted the common purpose of the Polish and German defenders of the capitalist order when it came to persecuting the left. Then again, laziness and incompetence must also have been a factor, as Grossman's association with the People's University and imprisonment were common knowledge in Warsaw.[24] Because the police had been sniffing around the institute for some time, Grünberg anticipated their objections and gave assurances that Grossman "would refrain from all political activity in Germany and engage exclusively in scientific work."[25] Nor was the Faculty impressed by police attempts to interfere in university affairs. It resolved that

> The Faculty is not required to take political considerations into account or to give them significance in assessing questions related to *Habilitations*. It is, rather, solely to assess
> 1. The scholarly capacity of the applicant
> 2. His personal merit to be a member of the teaching body of a university.[26]

When Prussian officials still refused to budge, the Faculty again voiced its support for Grossman. Carl Grünberg and the university went over the heads of the local authorities by providing the Prussian minister for science, culture, and education with the names of a series of people who could provide an expert opinion on this troublesome fellow.[27] Grossman was, in fact, quite open about his political views, but was, he claimed, not engaged in politics in Germany.

The liberal political climate in Frankfurt and its university, the fact that, while anticommunist, the social democratic government of Prussia was not hostile to Marxism per se, and Grossman's own restraint eventually defeated the reactionary reflexes of Prussian officialdom. In the meantime, Grünberg raised his protégé's profile in German academic circles in a different way, arranging for his old associate Stefan Bauer to review Grossman's book on Sismondi for the *Archiv für die Geschichte des Sozialismus und der Arbeiterbewegung*. The review was overwhelmingly negative. But it was publicity and some of the criticisms were contradicted by Bauer's own evidence.[28]

By early 1927, the way to Grossman's *Habilitation* was open. In January, Professors Franz Oppenheimer and Grünberg provided expert reports on his work. In assessing Grossman's monograph on Sismondi, Oppenheimer, a social Zionist and a German patriot, made their political differences clear: he could not agree with Sismondi and Grossman that anarchy of production is indissolubly linked with the free trade economy. But his overall assessment was generous. "I do not hesitate," he wrote "to declare this little work outstanding. The author combines an unusual knowledge of the history of ideas with a thorough mastery of the theoretical foundations of the discipline and the gift for clear organization and presentation."[29]

Grünberg provided a supportive overview of Grossman's academic career and explained his move to Frankfurt am Main in very diplomatic terms: "As circumstances in Warsaw were not suitable for economic research, Grossmann decided to give up his activity there when I offered him a position as my assistant at the Institute for Social Research and—naturally assuming the agreement of the Faculty—raised the prospect of our Faculty granting him his *Habilitation* degree."[30] Demonstrating his own disinterestedness and professional competence, Grünberg expressed a reservation about the Sismondi study, reaffirming the orthodox assessment that Sismondi was *not* a socialist.

The *Habilitation* was finally awarded on March 28, 1927, for *Österreichs Handelspolitik* and a trial lecture on "Sismondi and classical political economy." From now on Grossman was a member of both the institute and the university. His inaugural lecture as a *Privatdozent,* exactly two months later, was on "Oresmius and Copernicus as monetary theorists (a contribution to the price revolution of the 14th and 16th Centuries)." Grossman had been interested in this subject since the early 1920s, at the latest. As the topic of his first university lecture in Germany, it was no doubt selected to demonstrate erudition to the university community and public authorities, without raising any questions about his political views. For the purposes of the university, another element of modest cultural camouflage, his identity was Germanized to "Heinrich Grossmann" and sometimes, even more teutonically, "Heinrich Großmann."[31]

Only in 1928, after his position in Germany had become more secure, did Grossman resign from his chair in Warsaw.[32] His mother's death, on May 14, 1928, at the age of seventy-five, severed another tie binding him to Poland.[33]

Whatever they thought of his politics, his Faculty colleagues had no cause to regret their initial support for Grossman. In mid-1929, the dean recommended his appointment to an ongoing post (*ausserordentlicher Professor*). He was also a member of the university's Academic Council from 1929 to 1933.[34]

Clearing the Ground

During World War I Grossman had discovered an aptitude for the application of conjectural methods to problems where there was "a lack of adequate materials."[35] His work on Marxist economic theory also made use of this skill. It considered likely outcomes on the basis of models where, because statistical collections were never entirely satisfactory and, in any case, not conducted on the basis of the labor theory of value, the supply of accurate data was limited.

Between the appearance of his study of the Duchy of Warsaw in 1925 and 1928 Grossman did not publish anything, nor did he start teaching at the University of Frankfurt until late 1927. He spent most of his time until November 1926 writing a large manuscript on Marxist economics, "The laws of development of 'pure' and empirical capitalism." He had begun the study in 1922 or 1923. But it encompassed work for his 1919 lecture on economic crises and even, perhaps, research on economic theory before the war. During the period to 1933, six interconnected publications on Marxist economics—a book, and five major articles—drew or built on this manuscript.[36]

Some of Grossman's teaching covered the same ground. Courses on "Conjuncture research and the problem of crises" and "Exercises in the history of value theories," in winter semester 1927–28, addressed issues at the center of his research for many years to come: capitalism's crisis tendencies and the originality of Marx's contribution to economics. The least overtly political subject Grossman taught was on "the theoretical bases of tariff and trade policy." It was probably recycled from the WWP. Thankfully, he no longer had to conduct introductory courses in descriptive economics, as he had in Warsaw.[37] His academic duties at the University of Frankfurt were specialized teaching and the supervision of doctoral students, several of whom had institute scholarships.[38] As a teacher he cut quite a figure. According to a former associate of the institute, he "would come to deliver lectures in Frankfurt with white gloves and a cane,"[39] his meticulous sense of dress complementing his self-confidence and concept of correct behavior.

The first published product of Grossman's major project on Marxist economics was a sustained critique of Fritz Sternberg's *Imperialism*, a large study of contemporary capitalism, which the institute had supported financially and was published by Malik in 1926.[40] Sternberg made a living as a publicist in the extensive socialist space between the SPD and KPD and, in response to the deficiencies he claimed to have found in Marx's work, formulated his own theories of the accumulation of capital, economic crises, the reserve army of labor, wages, the labor movement, and revolution.[41]

Imperialism had attracted considerable attention on the left, and its subject matter intersected with Grossman's work on economic crises (the longest chapter in Sternberg's book) and Marx's method. So Grossman took a break from the tasks directly associated with his own book to clear the way for it, by taking *Imperialism* apart in a long article in Grünberg's *Archiv*.

Grossman maintained that there was no connection between the economic analysis in *Imperialism* and its political stance. Sternberg did not see beyond the horizon of the early theorist of revisionism, Eduard Bernstein, accepting his critique of Marx's economics. Bernstein had argued that the severity of economic crises had diminished for generations; that the distribution of property had been decentralized rather than centralized; that class contradictions had declined, as workers' conditions improved; and particularly that the size of the capitalist and middle classes had increased absolutely and in proportion to the whole population. Sternberg agreed with all of this. But, because he justified socialism "as a categorical ethical postulate, the sole means to save humanity from falling into ahistoricity," rather than as a "necessary result of an historical process dominated by class struggle," he could still hold to a revolutionary standpoint in politics.[42]

Sternberg had no conception of Marx's method in *Capital* or his political outlook. Grossman's manuscript on "The laws of development of 'pure' and empirical capitalism," his monograph on Sismondi, and even the 1919 essay on economic crisis had already explained this method. *Capital* was far from being only a study of pure capitalism, whose conclusions did not apply to capitalism as it really existed. Marx, Grossman explained, progressively lifted the simplifying assumptions he made early in this work in order to grasp fundamental processes, as he introduced complicating factors, step by step, and the analysis came closer and closer to empirical capitalism.[43] This was something that Lenin had grasped in 1914–16, in the course of his studies of Hegel, influencing his recovery of Marxist politics.[44]

Sternberg's argument was not simply academic. Working-class consciousness, he maintained, had to be created by a socialist party and intellectuals, regardless of economic and political circumstances. He saw himself as rounding out Luxemburg's work. This was "a wicked misuse of the great fighter's name," Grossman wrote; she, like Marx, had argued that socialism was the product of capitalist development.[45] Behind this savage critique of Sternberg's position was irritation at a perversion of Marxism and Grossman's awareness, based on his own experience in building a socialist organization, that class consciousness and revolution can only grow out of the experience of struggle.

Both the German and Polish Communist parties had, at times, engaged in voluntarist policies that assumed revolution could be achieved through determined deeds, regardless of the circumstances. The German March Action of 1921 was one of the most serious of these adventures. The united front analysis of the Comintern subsequently had a salutary effect on the communist movement for a few years. But, in the course of the factional conflict in the Russian party that characterized the degeneration of the Russian revolution, the International's line lurched leftward again in 1924–25. Communist parties in several countries, including Poland and Germany, engaged in voluntarist rhetoric and activity. The results were declines in their memberships, influence, and credibility.

Against Sternberg's conception of revolution, Grossman quoted "a specialist in revolutionary matters and at the same time a Marxist."

> Marxists, said Lenin in 1915, know perfectly well that a revolution cannot be "made," that revolutions develop from crises and turns in history, which have matured objectively (independently of the will of parties and classes) . . . Marxism appraises interests on the basis of the class antagonisms and the class struggle which find expression in millions of facts of daily life . . . To the Marxist it is indisputable that a revolution is impossible without a revolutionary situation . . . For a revolution to break out, it is usually insufficient for the "lower classes not to want" [to live in the old way]; it is also necessary that the upper classes should be unable [to live in the old way], that is, that it becomes *objectively impossible* for the ruling classes to maintain their domination in an unchanged form. Secondly, that "the suffering and want of the oppressed classes have grown more acute than usual." Without these *objective changes,* which are independent of the will, not only of individual groups and parties, but even of individual classes, a revolution, as a general rule, is impossible. The totality of these objective changes is called a revolutionary situation. Only then is a further subjective condition of significance. This is not simply "revolutionary consciousness" (that cannot be created, moreover, simply by hammering the final goal into people's heads, in the absence of a revolutionary situation). It is, on the contrary, something quite different, "*the capacity of the revolutionary class for mass revolutionary action,*" which presupposes an *organization* of the unified will of the masses and *long experience* in everyday *class struggles.*[46]

Like Lukács, in his 1924 essay on the leader of the Russian revolution, Grossman endorsed Lenin's account of the circumstances under which a socialist revolution can be successful.[47] The JSDP and KPRP veteran counterposed Lenin's position to Sternberg's voluntarist argument and mistaken view that Marx believed revolution would be the automatic consequence of entirely economic forces.[48]

In fact, Marx's conception of the revolutionary process was a dialectical one, which Lenin, Lukács, and Grossman recovered and developed in complementary ways. Capitalism created the working class, forced it to defend its interests, and generated the circumstances under which it struggled against the capitalist class. In the course of its struggle, the proletariat could become aware that the destruction of capitalism was necessary for its self-liberation. A revolutionary party was essential to sustain and generalize working-class consciousness, gained through class struggle, and, under the right conditions, to coordinate revolution. As we have seen, Lukács used Hegelian language to express their common position: the working class was both the object and the subject of history.

Having dealt with Sternberg's politics, Grossman turned to his more strictly economic analysis, which misunderstood both the content of Marx's arguments and real economic processes.

According to Sternberg, the existence of surplus population (a reserve army of unemployed workers) is a precondition for the production of surplus value, and imperialism facilitates improved conditions for workers. Marx, however, had identified the fact that workers do not own means of production and so have to work for the capitalist class as the basic condition for the production of surplus value. He had also observed that, in the longer term, the absolute level of wages tends to rise, while they decline as a proportion of total output.[49] Sternberg's explanation of the determination of wages under capitalism did not allow for increases in the productivity of labor and hence increased exploitation alongside increases in real wages. Marx had dealt extensively with the factors that influenced the level of wages. So, to Sternberg's account, Grossman counterposed a basic lesson in Marxist economics.[50]

The lesson included the issues of imperialism and foreign trade. Sternberg (following Luxemburg) regarded non-capitalist markets as essential for the realization of surplus value. Without them, he thought, some commodities would remain unsold, as a purely capitalist economic system cannot provide a market for the whole of its own output. Marx had, however, in fact introduced foreign trade into his analysis, after showing how realization is *not* a problem for a closed capitalist system. The fundamental cause of economic crises, Grossman argued following Marx, is that capital accumulation itself undermines the valorization of capital (the creation of new value). Foreign trade is only one of a series of factors that can, for a time, blunt this contradiction.[51]

In addition to his critique of Sternberg, Grossman published two reviews in the *Archiv* in 1928. One was a very short and cursory account of a French book on the relationship between socialist theory and economic development.[52] The other dealt with the treatment of socialist economics in a book by his former colleague at the Austrian Scientific Committee for the War Economy, Othmar Spann, now a well-known advocate of corporatist nationalism.

Grossman's reason for reviewing Spann's book was its "wide distribution," which, however, could "only be explained by its function as a painless, because short and shallow, exam primer for thousands of students." Spann's discussion of socialism confused different schools and demonstrated a lack of clarity about what socialism was, let alone the specifics of Marx's position. Changes since the third edition of the book were, by and large, detrimental, notably the eradication of a mention of Grünberg's argument that socialism in the modern sense only emerged after the French revolution.

There were numerous factual and theoretical errors in Spann's account of the ideas of Saint Simon, Fourier, and Sismondi and especially Marx. To the claim, derived from Böhm-Bawerk, that the third volume of Marx's *Capital* contradicted the first, Grossman responded that they were written at the same time and, as he had explained before, that the first volume employed strong simplifying assumptions while the third dealt with concrete reality. In summary, it was "no normal artistic achievement [for Spann] to heap up so many mistakes, only the most serious of which can be emphasized here, in scarcely twenty pages."[53] Grossman's review complemented another by György Lukács in the same issue of the *Archiv*. Lukács dismantled Spann's attempt to provide a "sophisticated apology for fascism."[54]

The Law of Accumulation and Collapse of the Capitalist System

In 1929, *The Law of Accumulation and Collapse of the Capitalist System (also a Theory of Crises)* was issued as the first volume in the institute's monograph series. The book became and remains Grossman's best known work and attracted vastly more public attention during the 1920s and 1930s than any other publication by a member of the IfS.[55]

Grossman still maintained, as he had a decade before, that a theory of economic crisis and collapse was not just some added optional extra in the socialist critique of capitalism. Bernstein had correctly regarded the argument that capitalism was inherently prone to crisis and collapse as central to the logic of Marxism: "If the triumph of socialism were truly an immanent economic necessity, then it would have to be grounded in a proof of the inevitable economic breakdown of the present order of society." Denial that such a proof was possible constituted an important part of Bernstein's case against classical Marxism.[56]

If capitalism can go on forever, increasing the production of wealth all the time, then economic problems, at least, could either be overcome through working-class action to reallocate wealth or ameliorated into unpleasant but bearable irritants. In these circumstances, Grossman noted, the working class could just as easily reconcile itself with capitalism as voluntaristically attempt to realize socialism.[57]

Although his preface made it clear that he intended to focus on economic questions, Grossman did not regard politics as unimportant or as an automatic reflex of economics. On the contrary, he took precautions against such an interpretation of his work. "Because I deliberately confine myself to describing only the economic presuppositions of the breakdown of capitalism in this study, let me dispel any suspicion of 'pure economism' from the start. It is unnecessary to waste paper over the connection between economics and politics; that there is a connection is obvious. However, while Marxists have written extensively on the political revolution, they have neglected to deal theoretically with the economic aspect of the question and have failed to appreciate the true content of Marx's theory of breakdown. My sole concern is to fill this gap in the Marxist tradition."[58]

Lenin was clearly the preeminent figure among Marxists who "have written extensively on the political revolution." Grossman had embraced Lenin's renovation of Marx's politics and Lukács's recovery of Marxist philosophy. He argued that Marxist theory was now in greatest need of repair in the area of economics. As in his first publication on the proletariat and the Jewish question and his major study of Austrian trade policy, the deficiencies of previous understandings of the issues required a somewhat one-sided attention to specific topics and arguments, the approach Lenin called "bending the stick."[59] In this sense, Grossman's book, by emphasizing the importance of economic circumstances for a successful revolution, was a critique of leftist voluntarism and hence, tacitly, of the current Comintern line (see pages 145–46, below).[60]

Yet the fundamental argument of *The Law of Accumulation* was also directed against social democratic "neo-harmonists" such as Karl Kautsky, Rudolf Hilferding, and Otto Bauer, who believed that state action could eliminate economic crises, which they understood as the consequence of disproportions between different industries and departments of production. In their pre-war economic studies, they had refuted Bernstein by asserting there was no theory of collapse in Marx's account of capitalism.

During the 1920s, Hilferding and Bauer were leaders of the largest parties of the German-speaking working class. They formulated and justified the reformist policies of these organizations. Hilferding was an SPD member of the German parliament from 1924 until 1933 and German finance minister in 1923 and 1928–29. Bauer was the most important figure in Austrian social democracy after the war and Austrian foreign minister in 1918–19. Despite formal adherence to Marxist orthodoxies, therefore, they stood on the same ground as Bernstein and drew the same practical conclusions as the top officials and ideologists of labor and social democratic parties into the twenty-first century.[61]

Luxemburg had identified the logic of Bernstein's position and the centrality of a theory of economic breakdown to Marxism, in both her critique of reformism, *Social Reform and Revolution,* and her major economic work, *The Accumulation of capital.*[62] Grossman's book was designed, in the same spirit, to offer a coherent Marxist account of capitalism's vulnerability to crisis and collapse as a basis for revolutionary politics. Why then did he engage in extensive polemics against Luxemburg's economic analysis? The reason is given early in *The Law of Accumulation*:

> It was a great historical contribution of Rosa Luxemburg that she, in a conscious opposition to the distortions of the "neo-harmonists" adhered to the basic lesson of *Capital* and sought to reinforce it with the proof that the continued development of capitalism encounters absolute limits.
>
> Frankly Luxemburg's efforts failed . . .
>
> . . . Her own deduction of the necessary downfall of capitalism is not rooted in the immanent laws of the accumulation process, but in the transcendental fact of an absence of non-capitalist markets. Luxemburg shifts the crucial problem of capitalism from the sphere of production to that of circulation. Hence the form in which she conducts her proof of the absolute economic limits to capitalism comes close to the idea that the end of capitalism is a distant prospect because the capitalization of the non-capitalist countries is the task of centuries.[63]

Both Lukács and Grossman regarded her emphasis on capitalist collapse as correct. Lukács accepted Luxemburg's treatment of "the problem of accumulation" and rejected Bauer's critique of her position on purely political grounds.[64] Grossman, on the other hand, disproved her mistaken economic *arguments*, the most influential and systematic account of capitalist breakdown to date, in order to replace them with a more solid foundation for her *conclusions*.

In 1919, Grossman had explained the difficulty of simultaneously maintaining proportional output of use and exchange values as a source of economic crisis, even in a very abstract model of simple reproduction, where the scale of investment does not expand. He still adhered to this position. But *The Law of Accumulation* spelled out a new economic case for Luxemburg's political conclusions, within the framework of Grossman's thoroughly Leninist conception of working-class revolution.[65]

The book's key thesis is therefore only intelligible in the context of Grossman's commitment to a conception of Marxism shaped by his own experiences in the labor movement, the Russian revolution, and Lenin's political theory. At the same time, Grossman sometimes tailored the detailed *form* of his arguments in the light of more immediate political considerations. He was a close sympathizer of the Comintern and also recognized that the main audience for his ideas was among Communists. So, in an effort to ensure that his renovation of Marxist political economy would be understood without distortion, he took a number of precautions. These anticipated the reflex responses to his analysis by dogmatic adherents of the current party line.

In orthodox communist campaigns against Luxemburgism, her theory of economic collapse had been used to characterize Luxemburg as a proponent of the automatic collapse of the capitalist system, without the need for organized class struggles. Grossman endorsed this official view and carefully distinguished his own account of capitalism's tendency to break down from Luxemburg's.[66] In this respect, Grossman misleadingly counterposed Luxemburg to Lenin. But his approach to the two revolutionaries did not reproduce criticism of one (that, depending on the current line from Moscow, was sometimes qualified) and the total and unequivocal endorsement of the other that was typical of the communist movement by the end of the 1920s. On some questions, Grossman approved and invoked Luxemburg's judgment. On others he highlighted shortcomings in Lenin's thought.

The case Grossman made against Luxemburg's theory of breakdown, including the fact that it contradicted her own commitment to the class struggle, reproduced, unacknowledged, decisive points of Nikolai Bukharin's critique. By the time *The Law of Accumulation* was finished, however, Stalin was in the process of consolidating his control over the Russian state, and had turned on Bukharin and the right inside the Communist Party of the Soviet Union. Grossman's article against Sternberg had included favorable references to Bukharin. Now such comments would provoke condemnation by communist leaders and close off the possibility of dialogue on economic questions with members of the largest revolutionary current in the world. As a consequence, all explicit references to Bukharin in Grossman's book were critical.

THE LOGIC OF CAPITAL ACCUMULATION

The Law of Accumulation developed and was structured by the account of Marx's method that Grossman had outlined in earlier publications.[67] After surveying previous Marxist discussions of the question of capitalist collapse, the book moved from abstract to progressively more concrete levels of analysis. The second chapter examined the law of collapse when a number of simplifying assumptions were made. The third dealt with countertendencies to the law, as these simplifying assumptions were lifted. The conclusion considered the connections among capitalism's crisis tendency, the class struggle, and the concentration of capital. Throughout the book, Grossman offered critiques of the literature concerning Marx's position on various issues.

In his 1919 lecture and the study of Sismondi's economic theory, Grossman had maintained that the contradiction between use value and exchange value was vital to Marx's theory of crisis, a point neglected by earlier Marxists (on the labor theory of value, see pages 49, 94–95, 105–106, above).[68] An understanding of capitalist production as the contradictory unity of a labor process and a valorization process also lay at the heart of the different, but complementary argument that was the core of *The Law of Accumulation*. This argument focused on problems with valorization, rather than with maintaining proportional output.[69]

Commodities, as use values, satisfy human needs. The process of capitalist development involves the potentially unrestricted growth of the production of use values, given the capacity of human needs to expand and change. Production, however, is not undertaken to satisfy human needs, but to produce profits, that is, additional exchange value for capitalists. "From a purely technological aspect, as a labor process for the production of use values, nothing could impede the expansion of the forces of production. This expansion encounters a barrier in the shape of the valorization process, the fact that the elements of production figure as capital which must be valorized. If profit disappears the labor process is interrupted."[70]

Grossman demonstrated how this happens by using a reproduction scheme based on one elaborated by Bauer,[71] who in turn drew on Marx's model in the second volume of *Capital*. This model involves assumptions about the combination of constant capital (machinery, equipment, and raw materials) and variable capital (paid as wages) and generates a specific pattern of growth. In the first stage of his analysis of the tendency to capitalist collapse, Grossman employed the model because it abstracted from less fundamental aspects of the system such as momentary fluctuations in prices, deviations of prices from values, unevenness in the development of productivity, and the influence of foreign trade. These considerations could be reintroduced at later stages, as in Marx's analysis, once the basic features of capitalism had been exposed.

The choice of Bauer's model was, in part, a political one, designed to discredit Bauer's conclusions on the basis of his own assumptions. Bauer had realistically assumed a higher rate of accumulation of constant than variable capital. Capitalists try to reduce the value of the commodities they produce so that they can undercut their rivals. Increasing the productivity of their workers by introducing new and more expensive machinery and technology is generally an effective way of doing this. As total output grows, constant capital will tend to expand more rapidly than variable capital. So there will be a rise in the relative weight of constant capital in capitalists' total outlays, known as the organic composition of capital. It is the variable capital alone, however, that produces new value. As profits are measured against total outlays, a decline in the weight of value-creating variable capital will mean a fall in the rate of profit, if the rate of surplus value (the ratio of new value to the value of the labor power that created it) is held constant. To the extent that capitalism increases the productivity of human labor and accelerates the production of use values, it is therefore also characterized by a tendency for the rate of profit to fall. For Grossman, this tendency was the key to capitalist breakdown.

The rate of profit declined in Bauer's model. But he and his fellow neo-harmonists thought that the rate of profit could tend downward, indefinitely getting closer and closer to zero without ever disappearing entirely. Grossman demonstrated why this is not the case and his explanation remains important.

Bauer had let his model run for four years and argued that it demonstrated that capitalism could go on forever without crises, so long as the output of exchange values from different industries (simplified in the model to two departments of production, producing means of production and means of consumption) was kept in the correct ratios. Grossman simplified the model even further, eliminating distinct departments of production, and let it run for thirty-six years. He found that it encountered difficulties after year 34 and collapsed entirely in year 36.[72]

Beyond a certain point in the accumulation process, although the mass (total amount) of profit continues to rise, it is insufficient to sustain production. In the Bauer-Grossman model, the incentive for capitalist investment already begins to decline after twenty years, when the absolute amount of surplus value available for the private consumption of the capitalists has to fall, if the rate of accumulation of constant and variable capital is to be maintained. Confronted with such a situation, sane real-world capitalists start seeking other, more profitable outlets for investment, outside production, notably in speculative activity, and the export of loan capital.[73] In year 35 of the scheme, no surplus value is available for capitalists' private consumption and there is not even enough surplus value to cover investment in additional constant and variable capital, as specified in the rules of the model.

> So either working class wages have to be reduced or previous assumptions [of the model] must be broken. In particular the assumption that, with a 5% annual increase in population constant capital must accumulate at 10% a year if technological progress is to match population growth, has to be lifted . . . The tempo of accumulation must decline *from now on* and indeed slow down continuously and progressively. Accumulation cannot keep up with population growth. Fewer and fewer machines etc than are really required can be put in place, which means nothing else than that the development of the productive forces is constrained. As a consequence, from this year on an increasingly large reserve army [of unemployed workers] emerges. The slowing of the tempo of accumulation and the emergence of a reserve army occur, not as Bauer thinks, because wages have risen, but despite the fact that, in accord with our assumption, wages have been constant for the whole time![74]

Not only does the rate of profit in the Bauer-Grossman model fall, Grossman stressed, but the rate of growth of the mass of profit (which remains constant at 5 percent per annum, reflecting the rate of growth of variable capital) also falls behind the rate of growth of the total value of production, (which asymptotically approaches 10 percent per annum). So a point is eventually reached when the increase in the mass of profit is not large enough to cover the projected increase in investment, which is growing at a higher rate. The rate of profit cannot, therefore, fall indefinitely. Whatever the rate of accumulation assumed in the model, the rate of profit eventually declines to a level at which the mass of surplus value is not great enough to sustain that rate of accumulation.[75] It was this mechanism, which he saw as intrinsic to the process of capital accumulation, that Grossman regarded as "the decisively important" factor in Marx's theory of economic crisis and breakdown.[76] What is more, "the limits to accumulation are specifically capitalist limits and not limits in general. Social needs remain massively unsatisfied. Yet from the standpoint of capital there is superfluous capital because it cannot be valorized."[77]

Grossman developed a formula for calculating the point at which the model of accumulation breaks down, in order to highlight the factors that slow down or accelerate the collapse. The crisis is accelerated by a higher organic composition of capital and a faster rate of accumulation of constant capital. The effects of a rise in the rate of accumulation of variable capital are ambiguous, while a higher rate of surplus value slows down the tendency of capitalism to break down.[78]

The onset of a crisis, as a consequence of capitalism's tendency to break down, still does not mean that capitalism is doomed.

> Obviously, as Lenin correctly remarks, there are no absolutely hopeless situations. In the description I have proposed the breakdown does not necessarily have to work itself out directly. Its absolute realization may be interrupted by counteracting tendencies. In that case the absolute breakdown would be converted into a temporary crisis, after which the accumulation process picks up again on a new basis. In other words the valorization of the overaccumulated capital can be met through capital exports to countries at a lower stage of accumulation. Or a sharp devaluation of the constant capital during the crisis might improve the prospects for valorization. Or wage cuts could have the same effects in terms of warding off the catastrophe. But quite apart from the fact that all these situations violate the assumptions postulated in Bauer's scheme, these solutions would have a purely temporary impact. Restored accumulation will again generate the very same phenomena of overaccumulation and imperfect valorization.[79]

Before, in, and after *The Law of Accumulation*, the purpose of Grossman's argument was to establish the necessity for revolutionary practice and the context in which it could be successful: the relationship between objective and subjective factors in the revolution. Lenin's (and Grossman's) point about the mistake of identifying even deep crises as insoluble was that "the revolutionary parties must now 'prove' in practice that they have sufficient understanding and organization, contact with the exploited masses, and determination and skill to utilize this crisis for a successful and victorious revolution."[80]

By following Marx in progressively dropping the simplifying assumptions of his initial model, Grossman brought his analysis closer to concrete reality. With the introduction of offsetting mechanisms, capitalism's tendency to break down will take the form of recurring crises, rather than an uninterrupted collapse.[81] A crisis is, moreover, "from the standpoint of capitalist production, a healing process through which the valorization of capital is restored."[82] As part of the process of approaching the real world step by step, Grossman also brought the credit system into the discussion. This enabled him to identify the characteristic lower interest rates in the early stages of a recovery and, subsequently, rising levels of interest, as the pace of accumulation increased.[83]

Before extending his analysis to a more concrete level, however, Grossman noted that, according to Marx, crises would occur even under circumstances of simple reproduction (that is, when profits are not reinvested). While the process of capital accumulation was the decisive element in Marx's theory of crisis, the renewal of fixed capital, in particular, has a great influence on the periodicity of crises.[84] This was an issue Grossman had addressed in Warsaw, in "The Developmental Tendencies of Contemporary Capitalism."[85] Furthermore, he still insisted, as in 1919, "that proportional accumulation is a purely ideal case; a fiction that could actually prevail only accidentally. As a rule the actual process of accumulation is quite unequal in the various branches."[86]

COUNTERTENDENCIES

The third chapter in *The Law of Accumulation* examined modifying countertendencies to the tendency for the rate of profit to fall. Marx discussed these in *Capital* as he successively adjusted his initial, very abstract model, by incorporating more real-world elements, including the conscious and unconscious measures taken by capitalists and states to sustain or raise profit rates. "The capitalist's continual efforts to restore profitability might take the form of reorganizing the mechanism of capital internally (for instance, by cutting costs of production, or effecting economies in the use of energy, raw materials and labor power) or of recasting trade relations on the world market (international cartels, cheaper sources of raw material supply and so on). This involves groping attempts at a complete rationalization of all spheres of economic life."[87]

The process of capital accumulation itself lowers the value of both variable and constant capital. A consequence of the introduction of new technology and superior means of production is that commodities can be produced with the expenditure of less labor. This applies to both means of production and means of consumption (and hence labor power). If means of production are produced at a lower cost, the organic composition of capital will decline and the rate of profit will rise. To illustrate this point, Grossman presented and extended material about the German shipping industry from his 1919 presentation on crises.[88] Nevertheless, "the factors which bring about the tendency for the rate of profit to fall do indeed win the upper hand 'in the long run,' because in the end there really is an increase in the productive forces of all branches of industry."[89]

Cheapening the cost of variable capital increases the rate of surplus value, by reducing the proportion of the working day workers have to spend reproducing their labor power. The depression of wages below the value of labor power has a similar effect. Both raise the rate of surplus value, increasing the rate of profit and postponing the onset of crises. What is more, the tendency for the rate of profit to fall is accompanied by a tendency for the rate of surplus value to increase.[90] Desirable as the defense of working-class living standards is for its own sake, Grossman noted that "once this connection is clear we have a means of gauging the complete superficiality of those theoreticians in the trade unions who argue for wage increases as a means of surmounting the crisis by expanding the internal market."[91]

He identified a series of other factors that affect the rate of profit. Increasing the turnover time of capital means that it can give rise to more surplus value, by freeing a portion of money capital for productive investment. For example, more efficient transport or communication means that less money capital is tied up in raw materials, unfinished products, and completed commodities lying fallow in stockpiles or warehouses before they are sold.[92] New commodities may emerge whose organic composition of capital is lower than the average, giving rise to a higher average rate of profit.[93] The extension of capitalist production on the basis of existing technology—simple accumulation—will slow the tendency for the rate of profit to fall.[94] As the ability of productive capitalists to dominate the whole of the circuit of capital grows, they are in a better position to reduce deductions from surplus value, in the form of the claims of landowners (ground rent), commercial capitalists (commercial profit), and banks (interest).[95] Decreasing the income of intermediate social strata—bureaucrats and professionals, who are not involved in production—has like consequences.[96] The rationalization of public service bureaucracies and of legal, auditing, and other professional services are examples of this process. Moreover, "from the Marxist theory of accumulation," according to Grossman, "it follows that war and the destruction of capital values bound up with it weaken the breakdown and necessarily provide a new impetus to the accumulation of capital."[97]

Changes in the level of population, through the availability of labor power, influence capitalism's breakdown tendency. Capital accumulation increases the need for workers to valorize capital. Eventually the impossibility of this valorization, because population growth is too slow, gives rise to crisis and unemployment: "Unemployment was a consequence of insufficient population!"[98] The need for labor power pushes capitalists to attempt to extend the length of the working day, to seek supplementary sources of surplus value and labor on the world market.[99] The mercantilist preoccupation with population (examined in Grossman's own work on the origins of official statistics) and early colonial policy were not about finding *markets*. They were concerned with capitalist *production* and hence the need for labor. As much of the labor used in colonial capitalist production was extracted from slaves, Grossman developed, for the first time, Marx's comments on the importance of the slave trade for the emergence of capitalism in an account of the trade's origins and significance from the fifteenth century.[100] In doing this he drew on his earlier research on the economics of slavery.[101]

For Grossman, as for Luxemburg, "the growing tendency to break down and the strengthening of imperialism are merely two sides of the same empirical complex." He expanded the argument, previewed in his critique of Sternberg, that imperialism was a means of "*securing the flow of additional surplus value from outside*" a country. This counteracts the increasing difficulty capitalism has in overcoming crises of over-accumulation as the scope of capital accumulation grows stronger.[102] Just as the diversification of domestic economies into new areas of production expands the scope for creating surplus value by creating different use values (new kinds of commodities), so foreign trade slows the breakdown tendency by increasing the variety of use values. Foreign trade also raises profit rates by allowing greater economies in the scale of production and distribution.[103]

The formation of a world rate of profit means that trade involves the transfer of surplus value from less to more developed countries. Commodities produced with a lower organic composition of capital sell below their value, while those produced with a higher organic composition sell above theirs. This was a rigorous formulation of a theory of "unequal exchange," a term Grossman used long before the idea became fashionable in the 1970s.[104] "At advanced stages of accumulation, when it becomes more and more difficult to valorize the enormously accumulated capital, such transfers [from underdeveloped to developed countries] become a matter of life and death for capitalism. This explains the virulence of imperialist expansion in the late stage of capital accumulation."[105]

Other aspects of imperialism—the pursuit of cheap raw materials and efforts to achieve monopoly control over them, at the expense of competitors—also help overcome falling profit rates.[106] Grossman identified a phenomenon that still characterizes the aid programs of developed countries whose foreign loans are used to obtain orders for local industry at high prices, to the exclusion of competitors backed by other states.[107] The export of capital, in the form of loans, credits, and speculative investments, is driven by concern over the rate of profit.[108] At best, previous Marxist treatments of the subject, after Marx, had only provided empirical descriptions. Grossman wrote that this was true of Lenin's treatment of capital export, although "he makes many acute observations."[109] Rather than being directly related to the level of monopolization of industry, as Lenin suggested, capital export is a consequence of the lack of opportunities at home for adequate returns on investments of liquid funds, due to low profit rates and the inability of productive investments to increase the mass of surplus value, that is, of capitalism's tendency to break down.[110] Corporate gambling on the stock exchange has a similar logic.[111]

The current advanced stage of accumulation and obstacles to profitable new investment, Grossman argued, mean that, while capital export previously characterized the slump stage of the economic cycle, today it is an ongoing phenomenon. In this sense, Lenin's characterization of imperialism in terms of capital export was quite correct.[112] Grossman wrote in 1929, but his conclusions about imperialism still apply: "It is also, therefore, clear that the struggle for spheres for investment is also the greatest danger to world peace. That this does not involve prediction of the future should be clear to anyone who studies the methods of 'Dollar Diplomacy' with the appropriate attention."[113]

BREAKDOWN AND REVOLUTION

The final chapter of *The Law of Accumulation* (entirely missing from the English translation!) was designed to complete the transition from studying capitalism's breakdown tendency at a highly abstract, simplified level of analysis to a much more concrete account of its operation in the real world of contending classes. It returned to the book's fundamental concern, announced in its preface, with the economic aspect of political revolution: the implications of the breakdown tendency for the working-class ability to seize political power.

At the heart of the relationship between accumulation and class struggle is the question of workers' conditions of life. In his version of Bauer's model, Grossman demonstrated how real wages rise for a period but then run into an obstacle. "*Here is the objective limit of trade union action.* Beyond a certain point in accumulation, the surplus value available does not suffice to maintain accumulation at a given level of wages. Either wages must be depressed *below* their previous level—or accumulation must come to a halt, the breakdown of the capitalist mechanism. The development thus presses on, unfolding and sharpening the inner contradictions between capital and labor, until a resolution can only be achieved through *struggle.*"[114]

In this way Grossman integrated his previous analysis of capitalism's objective economic tendencies with the issue of class power and politics. For, under these circumstances, capital's success in the struggle means that wages are pushed down below the value of labor power and labor power cannot be fully renewed. "If the largest and most important force of production, human labor power, is thus excluded from the fruits of civilized progress, it is at the same time demonstrated that we are approaching ever closer to the situation which Marx and Engels already foresaw in the *Communist manifesto:* 'the bourgeoisie is unfit to rule because it is incompetent to assure an existence to its slaves within their slavery.' This is also the reason why wage slaves must necessarily rise against the system of wage slavery."[115]

Hilferding and other reformist economists argued that the theory of breakdown should be rejected because it led to the conclusion that the working class should fatalistically await the mechanical demise of capitalism. The relationship between capitalism's breakdown tendency and the class struggle is, according to Grossman, a more complicated and dialectical one. Class struggles over the level of exploitation shape the actual course of the system's tendency to break down. Which side, bosses or workers, wins in confrontations over wages and conditions has important implications for capitalism's ability to survive. If workers are successful in such conflicts,

> a decline in the rate of surplus value and consequently an *accelerated* breakdown of the capitalist system will occur . . . It is thus apparent that the idea of breakdown, necessary on objective grounds, definitely does not contradict the class struggle. Rather, the breakdown, despite its objectively given necessity, can be influenced by the living forces of the struggling classes to a large extent and leaves a certain scope for active class intervention.
>
> . . . Only now is it possible to understand why, at a high level of capital accumulation, every serious rise in wages encounters greater and greater difficulties, why every major *economic* struggle necessarily becomes a question of the existence of capitalism, a *question of political power.* (Note the English miners' struggle, 1926.)
>
> The struggle of the working class over everyday demands is thus bound up with its struggle over the final goal. The final goal for which the working class fights is not an ideal brought into the workers' movement "from outside" by speculative means, whose realization, independent of the struggles of the pres-

ent, is reserved for the distant future. It is, on the contrary, as the law of capitalism's breakdown presented here shows, a result of immediate everyday struggles
and its realization can be accelerated by these struggles.[116]

Grossman's explanation of the relationship between immediate struggles and
revolution recalls his argument against the opportunism of the Polish Social
Democratic Party in *Bundism in Galicia*. There he not only rejected the reformist
separation of the socialist goal from day-to-day struggles, but affirmed the role of
the working class as both a product and a creator of history.[117]

At the end of his 1929 book, Grossman sought to influence the shape of
working-class consciousness which he (and Lenin and Lukács) regarded as so
crucial for the success of the socialist revolution. He did so by demolishing the
economic foundations of the most influential reformist argument in the labor
movement in a line of reasoning based on Marx's critique of commodity
fetishism.

As both an economic theorist and parliamentary leader, Hilferding was a
particularly prominent advocate of a peaceful road to socialism. He maintained that there was a spontaneous evolution toward organized capitalism
with the concentration of capital and establishment of trusts and cartels. Such
a development increased the scope for planning under capitalism, as opposed
to competition, hence for eliminating economic crises due to the anarchy of
production. It was therefore possible for the working class to take state power
by parliamentary means and thus to control the economy, which was being
more and more centrally organized and directed by the capitalists. From this
perspective, the transition to socialism was already underway.[118]

Hilferding, Grossman observed, had a restricted understanding of competition: "The more free competition is replaced by monopoly organization on the
domestic market, the more competition sharpens on the world market. If a
river's flow is artificially blocked with a dam on one side of the stream, it
presses on with even less restraint on the side that is still open. Whether accumulation of capital within the capitalist mechanism occurs on the basis of
competition amongst individual entrepreneurs or a series of cartelized, capitalist production associations struggling against each other is irrelevant for the
emergence of the tendency to break down or crisis."[119] Capitalism is a global
system that makes effective planning in individual countries impossible.

If, as Grossman argued in the previous six hundred pages, capitalism's crisis
tendency does not arise directly from competition and the anarchy of production but rather from the over-accumulation of capital and its effects on the rate
of profit, then organized capitalism cannot resolve the underlying problem.[120]

Grossman ultimately attributed capitalism's breakdown tendency to the
contradiction between capitalist production as a labor process and as a process

driven by the creation of value through the exploitation of wage labor, that is, by the competitive pursuit of profits: "As a consequence of this *fundamentally dual structure,* capitalist production is characterized by insoluble conflicts. Irremediable systemic convulsions *necessarily arise from this dual character,* from the immanent contradiction between value and use value, between profitability and productivity, between limited possibilities for valorization and the unlimited development of the productive forces. This necessarily leads to overaccumulation and insufficient valorization, therefore to breakdown, to a final catastrophe for the entire system."[121]

Capitalist valorization also *conceals* the labor process. Both this fetishism of commodities—the way the surface appearance of commodity production obscures its fundamental mechanisms—and capitalism's tendency to break down therefore have their roots in the double nature of production under capitalism. Liberated from the constraints of profit making, Grossman argued, production could be organized on a social basis and become a technical labor process, without crises and without the mystification that arises from the commodity form: "Where the social interrelations amongst individual production processes are immediately present and planned, there is no room for the law of value, whose most important task consists in the production of these social interrelations. Social equilibrium, *calculated in advance,* no longer has to be restored *subsequently* by means of the mystical veil of value."[122]

Capitalism's crisis-prone logic and its mystification of that logic were core features of Grossman's and Lukács's understanding of Marxism, as both a critique of the established order and a practical theory of socialist revolution. *History and Class Consciousness,* however, focused on "the ideological problems of capitalism and its downfall" and did not "discuss the central importance of this problem for economics itself."[123] *The Law of Accumulation* directly complemented Lukács's analysis, by exploring the economic roots and implications of commodity fetishism and their relationship to capitalist crises and revolution. So Giacomo Marramao was absolutely right to point out that "it is no accident that it is precisely in Lukács's *History and class consciousness* that one finds the philosophical equivalent of Grossmann's great attempt at a critical-revolutionary re-appropriation of Marxian categories."[124] Just as Lukács restored contradictory class interests and perspectives to the center of Marxist philosophy, Grossman restated the way they had been at the center of Marx's economic theory. Both drew on Lenin. Their insights incorporated his re-appropriation of Marx's argument that the capitalist state had to be smashed through conscious working-class action, and the lessons of his work in building a political party that both grew out of and sustained working-class struggles.[125]

An Economic Theory without a Political Home

Grossman's book quickly attracted very widespread attention in the German-speaking world. Reviews appeared in at least five mainstream journals and the liberal daily *Frankfurter Zeitung*. The official theoretical journals of the German-speaking social democratic parties reviewed *The Law of Accumulation*, the German party's organ *Die Gesellschaft* doing so twice. It was also discussed in the long-established journal of the German party's right and a publication of its left. Sternberg devoted a whole book to refuting Grossman's work and vindicating his own *Imperialism*. Not only did the KPD's theoretical organ carry a long review, two substantial assessments appeared in the German-language journal of the Comintern. A little later, anti-Leninist Council Communists debated the significance of Grossman's account of economic crises.[126]

The book soon had some impact on audiences who could not read German. The German-American Council Communist Paul Mattick embraced Grossman's approach in 1931 and expounded it in the United States, in German and then in English.[127] A very favorable French review appeared in 1932. In it, Mohan Tazerout mentioned that a French translation was underway in Brussels. The following year, Jean Duret also offered a French account and superficial critique of Grossman's theory.[128]

Japanese Marxists were the first to benefit from a translation of the book. Although the Japanese labor movement suffered severe repression during the 1920s and 1930s, there was a significant Marxist current that included talented intellectuals. The Marxist scholar Professor Yoshitaro Hirano organized the translation of Grossman's book that was published in 1932.[129] The two had become friends when Hirano, who was close to the Japanese Communist Party, visited Germany in 1928 and 1929.[130]

The Law of Accumulation rapidly became a reference point in Marxist economics. But, a few exceptions aside, it encountered a hostile reception.

A brief description of Grossman's relationships with and comments, in his book, on eight of the people who subsequently reviewed it helps to explain their hostility. Helene Landau had been a supporter of the Polish Social Democratic Party when the Jewish Social Democratic Party of Galicia, under Grossman's leadership, split from it. Later she married Otto Bauer. The efforts of Professor Karl Muhs to refute Marx were given ungentle treatment in *The Law of Accumulation*, with its accessible and very aggressive polemical style.[131] Sternberg's views came in for a further drubbing in the book, on top of the essay razing his *Imperialism*. By comparison, Grossman's criticism of Alfred Braunthal, who worked for the social democratic Research Center for Economic Policy in Berlin, was mild. Emanuel Hugo Vogel was dismissed as a typical bourgeois economist who denied the periodicity of crises and the possibility of determining the length of their phases. Grossman briefly paraded the early work of the grand old man of German social democratic economics, Conrad Schmidt, as an example of the impoverished state of the Marxist theory of wages. Much more space was devoted to attacking the arguments of his colleague Franz Oppenheimer, though Grossman acknowledged him as "a sharp thinker."[132] On the other hand, he did not qualify his identification of Jenö Varga, the Hungarian Communist resident in Moscow, as an "epigone of Marx," whose arguments were self-contradictory.[133]

Broader political considerations, however, underpinned the way Grossman's book was received. It is easy to understand the hostile responses of bourgeois critics: Leonhard Miksch, in the daily organ of the Frankfurt bourgeoisie, Adolf Caspary and Emanuel Vogel, a reactionary like Karl Muhs (who was soon praising the National Socialist revolution),[134] social reformers like Franz Oppenheimer[135] or, for that matter, the social democrats. The contention that capitalism entails periodic and profound periods of economic crisis that generate revolutionary situations was bound to antagonize supporters of the existing order and advocates, even ostensibly Marxist ones, of reforming capitalism into socialism.

Communist attitudes were conditioned by the emergence of a dogma in economic theory, based on Stalin's unchallengeable utterances and paralleling developments in many other areas, as his dictatorial, state capitalist regime in Russia consolidated its power. In 1930 Stalin anointed Varga as the high priest of this dogma, which metamorphosed in line with the political requirements of the regime.

Many of the criticisms made of Grossman's book were based on politically expedient (deliberate or unintended) misrepresentations of his position. One, concocted by social democrats and Communists alike, that he had a mechanical conception of capitalist breakdown and the transition to socialism, became the standard case for dismissing his analysis.

There was an important exception to the hostile communist response to *The Law of Accumulation*. At the end of the 1920s, many Soviet economists were increasingly concerned about the subordination of economic analysis to the immediate political priorities of the Russian state. Spektator (Miron Isaakovich Nakhimson), who explained crises in terms of disproportion between spheres of production, was one of those who had attacked Varga's underconsumptionist explanation of capitalist crises.[136]

A Bundist from 1898 until 1922, Spektator had contributed over a hundred reviews and articles to *Die Neue Zeit*, the premier journal of the international

Marxist movement before World War I. Following the revolution he returned to Russia and, during the mid- and late 1920s, participated in important economic debates there. In addition to research and university teaching responsibilities, Nakhimson headed the Department of Statistics of the International Agrarian Institute in Moscow, which developed links with the Institute for Social Research in Frankfurt.[137] Like Grossman, Nakhimson drew attention to the importance of the turnover of fixed capital in economic crises. In *The Law of Accumulation,* Grossman had endorsed some of Nakhimson's positions and criticized others.[138] Spektator and his intellectual allies in the Soviet Union were happy to read the book. Their comrade in Frankfurt not only rejected Luxemburg's underconsumptionism (which Varga reproduced without acknowledgment)[139] and made sharp criticisms of Varga, but did so in a very prominent publication, from a standpoint that was not only Marxist but obviously sympathetic to communism. In November 1930, Grossman was made a member of the Agrarian Institute, in recognition of the value of his book.[140] He received the award just in time. "After 1931 Soviet writers would disagree with one another within the bounds of discourse established by Stalin and Varga, but rarely would they overstep them."[141] Nakhimson also invited Grossman to visit the Soviet Union, where Sergei Mitrofanovich Dubrovskii, the head of the Agrarian Institute, said: "Dear comrade Grossman, no one here takes Varga seriously."[142] But Soviet economists could not publicly defend views that contradicted Varga's. Even doing so in private was becoming risky.

The Law of Accumulation had anticipated the two main criticisms made of it. One was that the book expounded a theory of automatic breakdown. The other, that there were countervailing mechanisms to the tendency for the rate of profit to fall, Grossman not only recognized but made a cornerstone of the structure of *The Law of Accumulation* and its discussion of Marx's method. While his critics focused on the cheapening of constant and variable capital as mechanisms which offset falls in the rate of profit, Grossman had already identified not only these but numerous other processes that served to sustain or increase the rate of profit.

In articles published during the 1930s and 1940s Grossman tacitly replied to accusations (by Braunthal, the Council Communist Pannekoek, and the Communists "Kraus," Otto Bendikt, and Varga,) that he had a mechanical theory of capitalist collapse, which neglected the class struggle, and that there were flaws in Bauer's original scheme (by the social democrats Sternberg, Arkadij Gurland, and Hans Neisser). These responses will be considered in the context of his published essays. In correspondence during the early 1930s and unpublished notes Grossman also replied to criticisms of his book. He drafted rebuttals of Braunthal and Helene Bauer, in particular, refuting their assertions that his model was arbitrary, that it neglected the effects of the devaluation of constant and variable capital (as not only Braunthal and Helene Bauer, but also Vogel, Miksch, Muhs, and Neisser had claimed), and that it predicted capitalism would break down solely because of low profit rates. He addressed the implications of his analysis for the class struggle and commented on the positions of Varga, Pannekoek, and Korsch, in letters to Paul Mattick. Grossman saw no point in replying to objections to his analysis (by Schmidt, Vogel, Oppenheimer, Caspary, Miksch, and Muhs) based on the rejection of Marx's labor theory of value.

To the widespread criticism that he had failed to deal with the devaluation of constant and variable capital, Grossman responded that

> the Marxist concept of a progressively higher organic composition of capital entails two different conclusions. First, the development of the productivity of labor means that the same mass of living labor (L) can set in motion an ever larger mass of means of production, that, as a consequence, the progress of the human economy is expressed in a progressively higher *technical composition* [of capital], in the relative increase of MP [means of production] in relation to L.
>
> Second, with this technical progress, which is just another expression for the increase in the productivity of labor, the products of human labor (means of production and consumption) are *devalued,* that is cheapened. So we have two counterposed movements. On the one hand an ever *greater mass* of MP, on the other hand a *cheapening* of this mass of products.
>
> ... Now the question of which of the two tendencies—growth in the mass or devaluation, is stronger—that is, the question of whether devaluation occurs to the same extent as the growth in the mass of the MP and thus the growth in mass is paralyzed by the decline in value, or rather whether devaluation is not as great and consequently that despite the devaluation of the MP, *its value in relation to v* [variable capital] *grows,* cannot be abstractly, deductively decided and has to be decided through *empirical observation. Experience,* indeed the experience of more than one hundred years, teaches that the *value* of constant capital, thus also of the total capital, in relation to variable capital grows *more quickly* than variable, that is, in the relationship c:v, c [constant capital] grows *faster* than v.[143]

Grossman illustrated his case with U.S. statistics for the period 1849 to 1919, which he had already cited, in part, in *The Law of Accumulation.*[144] To make this point, Grossman also drew on Otto Bauer's observations about the relationship between the organic composition of capital and the ratio of variable capital plus surplus value (V) to the total value of production (the sum of constant and variable capital and surplus value, P). From this empirical demonstration, Grossman

moved on to reassert the connection between the tendency for the organic composition of capital to rise and capitalism's proneness to break down.

> If, then, Helene Bauer wants to contradict the tendency to collapse and show
> that, through the devaluation of capital the mass of surplus value in relation to
> this total capital is *not* exhausted, does *not decline,* she has to demonstrate the
> *incorrectness* of the empirical fact of the progressively higher organic composi-
> tion of capital or, to speak with Otto Bauer, she has to demonstrate that the *law*
> of the "decline of V/P is incorrect."
>
> It is an impermissible contradiction—thoughtlessness—to talk about the
> fact of the progressively higher organic composition of capital and at the same
> time to assert that *devaluations* neutralize the tendency to break down, i.e. to
> deny the fact of the higher organic composition of capital . . .
>
> But if the tendency to a higher organic composition of capital, that is to a rela-
> tive decline in living labor, exists then the tendency to break down results from the
> progress of capital accumulation and at a certain level a *continuously larger part* of
> the newly created value product will be accumulated as additional capital.[145]

The portion of surplus value that has to be invested to sustain the accumulation process "grows relative to the total mass of living labor and, with a corre-
spondingly large growth of constant capital, entirely swallows the *mass of value*
created by living labor, surplus value, and the wage fund."[146] Beyond this point,
accumulation cannot continue.

Having used Otto against Helene Bauer, Grossman restated the importance
of taking the use value side of the accumulation process into account. When
commodities are understood as both use values and exchange values, Otto's
utopia of proportional accumulation falls apart. "Let us assume that the entire
rural economy uses 1,000 electric ploughs (each with a value of £80=£80,000)
which are sufficient to work the available land. If productivity now doubles, so
that with the same labor 2,000 electric ploughs can be produced, then the rural
economy will not be able to buy them, as they are superfluous. Devaluation
must have the consequence that the rural economy now only buys 1,000
ploughs, each with a value of £40=£4,000. Consideration of devaluation shows
the unsaleability of the product, the disruption of all the proportions worked
out so arduously by Otto Bauer."[147]

In response to Braunthal's assertion that the devaluation of variable capital
and a higher rate of surplus value would counteract the long-term tendency
for the rate of profit to fall, Grossman, in another manuscript, asked for references and evidence. Braunthal had provided neither.[148] Elsewhere, he dealt
with Braunthal's joke that impoverishment of capitalists was central to his theory (also told by Helene Bauer and retold by Muhs), and again explained the

role of the class struggle and the place of Otto Bauer's reproduction scheme in his own work.

> Nowhere have I said that capitalism will go under due to the impoverishment of the capitalists. I showed, rather, that an increasingly large part of surplus value (Ac) is, under the assumptions of Bauer's scheme, devoted to accumulation. The remainder, available for the consumption of the capitalists and workers, does not suffice. As a consequence an increasingly sharp struggle between workers and entrepreneurs over the level of wages necessarily flares up. *If* workers continue to receive the same wage, then nothing *remains* for the entrepreneurs. If, however, entrepreneurs maintain and where possible even increase their living standard, then they force down the level of wages, i.e. from this point on the *impoverishment of the workers* necessarily sets in. That, however, drives the workers to revolution . . .
>
> Let us assume that Br. does not hide behind the hardly valid proposition that Bauer's scheme is calculated "indeed only for a short period," namely a period of 4 years (p. 300). In my critique of Bauer's equilibrium scheme, I give a variation of Bauer's scheme (on p. 225 of my book). It shows that with a higher organic composition of capital the reproduction process won't survive even for this "short period."[149]

In *The Law of Accumulation*, Grossman's starting point was a variant of Bauer's scheme. As he now reiterated, he had used this particular model precisely in order to refute Bauer's conclusions on the basis of Bauer's own assumptions. But Grossman proceeded to lift Bauer's assumptions in order to generalize the argument and to indicate the effect of the countertendencies to the tendency for profit rates to fall. In his correspondence with Paul Mattick, he repeated this point, linking it to his conception of the relationship between capitalism's tendency to break down and revolutionary class struggles, while refuting the accusation that his account of capitalist collapse was mechanical. "But I did not want to give the impression that I derive the breakdown tendency *from Bauer's* scheme . . . Bauer makes unrealistic, false assumptions and I just wanted to pursue his argument *ad absurdum* . . . In reality these assumptions do not apply. There are precisely struggles between workers and capitalists over the distribution of surplus value. It is insufficient for *both* an adequate level of wages *and* the required rate of accumulation. One can only be achieved at the expense of the other. Hence the intensification of class struggles. The development of the situation in the United States, England and Germany over the past two years confirms this diagnosis 100 per cent. I do not maintain that surplus value declines. It can grow. And nevertheless it is insufficient because accumulation (as it requires an ever greater organic composition) swallows *a continuously larger part* of the surplus value."[150]

If capitalists secure their income, then wages are insufficient and

> an *objectively revolutionary* situation arises: the system shows that it cannot secure the living conditions of the population. From this *objective* situation and *through it* the class struggle *intensifies.* That is, the *subjective* factor, whether the working class through its struggles is capable of overturning the system, only becomes significant with the objective situation in this phase of development. Obviously the idea that capitalism must break down "of itself" or "automatically," which Hilferding and other socialists (Braunthal) assert against my book, is far from being my position. It can only be overturned through the struggles of the working class.
>
> But I wanted to show that the class struggle alone is *not* sufficient. The *will* to overturn capitalism is not enough. Such a will cannot even arise in the *early phases* of capitalism. It would also be [in]effective *without* a revolutionary situation.[151] Only in the final phases of development do the objective conditions arise which bring about the *preconditions* for the *successful,* victorious intervention of the working class. Obviously, as a *dialectical* Marxist, I understand that both sides of the process, the objective and subjective elements influence each other *reciprocally.* In the class struggle these factors fuse. One cannot "wait" *until* the "objective" conditions are there and only *then* allow the "subjective" factors to come into play. That would be an inadequate, mechanical view, which is alien to me. But, *for the purposes* of the analysis, I had to use the process of abstract isolation of individual elements in order to show the essential function of each element. Lenin often talks of the revolutionary situation which has to be objectively given, as the precondition for the active, victorious intervention of the proletariat. The purpose of my breakdown theory was not to exclude this active intervention, but rather to show when and under what circumstances such an objectively given revolutionary situation can and does arise.
>
> Bauer's scheme is insufficient on many grounds . . . I wanted to demonstrate that the result of even this, his mistaken scheme is breakdown and not equilibrium. *I do not want, however, to identify myself with Bauer's scheme under any circumstances.*[152]

The objections to *The Law of Accumulation* advanced by the social democrats Helene Bauer and Alfred Braunthal were more serious and thorough than those in reviews by Communists and Council Communists. A Council Communist critique, which Mattick had forwarded, Grossman justifiably dismissed as "thoughtless playing with words" and repetition of his own observations about the processes that counter capitalism's tendency to break down.[153] Mattick also arranged for the first issue of the Council Communist *Proletarier* to be sent to Grossman in 1933. It included a discussion of crisis theory by "Ko"

(Karl Korsch). To Korsch's suggestion that crisis theory amounted to a Sorelian myth that gave heart to the proletariat, Grossman responded that the bourgeoisie "will always remain the superior masters of this territory." "Hitler showed exactly how far one can go with 'myths' alone and what one can achieve with them . . . We, however, do not want to deceive ourselves or others. As a consequence, our activity has to be based on a theoretical understanding of the tendencies of development i.e. on the objective course of events."[154]

Grossman expressed many of the defenses of his position, developed in manuscript responses to Braunthal and Helene Bauer and correspondence with Mattick, in the summer of 1932, in a course on "The problem of the average rate of profit in modern economic theory."[155] He also used a long essay in Elster's *Dictionary* to restate and clarify his innovations in Marxist economics. The essay was initially published as a pamphlet, in 1932, and is discussed below. In it and other, subsequent publications Grossman again stressed that his analysis, far from denying the significance of the class struggle, provided a context in which it could be understood and hence made more effective. But he made this point most concretely, in an unpublished note. "What was the year 1929 in the USA and the year 1931 in Germany and England if not a giant *breakdown?* The working class was not prepared for this. It did not have a Lenin, who awaited and worked towards such a moment. Rather, for decades it heard from Hilferding and Helene Bauer that a breakdown was impossible. Only such a disorientation of the working class made it possible for the ruling class to overcome the panic and to survive the breakdown."[156]

Grossman's personal situation gave him space to publicly advocate economic theories that did not accord with Stalinist orthodoxies and to formulate the kind of criticism of the communist movement implied in this note. For many Communists, dedication to the party and what they understood as the cause of the working class was more important than their own views on specific questions. The Stalinist leadership of the Comintern used this loyalty to stifle critical thinking and drive out dissidents. In order to remain in the movement, György Lukács, for example, distanced himself from his original and creative contributions to Marxist philosophical and social theory in the early 1920s and then from his 1928 theses on the political orientation of the Hungarian party, when these did not match the Comintern's changing line.[157]

The leadership of the International in Moscow declared in mid-1928 that a new, Third Period since the war had opened. The Comintern soon insisted on policies that made united struggles between social democratic and communist workers next to impossible. Revolution, the Comintern proclaimed, was on the immediate agenda; social democracy was the left wing of fascism and the main obstacle to socialist advance.[158]

In contrast to Lukács, Antonio Gramsci continued to develop Marxist theory at variance with the policies of the Communist International during the late 1920s and 1930s. It was, at least in part, a fascist jail that insulated him from Stalinism. Trotsky too kept alive the revolutionary Marxist tradition, continuing to expound his earlier insights, such as the theory of permanent revolution, and developed a systematic critique of Stalinism. The fact that he did so on the basis of his commitment to Marxism and ability to face reality, without any institutional buffer, was one of his most impressive achievements.

Well after the demise of the Russian revolution that had provided a vital impetus to his work, Grossman's well-paid job at the institute and position on the margin of the communist movement continued to allow him to recover Marx's economics as an aspect of the theory of working-class self-emancipation. Thanks to the policies of the German and especially the Polish authorities, Grossman—unlike Lukács who remained a member and, until 1929, a leader of the Hungarian party—was not subject to the discipline of a Communist Party from about 1925. Despite his continuing identification with the Soviet Union and the communist movement, he was little inclined to bend to the wind from Moscow in areas where he had expertise. His intellectual self-confidence, not to say arrogance—the product of a privileged upbringing and success in bourgeois institutions, reinforced by years of commitment to and experience in working-class struggles—was a further precondition for this stubborn attitude. Karl Wittfogel later remembered his colleague as "a very erudite man, but very enamored of himself."[159] Karl Korsch and Ilse Mattick both expressed similar assessments of Grossman's character.[160]

In *The Law of Accumulation*, Grossman disparaged "Marx's epigones of all colors, from the reformists to the Communists"[161] and he defended the book's argument for the rest of his life. But he did not use his considerable capacity for polemic and vituperation to reply to Varga's criticisms in public. This was not out of sympathy for the newly anointed Tsar of Russian economics. In a letter to Mattick in mid-1931, he explained that, incapable of responding to the criticisms of his own position in *The Law of Accumulation*, Varga had "preferred to abuse me in a Communist journal. He hasn't gone into my argumentation and objections with a single word. As soon as I have the time, I will write a critique of Varga and illuminate this puffed up statistician from closer up."[162] The illumination never came. It was not difficult for Grossman to see that its publication would probably lead communist officials to brand him as an enemy of the Soviet Union and the communist movement, cutting him off entirely from the political current with which he then sympathized and the largest audience of people who might be open to his ideas.[163]

After *The Law of Accumulation* appeared, Grossman published several related essays. Grünberg's *Archiv* carried what he labeled a "small *programmatic* work."[164] "The alteration of the Original Plan of Marx's *Capital* and Its Causes" dealt with much more than the differences between drafts of Marx's economic study. It returned to the question of Marx's method and its implications for his understanding of capitalism. In this sense the essay justified the method used in *The Law of Accumulation* and highlighted some of the book's most important conclusions. Work on the essay was reflected in Grossman's course on "The economic system of Marxism" in summer semester 1929.[165]

In his 1859 *Contribution to a Critique of Political Economy*, Marx foreshadowed that the structure of his study of capitalism would deal successively with capital, land ownership, wage labor, the state, foreign trade, and the world market. That is, it would reflect certain basic, empirical features of capitalism. But the four volumes of *Capital* (including *Theories of Surplus Value*) actually dealt with the capitalist production process, the circulation process of capital, the structure of the process as a whole, and the history of the theory. That is, the final presentation was much more theoretical, focusing on the functional forms taken by capital.[166]

Grossman had already identified the connection between Sismondi's reproduction scheme and his method of abstraction. Now, on the basis of Marx's correspondence, he pinpointed the decision to change the structure of *Capital* to July–August 1863, coinciding with Marx's elaboration of the reproduction scheme used in the second volume. The scheme involved a series of simplifying assumptions or abstractions made to highlight the creation of surplus value as the defining feature of capitalism.[167]

The abstractions Marx made in the first stages of his analysis included a focus on industrial capital, to the exclusion of circulation and the credit system; the assumption that commodities sold at their value and therefore the exclusion of foreign trade, fluctuations in supply, demand, and the value of money; exclusion of the different forms that surplus value takes (taxes, ground rent, interest, and commercial profit) apart from industrial profit; and the temporary assertion that society only consists of the two classes of capital and labor, whose relationship defines the capitalist production process.[168]

In the literature, there was a great deal of confusion about Marx's method. But Grossman conceded that György Lukács, unlike Luxemburg, had grasped it. Lukács had understood that Marx abstracted to a society without any classes but workers and capitalists, "for the sake of argument, i.e. to see the problem more clearly, before pressing forward to the larger question of the place of this problem within society as a whole."[169] But, Grossman contended against Lukács, *Capital* was not a fragment and Marx himself, rather than Luxemburg, undertook the return journey to the living whole, reintroducing into his now clarified analysis elements previously abstracted from. Subsequently, as *The Law of Accumulation* demonstrated, "to every simplifying, fictional assumption" in Marx's system, "there corresponds a subsequent modification."[170] Although neither Marx's preliminary text, eventually published as *Grundrisse*, nor later drafts of *Capital* were accessible to Grossman, his pioneering treatment of the logic of *Capital* is still widely acknowledged.[171]

The Institute after Grünberg's Illness

Following an incapacitating stroke, Carl Grünberg was unable to work from the start of 1928. In March 1929, just over a month after his sixty-eighth birthday, he was relieved of his university duties and became an emeritus professor.[172] "With no hope of attaining a professorship in the normal way, Horkheimer was pushing for the post of director, which brought with it the prospect of an accelerated academic career." Pollock deferred to his lifelong friend, and Horkheimer, with Felix Weil's support, took over as acting director in October 1930, to be formally installed when Grünberg's contract ran out in 1932.[173]

Horkheimer, Pollock, and Weil were Marxists. But "none of those belonging to the Horkheimer circle was politically active; none of them had his origins either in the labor movement or in Marxism."[174] Horkheimer's inaugural address as director, in January 1931, was extremely cautious, avoiding anything that might be regarded as politically controversial. He seemed from the start to be acting from the conviction that he was the bearer of a revolutionary message, the safe preservation of which through all dangers was the most important single task—even though this was at a period when the institute's Marxist orientation had been openly avowed by Grünberg and Weil, when the need was great, and when controversial messages could still gain a hearing.[175]

The Depression had begun at the end of 1929. Burdened by reparations and particularly reliant on capital inflow for growth, the German economy was devastated; millions of Germans were soon out of work. Political polarization reflected and intensified social tensions. Support for the KPD increased from 10.6 to 13.1 to 14.5 percent of the vote in the Reichstag elections of 1928, 1930, and July 1932. The Nazi vote exploded from 2.6 to 18.3 to 37.4 percent. At the end of June 1932, Grossman wrote: "Whether, after the elections in July, there will still be a possibility for Marxists to work here is uncertain. As a consequence of the split in the working class, the Nazis have a significant chance of victory. The German working class has so far failed to unite against the common enemy in a moment of mortal danger! The Nazi's victory would signify the crushing of the labor movement for 10–15 years . . . The German working class understands everything, knows everything—but it *does* just about nothing. Yet again we see the way in which knowledge alone is insufficient if there is no *will to struggle.*"[176]

Although "Frankfurt University was one of the few universities in Germany where the Nazis got their heads bloodied if they tried to occupy the main gates or provoke clashes with left-wing or Jewish students," Horkheimer still refrained from publicly defending socialism or democracy and even from condemning the National Socialists.[177]

The Institute for Social Research provided an excellent environment for Marxist studies, not least because its considerable resources could ensure a comfortable income for its employees. Grossman's relationship with Max Horkheimer therefore had profound implications for his activities and lifestyle. That relationship was for years a harmonious one. As the best known and most productive member of the IfS, Grossman was an important asset, even as Horkheimer slowly shifted the institute's research program away from economics, the history of the labor movement, and contemporary politics toward philosophy and cultural criticism. So the author of *The Law of Accumulation* was left to pursue his own research agenda.

From 1930, Grossman continued the work of his friend and teacher, Carl Grünberg by contributing to a major publishing project. This was the fourth edition of Ludwig Elster's *Wörterbuch der Volkswirtschaft* (Dictionary of Economics). In this large body of work, discussed below, Grossman brought his own perspectives on politics and Marxist economics to bear.

It seems that Grossman took over some of Grünberg's teaching responsibilities too, notably a course on the "Economic condition of the German working class 1848–1928." In 1929 and 1930, he also offered further courses that addressed pressing contemporary issues: the working class and its organizations, imperialism, and the world economic crisis.[178] But his interest in the history of political economy was apparent in a seminar on "Marx as a historian of economics" in summer 1930 and "Theoretical economic exercises associated with selected chapters of Marx's *Capital*" in summer 1931.[179] This teaching overlapped with Grossman's research for the second volume of *The Law of Accumulation*,[180] "Gold production in the reproduction schemes of Marx and Luxemburg" and "The value-price transformation in Marx and the problem of crises."[181]

Somewhat belatedly, early in 1932, Carl Grünberg's friends and colleagues published a volume to celebrate his seventieth birthday, which had been on February 10, 1931. Grossman's contribution was a study of gold production and reproduction schemes.[182] The essay criticized Luxemburg's use of Marx's reproduction scheme in the second volume of *Capital*. Luxemburg, Grossman asserted, had ripped it out of the context of Marx's method of progressively approaching the real world in his theory, depriving it of explanatory value.[183] A detailed refutation of the amendments Luxemburg proposed for Marx's reproduction model reinforced the case against her conception of Marx's method. She had argued that the production of money should be allocated to a special third, department of production (III), separate from those making means of production (I) and means of consumption (II). Grossman, who had begun to consider the place of money in Marx's reproduction model in December 1924 at the latest, demonstrated in detail that Marx had specifically addressed this issue, regarding the production of money as part of department I; that Luxemburg had not bothered to examine the implications of her proposal for the reproduction scheme as a whole; and that her version of the model was incompatible with its assumptions.[184]

Why did Grossman devote a whole article to an essentially technical argument? One reason was that, in an unacknowledged form, Luxemburg's flawed arguments had been incorporated into Stalinist orthodoxy by Jenö Varga.[185]

Grossman's critique of Luxemburg was therefore a tacit attack on Varga's theory of economic crisis, legitimized by a new assault on Luxemburgism that Stalin had initiated in 1931. Unlike the 1925 campaign, this operation turned into an attack on Luxemburg's entire contribution to Marxism and equated Luxemburgism with the crime of Trotskyism.[186] Grossman did not, however, question her other contributions to Marxist theory or her credentials as a revolutionary.

While his contribution to the *Festschrift* was an attack on a rival approach to economic theory, Grossman's work on the value-price transformation was, in part, a response to critics of *The Law of Accumulation*. In a letter to Paul Mattick in 1931 and in notes on criticisms of his book, Grossman identified the question of the relationship between values and prices as an important issue in the theory of economic crises. During the summer semester of 1932, he pursued this issue in a course on "The problem of the average rate of profit and modern economics." Some of the results of this inquiry remained unpublished, others appeared in the first issue of the institute's new journal, the *Zeitschrift für Sozialforschung,* which superseded Grünberg's *Archiv.*[187]

On the basis of a further discussion of Marx's method, the essay on the value-price transformation drew attention to the assumption, underlying Marx's reproduction scheme in the second volume of *Capital,* that commodities exchange between different departments of production (those producing means of production and means of consumption) at their value. As a consequence, in the model there were different rates of profit in different departments, given the uniform rate of exploitation.[188] Thus the rate of profit was lower in the more capital-intensive department.

In reality profit rates tend to equalize around a general, average rate of profit, across industries and departments; and, as a consequence, commodities do not exchange at their values. In the third volume of *Capital*, Marx explained this. The general rate of profit is established through competition. Capitalists in capital-intensive industries, that therefore have lower rates of profit if commodities are sold at their value, will tend to shift their capital and curtail their production. Shortages of the commodities they produce will lead to a deviation between these commodities' values and prices of production, which are bid up. As a consequence more surplus value is realized in such industries than was produced there and their profitability improves. The opposite process takes place in labor-intensive industries. Overall, prices of production tend to deviate from values to the extent necessary to equalize the rate of profit across an economy. Commodities' market prices fluctuate around these prices of production.[189] In other words, prices deviate from values, though in a systematic way.

The chain of argument from values through prices of production to market prices provides the means to understand both the logic and empirical reality of capitalism. Grossman pointed out that, in thirty years of discussion of the problems of accumulation and crisis, no one had taken account of this role of competition in the formation of the average rate of profit. He also insisted that this process has implications for the nature of the common concerns of the capitalist class. Individual capitalists have an interest in the exploitation of the working class as a whole, as the profit they make is determined by the average rate of profit, not solely by the amount of surplus value extracted in their own enterprise.[190]

The efforts to explain economic crises in terms of disproportion between spheres of production, from Mikhail Tugan-Baranovsky's early discussion through to Bukharin and Sternberg, Grossman noted, were all couched in terms of a reproduction scheme in which commodities exchanged at their values before the introduction of the general rate of profit. Yet the proportionality necessary to sustain capital accumulation is one established on the basis of prices of production/market prices. "It is different in my book, which is concerned with explaining the primary, general crises of overaccumulation that embrace all spheres of production at the same time. For society as a whole 'the distinction between values and prices of production loses all significance' ... as in this case they are of the same magnitude."[191]

In his book, Grossman had demonstrated that the tendency to collapse was a feature of capitalism at a high level of abstraction, that of capital in general. His most abstract model excluded competition, in the sense of market fluctuations in prices and, more profoundly, the mechanism of competition that establishes the average rate of profit and hence the deviation of prices of production from values. This was a tacit response to Gurland and Neisser's objections that he had based his argument on Bauer's faulty reproduction scheme, and failed to take into account the equalization of profit rates and hence the transformation of values into prices of production.[192] In fact, Grossman's *modified* version of Bauer's scheme did not include separate departments of production. The different rates of profit in the two departments of Bauer's original model meant that it was only applicable at the value level of analysis. Grossman's more abstract scheme, in contrast, was capable of representing developments in value or price of production terms.[193]

Such objections, Grossman proceeded to show, did apply to the use of the reproduction schemes in theories of economic crises based on disproportionality.[194] "How then could the analysis of a value scheme demonstrate to us the necessity of the proportionality or disproportionality of commodity exchange under capitalism, if the proportional relations so carefully worked out in the value scheme are subsequently and of necessity overturned by the tendency for profit rates to equalize and the consequent redivision of surplus value!"[195]

Theorists who attributed crises to disproportionality mistakenly focused on the value reproduction scheme. They overstated its significance, regarding it as an expression of reality rather than an abstraction. Both Luxemburg and Bauer, in his critique of her, made this mistake. The problem of realizing surplus value, which Luxemburg identified, may be resolved precisely by the formation of the general rate of profit and the exchange of commodities at their prices of production. Otto Bauer transferred surplus value from one department to another in his demonstration that a production scheme that underwent proportional growth could be specified. Gurland and Sternberg objected that he gave no explanation of how this could occur. Helene Bauer tried to justify the transfer with reference to the credit system, which simply did not exist in the model at this level of abstraction. The transfer could be readily explained, however, if an average rate of profit was established and commodities exchange not at their values (as in Bauer's original model) but at their prices of production.[196]

The neglect of prices of production in recent discussions, Grossman argued, detracted from Marx's achievement in demonstrating how the average rate of profit forms. Classical economists, notably Ricardo and Malthus, had observed the phenomenon but were unable to reconcile it with a labor theory of value. Marx's important innovation and its implications were just as neglected by the neo-harmonists Bauer, Hilferding, and Kautsky, who believed crisis-free growth was possible, as by Luxemburg and her supporters, or Bukharin and other communist theorists. Instead of taking Marxism forward, they took it back to the point at which the post-Ricardian school had failed around 1850.[197] Grossman's attack on Bukharin, now a vulnerable and marginal, though still publicly prominent figure in Russia, here provided cover for criticism of official communist economics and the custodian of its Stalinist orthodoxy, Varga.

In two unpublished manuscripts, also products of his research on the transformation problem, Grossman criticized Ladislaus von Bortkiewicz's approach to the transformation of values into prices on the ground that it ignored Marx's method of abstraction. Grossman explained that the money Marx had employed in his exposition of the transformation was "not real, but an ideal standard constructed for the purposes of exact scientific research." This refuted Bortkiewicz's procedure of treating money/gold like other commodities, which led to a result that contradicted Marx's assumption that the total value of commodities before the transformation equaled the total of their prices of production after it.[198]

Manuscript student notes on Grossman's course on "The problem of the average rate of profit" included an extremely sketchy and seemingly flawed alternative to Bortkiewicz's and Natalie Moskowska's solutions to the transformation problem.[199] In developing an argument from *The Law of Accumulation*, the student notes were more illuminating. In the book, Grossman had identified unequal exchange as a mechanism through which surplus value was transferred from less developed to more developed countries. He now fleshed out the connection between this process and the transformation of values into prices of production. Contrary to Luxemburg's contention that surplus value from capitalist countries can only be realized in non-capitalist countries, Grossman maintained that "the opposite is the case. A part of m [surplus value] from countries with a lower organic composition of capital is transferred to countries with a higher organic composition. In reality a reverse movement of m [to that proposed by Luxemburg] is apparent. The political expression of this economic occurrence is the colonial policy of the large capitalist countries."[200]

Grossman's Politics in Germany

Like millions of others involved in the international workers' movement, Grossman continued to support the zigzags of official communism, as the Soviet state and Comintern became instruments serving the interests of the new bureaucratic capitalist class that emerged from the degeneration of the Russian revolution. There were, however, some who rejected the Stalinization of the Comintern and its component parties. Among graduate students at the institute during the late 1920s and early 1930s, there were Brandlerites (right Communists hostile to the Comintern's Third Period line), Trotskyists, and Council Communists (who rejected any involvement in parliamentary institutions and the idea that the working class needed a revolutionary party).[201]

Although he sometimes adjusted the form or emphasis of arguments in his publications to match the shifting political line of the Comintern, Grossman did not change his basic understanding of Marxist theory. Unlike communist hacks, he was prepared both to make arguments that contradicted official party positions and to draw attentions to weaknesses in Lenin's writings. He was not a devotee of the Stalinist cult of Lenin. Nor did he shun political contact with revolutionaries outside the communist movement.

In his letters to the Council Communist Paul Mattick, Grossman was more explicit about his political views than in his publications. The letters also demonstrated the interaction between his political commitments and personal relationships. In starting the correspondence, Mattick expressed his admiration for *The Law of Accumulation* and posed questions about economic theory.[202]

Soon Mattick revealed his antiparliamentary politics and invited Grossman to collaborate with his newspaper. Grossman's next letter was explicit, both about his desire for continued contact with Mattick and about the issues over which they disagreed. If you want to be consistently antiparliamentary, Grossman insisted, you shouldn't publish a legal newspaper like the *Chicagoer Arbeiter Zeitung.* "The difference between us, the revolutionary movement, and the parliamentary betrayers is that we know that *things will not go on this way forever.* The time will come when the ruling classes will eliminate freedom of the press and of assembly. We are prepared for that and respond with an illegal press, with illegal meetings. In Germany over the last months, 73 Communist newspapers have been forbidden by emergency decree."[203] His identification with the KPD was clear. Grossman went on to respond at length to a number of economic questions Mattick had posed, and then politely declined to contribute to *Chicagoer Arbeiter Zeitung.*[204] A friendly and apparently sporadic correspondence nevertheless continued through two significant shifts in Grossman's political outlook, until he moved to the United States in 1937.[205]

Despite the need to maintain a low political profile in Germany, the increasing polarization of German politics during the early 1930s led Grossman to take public positions on some issues. In 1931, for example he, Grünberg, Horkheimer, Theodor Adorno, Albert Einstein, Oppenheimer, and seventy-four other German academics with democratic or left-wing sympathies signed a petition condemning the attitude of the professional association of German university teachers to the statistician Emil Gumbel. The association, reflecting the predominance of conservative and reactionary views among university staff and administrators, had approved of a campaign by ultra-nationalist and Nazi students against his appointment as a junior professor at the University of Heidelberg. They objected because Gumbel was a left-wing social democrat, prominent as a pacifist and author of publications exposing the activities of right-wing death squads and other clandestine paramilitary organizations in Germany. The university sacked Gumbel and withdrew his license to teach in August 1932.[206]

Grossman's Stalinist sympathies were apparent during his trip to the Soviet Union. He led a study tour of twenty-four economists and engineers, organized by the Berlin-based Working Group for the Study of the Soviet Planned Economy (Arplan), from August 20 to September 12, 1932. A noncommunist participant counted Grossman, who was on the Berlin-based organization's committee of management, among Arplan's Communists, along with György Lukács and Karl Wittfogel.[207]

The Soviet Union impressed Grossman. But what he saw there was carefully choreographed by the Russian authorities: during their brief stay in Moscow, for example, his group attended four theater productions. Many other tourists, including the leading English Fabians Sidney and Beatrice Webb, whose commitment to gradual reform through the Labor Party was anything but communist, responded in a similar way. According to a transcript later turned up by the Nazis' Principle Imperial Security Office, Grossman participated in a discussion at the offices of Gosplan (the central planning agency) in Kharkov. Responding to some critical questions about Soviet planning by other members of his group, he said, "Today we can only consider the planned economy and in doing so can easily be burdened by private economic concepts. We come to learn."[208]

Some of Grossman's actions and writings provided evidence of the contradiction between his commitments to the USSR and his Marxist understanding of capitalism. Thus he declined an invitation to work at the University of Moscow because of Varga's hostility to his theories.[209] The defense of the USSR was one thing, economic theory another. In his 1932 essay on the transformation problem, Grossman acknowledged that I. I. Rubin had shared his conception of Marx's method: value and price of production theories relate not to different kinds of economy but different levels of analysis of the same capitalist economy. On the other hand, Rubin had failed to recognize implications of the transformation for the problem of crises.[210] These observations were not just a matter of referring to a colleague's arguments. They had political implications. Well before the publication of Grossman's article, the Soviet authorities had banned all public discussion of Rubin's theories or "Rubinism." In 1931 Rubin, a former Bundist, was sentenced to five years imprisonment in a show trial of "Mensheviks."[211] Grossman may have become a Stalinist, but he was one who had reservations about aspects of the party line and was not prepared to follow it in all things.

Already tired when he left Frankfurt, Grossman was ill when he returned from the exhausting trip to the USSR. After his recovery, he offered a course on the "Economic development of the Soviet Union (from War Communism to the Second Five Year Plan)" in winter semester 1932–33.[212] He was enthusiastic about what he had seen in Russia and this led to his most public political act in Germany.

On January 20, 1933, he defended the Soviet Union at a public meeting of two thousand people in Frankfurt's Saxophonsaal, ten days before Hitler became chancellor of Germany. Hannes Meyer, the former head of the Bauhaus, was reporting on his experiences after spending several years as an architect in the USSR. In the subsequent discussion, F. Jaspert, another German specialist who had worked in Russia, suggested that something wasn't right there. Also recently returned from the USSR, Grossman according to his own account "exposed Mr Jaspers [sic], who had defamed the Soviet Union in long articles in the *Frankfurter Zeitung*, as a liar."[213] In the newspaper, Jaspert had provided an entirely plausible account of the ugly realities of Soviet planning.[214]

Grossman's political attitudes and the scope of his interests during the early 1930s were also apparent in his contributions to Elster's *Dictionary*, a standard reference work on economic institutions and concepts. While Horkheimer took over Grünberg's job at the head of the institute, Grossman was, in an important sense, his intellectual successor. Grünberg had contributed entries on socialism, communism, and anarchism to earlier editions of the *Dictionary*.[215] After a long interval, a major expansion and revision was planned for the fourth edition, to be published between 1931 and 1933.[216]

When Grünberg became ill, his friend took over the job in 1930. The work required voluminous research, consumed a great deal of time, and had very tight deadlines.[217] Grossman's encyclopedic reading and interests over decades enabled him to draw on extensive literatures, including primary texts. He wrote thirteen biographical entries (the longest, of more than three densely printed pages, on Lenin) and substantial interpretative essays on anarchism, Bolshevism, the Second and Third Internationals, and the development of Marxism since Marx's death. He also updated and revised Grünberg's essays on Christian and religious socialism, and socialist parties.[218]

Several of his university courses provided testing grounds for Grossman's work on *Dictionary* entries. His teaching on "The history of socialism and anarchism" in summer semester 1931 and perhaps "On the theory and history of the German trade union movement" in winter semester 1931–32 dealt with topics he wrote on for the *Dictionary*. "The economic system of Karl Marx and its subsequent development 1883–1933" in winter semester 1932–33 and his essay in the *Dictionary* on this topic, drew on a course he had offered at the WWP in 1923.[219]

Other contributions to Elster's standard German reference work were overwhelmingly presented in blacks, grays, and blues by conservative and reactionary professors. Grossman provided readers with concise and clear information on both the development of the labor movement and Marxist theory, written in bright but nuanced shades of red.

A communist critique of social democracy was apparent in his essays on social democratic and communist ideas and parties, and several biographical entries. Grossman updated Grünberg's 1911 work on socialist parties, surveying developments in fifteen countries. He kept strictly to his bargain with the authorities in Poland about not mixing in Polish politics: the essay surveyed Rumania, with its far younger and less powerful labor movement but did not mention Poland. When many of the narratives about national social democratic parties reached the start of World War I, Grünberg's detached style gave way to a more forceful partisanship. For example, Grossman wrote that Austrian social democracy was, "like the German Social Democratic Party, always ready to pursue a policy of compromise with and toleration of bourgeois reaction. This contradiction between verbal radicalism and opportunist practice was clearest in the speech by Otto Bauer, the leading thinker of Austrian S[ocial Democracy], at the most recent Congress of the Second International in Vienna (1931)."[220] A particular hostility to Bauer, as an economic theorist and, especially before the war, as an apologist for the nationalism of the Austrian party also inspired this comment.

In his assessment of Austrian social democracy's position on the national question Grossman was critical of the views he had expounded as a leader of the Jewish Social Democratic Party of Galicia. Now he argued that "the national program adopted in Brünn (1899) carried the furious national conflicts in the bourgeois camp into the labor movement." The entry on Bolshevism outlined, without comment, Lenin's critique of the Bund's demand that the Russian Social Democratic Labor Party should adopt a federal structure.[221]

Eugene Debs, Jean Jaurès, and Sorel appealed to Grossman because of their devotion to the class struggle and class principles. His appreciation of Jaurès, for whom he had retained a soft spot since visiting Paris before World War I, contrasted with the standard communist assessment, following Lenin, of the French socialist as simply a reformist.[222] Grossman's sympathies were also unmistakable when he dealt with the development of the international communist movement. The entry on Lenin provided a lucid and persuasive outline, not only of the Russian revolutionary's political activity but also his contributions to Marxist theory on the question of political organization, the role of workers councils/soviets in the revolution, and revolutionary tactics.[223]

Far from complying with the rising leadership cult in Russia, Grossman's account of the history of the Bolshevik Party hardly mentioned Stalin at all. Nor did it pretend that Trotsky had played no role in the Russian revolution and indulge in the kind of hysterical denunciations of the exiled revolutionary that were now characteristic of Soviet historiography. The essay on socialist and communist parties even cited Trotsky on Austrian politics.[224] But in relation to both contemporary domestic policy in Russia and the role of the Comintern, Grossman fully accepted the official communist line. The entry on Bolshevism offered an uncritical account of the wonders of collectivization and the first five-year plan, and an orthodox Stalinist critique of Trotsky's attitude to industrialization.[225]

A friendly treatment of communism in a mainstream reference work was a remarkable occurrence. So it was not surprising, as Grossman later recalled, that KPD leaders were grateful "for my essay 'Bolshevism,' as I had so effectively supported the cause in such a place."[226] His essay on the Third International labeled the program adopted at its Sixth Congress in 1928, as Stalin consolidated his power in Russia and the Comintern, "one of the most significant documents in the history of the modern workers' movement, summarizing the whole knowledge and experience of the proletariat's revolutionary struggles."[227]

The most significant entry by Grossman in Elster's *Dictionary* was his survey of Marxism after Marx. He "worked 15–18 hour days for 6 weeks just to finish the essay" before departing on his tour of the Soviet Union. Prior to its appearance in the *Dictionary,* the essay was published separately as a pamphlet, *Fifty Years of Struggle over Marxism 1883–1932.* This was a much larger publication than the articles with which Grossman had marked the fortieth anniversary of Marx's death. His friend, the communist professor Yoshitaro Hirano, translated and introduced the essay for a Japanese audience in 1933.[228]

Following Lenin's argument, the study located the material basis of reformism in the emergence of a labor aristocracy, bought off with spoils from imperialism. It then outlined Bernstein's critique of Marx and the influence of neo-Kantian ethical socialism in the social democratic movement. The subsequent treatment of Luxemburg's contribution to the campaign against revisionism was very positive. The entry also examined reformist theory during the war, notably Karl Renner's treatment of the state, and summarized Grossman's own earlier critique of the neo-harmonist economic theories of Hilferding, Bauer, and Kautsky.[229]

After settling accounts with social democratic revisionism before and after World War I, "The Development of Marxism after Marx" outlined the revival of revolutionary Marxism, beginning with a sketch of the development of historical materialism from the late 1880s. In listing Marxist approaches to a wide range of topics, he included his own work on Austria's trade policy, the origins of official statistics in Austria and the Duchy of Warsaw, for the light they shed on the transition from the feudal to the modern state in the eighteenth century. Wittfogel's 1931 study of China and Horkheimer's "A New Concept of Ideology?" were also featured. The essay praised Lukács's *History and Class Consciousness* in particular, although it remained out of favor in the Comintern and had been repudiated by its author. Grossman's survey did not mention Stalin at all—unthinkable in a Soviet or official communist treatment of such a topic, given the extent of the Stalin cult by 1932.[230]

The sections of the essay that dealt with the problems of imperialism and war and the end of capitalism included substantial recapitulations of Grossman's arguments in *The Law of Accumulation*.[231] He counterposed his own account of capitalist crises and breakdown, deriving from the tendency for the rate of profit to fall, to Bukharin's general comments, the focus on problems of realization by Luxemburg and others (without mentioning Varga), and the disproportionality school, deriving from Tugan-Baranovsky.[232]

At high levels of capital accumulation, he explained, even if the absolute mass of surplus value was still rising, the decline in the *relative* mass of surplus value would eventually reach a point where, if the accumulation of constant capital was to be maintained, capitalists would have to try to reduce their outlays on variable capital or their own consumption. This would provoke sharp class struggles. Should bosses generally be successful in these, labor power would not be fully reproduced, that is, the working class would be paid less than the value of its labor power. If workers maintained their living standards, then the rate of accumulation would slow and technological development would stagnate. Because accumulation takes the form of investment in concrete use values, it will ultimately become impossible to invest the arbitrarily small fragment of additional surplus value produced as the rate of profit declines.[233]

Counter-tendencies can temporarily offset the decline in the rate of profit and moderate crises so that they do not result in total economic collapse. But the countertendencies become progressively weaker. "If crisis, for him [Grossman], is a tendency to break down that has not fully unfolded, *then the breakdown of capitalism is nothing but a crisis that has not been limited by countertendencies.*" Grossman went on to emphasize, in what was clearly a response to critics of his book, that

for the proletariat, it can never be a matter of a fatalistic policy of waiting, that is without actively intervening, for the "automatic" collapse. Old regimes never "fall" by themselves, even during periods of crisis, if they are not, precisely, "overturned" (Lenin). The point of a Marxist theory of breakdown, according to Grossmann, consists only in the need to reject voluntarism and putschism, which regard revolution as possible at any time, dependent only on the subjective desire of revolutionaries, without considering whether the *situation is objectively revolutionary.* The meaning of a Marxist theory of breakdown is that the revolutionary action of the proletariat receives its strongest impulse only when the existing system is objectively shaken. This, at the same time, creates the conditions for successfully overcoming the resistance of the ruling classes.[234]

6

Exile and Political Reassessments

Hitler became chancellor of Germany on January 30, 1933. There was no serious working-class mobilization against the Nazis as they took power by formally legal means and then intimidated, jailed, and murdered their political opponents and destroyed the organized labor movement. For the leadership of the Social Democratic Party, such a mobilization would have challenged the cherished Weimar Constitution. The suicidal sectarianism of the Comintern's Third Period policy toward social democracy made cooperation between communist and social democratic workers next to impossible, even to resist the Nazis. After the National Socialist takeover, the German Communist Party held fast to this line for over a year, believing Hitler would soon discredit himself, opening the way to revolution.[1]

The institute under Horkheimer had made systematic preparations against a Nazi takeover. Almost all its assets were invested outside Germany. Its headquarters were rapidly transferred to Geneva, where a branch office had been set up in 1930.[2] Grossman left for Paris on March 4.[3] Nine days later, the police searched and sealed the offices of the IfS. Soon the National Socialist Student Organization and State Police took over several of its rooms for their own use.[4]

In early April, the University Senate severed connections with the institute, while continuing to use the lower two floors of the IfS building. But the Economics and Social Science Faculty approved Grossman's application, from Paris, to undertake research rather than to teach at the university, during the summer semester.[5] In September he applied for leave in the winter semester too.[6] But the Nazis had already passed the Law for the Reestablishment of the Professional Civil Service on April 7. This expelled Jews from public employment and honorary posts, including at universities. The Prussian Ministry for

Science, Art, and Education formally purged Grossman, by withdrawing his license to teach on December 18, 1933, on the grounds that he was not an Aryan. This was despite the exemption from this provision of the law for Jews who had fought in the armed forces of an ally of the German Reich in World War I.[7] But the Nazis were not ones for legal niceties. In any case, the law also provided for dismissals on political grounds. A supplementary law in July sacked all civil servants who belonged to any party or organization that supported the aims of communism, Marxism, or social democracy.

Grossman's work in Paris was hampered by the German police, who had confiscated two chests of manuscripts from a forwarding agent in Frankfurt. The boxes contained his inaugural professorial lecture, a history of slavery from the early Christian era to the present, work for the second volume of his crisis book, and notes on the theory of statistics.

He lied and did whatever else was necessary to extract his papers from the clutches of the Nazis, writing to the dean of his Faculty in Frankfurt, that "they do not contain a single line with a political content."[8] Grossman's Polish citizenship proved useful. The Polish Consul's intervention was decisive in having the boxes released.[9] But it took until October 1934 before he succeeded in retrieving part of his library. "All 'socialist' works by Marx, Engels, Jaurés, Lassalle, Mehring, Kautsky, and your book with the dedication, too, were confiscated" he wrote to his friend Max Beer, who had worked at the institute in Frankfurt for a period, "and they confiscated along with them books that were not 'suspect,' if they were valuable." He also lost access to the documents he had donated to the institute's archive.[10]

Grossman lived in several hotels before moving into "an expensive *atelier*" at 12 rue Victor Considérant, by the Montparnasse Cemetery. A solid socialist address, he later explained to his friend Christina Stead, as Considérant was the leader of the Fourierist utopian socialists from 1837.[11] Both residences were less than a kilometer and a half's stroll from the institute's office. They were close to Montparnasse, the center of Paris's most vibrant artistic movements both when Henryk and Janka had lived in the city and also during the period between the wars. Through the painter Moïse Kisling at least, Grossman maintained contact with that milieu.[12] He found La Coupole restaurant, in Montparnasse, particularly congenial.[13]

The decisions to move to Paris and stay there for close to three years contrasted with the trajectory of Grossman's colleagues, most of whom initially went to Geneva and then, from 1934, to New York. Columbia University provided the IfS, known in the United States as the Institute of Social Research, with office space, while institute members participated in some university activities, such as seminars and extension courses.

Grossman missed contact with his friends at the institute, but his French (as opposed to his English) was excellent and it was easier to stay in touch with the political and academic life of Europe from Paris than New York. True, he had last lived there two decades ago, but he knew Paris and was familiar with its geography and its resources for researchers from his previous long stay. Most important, the institute had a branch office in Paris, in rooms at the École Normale Supérieure at rue d'Ulm in the 5th Arrondissement, not far from the Sorbonne campus of the University of Paris. The city was particularly important to the IfS because the Parisian publishing house Alcan issued the institute's journal, the *Zeitschrift für Sozialforschung* (*ZfS*), from 1934.

Friends and acquaintances, from before and after the war, also lived in Paris. The distinguished historian of economic thought at the Sorbonne, Charles Rist, for example, had written to praise his book on Sismondi and had published reviews in Grünberg's *Archiv*.[14] There were many people, German and French, including dissident Communists with whom Grossman could discuss what had gone wrong in Germany. He participated in the German antifascist movement in exile.[15]

Other friends visited from abroad. In May 1935, Grossman's lifelong confidant, Oskar Kurz, came to see his cousin.[16] His former student, Walter Braeuer, called in later that year and again in 1936, just before Grossman left for London. Nevertheless Braeuer's old professor "invited me to a cafe and we spoke for two hours."[17] There were soon new colleagues and friends. Among academics were a historian associated with *Annales,* Lucie Varga, whose husband was the German historian of science Franz Borkenau, and the Spanish philosopher Blas Ramos Sobrino. Grossman often met another historian of science, Alexandre Koyré, who contributed reviews to the *ZfS*.[18] Auguste Cornu became a good friend. As a sympathizer of the international, antipatriotic Zimmerwald movement during the war, Cornu had been a founding member of the French Communist Party in 1921. He was an expert on Marx's early intellectual and political development. Like the *ZfS*, his books were published by Alcan. Conservative university authorities denied him an academic post, despite his doctorat d'état, because he was a Communist.[19]

Although separated from the institute's head office in Geneva and then New York, Grossman continued to draw his salary and to work on projects formulated in correspondence with Horkheimer. His initial priority in Paris was the preparation of a revised, French edition of *The Law of Accumulation*. But this was hampered by the confiscation of his manuscripts and library, and lack of access to relevant research materials, due to the reactionary collection policy of the French National Library.[20] During 1934, Grossman abandoned the idea of a French translation of his book but persevered with research for its sequel.[21]

Meanwhile, he wrote two reviews for the *ZfS* and a contribution to an encyclopedia edited in the United States, all concerning Sismondi. His brief review of Elie Halévy's selection of Sismondi's writings was favorable. It did suggest, however, that Halévy's introduction had missed the opportunity to point out how "the different underconsumption theories, which circulate widely in the contemporary labor movement and elsewhere (e.g. L. Boudin, H. Cunow, K. Kautsky, Rosa Luxemburg, the CGT [trade union federation] in France etc.), despite their Marxist terminological disguise, in reality indicate a renaissance of Sismondi's approach to crisis theory."[22]

Grossman probably read the Halévy selection while preparing the entry on Sismondi for the *Encyclopedia of the Social Sciences*. This drew extensively on his own earlier treatment of Sismondi's economic thought, but also discussed the Swiss economist's researches in French and particularly medieval Italian history, and the way he and Madame de Staël "paved the way" for the modern sociology of literature.

In his monograph ten years before, Grossman had not examined Sismondi's treatment of foreign trade, and had argued that it was superficial to regard problems of income distribution and the low level of workers' consumption as the Swiss economist's most important explanation of economic crises.[23] The *Encyclopedia* article, however, stated that Sismondi had regarded "the necessity of continuous [capitalist] expansion and conquest of new outlets, resulting from the restriction of the internal market" as an inherent characteristic of capitalism overlooked by the classical economists. It also acknowledged Sismondi's underconsumptionism, which Kautsky and Luxemburg had adopted, and endorsed Lenin's critique of this approach. Grossman now stressed that for Sismondi "the deeper cause of underconsumption" and crises was "the fact that in a capitalistic society the extent and direction of economic activity are determined by exchange value" rather on the basis of social need.[24]

The second contribution to the *ZfS* that Grossman wrote in this period was a very short and unfavorable review of Robert Bordaz's book on Marxist economics. Bordaz, Grossman argued, demonstrated impressive ignorance of the history of political economy and Marx's account of capitalism. Bordaz's version of Marxist crisis theory was "a paraphrase of Sismondi's teachings."[25]

In March 1934, on Horkheimer's request, Grossman began writing a review of an entirely different order: a long critique of Franz Borkenau's book on the origins of the bourgeois worldview.[26]

After gaining his doctorate, Borkenau had worked for the Communist International in Berlin, under Jenö Varga, and then for the Western European Bureau of the International.[27] Expelled from the Communist Party in 1929 for his criticism of the Third Period line, he supported Heinrich Brandler and August

Thalheimer's KPD-Opposition. Borkenau's move to Frankfurt, on an institute scholarship to write a study of the emergence of the modern conception of the world, had significantly strengthened this right communist organization in the city, at a time when Grossman was still a strong supporter of the KPD.[28]

The need for a critical review of this book, published by the IfS, arose from concern in the institute that Borkenau's analysis was neither Marxist nor accurate.[29] The first chapter, which related intellectual developments to the emergence of manufacturing, was only inserted after criticisms from the institute, provoked by Grossman, who drew on his investigations of Renaissance thought.[30]

Without satisfactory resources to extend his study of crisis theory, Grossman became engrossed in work on the review of Borkenau's book. Its scope expanded dramatically. In October 1934, he told Paul Mattick that "the problem of the origins of mechanistic thought has so gripped me and taken up all of my efforts that I have spent almost all of my time for months in the Bibliothèque Nationale in the literature of the 16th and 17th Centuries . . . When I eventually finish writing it up, it will be, I hope, a nice contribution to the materialist conception of history and not in the form of general babble, à la Bukharin, but as *concrete* historical research."[31] Two and a half months later, he wrote to Max Beer that "I give the first—so far as I know—outline of a materialist history of mechanics from the 14th century to Descartes."[32]

In fact, a Russian Marxist had made an important contribution in this area in 1931. Boris Hessen delivered a paper to the International Congress of the History of Science and Technology in London, on the social and economic roots of Newton's *Principia*. His study overlapped in method and content with Grossman's critique of Borkenau. By 1937, Grossman was not only aware of Hessen's study but regarded it as complementing his own work and defended it against criticisms.[33]

The extensive original research Grossman undertook for his review delayed its completion. He wrote *three* substantial essays against Borkenau. Two, "Capitalism in the Period of the Renaissance" and "Manufacturing from the 16th to 18th Centuries," demolished Borkenau's contention that modern mechanics dated from the middle of the seventeenth century and could be explained in terms of the emerging division of labor in manufacturing. In fact, mechanics was developed in the fifteenth century, while manufacturing emerged in the second half of the eighteenth century![34] The third essay shredded Max Weber's argument, regurgitated by Borkenau, that capitalism was a consequence of the Protestant reformation.[35] After initially agreeing to publish two essays, Horkheimer put his foot down, asking Grossman to produce what "I originally asked for . . . by December 15 at the latest."[36]

To meet the deadline Grossman worked twelve and more hours a day for two months. "For years no work, neither my crisis book nor the Elster articles which had to be written quite quickly," he wrote to Horkheimer, "has required as much effort as the Borkenau essay. It made me ill and nervous." The scale of his output contributed to his nerves. It proved impossible to compress his studies into thirty-two to forty-eight pages, even after discarding almost all of the critique of Weber, and he told Horkheimer that "*it was an unachievable task that you set me.*" Nevertheless, "the essay finishes Borkenau off. But he was a secondary consideration for me. I not only offer a critique, but show *positively* how the problem can be solved."[37] In January 1935, Grossman submitted an essay that eventually occupied seventy pages of the journal, despite the use of very small type for some passages. Yet Grossman's insistent cajoling of Horkheimer to publish this long essay was justified. "The Social Foundations of Mechanical Philosophy and Manufacture" remains a reference point for historians of science.[38]

Grossman's review contrasted key elements of Borkenau's case with original sources and widely accepted scholarly conclusions about the nature and timing of both the development of modern science, especially mechanics, and the origins and stages in the evolution of capitalist manufacture. Borkenau asserted that there was a connection between the emergence of a detailed division of labor in production and the rise of modern physics. But he provided no evidence of this. So "the reduction of the elements of the mechanistic world [view] to the division of labor in manufacture proves to be decorative, 'materialistically' adorning the genesis of mechanistic philosophy, but by no means serving as a means of analysis."[39]

There was, however, plenty of evidence, notably in discoveries made by Leonardo da Vinci and René Descartes, for Grossman's own position. In 1919, he had stressed the importance of abstracting from distracting appearances in order to get to the fundamental process involved in economic crises, drawing an analogy with the scientific approach applied by physicists who abstracted from the effects of the air when investigating falling bodies. This understanding of scientific method allowed him to explain the logic of Marx's argument in *Capital* and the book's structure. Now, with the assistance of Marx's comments about machinery in *Capital,* he applied the same insight to the history of science, demonstrating that constructing, working with, and observing machines had made it possible to set aside some of the concrete appearances of physical phenomena—complicated by different kinds of motion and friction, for example—to identify abstract mechanical work. The material foundations of mechanics and the mechanistic worldview therefore lay in the impetus given by capitalism to the invention of new machines.[40] Borkenau, on the other hand, wanted to "understand the basic architectural form of a building by explaining the character of the sixth floor in terms of the structure of the fifth, without considering the foundations or the intermediate floors."[41]

Although the argument in Grossman's essay was thoroughly Marxist, there was no mention of Marx in its conclusion, which stressed the connections between ideas and the forces and relations of production; already following a timid editorial policy of scaling down the institute's Marxist reputation, Horkheimer deleted Marx's name and references to him.[42]

By way of contrast, Grossman's response to Horkheimer's very expansive praise for the article[43] indicated his continuing political engagement: "We all fight for the great proletarian cause. But since the destruction of the labor movement, a satisfaction which every fighter gained earlier—before the world war—from recognition within the movement is no longer possible. So one is happy to find satisfaction in the narrow circle with which one is bound and from that gains encouragement for further work."[44]

Following his work on the history of science, Grossman wanted to relax for a while but "various 'domestic' worries, which I have never lacked, leave me no leisure."[45] These worries may have been occasioned by his relationship with a young French woman. At least for a period, according to Christina Stead, his stay in Paris with the enjoyment of cafés, cycling, and the woman's company was an idyll.[46]

Within a few weeks of finishing his Borkenau review, however, Grossman wanted "to get back to volume II of my book," whose main focus would be on the necessity of crises, even under circumstances of simple reproduction. An appendix tackling the critics of the first volume would be attached.[47] But the heat during the height of summer made working difficult.

So Grossman decided to take a trip to Spain. His friend, the Marxist philosopher of law Blas Ramos Sobrino, had invited him to spend a couple of weeks at his country villa, sixty kilometers from Valladolid. Despite frequent temperatures around 35° C, Grossman spent his summer holidays on a three thousand kilometer recreational and study trip through Spain.[48]

The origins of modern science were still on his mind. From Valencia, he wrote a long letter, with diagrams, to Pollock and Horkheimer about ancient and medieval machines and their relationship to the theory of mechanics. Marx had argued that in a society based on slave production, there was no impetus to economize on the expenditure of human labor by developing mechanics. Yet certain kinds of machines were known in the ancient world. Now a visit to the National Archaeological Museum in Madrid prompted Grossman to recognize that ancient machines were not designed to replace slave labor, but to perform tasks that simple human labor could not undertake.[49]

Political Reassessments

The move to Paris and intensive research did not prevent Grossman from keeping up with political events or from rethinking some of his views. The Nazi victory and failure of the German labor movement led him and many other Communists, including Trotsky, to reassess their political positions and attitudes to the official communist movement.[50] The outlook of Horkheimer and his closest associates also shifted during the 1930s.

Grossman did not publish his ideas about the communist movement, the Soviet Union, or Stalinism after 1933. But, already aware of deficiencies in the policies of the KPD in 1932, his very critical attitude after the Nazi takeover was clear in letters to Paul Mattick until 1935. Shortly after leaving Germany, Grossman wrote: "The KPD certainly made major mistakes, and the 'leaders' installed by Moscow—in reality mere puppets—bear the principal blame. But despite everything! Forced into illegality by Hitler and forced to fight for its life, the Party will come out of this fight *purified* and strengthened, with new, better leaders. As things stand in Germany *only* the new KPD can be a point of crystallization for a serious struggle for power and for the overthrow of fascism! Anything else is a criminal utopia!"[51]

Like Trotsky, however, he soon gave up hope that change could come from within the KPD. "All independent men, capable of thinking on their own were thrown out of the Party. What remained was a bureaucracy that slavishly subordinated itself to Moscow. No revolution can be made on command from Moscow."[52] In mid-1933 Grossman sent Mattick a very recent essay by Trotsky which argued that the Comintern's Third Period policies had contributed to the defeat of the German working class by preventing a united fight by communist and social democratic workers. Now Grossman wanted to have contact with all active working-class groups resisting Hitler.[53] Late in the year he attacked the German Communist Party's sectarian policies. Its leaders could not fulfill elementary educational duties because "instead of clarifying issues, generating knowledge and understanding they *only complained*. Independent thought became impossible, because they immediately scented 'deviation' in it and the best comrades, most ready for self-sacrifice and tried in struggle, were labeled lackeys of the bourgeoisie. If the bourgeois revolution in France sent its own fighters to the guillotine, physically put them to death, proletarian fighters who think independently and search out the correct path are now morally put to death."[54] It wasn't long before large numbers of veteran revolutionary campaigners, KPD members among them, were executed in Russia too.

Grossman sought to clarify the issues involved in the destruction of the German labor movement by participating in a discussion group. It paid particular attention to the question of "why in 1918/19, 1920, 1923 etc all the objectively given revolutionary opportunities were missed! Why the revolutionary elements always remain isolated!" Among those who participated were Paul Frölich and Jacob Walcher, founding members of the KPD who had become leaders of the Socialist Workers Party (SAP). A left-wing breakaway from the SPD in 1931, the SAP had about 17,500 members in January 1933. With the international Trotskyist movement and two Dutch organizations, the SAP issued a joint call for the establishment of a new, Fourth International on August 26, 1933. Subsequently, however, the party moved to the right and became very critical of Trotsky and his adherents.[55]

In the wake of the Nazi takeover in Germany and the destruction of democracy in Austria, Stalin and hence the Communist International eventually abandoned the Third Period policy. It was replaced by the Soviet Union's pursuit of alliances with France and Britain against Germany. In the Comintern this took the form of a new Popular Front line in 1934–35, which sought reconciliation not only with social democratic but also liberal and, eventually, conservative but "patriotic" bourgeois parties.[56]

Grossman's initial assessment of the international turn to the right had a very Trotskyist flavor and recognized that class collaboration did not serve workers' interests. "Now, after the collapse of the IIIrd International because of events in Germany, in January 1933, an even more wretched policy follows—the Communist movement is subordinated to the Soviet Union's foreign policy and need for peace. The result: unprincipled opportunism in current policies in all countries. Nevertheless, I think that the working class will awake. A new world war rapidly approaches. It will end with a series of revolutionary uprisings."[57]

To Max Beer, he expressed similar sentiments and an attitude toward Trotskyism like that of the SAP at the time. The international Trotskyist movement had recently lost two of its most influential European sections, in Greece and Spain, and the small French section had split over a decision to enter the Socialist Party. "Sadly, the political situation is hopeless. The IIIrd International morally bankrupt, Trotskyism having perished miserably, other little groups without hope in the future of the workers' movement. In short we have to start the whole work from the beginning. But despite all this I am an *optimist* because the *objective* economic situation of capitalism is hopeless."[58] Grossman let Horkheimer, with his more abstract concerns, know that "I gave up the hope that the Muscovites would indicate a fruitful path in the area of philosophy. Over there, Stalin has to be celebrated as the greatest philosopher, the greatest economist, the greatest thinker in general."[59]

He soon referred to the contemporary degeneration of Russian planning and some of its results, "which have nothing to do with the socialist economy," while affirming its underlying principles.[60] In October 1935, Grossman wrote to Mattick that "the Stalinist bureaucracy doesn't please me either. I also have much, very much to confirm this." But because private property and private accumulation did not exist there he rejected Mattick's (in reality accurate) assertion that surplus value was extracted from workers in the USSR as sectarian. "Here in Europe everyone knows that the defeat of the Soviet Union would throw the workers' movement back 50 years. So one cannot *fight against* the SU as a 'surplus value producing state'; we have, rather, to *defend* the SU from the external enemy with all available means."[61]

Core members of the institute agreed that the international situation was appalling. Trying to raise Grossman's spirits in 1937, Leo Löwenthal, a member of the IfS since 1930, whom Horkheimer entrusted with particular responsibilities for editing its journal, wrote: "The only thing we have is to make that imagination [in thinking and feeling] useful for the theoretical goals which are dear to us."[62]

For Horkheimer's circle, a preoccupation with theory (substituting for religion as the "heart of a heartless world") provided consolation, as the miseries arising from capitalism, Hitler, and Stalin intensified from the mid-1930s. Grossman had a more Marxist orientation, the result of personal experiences that Horkheimer and his intimates did not share, believing that it was necessary to rebuild the workers' movement and that capitalism's own material contradictions, especially its proneness to economic crises, would make this possible. In other words, he remained committed to the recovery of Marxism to which he, Lenin, and Lukács had already made major contributions. For a few years, there was consistency between this commitment and his attitude to the Soviet Union, that is, his recognition that there had been a Stalinist counter-revolution in the USSR. But Grossman abandoned his negative views about the Soviet Union between October 1935 and November 1936, a period that saw the high points of the Communist International's Popular Front strategy.[63]

A Popular Front of radical Republicans, Socialists, Communists, and, to their left, the smaller Partido Obrero de Unificación Marxista (POUM, Workers' Party of Marxist Unification) won the Spanish elections in February 1936. An upsurge in class struggle followed. A similar wave of strike action occurred in May 1936 after the election of a Popular Front government in France, under Socialist Premier Léon Blum. The largest wave of industrial action in French history, culminating in widespread factory occupations, won workers large wage rises, shorter working hours, and, a breakthrough of international significance, paid annual leave.[64]

Franco's military uprising against the government of the Spanish Republic, on July 19, triggered a revolution. Workers' committees took over much of production, distribution, and public administration in regions where the coup had been repelled.[65] To avoid disturbing possible allies in France and England, the Comintern insisted that the civil war was about the defense of bourgeois democracy and that socialism was not on the agenda in Spain. The Spanish Communist Party and the Soviet Union (through Comintern personnel in Spain and its supply of arms to the Republic) used their influence to contain and undermine the institutions of workers' power. From May 1937, the Republican government and Spanish Communists actively suppressed the revolution, the POUM, and other organizations on the far left.

Despite the counter-revolutionary politics of the Spanish Communist Party, most ordinary Communists around the world still saw themselves as revolutionaries and their organizations' policies as a purely tactical matter.[66] The party and the Soviet Union, after all, supported the Republic's military effort against Franco's reactionary insurgents. While Nazi Germany and fascist Italy provided aid to Franco, Britain and France respected a formal international ban on the supply of arms to either side.

Grossman had condemned the new Popular Front strategy in France as early as November 1934, but events in Spain seem to have changed his mind about the Soviet Union and the communist movement. His response was conditioned by friendship with Ramos Sobrino and his recent trip to Valladolid and other parts of Spain. Valladolid fell to Franco's military coup on the first day. Here "the repression in Old Castile reached its maximum severity." Thousands of leftists and Republicans were executed, though Ramos Sobrino escaped.[67] In early 1936 the SAP also adopted a favorable attitude to the Popular Front tactic, although Grossman moved much farther toward to the politics of the Comintern.[68]

In late 1936 Borkenau delivered a public lecture to the Sociological Society in London about a trip he had recently made through Republican Spain. It confirmed Grossman's suspicions about him. To Horkheimer, Grossman denounced Borkenau for taking a "position against the [Republican] regime in Madrid." He was "in short, a dangerous fellow, a pronounced fascist!"[69] While the object of this attack was critical of the policies of the Popular Front government and had moved a long way from Marxism toward conservative liberalism, Borkenau was far from being a supporter of Franco. His book, *The Spanish Cockpit*, soon provided an objective description of the Stalinists' suppression of the revolution and radical left in Spain.[70] But Borkenau's liberal politics meant that many on the left were skeptical about his account of Spanish events.

Grossman's own views were now, in practice, "subordinated to the Soviet Union's foreign policy and need for peace." He accepted the Popular Front analysis that not revolution but only an alliance involving the communist movement, the USSR, and bourgeois democrats could provide an alternative to Franco. Emotional responses rather than independent analysis governed Grossman's attitude to the civil war in Spain. In December 1937, he wrote to Horkheimer that "I am under the influence of an event. A few weeks ago I was invited to a cocktail party at an Englishman's home, where I made the acquaintance of a Mrs Holand [sic]. She told me that her husband had gone to Madrid as a pilot. (He was a captain *of British Air Force* [English in the original]). I asked if he is a socialist. 'No, but he hates the fascists.' On the 16th, the newspapers brought the news that Holland had been shot down in his bomber! He has left behind a daughter!"[71]

From 1936 Grossman was an uncritical supporter of Russian foreign and domestic policy. Ilse Mattick (born Ilse Hamm), a friend from the late 1930s, remembered him as "a Stalinist down to the bone," espousing an "undying love of Stalin." He knew what was going on in Russia but thought it was right.[72] Among those murdered by Stalin were Karl Radek, Grossman's comrade in student politics, and Miron Isaakovich Nakhimson, who had invited him to the Soviet Union.[73] Yet in the belief that the Soviet Union was the only effective bulwark against fascism, he accepted the purges and Stalin's realpolitik as necessary to preserve the Russian state.

However, Grossman still did not toe the line on all questions of Marxist theory. The contradiction between his views on Russia and his commitment to certain basic Marxist propositions concerning the relationship between working-class self-activity and socialism reemerged. The support of the IfS, tremendous intellectual self-assurance, and confidence that Communists would eventually be persuaded by his arguments meant that, despite his delusions about the USSR, he continued to defend his heretical approach to crisis theory and to write studies that more consistent Stalinists were incapable of producing.

London and Economic Research

As early as September 1933, Grossman anticipated that war and the prospect of being interned in France might force him to leave Paris.[74] England, even though the Conservatives were in office, would be safer. He had already understood English in 1917, at the latest, so he could get by in London, although he always spoke the language with a strong accent and wrote it idiosyncratically.[75]

The institute had a small branch in London, run by the Marxist sociologist Jay Rumney (originally Jacob Rumyanek),[76] who became a friend of Grossman's. What is more, the city had the huge additional advantage, for research purposes, of the British Museum. Once he had completed his critique of Borkenau's book, the problem of the conservative collection policies of the Bibliothèque Nationale in Paris had reasserted itself. Grossman missed daily contact with his colleagues at the institute and looked forward to a reunion with them. Like Horkheimer, he regarded London as a stepping-stone to New York.[77]

Grossman started making preparations to move to London in 1935. Before deciding to leave Paris permanently, he made a two-week trip to investigate living arrangements across the English Channel. He contacted his friend Max Beer to ask for his support and that of the eminent economic historian and social reformer Professor Richard Tawney, with whom Grossman had already corresponded, in obtaining a visa.[78]

The reconnaissance proved successful, but the process of moving was drawn out and Grossman did not leave Paris until January 1936. Even then he left ten boxes of books behind with friends in Paris and it took weeks to find a decent place to live in London.

At first he stayed at 60 Belsize Park, then close by in a cultured boarding house at 9 Belsize Avenue, "where I can invite someone to tea."[79] Hampstead Heath was less than a kilometer away and, beyond it, Rumney's home in Highgate and Marx's grave in Highgate Cemetery. Grossman enjoyed strolls on the Heath and in Regents Park, particularly in the spring. After a short walk from home to the Belsize Park tube station, the Edgware Line took him straight to Euston Station, near the University of London and the British Museum, where he conducted much of his research.[80] London agreed with Grossman. After an initial depression, he settled in and felt "really good and immediately got stuck into work. For weeks I sit from 9.30 every day (I leave home at 9) until 4–4.30 in the British Museum. This week I also began to visit the library of the London School of Economics. I have not had such a good atmosphere for work as the reading room of the British Museum since Frankfurt. When I compare this with Paris, a real fight over every book, I regret that I did not come here earlier! And the pleasantness of the people too."[81] English academics offered a much warmer reception than Parisian professors. Harold Laski of the London School of Economics was well disposed to the institute and its members. Tawney, also of the LSE, invited Grossman to tea. He concluded that he had stayed in Paris "too long."[82]

In London Grossman's work focused on economic questions. For a while, in 1936, he was "fully caught up in 'money,' that is basically the money literature."[83] But before October 1936, he wrote four pages on the relationship between economic crises and fascism, and on the ineffectiveness of policies, like those of León Blum's Popular Front government in France, inspired by underconsumptionist theories. The result was a particularly concrete explanation of contemporary developments, based on his own theory of economic crises.

How is a crisis overcome? Not in any place or *at any time* through a sudden increase in the *purchasing power of consumers,* following which a boom sets in. In reality we see something entirely different: hundreds of attempts, of a partial or general nature, are made to restore *profitability,* that is to increase the difference between costs and prices . . . [One way to do this is by] reducing capital costs of machines, raw materials, *pushing down interest,* reducing taxes, reducing social services—and most importantly *pushing down wages!*

The other way is to increase prices by extending credit, destroying part of the product or restricting part of production . . .

Both paths are often taken at the same time. The *slowness* of the recovery confirms my theory that the duration of the crisis cannot be predicted and calculated, let alone the duration of the boom! . . . It depends on how quickly or slowly entrepreneurs identify where to make improvements, on the response of the government (reductions in interest and tax), on the strength or resistance of workers' organizations in relation to wage reductions, on the strength of cartels in relation to reductions in the prices of machines and raw materials, etc . . . If [workers] are tough in defending themselves, they slow the implementation of wage cuts—and thus the restoration of businesses' *profitability.*[84]

. . . Precisely in these developed countries with strong workers organizations fascism comes to the aid of capitalism.

. . . That is the role of German fascism. Wages, which were 44 billion Marks in 1928, fell (with roughly the same number of people employed) to 31 billion in 1935, i.e. by 13 billion or 30%. When the increases in the prices of food, clothing etc are taken into account, real wages fell even more, about 35–40%. And exactly for this reason profitability grew . . . i.e. to that extent the crisis was overcome!

Those who want increases in the purchasing power of workers do not operate in the real world and its causal relations, but in that of utopian "demands" which totally block the path to understanding fascism and its entire policy for saving capitalism.

The capitalist crisis is to be overcome, on the basis of capitalism, by demanding non-capitalist methods of distribution! One teaches the capitalists that, by forcing down wages they mistake their own interests. One advises them to *increase* wages—in their own interests!

But the "stupid" capitalists do not pay much attention to this advice. They seek to overcome the crisis through *wage cuts* and, to the extent that they succeed, *profitability* is restored pro rata and hence the ability of capitalist enterprise to function.[85]

Reflationary efforts in the United States, England, and Germany, Grossman later pointed out to Horkheimer, did not start by raising the working class's purchasing power, but on the contrary by openly or covertly *reducing the level of wages.* According to Premier Blum's underconsumptionist theory, the increases in wages and reductions in working hours won by French workers and supported by the government should have reflated the economy. In fact these policies "resulted in inflation and the uncompetitiveness of French industry. In short the failure of reflation. He had to take back the wage rises. As this was impossible, he stumbled into devaluation as a way out of the problem by cutting wages covertly . . . I believe that the thorough internment of underconsumptionist theory is important!"[86] In March 1937, Blum announced a pause in his entire reform program; on June 22 his government resigned. For Grossman, the "Blum experiment" demonstrated that "theory is, after all, not unworldly brooding, it should draw from experience! In the light of the facts, this experiment shows that purchasing power theory, i.e. underconsumptionist doctrine, suffers from a scandalous bankruptcy."[87]

Grossman did not develop these insights further, for where could he publish them, given that the *ZfS* "now has more sociological and less economic" content?[88] Another economic project, however, gave rise to a substantial study. Horkheimer suggested using the methodological part of his work on crises for an article to appear in a 1937 issue of the journal.[89] But Grossman, who had already celebrated a previous decadal anniversary of the publication of the first volume of *Capital*,[90] proposed a long and original piece to mark the book's seventieth birthday. It would argue that Marx had not perfected but rather revolutionized classical political economy, and identify the new features that differentiated his work from that of his predecessors and successors.[91]

In writing this piece, Grossman made use of research he had already done by 1926 (at the latest) and preparations for a course specifically on the relationship between Marx and Ricardo in 1928, as well as his own published studies.[92] Though concerned about the article's possible length and suggesting that the treatment of Marx's relationship to his successors could be left out, Horkheimer strongly approved of the suggestion.[93] This response was hardly surprising, as, consciously or unconsciously, Grossman was developing and radicalizing themes Horkheimer had addressed in a letter a year earlier and in the article "On the Problem of Truth."[94]

The letter had included a long summary of the article, contrasting traditional and dialectical logic. The example Horkheimer had used was Marx's incorporation of the categories of classical economics into a new theoretical structure that contradicted the static theory in which they had arisen. The summary noted how in Marx "concrete tendencies which drive towards decline are derived from the 'first' simple and general concepts, in a closed logical structure."[95] This, in turn, reflected Grossman's views about Marx's method.[96] Horkheimer was not a principal influence on Grossman, nor Grossman on Horkheimer. But, during the mid-1930s, their relationship was not just a matter of mutual support; their exchanges were also fruitful on both sides.

There were, however, major and growing differences between the political perspectives and temperaments of Grossman and Horkheimer. Thus the old Marxist militant recommended that a collection of Horkheimer's essays from the *ZfS* should be published as a book, so that wider circles could read his work. The journal was, unfortunately, rather inaccessible. He was pushing the institute's director toward greater practical political engagement: "Really, from an activist standpoint, you should be interested in confronting broad layers of young people. One should never forget that the victory of Cartesianism was not simply achieved through the power of pure thought but was supported in the university by the fists and clubs of Dutch students, who answered the brutal force of scholasticism with the similar force of their fists!"[97]

This commitment to practical polemics was apparent in Grossman's own published work, as far back as his involvement with the JSDP. His preference for participating in political and intellectual debates in a direct, open, and even blunt way was thoroughly out of sympathy with Horkheimer's approach to the institute's public profile. The director did not want to stir up hostility, especially in the United States, by proclaiming Marxist sympathies too openly. Over the following years, Horkheimer's concern to maintain a respectable front intensified and his political outlook shifted. When, in late 1938, the Marxist philosopher Ernst Bloch sought a position with the institute in New York, "Horkheimer said, quite openly, that Bloch's political views were too communist to make his appointment possible."[98]

Grossman's reference to the "fists and clubs of Dutch students" also provided a hint of concern about a question that Horkheimer had dealt with rather coyly. His article, "The Latest Attack on Metaphysics," mentioned that science had abandoned religious conceptions in the early seventeenth century, but did not explain how and why this had happened. It was, as Grossman emphasized, a matter of physical as well as intellectual struggle. The same issues arose in relation to contemporary revolutionary strategy. Horkheimer had accounted for the origins of "the dialectical theory of society"—code for Marxism—in the "will for a more human existence," in which "a higher spontaneity" is possible.[99]

Citing Marx's account of historical materialism in the preface and postscript to *Capital,* Grossman insisted that the laws of capitalist production are less determined by than determining human desires, consciousnesses, and views. "I know very well that these sentences do not contradict activism. But this is precisely, therefore, a problem that should be dealt with in an essay like yours." Grossman referred to Marx's *Economic and Philosophical Manuscripts* of 1844, recently published for the first time, to support the argument that people can only realize their species-being and employ their species-powers under socialism. In the prehistory of humanity, before socialism is achieved, the conditions of production alienate people from their nature and their capacities: capitalism stunts their development.[100] The structure of society subordinates conscious decision-making to economic laws.

Grossman wanted Horkheimer to provide an explicit account of how people can consciously shape society, given that the logic of capital accumulation seems to rule this out. For Grossman, with his experience in working-class organizations and competence in economic theory, two elements in such an explanation were obvious: class struggle and economic crisis. But Horkheimer's vagueness about the "will for a more human existence" signaled that he was moving away from Marxism. In the postscript to his letter, Grossman wrote: "I would be very pleased to hear your view on this point." Horkheimer did not respond.[101]

While living in Paris and London, Grossman took his other responsibilities to the institute seriously, maintaining involvement through contact with Horkheimer, Löwenthal, and Pollock. He kept Horkheimer informed about developments affecting the IfS and its reputation, sending articles and book reviews clipped from newspapers. In 1933 he encouraged Paul Mattick to promote contact between the U.S. Marxist philosopher Sidney Hook and Horkheimer.[102]

Particularly through his warm correspondence with Leo Löwenthal, its editor, Grossman also assisted with the publication of the *ZfS*. He liaised with Koyré about an article, commented on manuscripts submitted by Mattick, Emil Grünberg (Carl's son), Max Beer, and Walter Braeuer, and suggested books that could be reviewed.[103] At least initially, Grossman facilitated the publication of Mattick's reviews in the journal.

On intellectual matters, Grossman was ruthlessly honest with his friends. The essay Braeuer had submitted to the journal was, he reported, "worthless," as he had told Braeuer himself.[104] When Löwenthal asked for comments on a draft of his own review of a book about the historical significance of the invention of the horse harness, Grossman observed that his colleague was writing about a topic which "you have not mastered" and giving credence to a preposterous argument.[105] To reinforce this point, in a subsequent letter, Grossman explained the difference between Marxism and technological determinism. The published review did not, however, indicate that Löwenthal had accepted this somewhat brutal advice.[106]

Grossman also made observations about several articles after their publication in the journal. He praised many of Horkheimer's contributions, but was very critical of an article on jazz by "Hektor Rottweiler." This guard dog of high culture rejected jazz as a capitalist commodity that reinforced alienation and the subjection of the individual to the collective. "I must confess," Grossman wrote, "that the essay by Rottweiler (whom I don't know) seems entirely mistaken. Too much uninteresting technical shoptalk, behind which there is almost no sociological analysis. We all knew that jazz did not come out of Africa but was produced in capitalist centers." Without a serious discussion of the social history and contemporary context of jazz, he implied, the combination of an analysis of its musical characteristics and abstract comments about its commodity form were hardly the basis for drawing serious conclusions.[107]

In reply to Grossman, Horkheimer strongly endorsed the article and revealed, in confidence, that Teddy Wiesengrund (Theodor Adorno) was the author. Grossman had some understanding of this area. He may not have had Adorno's professional musical training, but classical music was one of the pleasures of his life. He diplomatically reaffirmed his position in a reply to Horkheimer. "Dr. Schön," his wife, and "Mathias Seiber" had recently visited. It was not just himself, he gave Horkheimer to understand, who was critical of the jazz article.[108] Ernst Schoen had not only been the cultural director of Southwest German Radio, but was also a musician. Mátyás Seiber, the Hungarian cellist and composer, had taught a famous class in the theory and practice of jazz at Hoch's Conservatory in Frankfurt.

Work, leisure, and politics were intertwined for Grossman. The best-seller *Gone with the Wind* related to his research on slavery. The author, Margaret Mitchell, he wrote to Horkheimer,

> knows the milieu of the slaveholders and plantation owners and accurately shows that the loss of the war against the Yankees signified a real social revolution for the plantation owners. What she presents entirely falsely is the situation of the Negroes. What she presents is just the *house Negroes,* for personal service, and here too (even if the situation of these Negroes was better) she idealized things too much. Slavery demoralized not only the enslaved but also their masters. It wasn't as "nice" as Mitchell wants it. It wasn't so seldom that when guests visited, one said "good night" offering them not only a candle but, as an expression of hospitality, an attractive slave woman too . . .
>
> But the main issue in the problem was not house slaves but *plantation slaves.* You don't get a word out of Mitchell about this—only a gentle reminder in the refusal of the house slaves to work in the fields because that they weren't "field hands" . . .
>
> And indeed the supply of slaves: the slave *trade* and slave *smuggling* with all their horrors. Finally slave breeding. Slave breeding factories existed, where

slaves were produced as pigs or horses are raised today on farms. Sweet Mitchell doesn't breathe a tiny word about any of this.

Not to mention the peculiar morality that Mrs Mitchell justifies: shoot a vagabond marauder just because he *wanted* to steal. Naturally her Captain Butler immediately gives her absolution. Skarlett didn't have *any other alternative!*

Where it is a matter of maintaining the elevated social position of landowners, any ruthlessness is justified to avoid being declassed!

. . . The book is interesting, in places exciting—it doesn't have any artistic value.[109]

The following year, Grossman's interest in slavery was expressed rather differently, in a published review of a recent collection of Marx and Engels' writings on the U.S. Civil War. He offered a lucid outline of their analysis of the conflict, emphasizing that, although other issues were involved, it was fundamentally about the incompatibility of production relations based on slavery and on free labor.[110]

Although he was able to get on with economic research and establish a small circle of friends in London, Grossman was delighted to receive Horkheimer's invitation to go to New York in the autumn of 1937. He planned to visit the United States in October, initially on a tourist visa. "I don't have to reassure you how much I am looking forward to this, not only on objective grounds, although I hope to gain considerable stimulation for my work through discussions."[111] After the good initial reception, England had disappointed him. As early as November 1936 he agreed that England had "*no art* (neither painting nor architecture nor music),"[112] perhaps he had taken his summer vacation in the Netherlands for this reason. His ironic sense of humor was apparent when he later wrote: "The English mentality—I haven't seen anything so narrow minded for ages—is *à la longue* unbearable. . . A small clique of conservatives knows how to impose their manners, mode of life and thought on the great mass of the people. Everyone only wants to be 'a gentleman' and becomes one by wearing white flannel trousers on Sunday and playing tennis and only speaking in short, disjointed words, but if possible remaining silent. The silence of the cemetery!"[113]

So Grossman, committed to the institute, active on its behalf, and keen to contribute to its activities, was "looking forward a great deal to being in the circle of old Frankfurt friends again."[114] Horkheimer's feelings, expressed to Adorno in early 1937, were not so warm: "we have always regarded him, however, as a loner."[115]

On October 14, 1937, Grossman landed in New York and quickly contributed theses to an institute seminar series on monopoly capitalism.[116] His observations drew on arguments in *The Law of Accumulation,* highlighting the declining ratio between the mass of profit and accumulated capital that leads to foreign investment. If the rate of accumulation is sustained, an ever smaller proportion and eventually declining mass of surplus value is available for the consumption of capitalists, who consequently seek to sustain their living standards by cutting wages and hence sharpening the class struggle. Lower rates of profit on borrowed capital lead to financial crises for borrower countries and debt reduction through currency devaluation. The same conditions result in greater centralization and concentration of capital as different sectors try to achieve higher prices and profitability at the expense of their customers. Tariff walls, abandonment of the gold standard, as countries seek to reduce the prices of their products through currency devaluation and regulation, are means of international competition that split the world market into separate territories. Devaluations also serve to undermine wages in countries with strong trade unions. Capitalism moves from a phase of expansion to one of contraction, when the profitability of a small minority of owners is achieved at the expense of higher levels of unused capacity in heavy industry, the destruction of large amounts of commodities and capital, the restriction of agricultural production, and the denial of minimal conditions of existence to the masses of the unemployed.[117]

Experience of the seminar, the institute in New York, and the city itself dissolved any reservations Grossman may have had about remaining in America. But, because he had entered the United States on a visitor's visa, he had to leave in order to return on a more permanent basis. He took a cruise to Havana, in April 1938, anticipating a very brief stay to deal with the bureaucratic formalities involved in getting an immigrant visa.

There were unexpected delays. The problem was that Grossman, unlike other members of the institute, had a Polish rather than a German passport. Warsaw had to be telegraphed about a visa number. Initially, Grossman went swimming and took in the sights until it was sorted out. "The tropical fruits and fantastically beautiful colors of the sea. Here you can understand the splendid colors of a Gauguin. One is bewitched by this natural splendor." "Cuban women exceptionally beautiful in the magnificence of their bodies and the rhythm of their walk." He also reported to his colleagues in New York impressions of the economic and cultural dependence of Cuba on the United States, living standards, the related extent of prostitution and, on the basis of the large range of Spanish language newspapers, magazines, and books, the vibrancy of Cuban intellectual life.[118]

The visa formalities did not, however, go smoothly. Nor, as Grossman had not taught in the last two years, did the immigration regulations recognize his professorial status. Having fled the Nazis' racism in Germany, the racism of the U.S. ruling class—in the form of the Johnson-Lodge Immigration Act[119]—was keeping him offshore on the other side of the Atlantic. Confronted by the prospect of a delay of weeks, he became depressed and, on top of this, suffered from sunburn. There was no garden nearby with trees under which he could read: "Yes, the palms are very attractive, but they don't provide any shade or moisture." Grossman's enthusiasm for his work, new experiences, and life were always matched by a capacity for gloom. In letters to Löwenthal, in whom he confided more than Horkheimer, he had mentioned periods of depression triggered by news of the defeat of the workers' rising in Vienna in early 1934; unexplained circumstances later in the year; then problems with finding lodgings and the rainy London climate in 1936.[120]

Members of the institute provided practical assistance and moral support for their stranded associate's campaign to get a visa. Horkheimer passed on advice "that you appear to the consul with a cheerful expression and conduct yourself with the courteousness of a Polish grandee, which is in any case typical of you, and in no way betray your depression." When the visa finally came through, after three weeks, Pollock sent a congratulatory telegram, from "Horkheimer and the others."[121]

After arriving back in New York on May 10,[122] Grossman eventually set up house in a three-room apartment at 64/521 West 111 Street, within a kilometer of the institute's offices at 429 West 117th, Columbia University, and Central Park. Without a room at the institute, he worked from home and kept his library there. Less than a month after his return to the United States, he applied for first citizenship papers, although he never sought to be naturalized.[123]

Ilse Hamm, a young German exile he befriended in New York, remembered him as a very private person, with a deep feeling for the classical art of the eighteenth and nineteenth centuries and a serious interest in music. He was very knowledgeable and interesting to listen to, she found, though one did not get much of an opportunity to engage in discussion, as he was extremely full of himself and very vain: the bookshelves around the room in which he entertained visitors contained the books he had written in fancy parchment bindings. He "couldn't bear it if his socks didn't match his curtains." But Grossman was also generous and kind: patient and considerate in helping her to get her bearings in the United States.[124]

With Grossman's help one of his closest and oldest friends also joined him in New York.[125] On the annexation of Austria by Nazi Germany, his cousin the social democratic medical practitioner Oskar Kurz was arrested simply because he was Jewish. Like many other Austrian Jews, he left the country soon after his release.[126]

In the New World

The dominant theoretical perspectives at the institute, that is, Horkheimer's views, were still changing when Grossman settled in New York. This had important implications for their relationship. From the late 1920s Horkheimer's writing had concentrated on critiques of contemporary philosophy from a Marxist standpoint and, as we have seen, Grossman had a high regard for this work. But in an important 1937 essay, "Traditional and Critical Theory," the institute's director separated dialectical thought from the working class and its experience.[127]

Over the next three years, Horkheimer's outlook became increasingly conservative. He abandoned historical materialism and the idea that the working class could liberate society. Theodor Adorno became his closest collaborator.[128] Their work together was pessimistic, aphoristic, hostile to the Marxist project of human liberation through conscious class struggle. Indeed, they rejected the entire enlightenment commitment to a scientific understanding of the world. When Horkheimer departed New York to live in Los Angeles from April 1941, he left behind not only administrative duties—delegated to Pollock—but also most of what remained of his previous political commitments.

In New York, before Horkheimer's departure, Grossman was far from being a part of the inner institute circle that sympathized with its director's views. The Marxist economist's work was, nevertheless, initially regarded as significant for the IfS. A list of books by members of the institute, to be completed between mid-1938 and 1940, featured Grossman's second volume on crisis theory, which would demonstrate that even in a static economy the uneven pace of replacement of fixed capital was a factor giving rise to crises.[129] But, having incorporated many of the results planned for the second volume into the essay on Marx's relationship with his predecessors, from 1939 Grossman mainly worked on different projects, among them a study of the origins of modern science and a book on the social structure of society in the thirteenth and fourteenth centuries and the beginnings of bourgeois society.[130]

Grossman's international reputation was still an asset for the institute, given the limited public recognition of its other members. His work had been translated into Japanese, Czech, and, thanks to the efforts of Yugoslav Marxists, Serbo-Croatian. Believing that he was destitute after fleeing from Nazi Germany, the comrades in Belgrade had even offered to send Grossman monthly financial contributions. Spanish Marxists had also established contact in 1933.[131] Awareness of his work in Marxist theory also spread in the United States, partly because he and other left-wing German academics now lived there. Without fully grasping it, a Howard University academic in 1939 attempted to employ Grossman's explanation of the method used in *Capital* in an article on Marx's treatment of the middle class.[132]

Two influential and very widely circulated U.S. surveys of Marxist economics were far more significant in drawing attention to his work. While unconvinced by his arguments about economic crises, William Blake, from 1942 a personal friend, acknowledged Grossman as "a true scholar and economist and a deep student of Marx" in his 1939 *Elements of Marxian Economic Theory and Its Criticism*. Blake endorsed Grossman's explanation of the structure of *Capital*.[133] Paul Sweezy's *The Theory of Capitalist Development* addressed these issues too, along with Grossman's account of imperialism.[134]

Relations with Horkheimer and other members of the institute continued to be pleasant during the late 1930s and Grossman happily participated in joint activities.[135] He also found new friends and contacts in New York. Between 1938 and 1940, the German philosopher and fellow communist sympathizer Ernst Bloch was in the city and associated, like Grossman, with the circles of émigré German communist intellectuals, which expanded after the Nazi victory over France in 1940.[136] Grossman provided some assistance to Edgar Zilsel, a younger, Austrian historian of science, among others.[137] One of Grossman's pleasures was entertaining his colleagues and other people at "tea evenings" in his apartment.[138] Another was photography, though he conceded to the professional photographer Lotte Jacobi, whose work he purchased and with whom he corresponded, that his efforts were nowhere near as artistically successful as hers.[139]

Grossman had particularly warm feelings for the Löwenthal family, especially Leo's son Daniel, whose stamp collecting he assisted. Even while trapped in Havana, Grossman sent "a few Russian and Cuban stamps, which I received from a Russian friend here." Later, in response to Löwenthal's concern that some stamps had been purchased as a gift for his son, Grossman replied, "In relation to the stamps for Daniel, you are in error. I lie often and with pleasure. When I tell the truth, however, no one believes me."[140]

While conducting small classes for students associated with Columbia University in his apartment for a period until late 1941,[141] Grossman remained a diligent member of the IfS. Between 1938 and 1942 he wrote nine book reviews for the institute's journal, in addition to polishing the long article on the essence of Marx's originality and researching other topics. One review was his summary of Marx and Engels on the Civil War in the United States. Two dealt with issues in the history of science. Six were related to crisis theory.[142] In these, he expressed a consistent Marxist perspective, which is more than can be said of many of the other contributions to the journal that dealt with economic issues.

This Marxist outlook was apparent in Grossman's correspondence with colleagues from his vacation explorations of the north-east of the United States.
He not only sent postcards, but generalized from his experiences and investigations, as he had during his trips to Spain and Cuba. Apart from mentioning
horse riding, rowing, and more sunburn, he reported from upstate New York
in August 1938 on his visit to the historic ruins at Fort Ticonderoga, a site of
battles during the Anglo-French War and the American Revolution. "Unfortunately, the museum does not keep the scalps the Indians took from the French
for which they received money from the English! A pity, they would have been
a nice illustration of historical morality and virtue!"[143]

In the summer of 1939 he wrote about the sociology of resorts, particularly
contrasts between sexual relations at Tallwood, on Lake Maranacook in Maine,
and Timberlands in the Adirondaks.

> Here [in Tallwood] flirting and the sexual question only play a subordinate
> role—in the tradition of flirting in summer resorts. What I saw in Timberland is
> an organized market—demand and supply—no flirting, no "romance," as por-
> trayed in the film *Have a nice time.* Everything is "rationalized" to the point of
> being out of control. The specific economic circumstances under which such an
> organized market for sexual life arises: the era of the secretary who has no
> prospect of marrying. Nor does she wait for a husband—but is determined to
> use her youth up on amusement. No old fashioned "romance," no. They are
> beyond that. No ties lasting longer than several days! They want to have a free
> hand: they look for a different partner for the afternoon and yet another for the
> night. Intellectual qualities don't play any role at all: the *girls* look at a man with
> the eye of a slave trader: a man must be *big and strong.*
>
> You can imagine the future, when these features are generally dominant! 20
> year old *girls* are sarcastic or even cynical *in puncto* "love." They don't know any-
> thing about it. They only know sex. For the man that is very convenient. From a
> social standpoint it is a catastrophe. I believe a symptom of a declining capitalist
> world.[144]

Although dramatized for humorous effect, Grossman was obviously scandal-
ized by what the young Jewish women at Timberland were up to. It was worlds
away from his "Central European gallantry: the hand kissing and bowing."[145] His
own relationships, however, had not been and were still not entirely conventional. In New York he had a lover for a number of years and mentioned their
relationship to Ilse Hamm, who thought "he accumulated women because of his
ego, but did not necessarily like them." As a platonic friend, he tried to dissuade
Ilse from marrying Paul Mattick, because "he is a sectarian." But "Sectarian or
not, he was always cordial and thoughtful in relation to Paul (+ me)."[146]

Theoretical, political, and financial factors eventually converged to create tensions in relations between Grossman and his colleagues at the institute. Horkheimer, Weil, Pollock, and Löwenthal can be understood as traditional intellectuals, among the more modest of the working class's ideological conquests, at least for a time attracted to Marxism in the course of the upheavals at the end of World War I, but without experience of the organized labor movement. Theodor Adorno, somewhat younger, had an even more abstract appreciation of Marxism. By the late 1930s, their Marxist publications were not well known. In this respect, the sunk costs of their intellectual investments in Marxism were relatively low. Following the counter-revolution in Russia and the rise of the Nazis, they drifted away from a materialist perspective. "In the 1940s, Horkheimer and Adorno depart[ed] from the Marxist theoretical tradition," which was still evident in their earlier critical theory phase, to focus on "the world-historical drama of the active confrontation of the human species with nature."[147] Leo Löwenthal later recalled, "We didn't feel that we had deserted the revolution, but rather that the revolution had deserted us."[148]

Grossman responded to the defeat of the Russian revolution and the German labor movement very differently. An organic intellectual of the working class at an early age, he was recognized internationally for his contributions to Marxist theory, despite widespread criticism of his account of economic crises. Experience of several periods of advance and retreat in the class struggle equipped him to deal with the appalling setbacks of the 1930s. Henryk Grossman continued to advocate working class revolution, even if his position was distorted by illusions in the Soviet Union. There remained a close connection between his commitment to working-class self-emancipation and his contributions to Marxist economics and crisis theory. Where Horkheimer's Frankfurt school gave up historical materialism and belief in the working class's ability to liberate humanity, Grossman deluded himself that these were compatible with Stalinism and hoped to convince Communists of the correctness of his views on economics.[149]

Growing intellectual differences between Grossman and Horkheimer and his circle were compounded by the state of the institute's finances. The very impressive resources of the IfS survived not only the Depression but exile in excellent condition; Lukács called the institute the "Abyss Grand Hotel."[150] Grossman received welcome New Year bonuses in 1935 and 1936, on top of his normal salary.[151] His income in 1940 was $2,857, well over twice the level of average earnings for full-time employees.[152] But the institute's investment strategy, formulated by Pollock, ran into difficulties in the late 1930s.[153] The problems coincided with the 1938 downturn in the U.S. economy, which, according to Pollock's theory of organized capitalism, should not have happened.

The institute's financial crisis led to staff cuts. As director, Horkheimer still acted on the belief that the supreme task of the IfS was to preserve his own well-being and hence capacity to produce theory. Horkheimer's and Pollock's deliberate disinformation and divide and rule tactics created stress and uncertainty among institute members. "Many of the staff were left confused and insecure by more or less secretive hints dropped about the Institute's impending financial collapse, and by obscure reductions in their salaries."[154]

Even those with unquestioned personal loyalty to the institute's managers were not spared. "After a discussion with Pollock in September 1941, Löwenthal was left in tears because Pollock had told him about plans for his future in such an unfriendly way, and Adorno was very disturbed that everything had been left hanging in the air for months."[155]

The Hitler-Stalin Pact and the outbreak of World War II led Horkheimer to make more open and sweeping criticisms of the Soviet Union as an authoritarian state.[156] While Stalin's foreign policy in this period disillusioned large numbers of Communist Party members and sympathizers, it did not alter Grossman's attitude to Russia. He accepted the pact, the partition of Poland between Germany and Russia, and Stalin's occupation of the Baltic states and Finland as maneuvers necessary to preserve the Soviet Union. A major political gulf therefore opened up between Grossman and the group around Horkheimer, who were appalled by this turn in Soviet foreign policy. Grossman took issue not only with their criticism of Stalinism but also their increasingly conservative perspectives.[157]

When a proposal for a project on "Cultural Aspects of National Socialism" was put to the Rockefeller foundation in early 1941, Grossman was not to be a principal contributor, only "an adviser for economic history, statistics, and economics for all sections where such problems may enter."[158] This marginalization was one of the factors that led to a turning point in his relations with the institute. Grossman was angry about this and over the fact that his pay had been cut by 16 percent.[159] He accused Pollock of a series of affronts and of having opposed his move from London to New York. At Grossman's birthday party, on April 14, 1941, there was a confrontation between the two economists, the "60th birthday incident."[160] Given Pollock's modus operandi, this may well have been a deliberate provocation to discourage Grossman from continuing his association with the institute. But he was the veteran of PPSD chicanery more sophisticated than this, undertaken by far more experienced and competent operators: Horkheimer and Pollock would not get him off the IfS payroll so easily. He withdrew from most forms of collaboration with the institute, but did not resign.

Capitalist Dynamics and Evolutionist Economics

Grossman had sent a long draft of his article, originally planned for the seventieth anniversary of *Capital*, to New York by May 1937. It remained unpublished, largely because issues of the *ZfS* consistently failed to appear on time and then because of the Nazi occupation of Paris.[161] By 1939, Horkheimer and Adorno, in particular, had concluded that Marxist economics was significant not as a means to understand concrete developments in capitalist societies but only as an ironic demonstration of its contradictions.[162] In November 1941, Grossman called an end to the delays. He threatened that, if the essay did not appear by Christmas, it would be published as a book in English, with a preface explaining how the institute had sabotaged it for two years.[163] A version of the study was, at least in part, translated, but the institute finally issued eighty duplicated copies of *Marx, Classical Political Economy and the Problem of Dynamics* (*Dynamics*) in German, dated 1941.[164]

Löwenthal was responsible for publishing the essay and had to bear the brunt of Grossman's outrage at the postponements of its publication. He had a low opinion of *Dynamics* and described the economist to Horkheimer as "totally meshugge [crazy]" and "psychotic."[165] In a later, self-contradictory outburst, he maintained that Grossman "is obsessed with monomaniac ideas of persecution. I think we should pension him off by October 1st."[166] Horkheimer thought Grossman "a bit crazy" but was, from California, far less vehement about him.[167]

As a sequel to *The Law of Accumulation*, presenting the arguments Grossman had earlier foreshadowed for the second volume of the book,[168] *Dynamics* identified and vindicated Marx's fundamental contribution to the understanding of the capitalist economy and his relationship to classical political economy. The essay dealt with two related issues. The first was the importance of the dialectic between use and exchange value, a topic neglected in the preceding Marxist literature and at the heart of Grossman's recovery of the revolutionary element in Marx's economic theory. His analysis of this question drew on insights already expressed in his 1919 lecture, years of subsequent teaching, and publications on Marx's economic theory and place in the history of economic thought.[169] The second issue was Marx's conception of capitalism as a dynamic system.

A sketch of four phases Marx had distinguished in the history of political economy and its relationship to class conflicts opened the study. The first phase, of classical political economy inspired by the struggle of the emerging industrial bourgeoisie against the old feudal order, gave rise to important insights into the nature of capitalism, notably the distinction between productive and unproductive labor and a labor theory of value. The subsequent three phases, of vulgar political economy, retreated from these achievements as the bourgeoisie began to participate in state power, and coped with the first working-class organizations and then serious conflicts with workers. Particularly after 1848, bourgeois political economists tended to retreat into the atheoretical descriptions of the historical school or a purely subjective theory of value, which gave rise, from the 1870s, to the mathematized, marginalist economics that still dominates the profession in the twenty-first century.[170]

Marx, Grossman explained, had neither completed Ricardo's system, nor undertaken a socialist critique of capitalism using Ricardo's concepts. In fact, Marx regarded the classical economists' preoccupation with the law of value—the idea that commodities exchange in accord with the amount of labor embodied in them—as accepting the mystified appearance of capitalism which, by focusing on exchange value and the market, passed over the unequal relations between workers and capitalists in production. "The point is not to eliminate the mystifying factor and substitute another category for it, but rather to explain the necessary connection between the two and hence what is deceptive in the phenomenon of value. Because capitalist reality is a dual reality, possessing a mystifying and a non-mystifying side, which are bound together into a concrete unity, any theory which reflects this reality must likewise be a unity of opposites."[171]

In 1923 and 1924, Korsch, Lukács, and Grossman himself had seen a fundamental achievement of Marx's analysis in its ability to account for both the material *realities* and the fetishized surface *appearances* of capitalism, for both the logic of capital accumulation and the mystifications of bourgeois economics.[172] One of Marx's key insights, which had made this possible, was to understand the production process as the unity of a labor process (creating use values) and a valorization process (creating value and hence exchange value).[173] Marx had identified the contrast between labor and labor power, the use value and exchange value sides of workers selling their ability to work, as his "decisive discovery" and the foundation of his understanding of the capitalist mode of production.[174]

In 1936, Grossman had explained to Horkheimer that Marx wanted not to complete but rather to revolutionize the categories of classical political economy. His discovery extended beyond identifying the use value and exchange value sides of human labor to an analysis of the dual character of the commodity, the production process, the reproduction of social capital, capital itself, and the organic composition of capital.[175] In his essay, Grossman pointed out that understanding the two-fold nature of economic phenomena entails criticism of "previous theory for only looking at individual, isolated sectors, instead of grasping the concrete totality of economic relations." Furthermore, "Marx's critique of Ricardo's categories of value, and the changes he made closely resembles Marx's critique and transformation of Hegel's dialectic."[176]

In a draft of *Dynamics,* the affinities between Grossman's approach to Marxist economics, Korsch's and Lukács's contributions to Marxist philosophy, and also Lenin's recovery of Marxist politics was particularly apparent. All returned to Marx by identifying the working class dialectically not only as an object of the historical process but also as a creative subject. Grossman insisted that "in the labor process, labor takes the form not of a tool, but 'labor itself appears as *the dominant activity*,' here the world of objects does not control labor; rather all of the means of production are subordinate to labor."[177]

His lecture to the Academy of Sciences had already outlined the argument now spelled out in more detail. The contradiction between the use and exchange value aspects of commodities, when these commodities take the form of capital, gives rise to "the necessity of periodic crises at the stage of simple reproduction."[178] That contradiction also underpinned the main point he had made in *The Law of Accumulation.*

> When seen in connection with the presentation of the development of the productive power of labor in Volume I, the presentation of the tendency of the rate of profit to fall in Volume III of *Capital* shows that Marx also derives this category from the dual character of labor, namely the inverse movement of the mass of use values and values as a consequence of the increase in the productive power of labor: the richer a society becomes, the greater the development of the productive power of labor, the larger the volume of useful articles which can be manufactured in a given period of labor; however, at the same time, the value of these articles becomes smaller. And since the development of the productive power of labor means that a constantly growing mass of means of production (MP) is set in motion by a relatively constantly falling mass of labor (L), the unpaid portion of labor (surplus value or profit) must progressively fall.[179]

Classical political economy and its mainstream successors were misleading because they focused on the value side of economic activity, excluding the real labor process. Yet, "the life of the working class depends on the mass of use-values which can be bought with a capital," because its survival requires the consumption of specific use values (food, clothing, shelter, etc.). As Marx wrote, "By denying the importance of gross revenue, i.e. the volume of production and consumption—apart from the [value-]surplus—and hence denying the importance of life itself, political economy's abstraction reaches the peak of infamy."[180] But it was with the flight from concepts that might threaten prevailing property relations, into psychology—the subjective theory of value—and efforts to turn economics into an exact science by means of mathematics, that political economy reached a peak of abstraction.[181]

The second major issue in *Dynamics,* already noted in *The Law of Accumulation,* was the contrast between the dynamic nature of Marx's economic system and the static approach of contemporary marginalist economics.[182] It was and remains one of the most impressive critiques of the methodological underpinnings of the body of ideas known as economics in most universities and the media.[183]

Grossman established how and why mainstream mathematical economics simply cannot fully encompass capitalist social relations. Both the Austrian and neoclassical schools share the marginalist assumption that consumer demand is the determining element and that economies tend to reach a meaningful equilibrium.[184] Behind their appeal to equilibrium lies "the need to justify the existing social order as a 'reasonable,' 'self-regulating' mechanism, in the context of which the concept of 'self-regulation' was intended to direct attention away from the actually prevailing chaos of the destruction of capital, bankruptcy of firms and factories, mass unemployment, insufficient capital investment, currency crises, and the arbitrary distribution of wealth."[185]

Marx had recognized that the dual nature of the production process gave rise to disequilibrium rather than equilibrium, and that this was the key to the dynamic of the capitalist system.[186] His approach necessarily incorporated the dimension of time (excluded from the dominant theory): capital is advanced as money, a representation of exchange value, but has to be successively transformed into elements of production and then finished products. The periods of time during which capital, in its circuit, assumes the forms of different use values affect the rate of profit.[187]

Within this framework, Grossman argued, an equilibrium situation will only be possible if a number of implausible conditions are met. The exchange values of commodities and the techniques with which they are produced (as use values) will have to remain constant. The turnover times of fixed and circulating capital in different industries will have to be the same, despite the fact that the lives of different commodities (as use values) have different durations. Difficulties in meeting these conditions already arise under simple reproduction, where the scale of output does not increase, even before the complication of capital accumulation is introduced.[188]

Then there is the problem of achieving simultaneous equilibrium in the valorization process and the labor process.[189] "The influence of the dominant theory has meant," however "that Marxist literature has also dealt with the problem of equilibrium—insofar as its conditions are specified in Marx's

'Tableau Economique' [his reproduction schemes in volume 2 of *Capital*]—exclusively in terms of value. (Kautsky, Hilferding, Bauer, Luxemburg, Bukharin)."[190] Marx, on the other hand, insisted there has to be a technical as well as a value proportionality in production: the value of means of consumption and the value of means of production not only have to be produced in the right ratios, the specific machines and raw materials employed at different stages of production and the specific goods workers consume to sustain life also have to be produced in the correct proportions. "Marx shows that the value-equilibrium, which is asserted by all static theories, and which the economy is supposed to tend towards, can only be established by chance or exception. This is because the technical labor-process gives rise to resistances and blockages of an objective and enduring kind which, in principle, exclude the establishment of such an equilibrium."[191]

At greater length than in his early presentation on crises, Grossman also explained how the price mechanism, under conditions of large-scale and concentrated production, could intensify economic disequilibrium as firms compete for market share by increasing output and using new technology, even in the face of declining demand.[192] The expansion of production and the resulting increase in the organic composition of capital reduce the likelihood of simultaneous equilibrium in the valorization and labor processes even further.[193] Other features of capitalist production have the same effect. The normally uneven advances in the techniques of production in different industries will stand in the way of proportional expansion across the economy. The material characteristics of production mean, furthermore, that there is a minimum amount of accumulated value that has to be invested in specific sectors.[194] For example, the surplus value accumulated over a year may be sufficient to expand a clothing factory by an additional number of cutting and sewing machines. But a steel mill may have to accumulate over several years before it can invest in a new furnace and related equipment.

Finally, "a uniform proportional expansion of all the spheres of production rests on the hidden assumption that demand (consumption) can also be expanded in an even and proportional manner." This was an argument Grossman developed in response to Helene Bauer's critique of *The Law of Accumulation*. "No one who finds two tractors sufficient for the cultivation of their land will buy four simply because their price has fallen by half, as the demand for tractors—all things being equal—is not a function of their price, but of the acreage of land."[195]

"All these moments," Grossman concluded, "serve to make a uniformity of motion of the technical and value aspects impossible to achieve, and to hinder the dual proportioning of the development of the productive apparatus, in both value and quantitative terms, which is postulated by economic theory as the condition for 'equilibrium' . . . Under such circumstances equilibrium, the 'rule' which is presupposed by political economy, can, as it were, only occur by chance within the general irregularity, as a momentary transitory point in the midst of constant disequilibrium."[196]

Although the publication of Grossman's impressive essay removed an immediate irritation in his relations with the institute, it did nothing to reduce the underlying tensions.[197] When Horkheimer wrote in a friendly tone, in April 1943, telling him about an institute project on anti-Semitism in the United States, funded by the conservative American Jewish Committee, Grossman was unimpressed. Having thanked Horkheimer for his birthday greetings and a bottle of Scotch, he replied that he did not know "if you are interested in the Jewish Project only in so far as several thousand dollars can be earned through it." In any case, "I am deeply convinced that now is not the time for theoretical studies of anti-Semitism. It is time for swift *political* action by Jews. We are well enough informed about the motives behind fascist, anti-Semitic agitation. One must and can *act*. If Jews don't do that, no theoretical project (even the best imaginable) will help and Jews will have to expect many evil experiences."[198]

The political hostilities were mutual. Horkheimer, Pollock, and Weil grew concerned that the publisher of Grossman's planned English edition of *Dynamics* might be procommunist. That could discredit the institute.[199] For Horkheimer this was now more than a matter of public appearances: over the previous decade, his caution had evolved into a desire for apolitical respectability, associated with distaste for left-wing engagement.[200]

A very large, early draft of *Dynamics* had dealt with the question of whether one of Marx's original contributions had been to historicize economics. But this material was pruned out before publication.[201] It was extended and developed in "The Evolutionist Revolt against Classical Economics,"[202] which Horkheimer labeled "a most rotten piece of work."[203] Like *Dynamics*, Grossman's latest study clarified the originality of Marx's contribution to social theory. It challenged two false conceptions: that Marx was the first to introduce a historical perspective into economics; and that this was due to the influence of Hegel on Marx. Much of the essay dealt with the question of "how dynamic or evolutionary thinking actually entered the field of economics."[204]

The most influential works of classical political economy, including those of Adam Smith and Ricardo, did not recognize that economic development took the form of successive modes of production. "The classicists took a rationalistic rather than a genetic approach to the past. All previous societies were measured with the rational yardstick of free trade. That is why they knew of only two ideal states: the 'original state of things', occurring before the fall from grace, as it were, and the bourgeois state in their own days, of more or less free trade and competition."[205]

There were theorists outside the mainstream of political economy, in both France and England, whose views were shaped by the political revolutions in America and France, and the industrial revolution in England. So, "the subject of our analysis is a current of thinking which emerged in the social sciences during the last third of the eighteenth century and became triumphant during the first half of the nineteenth century: the concept of the evolution of human society through a succession of stages, each superior to the preceding one."[206]

The study elegantly integrated material from the work of six political economists and the English translation, for which Grossman paid $120, was very lucid.[207.]

"It is apparent," Grossman concluded on the basis of his survey, "that by the time Karl Marx (1818–83) began his work, in the forties of the last century, the application of evolutionary concepts to economic institutions and the formulation of the doctrine that economic systems are historical in character had been basically accomplished. Marx himself pointed that out repeatedly, though it was left to him to complete and sharpen the analysis."[208]

Marx's evolutionist precursors were capable of "the generalization of an empirically and inductively constructed series of particular observations." This was analogous to the method of the historical school, within which Grossman had concealed the Marxist underpinnings of his study of Austria's trade policy. But, "unlike the discredited school of Roscher, who substituted for theoretical laws an unthinking, chronological accumulation of unanalyzed descriptive material, [Richard] Jones considered it his function to test and correct the prevalent theories against actual historical developments and to formulate concrete experience into new theoretical viewpoints and categories."[209]

In contrast to the earlier evolutionists, Marx shared Hegel's dialectical concept of the development of the cultural whole, the totality of modern bourgeois society, as the object of his analysis: "Every present moment contains both the past, which has led to it logically and historically, and the elements of further development in the future"; so "to understand things it is necessary to grasp them genetically, in their successive transformations, and thus to discover their essence, their 'notion' (*Begriff*)."[210] Marx, like Sismondi and Jones, saw development as "an objective process of history, whereby each historical period or social structure is *marked by specific objective tendencies*," while for Hegel the essence of development was "the progress within man's *consciousness of the idea of freedom*."[211] Without using the expressions, Grossman therefore distinguished between the materialism of the evolutionist political economists and Hegel's idealism.[212]

"By attributing to Marx the first application of evolutionary thinking to economics, critics have obliterated the original contribution that Marx really did make to our understanding of history and the specific differences between Marx and his predecessors."[213] According to Grossman, an account of how transitions between economic systems occur was part of that contribution. This had a number of aspects.

One was showing how the old mode of production gives rise to forces that lead to its own supersession: "Newer, higher relations of production never appear before the material conditions of their existence have matured in the womb of the old society."[214] "For the first time in the history of ideas we encounter a theory which combines the evolutionary and revolutionary elements in an original manner to form a meaningful unit."[215] Revolution becomes necessary because legal property relations and political power do not change at the same pace as the productive forces; all "are subject to the law of uneven development."[216]

Another original feature of Marx's theory was his demonstration that capitalism necessarily suffers a tendency to break down. This Grossman identified with his own (and Marx's) account of economic crisis. Recapitulating the Leninist analysis of *The Law of Accumulation* and entries in Elster's dictionary,[217] he maintained "that no economic system, no matter how weakened collapses by itself in automatic fashion. It must be 'overthrown' . . . 'Historical necessity' does not operate automatically but requires the active participation of the working class in the historical process . . . The main result of Marx's doctrine is the clarification of the historical role of the proletariat as the carrier of the transformative principle and the creator of the socialist society . . . In changing the historical *object*, the *subject* changes himself. Thus the education of the working class to its historical mission must be achieved not by theories brought from outside but by the everyday practice of the class struggle"[218]

*   *   *

As a young revolutionary leader, almost four decades earlier, Grossman had also emphasized the centrality of class struggle both to the formation of working-class consciousness and to revolution. Here, however, he used particularly clear, Lukácsian/Hegelian terms. In his dialectical concept of history, Marx "follows Hegel, for whom history has both an objective and a subjective meaning, the history of human activity (*historia rerum gestarum*) and human activity itself (*res gestas*)."[219]

Grossman had modified aspects of his essay in light of comments Horkheimer sent him, though not the basic argument or conclusions.[220] Its treatment of Hegel was soon praised by an anonymous reviewer in an early issue of Dwight Macdonald's *Politics*. In 1945, an academic at Columbia University recommended the essay as "an ·excellent discussion" of Marx's approach to history.[221] This "most rotten piece of work" was republished twice during the early 1990s, in collections on Marx's thought and Richard Jones's economics.[222]

An Independent Scholar

By 1943, the core staff of the institute had been drastically reduced, with only Horkheimer and Adorno in a position to devote significant time to their own research. Grossman, whose politics and age made the prospects of alternative employment dim, refused to be intimidated or cajoled off the payroll.

Eventually, changes in the institute's structure and Grossman's unfriendly comments in conversations about it led Horkheimer to sack him. The director informed him, in March 1944, that the institute was severing relations because of his hostile behavior.

Grossman's misdemeanors were manifold. He had said nasty things about the institute, allegedly describing it, in private, as "those swine at 429," "the seat of capitalistic reaction," and "those slanderers of the Soviet Union." He had not participated in institute activities for two years. These activities now mainly consisted of the work of Horkheimer and Adorno, in California, and a project on anti-Semitism with which Grossman had not been associated, even before relations had broken down. He had ungratefully failed to acknowledge the institute in "The Evolutionist Revolt," the essay Horkheimer had condemned. Although no longer a member of the IfS, Grossman was, Horkheimer conceded, to receive a voluntary fellowship to support his scholarly work.[223]

The uncooperative former member of the institute soon returned the first check under the new arrangements, because the "marginal notation 'Fellowship $200.'" was written on it. Such a designation, he contended, undermined his legal rights as a lifelong *member* of the institute.[224] While insisting on Grossman's changed status, Pollock conceded that the Social Studies Association Inc, the foundation that held the institute's funds, would provide a year's notice before any change in financial arrangements.[225]

Denied any compensation from the institute for wartime inflation, Grossman tried unsuccessfully to offset his rapidly falling real income by means of tax minimization. He told the Department of Taxation that his grant-in-aid was not a salary and was therefore not taxable. It was only a coincidence that the size of the monthly grant was the same as his former rate of pay.[226]

Although Horkheimer's support and comments during the 1930s had assisted Grossman's work, they had not changed his basic Marxist stance, adopted early in the twentieth century; his methodology in economics, most thoroughly worked out during the 1920s; or his Stalinist views, readopted in the mid-1930s. Grossman, detecting and rejecting the thrust of Horkheimer's evolution in the early 1940s, continued to adhere to these views after the institute cut him loose.

7

From Independent Scholar
to East German Professor

After his break with the institute, Grossman was depressed for a period. Members of the Horkheimer circle thought that he "led a lonely and isolated existence" in New York.[1] The Australian novelist Christina Stead, who was just getting to know him in 1942, initially conveyed a similar impression to her partner, the Jewish American financial analyst, economist, and writer Bill Blake.

> I saw Count Chatterbox yesterday: he is much bowed, tired, much about "sabotage," poor gink. You know, I believe him. His anxiety to see me was out of utter loneliness, he was apparently counting on spending the summer with you going over his notes. Does not know where to go for the summer. Likes to lie on the beach but is afraid FBI won't let foreigners go on the beach. Went to the White Mtns last time and hated it—"some little hills" and "a lot of old people, they went to bed at 9 and turned off the lights." He asked if there was a café. Oh, yes: and they showed him. A milk bar. He talked for hours: would be talking still if I had not invented telephone call and fictitious date with "Dr. Libenson." He wants to marry you, adopt you and make you his carry-all of confidences. Can't make out why he didn't marry a brilliant woman. He is not averse to marriage, women, sex; quite the opposite I should say. Perhaps an unhappy marriage in the background. He needs a wife like nothing else.
>
> . . . Poor lost man. He cannot get over his insignificance here when he was such a figure, a celebrated scholar, in Europe . . . What he misses most of all are his workshop of brilliant young men and the CAFÉ; of course the two go together. "The Café" keeps cropping up amongst Descartes' ideas and the wherefore of the ancient Greeks.[2]

Stead, Blake, and Grossman had a shared political outlook. They were dedicated supporters of the Soviet Union and members of the Joint Anti-Fascist

Refugee Committee, originally set up to assist Republicans fleeing from Spain.[3] Blake was an active and effective fundraiser for communist causes. The two men had a common interest in Marxist economic theory and their extensive correspondence helped Blake prepare a book on imperialism.[4]

Even in 1942, when his own employment situation and international political conditions were no cause for joy, Christina described another side of Grossman. "He's crazy as a bedbug is our Grossman, wild, excitable . . . but sane, cheerful, brave . . . a splendid fellow, though quite a trial as a conversationalist. He does not give a tuppenny damn for me and my affairs: nothing in the world counts but his work, 'Grossman's Works.' O.K.! I am not the one to complain!"[5] He had a good sense of humor: "'Diss iss *GROSSMAN*: I like very much to invite you and Ruth [Blake's daughter] to Teatr one evening. I want to thank you very much for your book: it is a great honor for me to read diss inscription. I am reading it: very much it iss a very harrd lecture forr me.' . . . I told him *his* books were a very harrd lecture forr me. He relished this joke. (I don't mean I mocked his actual language.)"[6]

After more contact, Christina remarked that he was "a marvelous companion," so long as he was "not in one of his black or silly moods." By 1946 the relationship between Henryk, Christina, and Bill was very close. "Why doesn't LETTY FOX [her novel] sell like mad," she wrote to Bill, hoping they could all go to Europe together, "and then we could all (three) be over there?"[7]

"I am reading with passion (but in small daily doses) Letty Fox;" he later wrote, "in small doses, to avoid to crush my 'moral' prejudices, as Christina warned me *not* to read the book."[8] "The novel followed the life and loves of Letty Fox, a young woman in New York. Grossman found Letty less appealing than her little sister. "Letty is for me too much passive, waiting for the first serious proposition, and marry the man who make the proposition. I prefer little Jacky who loves Godynch in spite of that everything in him is repugnant. She reacts emotionally not with brain like Letty."[9] The character of Simon Godynch, a Nobel Prize–winning professor, was based on Grossman.

Grossman's sense of honor, an aspect of his moral prejudices, and his own importance were functioning when he remonstrated with Bill for making inquiries, after World War II, about an academic post for him in Belgium:

> In general, you both, are excellent psychologists, so in this special case, I regard it as a little unpsychological effort of Bill to propose me for a professorship there. Bill, have you forgotten, what I wrote about the last Congress of the Second International in Vienna 1931, and specially about the Chairman of this Internat—Mr de Brouckère? Every word, I wrote, is true. These gentlemen never protested, because they know, that every word, I wrote, is exact. But no,

you, dear Bill, you gave them a cheap opportunity for revenge and humiliation for you and me. (Please, Bill read again in *Wörterbuch der Volkswirtschaft* vol. II. p 16–17, art. 'Internationale'.)[10]

Henryk, still in New York after Christina and Bill had returned to Europe in 1947, wrote at the close of a letter: "Dear Bill, you mention your friendship. You should be sure that I have the same feeling. Sometime to me superfluous to express how much I love you and Christina. You must have the feelings; the words are unable to express the real things."[11] Eventually Blake referred to Grossman as his brother and Stead would describe him as "one of the men who meant something to me."[12]

Christina and Bill were not Grossman's only intimate companions in the United States. Nazism and the war had driven long-standing and very close friends to New York: not only his cousin Oskar Kurz, but also Rafał Taubenschlag, Grossman's contemporary at the Jagiellonian University in Kraków, who became a research professor at Columbia University and worked on the history of Greek and Roman law in Egypt.[13] The two old scholars dined with each other regularly at the Waldorf Astoria Hotel and socialized together with other friends. For a period, Taubenschlag visited Grossman every Sunday morning.[14] The Franco-Polish painter from Kraków, Moïse Kisling, who lived in New York from 1940 to 1946, stayed in touch.[15] Alexandre Koyré and other contacts from Paris were in New York during the war too.

Among German and Polish exiles in New York, Grossman found old acquaintances and friends, and made new ones. There were former colleagues from Frankfurt, such as Carl Grünberg's son Emil, the Christian socialists Eduard Heimann, an economist, employed at the New School for Social Research, and Paul Tillich, a theologian at Union Theological Seminary. Grossman tried to get to know the Marxist art critic and historian Max Raphael better, inviting him over for an evening.[16]

By the mid-1940s, Grossman's wide social circle only intersected with the periphery of the institute.[17] After the break with Horkheimer, Grossman was immune to his flattery.[18] Stead wrote in April 1944 that "we had a long cozy chat about Institut who are a lot of leetle boogbeds, I am told. He became a bit dubious about 'boogbeds' after a while and asked if that was right."[19] What, after all, was the value of compliments from bedbugs? Nor did Grossman admire Herbert Marcuse, Otto Kirchheimer, and Franz Neumann, members of the outer institute milieu who worked for U.S. government intelligence agencies during and after the war. Neumann's appointment to a chair at Columbia, in 1947, was greeted in a less than generous spirit: "Never was a man with less theoretical ability than he. A second class attorney. But he knows business."[20]

Association with Horkheimer did not, however, damn everyone. Grossman sustained friendships with some people he knew through the institute: Alice Maier, Horkheimer's secretary, her husband Joe, who had a scholarship at the institute before its financial crisis, and the Rumneys.[21] Having moved to the United States in 1938, Jay Rumney, who had been the institute's representative in London, soon took up a post in the Sociology Department at Rutgers University, where Joe Maier was later employed too.

A wide correspondence kept Grossman in contact with friends and colleagues around the world. He was in touch, for example, with the exiled Spanish communist professor and translator of *Capital*, Wenceslao Roces Suárez, in Mexico. After the end of the war he also exchanged letters with people in many European countries. One consequence was the publication in Prague of an extract from Grossman's "The Evolutionist Revolt against Classical Economics," in an authorized translation by Jiří Stolz.[22]

In New York, Grossman lived in a three-room apartment with his library of "about 2,500 books."[23] Christina's description after her first visit suggested that he wasn't much of a housekeeper or good at looking after himself.

> Largish, ill kept, unrestored apartment; large sitting room two small rooms knocked into one, weather stains, bad air, smell of paint, old carpet, dust, etc. He did not notice. Now see it is possible for him to have breathed air from kitchen (gas) and not noticed it. He is red skinned, eyes reddish, has bad cough and headache; takes aspirin all the time says it is from his night-cough which comes on him with the cold at about 3 in the morning when no heat at all. Did not see the bedroom but judge very untidy; his paper-filing system "Wolfinger." Very hospitable generous, quaint: wanted to make us take back beer and baloney. Gave us sherry, ginger ale etc. Dust everywhere, excellent scholar's library reminded me of worst corners of Bent St. He said Yes but mere remnant of library.[24]

Aspirin was hardly the best cure-all for someone who had kidney and stomach problems. But the drug may have had some longer-term benefit as he suffered a stroke while in New York.[25] Despite the dust, Grossman took greater care of his collection of books, a tool for politics and work, than his own health. Rebuilding his library by visiting second-hand book stores was also one of his recreations. Christina "showed him the old secondhand bookshops. He asked where. Says he hungers for them, the joy of coming home with three for 25c . . . and why they hated Riazanov in Europe: he took all the valuable books in his pockets and under his shirt for Soviet Russia and the scholars couldn't pick them up, 3 for 5. Too bad."[26]

Preparing for their departure to Europe in 1946, she and Bill sold many of their books to a pleasant Barnes and Noble representative. She suggested Henryk might do the same at some stage. He wasn't interested.[27] His books were not only a resource for his own work. A year later, contemplating a return to a Germany denuded of socialist literature by the Nazis, he wrote to his former student Walter Braeuer: "My earlier library in Frankfurt/Main was stolen from me by the Hitlerites, but I was in the position to slowly build up a new one. *I want to bring it with me.* The participants in my seminars must have the opportunity to read the books and my library would be at their disposal."[28]

In addition to research and politics, in New York music continued to play an important part in Grossman's life. He was delighted with Christina and Bill's parting gift, on leaving for Europe, of Beethoven's quartets, quintets, and sextets on records: "It is a real pleasure to have them at hand."[29] Soon he sent them a report about "a charming evening; a musical soirée" with mutual friends.[30]

Along with the remnants of the library he had been able to bring from Europe, Grossman had other mementos. A copy, possibly painted by Janina, of a work in the Louvre hung in his apartment.[31]

News from Poland was another reason for Grossman's black moods. Janina and their son Jan, who worked with the resistance in Warsaw, had been murdered in Auschwitz in 1943; Henryk's brother and sister-in-law in another death camp.[32] It seems that his other son, Stanisław, had died earlier.[33] He no longer had any family in Poland.

Some people Grossman cared about had survived in Europe. Walter Braeuer was in concentration camps for years. He reestablished contact with his old professor, in March 1947, and mentioned the impoverished state of Germany. Grossman started sending him parcels of food and other essentials, as he did to a friend in Belgrade.[34] Although his income was modest and declining, financial security and, for that matter, his health were less of a priority for Grossman than loyalty to friends, to whom he gave generous gifts.[35] In 1942, for example, he had written off a debt equivalent to more than a month of his salary to his attorney friend, Hermann Thorn, whose wife was ill.[36] Elegant clothing also remained important for Henryk. As it began to get cold in late 1946 Christina told Bill Blake that he "has a new winter coat, which he is showing everyone, dark blue, very nice, but not very warm."[37]

Grossman was still capable of infecting others with his enthusiasm about ideas and politics, explaining complex issues, and convincing them in argument. Early in their acquaintance Stead was impressed: "Then he sets out to explain Akkumulations-Theorie to muh! Let me tell you one thing—in his atrocious English he makes himself clear and interesting. He is a born expositor and teacher."[38] Under Grossman's influence Oskar Kurz, at the age of about sixty, abandoned his lifelong commitment to the Austrian Social Democratic Party for a communist perspective.[39]

After considerable efforts on Christina's part and reluctance on Henryk's, she prompted him to reflect on his political commitment.

> Approaching the subject of what emotional or other attitude a Bolshevik really has, I finally got at it, in a purely accidental manner. He has no love for the poor, or the masses, nor for any "people" in general. Otherwise, says he, how could you shoot your enemies and wish to abolish the upper classes? The result would be patience and resignation . . . Then why do you make this sacrifice, or they, say I (in effect). I do not sacrifice myself, I sacrifice the rich, he said (Acclamation!) Back to the fray: so what does he feel? "I feel as if I saw a dangerous badly made deadly machine running down the street, when it gets to that corner it is going to explode and kill everyone and I must stop it: Once you feel this it gives you great strength, you have no idea there is no limit to the strength it gives you."[40]

This concrete simile recalled György Lukács's more elevated account of the revolutionary role of the working class, an account that had emphasized, as Grossman did, the significance of capitalist crisis in the revolutionary process: "When the moment of transition to the 'realm of freedom' arrives this will become apparent because the blind forces really will hurtle blindly towards the abyss, and only the conscious will of the proletariat will be able to save mankind from the impending catastrophe. In other words, when the final economic crisis of capitalism develops, *the fate of the revolution (and with it the fate of mankind) will depend on the ideological maturity of the proletariat, i.e. on its class consciousness.*"[41]

In the United States, Grossman kept up with daily political developments by reading, clipping, and filing material from a range of newspapers.[42] He belonged to several organizations, in which radicals in the exiled Polish and German communities played prominent roles.

The Polish economist Oskar Lange and Grossman were already acquainted in 1938. After the German invasion of Russia terminated the German-Soviet agreement in 1939 to partition Poland, Lange became one of the leaders of pro-Soviet Polish-Americans.[43] He and, much less prominently, Grossman were both involved in the left-wing Alliance of Polish Democrats.[44] Lange became the ambassador of Poland in Washington in 1945 and later its representative on the United Nations Security Council. According to Lange, Grossman was open-minded and cultured, in general, but very dogmatic whenever one started to talk about social democracy, the evolution of capitalism, and so on.[45] While a socialist, Lange was no Marxist, justifying socialist policies on the basis of mainstream neoclassical economics. Grossman probably found him dogmatic on economic questions too.

Cocktail parties with Polish friends were a feature of Grossman's social life and he attended the functions of a Polish workers' organization.[46] In 1948 he met some people who remembered him from his activities as chairperson of the People's University in Warsaw, during the early 1920s: "Pleasant memories!"[47] Stead's short story based on Grossman's conflict with the Khasidic notables of Chrzanów in 1906 suggests that a worker from his JSDP days paid him a visit too.[48]

Following the fall of France in 1940, some German Communists and communist sympathizers had escaped to North America. After his break with the institute, they provided Grossman with a new milieu for political discussion and friendship. "In the USA," he later reported, "I belonged to a group of antifascists to which Gerhart Eisler and Albert Schreiner also belonged. I gave lectures for workers and took part in discussions in antifascist circles until the reactionary turn in US politics made further activity impossible for me."[49] Eisler and Schreiner were the senior German Communists in the United States.

Eisler (brother of the composer and Brecht collaborator Hanns) was, during the 1920s and early 1930s, an influential official and journalist in the German Party (KPD); from 1933 to 1936, he was the Communist International's on-the-spot minder of the Communist Party of the USA. He was the top KPD official in the United States after his return. Grossman had more contact with Albert Schreiner, a cofounder of the KPD and veteran of the Spanish Civil War, and other German exiles very sympathetic to or in the KPD.[50] By 1948, he was particularly close to the journalist Hermann Budzislawski and his wife Hanna.[51] Hermann had held communist opinions, if not a party card, since the early 1930s. From 1934 he had been the editor of the influential literary and political journal *Die Neue Weltbühne* in Prague and then Paris. From mid-1941 Budzislawski worked for the influential U.S. columnist Dorothy Thompson, as a researcher and ghost writer. Alexander Kupferman, known as Friedrich Georg Alexan, who had also been involved in antifascist literary activity in France, was another friend.

Unlike Eisler, Schreiner, Alexan, and Budzislawski, another of Grossman's New York associates, Felix Boenheim, had moved to the United States as early as 1935. He was a socialist medical practitioner and a veteran of the revolutionary Bavarian council republic of 1919. The "New York colony" of Germans aligned with the KPD also included the philosopher Ernst Bloch, Albert Norden, who had been a senior communist journalist in Germany, and the publisher Wieland Herzfelde.[52]

Many of the colony's members were involved, like Grossman, Stead, and Blake, in the Joint Anti-Fascist Refugee Committee and Die Tribüne für freie Deutsche Literatur (the Tribune for Free German Literature), a literary organization of the German left in the United States. As the Tribune's secretary, Alexan was its driving force. He organized antifascist events, like presentations by authors, theater performances, and art prints.[53]

Alongside Aaron Copland, Alfred Döblin, Albert Einstein, Reinhold Niebuhr, Paul Robeson, Jean Renoir, and Upton Sinclair, Grossman was a member of the illustrious honorary committee for the Tribune's literary and musical celebration of the novelist Thomas Mann's seventieth birthday in June 1945. Other members of the committee whom Grossman knew personally included the Yiddish writer Sholem Asch, a contributor to the *Sotsial-demokrat* in Kraków before World War I, Stead, Blake, Boenheim, Bloch, Budzislawski, and Herzfelde.[54]

Playfair and Descartes

Overlapping with politics, Grossman's main priority was his research and writing. In his first, short letter to Walter Braeuer, after learning that he had survived the camps, Grossman mentioned the murder of his wife and son by the Nazis. To this sad news and expressions of sympathy, he added a postscript: had Braeuer seen his latest articles?[55]

As recorded by Christina Stead, Henryk's normal routine was severe. "He reads books about seven hours a day and works in the evening too." Sometimes he pushed himself still harder. Later Stead reported he "only works eight hours a day when he has no book coming out, but when an article or book is coming out, he works fourteen or fifteen." She was concerned that "he's going to work himself to death, I can see it, because anyone can see he can no longer stand such labor."[56] From 1947, there were signs that his health was also being undermined by Parkinson's disease.[57]

Dividing his research time among the New York Public and Columbia University Libraries, and his apartment, Grossman worked on Descartes, mathematical economics, and the development of machinery in the ancient world. He also reworked the essay on dynamics for an English edition, making changes "to appeal to Americans, to give them at first what they call 'facts, facts.'" It did not appear in print. A short Polish manuscript written in 1945 on the situation of the American bourgeoisie and American capitalism went unpublished too.[58]

In 1946 Grossman reported to his former colleagues at the institute that he had completed a book on Descartes and was working on another, which dealt with Marx's economics.[59] The Descartes book incorporated work Grossman had conducted since the 1930s on the earliest development of capitalism and extended his studies of Descartes for "The Social Foundations of Mechanical Philosophy and Manufacture." It showed "that *The Geometry* is not so much a mathematical work as an original philosophical method . . . which in the form of an equation will enable every man in the street, who can read and write and has had no special education, to discern the highest truths . . . Descartes came to this idea, as I demonstrate, thanks to the influence of contemporary machinery. He invented two machines for polishing lenses, himself, and from this experience he became convinced that simplified, mechanized labor can do work better than schooled but individually different people."[60]

In a summary of this argument, Grossman identified the reason for his sympathy with Descartes' position, in the political logic of a recent parallel. "We encounter here in Descartes similar ideas to those which Lenin later developed in relation to the state and the functions of administration: 'On the basis of capitalist culture the great majority of functions of the old state have become enormously *simplified*.' That makes it possible for Lenin to call for them to be torn out of the narrow circles of political specialists and professional politicians 'as a special function of a special social class'; through their simplification 'they will be quite within the reach of *every literate person*'. 'The constant simplification of the functions will admit of their *being performed by each*, in turn.'"[61]

A longer manuscript in English also dealt with the relationship between Descartes' innovations and the development of machines, from the twelfth to the sixteenth century,[62] and incorporated insights from Grossman's work on slavery. Although "the ancients had produced many wonderful automatic devices," "with exceptions antiquity did not bequeath to us any labor-saving devices." This was because "slavery can be regarded as *an economic perpetuum mobile*, as a natural machine that continuously supplies energy without costing anything. Hence there was no social need for artificial labor-saving machines." The rise of production by means of free labor, in the twelfth and thirteenth centuries "explains why at the very time that the ancient *perpetuum mobile* disappeared, the longing for an artificial *perpetuum mobile* arose and attempts to construct one were made." While a mechanical *perpetuum mobile* is an impossibility, the same period saw new inventions and new applications of old ones that at least economized on the use of human labor.[63]

The only article by Grossman published in the period after Horkheimer threw him out of the institute was "William Playfair, the Earliest Theorist of Capitalist Development."[64] He wrote it in a couple of months during early 1947.[65] "Initially," Grossman told Rafał Taubenschlag, who had returned to Warsaw, "I thought of publishing it with the Kraków Academy of Sciences.

Being afraid that the process could take too long, due to all these approvals necessary, I decided to send it to England. Out of the rain and into the gutter! There is a shortage of paper, printing blocks etc. in England. In short, publishing this article (ten thousand words) is taking for ever."[66] To secure the article's publication Grossman had sought the assistance of Harold Laski, through Bill Blake who was then living in England.[67] Another old contact, Richard Tawney, may have played a role too. He was on the editorial board of the *Economic History Review*, where the essay eventually appeared in 1948.

The article, while presenting a self-contained argument, supplemented Grossman's study of Sismondi and the conclusions of his most recent publications on the history of political economy, "Marx, Classical Political Economy and the Problem of Dynamics" and "The Evolutionist Revolt against Classical Economics."[68] Playfair reported tendencies for capital to concentrate in a few hands, for the productive classes to become impoverished, and for the middle classes to disappear.[69] In this he anticipated Sismondi's account of such trends by fourteen years. But the English economist's most interesting observation predated its rediscovery by a century.

Countries reach a point in their development from poor agricultural producers to rich industrial nations when more capital is available than can be profitably invested. This, Playfair maintained, was typical for modern nations at a particular stage of development and ushered in a period of moral and economic decline. Playfair reconciled this conclusion with his conservative political inclinations by drawing attention to counteracting tendencies in capitalism that might, particularly when promoted by government, postpone the primary tendency to suffer disintegration and decay. These counteracting tendencies were "export of commodities and of capital, decentralization of capital, further various forms of unproductive expenditure and waste." The most effective was the export of capital. Or, if capital was invested at home, the resulting products had to be exported.[70]

"Only at the beginning of the twentieth century was the problem raised again by J. A. Hobson, whose work gave rise to a whole literature."[71] Grossman's comment undoubtedly referred to Lenin's *Imperialism: The Highest Stage of Capitalism*, which drew heavily on Hobson.

The relationship Grossman established in his study of Playfair between the ideas of classical political economy and Marx was weaker than those he highlighted in his discussions of dynamics and the evolutionist revolt. While his latest article did mention Marx, it contained no substantive discussion of the *content* of Marx's theory. Playfair, for example, anticipated Marx's employment of the methodology of tendency and countertendency. But Grossman did not explain Marx's distinctive application of this method. The article was less satisfying than Grossman's publications in the early 1940s in several additional ways.

It was stylistically inferior. This was a matter of both the quality of the translation and avoidable weaknesses in the organization of the material and the presentation of the argument. More significant, the earlier essays highlighted issues of importance to Marxist strategy: the impossibility of sustained capitalist equilibrium, in the essay on dynamics; the role of working-class self-activity and revolution in the transition from capitalism to socialism, in the study of Marx and his evolutionist forerunners. The closest equivalent in the Playfair essay was a brief reference to the process of socialization under capitalism as a prelude to a socialist economy. Nor did Grossman take advantage of an opportunity to discuss the role of the working class in the achievement of socialism. The length of the article and concern to find an outlet for its publication in a mainstream academic journal were grounds for political caution.

Something less conscious may also have been at work. After World War II, Stalinists believed that socialism was being introduced into eastern Europe and especially the Russian-occupied zone of Germany on the bayonets of the Red Army, rather than through proletarian revolution. If Grossman had discussed working-class self-activity as an aspect of his economic theory the contradiction with his Stalinist ideas would have been glaring. Perhaps for this reason, he regarded his most recent essay as more suitable for publication in German than the article on the evolutionist revolt.[72]

That Grossman was quite aware of the rigidity of Stalinist dogma was apparent in his advice about Bill Blake's book on imperialism. Despite their shared admiration for the Soviet Union and its policies, Grossman wrote: "In your book you should *avoid any direct criticism* of Lenin. You can make your different view clear, without attacking him—otherwise your book will be doomed as heretic. You can say 'older Marxian theorist told this that. Today situation is changed', etc."[73]

After the war, Grossman's earlier economic work attracted very limited attention in the United States. In a 1948 survey of theories of imperialism, Columbia University academic Earle Winslow, as Paul Sweezy had in 1942, criticized Grossman's crisis theory, but identified him as "a Marxist of real originality."[74] Increasing and realistic pessimism about politics in the United States and the prospects of finding a wider audience for his work there reinforced Grossman's illusions about the emerging Soviet bloc. In 1947 he was not keen on Bill Blake's suggestion that he respond to Sweezy's critique of *The Law of Accumulation*. "It is not so important for me to write a letter against the distortions of Mr Sweezy. If I will not be able to publish an English book on Marx, such a letter will not help. If I will publish a book, then I will crush him all bones and the reader will be able to judge himself which book gives really superior interpretation of Marx theory."[75]

Back to Germany

There is a long tradition of antisocialist hysteria in the United States. This was cranked up again by the media and government in the late 1930s. The U.S. House of Representatives set up a Committee on Un-American Activities (HUAC) in 1938, to promote a virulently anticommunist atmosphere. Laws in 1939 and 1940 banned federal employees from membership of organizations that advocated the overthrow of the U.S. government, then made it illegal to belong to such bodies and subjected foreigners to close supervision. Grossman expressed concerns to Stead and Blake in 1942 that the Federal Bureau of Investigation might regard a summer holiday at the beach as suspicious. He thought that neighbors might denounce him as a Marxist if they overheard tutorials with Columbia students, which he conducted at home. On first sight these worries might seem delusional.[76] They weren't. The FBI began to take an interest in him as a suspicious foreigner in 1940, while he was taking his summer vacation at Hyannis on Cape Cod, Massachusetts. The New York police informed FBI Director J. E. Hoover that "Dr. Henry R. Grossman supposed to be a professor . . . has all kinds of data regarding the location of harbors, etc . . . It is believed that part of his identification is phony and he is being checked with Fifth Column activities."[77]

According to the special agent who observed Grossman on his way home, he was in pretty good shape, looking only forty-five or fifty years old and weighing about 145 pounds (66 kilograms), was well tanned, wore a gray tweed suit, and was traveling with two young female acquaintances. His features were "typically Jewish or Dutch"![78] Having identified Grossman as a possible *German* spy, the FBI apparently failed to discover their subject's communist associations.

From 1945, as the wartime alliance between the United States and USSR began to break down, HUAC and other agencies expanded their surveillance of subversives and foreigners. Anticommunism was a useful tool to conflate any form of militancy with the foreign policy of the Soviet Union, and to mobilize the U.S. population against both. These circumstances colored Grossman's darker moments. His experience of arrest in Poland for communist associations, flight from Nazi Germany, and obvious foreign accent made him feel vulnerable. Grossman's financial situation was also increasingly precarious. As inflation surged after the war, the value of his fixed income declined. It was equivalent to more than twice the average earnings of full-time employees in 1940, but only 86 percent in 1948.[79]

In 1946, with the Cold War chill already apparent, Grossman was thinking about leaving the United States. His approach was sensibly cautious: "he would want the money to come back if it was not the right atmosphere etc."[80]

In October 1946 Gerhart Eisler, on the verge of leaving the United States for Germany, was arrested. Congressman Richard Nixon, whose electoral success was based on red baiting, made his national reputation through HUAC and used his first speech, in February 1947, to denounce Eisler as a Russian spy. The communist leader was sentenced to a year in jail for contempt of Congress.[81] A few weeks after Nixon's speech, Grossman wrote: "here everything develops— 'according to plan.' Anti-labor legislation in preparation."[82] He informed Braeuer in the Soviet Occupation Zone of Germany that "Marxism is designated a crime and one can only make a career if one writes *against* Marx."[83]

Albert Schreiner had managed to return to Berlin in December 1946. There he was an official responsible for education policy in the Soviet Zone. In September 1947, he took up a chair in Political Science and International Relations at the University of Leipzig.[84] With Oskar Kurz planning to set off for Vienna, in June 1947 Henryk wrote to Christina and Bill that Taubenschlag had already departed, "Again an friend less."[85] He let the German Central Administration for Education in the Soviet Zone know, probably through Schreiner, that he was interested in a professorship in Berlin or Leipzig.[86]

The prospect of teaching in socialist Germany was attractive. "I want to make my small contribution to the construction of a new better Germany," where "I would regard it as my particular mission to win hundreds, yes, thousands of the youth of a large city for the idea of Marxism and for the ideals that we fight for in practice."[87] Grossman asked Rafał Taubenschlag, also in his sixties, how he coped with lectures. "Don't you get tired? How do you find the new generation of students in the new Poland? I am extremely interested in this question!"[88]

But Grossman's instincts and touch as a teacher and academic supervisor were still sure. A suggestion to Bill Blake that his plans for the book on imperialism were perhaps overambitious was followed by a nudge toward a tighter definition of the project: "I would be curious to know how you would characterize in two or three sentences the leading idea of your book: what do you wish to prove or disprove. Have you already such idea—or will she be only the result of your research?" In a professorial tone, after a very faint praise for a lightweight article on the economics of the music industry in the United States, he chided Walter Braeuer, "but it surprises me that you waste your time with such articles, instead of concentrating on economic problems. Escapism?"[89]

Learning that Grossman was thinking of returning to Europe, Braeuer and his wife suggested that he could live with them and teach in Rostock, where Braeuer was a *Dozent* (lecturer) and soon became a professor. But life in the provincial town on the Baltic was not appealing. Grossman understood his own character, social situation, and needs, and how to deal with them. "I would feel bad in a small town. I do not have a family; wife and son were murdered by the Hitlerites. I cannot always work at home and be alone. I need to have the possibility of going to symphony concerts or the theater."[90]

In February 1948, Braeuer heard that an official invitation from the University of Leipzig was in preparation.[91] Schreiner was actively recruiting exiles in the United States for his new employer: Hermann Budzislawski, Boenheim, Bloch, Herzfelde, and the anthropologist Julius Lips, among others, took up professorial posts there in 1948–49.[92]

Through Budzislawski and Alexan, Schreiner sounded Grossman out about going to Leipzig.[93] This was a welcome prospect. Leipzig was not Berlin, with its theaters, concerts, and museums, but it was the second largest city in the Soviet Zone. The University of Leipzig was one of the oldest and largest in Germany, and had been established in 1408, almost four centuries before the university in Berlin. Grossman was probably unaware of a different set of advantages presented by Leipzig. For the time being, the political and cultural atmosphere in the province of Saxony and especially at the University of Leipzig was more open and less dogmatic than in Berlin, the seat of both the Russian occupying authorities and the central German administration of east Germany.

When discussing his move to Leipzig, Grossman particularly asked Schreiner for housing near Budzislawski, "in order not to feel alone,"[94] but there were other familiar figures at the university. The economist Georg Mayer had recently moved from Hessen, in the U.S. Zone of Occupation, to take up a chair in Leipzig. He had been a fellow cofounder of Arplan, which had sponsored Grossman's 1932 tour of the Soviet Union.

An aspect of the Cold War conflict was the competing efforts of the emerging German states to attract famous and sympathetic academic and literary figures from Nazi-imposed exile to their territories. West German authorities and the University of Frankfurt were eager to demonstrate their commitment to democracy by persuading Max Horkheimer to return to his chair in philosophy. The decisions of left-wing academics, writers, and artists to settle in east Germany buttressed the socialist pretensions of the regime there.

Immediate practical considerations also motivated the east German authorities to recruit Grossman and other exiles. The Russian and local German administrations had dismissed perhaps 200,000 former Nazis and Nazi-sympathizers from their jobs in east Germany by 1948.[95] This and departures for the West had particularly serious consequences in the universities, which lost three-quarters of their professors and four-fifths of their junior academics.[96] At a meeting of the staff of the new Social Science Faculty in Leipzig, Fritz

Behrens, a Communist, had concluded that "only one thing will help us: a troop of Jewish emigrants from America must come here."[97] In putting this strategy into practice, Schreiner dealt personally with arrangements for the visas and accommodation of friends from the United States he had recruited.[98]

Leipzig employed more socialist academics who had survived the Nazi period in western exile or inside Germany than any other east German university. Apart from Behrens' strategy, two factors apparently contributed to this pattern. On the one hand, the Soviet administration saw the emergence of an intellectual center in Leipzig as a counterweight to Berlin. On the other, the communist authorities regarded socialist professors who had survived in Germany or western exile—as opposed to those who had been through the Stalinist mill in Russia—as less reliable aspirants for posts in the capital, where it would be easier for them to win influence and political orthodoxy was more highly valued.[99]

The political concerns of the government of Saxony, the Soviet military administration, and the central communist authorities in east Germany delayed the dispatch of the official offer of a chair to Grossman. This worried him.[100] The proposal to appoint him also had to grind through the slow wheels of the university, whose structures were still in flux. Behrens became the dean of the Social Science (Gesellschaftswissenschaftliche) Faculty, set up to promote socialist scholarship. His professorship, however, was in the old Economics and Social Science (Wirtschafts- und Sozialwissenschaftliche) Faculty. Although, in accord with the Stalinist orthodoxy, he regarded both Grossman's and Luxemburg's theories of economic crisis as mechanical,[101] Behrens wanted to increase the influence of socialists in the old Faculty by recruiting Grossman to its last vacant chair. By 1948, the representatives of the new order in Germany were more confident about extending their influence into the bastions of conservatism. Gerhard Menz, dean of the Economics and Social Science Faculty, wanted a financial economist rather than another Marxist professor of political economy, like Behrens. He argued that Grossman should go to the new Faculty. Eventually Behrens, with his excellent party connections, won the debate.[102]

Like being stranded in Havana, months of waiting for the formal invitation to take up a professorship in Leipzig stressed and depressed Grossman. The tone of a letter he wrote to Walter Braeuer, probably his most trusted contact in Germany, reflected his anxiety. Grossman indulged in self-justification and even made an implicit accusation against his former student, when he suggested that the delay might be due to the unorthodox analysis in *The Law of Accumulation*. However, when Braeuer responded, hurt, Grossman hurried to thank him for his support and reassured him that "I only gave expression to the disappointment that the struggle for Marxism over my whole life apparently signifies nothing because I have a different view on this or that theoretical point."[103]

The invitation to take up the chair in the Faculty of Economics and Social Science in Leipzig was finally issued in August 1948, two months after the start of the Berlin Blockade. It was quickly accepted and covered in the east German press. But, in the context of plunging Cold War temperatures, this was another reason for the new appointee to worry: "the article in which I am mentioned *can* do damage. I am astounded that the correspondent does not realize this. I am sure that he has the best of intentions, but the note can have the effect of a denunciation."[104] Both Henryk "Großmann" and Hermann Budzislawski were listed in the university calendar for winter semester 1948–49, at their New York addresses.[105] In 1949, the Social Science Faculty absorbed the Economics and Social Science Faculty and Julius Lips became the first socialist rector of the University of Leipzig.[106] The new Stalinist order was conquering the universities.

Grossman was a major catch for Leipzig and "socialist" eastern Germany. He was the Marxist economist with the highest, independent, and truly international reputation in the immediate postwar period. Unlike Jenö Varga, who was well known because he had been Stalin's man in economics for twenty years, Grossman's standing did not depend on his political or institutional affiliations and extended well beyond the ranks of communist parties. This was despite the fact that his views on crisis theory had few supporters. His stature, like that of Brecht or Ernst Bloch, contributed to the credibility of the administration in eastern Germany and the state government in Saxony, less dominated than the German authorities in Berlin by senior apparatchiks who had spent two decades in Moscow.

While the possibilities of a post in Germany were still being explored, Taubenschlag and Grossman unsuccessfully put out feelers, through Oskar Lange, about openings in Poland for the former president of the People's University and professor at the Free University.[107] Shortly before his departure for Europe, where he would visit Taubenschlag en route to Leipzig, he still asked his old friend "about the reason for the matter of my professorship getting stuck."[108] It may be that to the Polish United Workers (i.e. Communist) Party—purged so many times of Luxemburgist elements and even dissolved by Stalin in 1938—anyone who had made any favorable comments about Luxemburg in the past thirty years was suspect,[109] let alone someone whose international reputation (made in Germany!) rested on a theory criticized in the pages of the Comintern's journal.

Grossman's attitude to Poland was influenced by other factors too. He was a Stalinist, but not always an orthodox one. He accepted the need for a communist-dominated government in Poland, but not the official fiction that the coalition that held office after the (coerced and rigged) January 1947 elections had majority support.[110]

Passing through Poland on his way to east Germany, Grossman received the offer of a post in Warsaw. "But for personal and objective reasons I could not accept. The personal reason is that my wife and son were gassed in Auschwitz, my brother and his wife in another modern furnace and at every step and turn I would remember this. I could not feel well in Poland. The objective reason is that in the Eastern Zone of Germany, the socialist permeation of courses is so much more advanced than in Poland. They are not routine courses but a real step towards the socialist permeation of teaching. For me, as a Marxist this is a decisive circumstance."[111]

From early 1948, the institute's objectives and Grossman's coincided in one respect. In April, when Horkheimer set off on a trip to Europe, funded by the Ford Foundation, to take up a guest professorship in Frankfurt and examine the prospects for a permanent return across the Atlantic, Pollock suggested that an effort be made to get rid of the institute's problematic dependant.[112] The prospect of a lump sum pay-out appealed to Grossman. It would cover the considerable cost of travel and freighting his library to Europe, fund the shipment of food packages to himself and the Braeuers in Germany for a year or so, and provide some security if matters did not go well in Leipzig. Grossman managed to extract $4,800, twice his annual salary, plus $500 to cover the transport of his library to Europe, from the institute. Compared to the $20,000 it cost to terminate the contract of the psychiatrist Erich Fromm in 1939, this was a stunning bargain.[113]

As Grossman was preparing his departure, in December 1948, Jay Rumney recommended that a young academic, Chimen Abramsky, meet him in New York. They had long conversations on six occasions. Abramsky observed that Grossman "lived in poverty in New York" and was not interested in Jewish matters but "found him a most charming person with an encyclopedic range of knowledge."[114]

Grossman embarked on the *Batory,* a Polish freighter bound for Gdynia in February 1949.[115] Friends farewelled and photographed him that morning. Alice Maier sent copies of the picture to him, the Rumneys, and Herman Thorn.[116] Gerhart Eisler, out of prison on $20,000 bail, managed to slip out of the United States on the same boat a few months later accompanied, as cover, by Friedrich Alexan's young daughter.

In Leipzig

The trip to Leipzig in winter took its toll on Grossman, who also had to worry about his books, household goods, and presents for friends (including women's shoes for Leni Braeuer, Walter's wife, and medicine for a colleague at the university—stolen during a customs check on the Polish-German border), which he brought with him.[117] In Berlin, a journalist photographed Henryk for the east German press. He looked haggard and unwell. He is less tired in another photo of similar vintage, which is on this book's frontispiece. But in both the right side of his face seems to have been affected by a stroke.[118]

The reception for the new professor of political economy and director of the Economic Planning Institute was fulsome.[119] Although little of the war damage to the housing stock had been repaired, in Leipzig "a very attractive, splendidly equipped apartment awaited me" at Schlößchenweg 6. Bill Blake later wrote: "he lives beautifully, really like a prince . . . in a rococo palatial apartment house opposite a beautiful park," with a "lovely room facing the wood and brook with a small terre-plein nicely managed into a quinconce: an ideal workroom."[120] Among Henryk's memorabilia on display was a photograph of a painting by Janka "showing him as a Polish nobleman in native costume when he was in his twenties."[121] Reflecting the importance of music in his life, he also acquired a grand piano.[122]

Just as Albert Schreiner had reassured him it would, the apartment was near the Budzislawskis' home. "Frau Professor Budzislawski took on to her narrow shoulders the difficult burden of finding an apartment, dealing with the tradesmen (painter, electrician, carpenter etc) arranging furniture, carpets, bedclothes and even finding an old housekeeper who cleans the apartment and cooks my meals." Bookshelves were made for his library.[123]

Both the university and the government of Saxony treated Grossman very well financially and made tributes to his achievements.[124] His normal monthly salary was equivalent to U.S. $260, more than his income in New York, a substantial chunk of which had immediately been paid on rent. On his birthday, April 14, Professor Behrens made a speech and he received presents, flowers, and plants from co-workers at the Economic Planning Institute. Soon the Social Science Faculty, in the person of its new dean, Albert Schreiner, suggested that Grossman be nominated for the National Prize for Science and Technology in recognition of his scientific achievements.[125]

Karl Heinz Lange, who was a student in Leipzig at the time, remembered that the inaugural lectures of scholars who had returned from emigration were important public events:

> They were understood as confirmation that we were on the right side.
>
> Henryk Grossmann's inaugural address took place in the large lecture hall in the Economics and Social Science Faculty building (previously the Commercial College, today Geschwister-Scholl-Haus). Grossmann was already at that time a very old, infirm-looking man, obviously suffering from Parkinson's disease, but he was, given our circumstances, strikingly well dressed.

In addition to the then Dean of the Faculty, Fritz Behrens, Hans Maier [sic] and Ernst Bloch welcomed him in very personal speeches. Both said their entire understanding of economics was thanks to Henryk Grossman, formerly of Frankfurt am Main. He was one of the greatest contemporary German economists. Fritz Behrens hoped for the enrichment and vitalization of scholarly controversy.[126]

Invigorated by his new environment, Grossman threw himself into politics, teaching, and social activity. By early June he was planning to organize a series of lectures by visiting professors from the west zone,[127] the Soviet Union having lifted the blockade of Berlin on May 12, 1949. Grossman's hope to promote intellectual exchange between east and west Germany was very much in accord with this shift in policy, which he also anticipated might accelerate the delivery of the regular food packages from the United States he had arranged before his departure.[128]

The day the blockade was lifted, Grossman cited the pressure of work and the possible impropriety of Leni Braeuer staying in his apartment as grounds for delaying her planned trip to Leipzig. This led to strained relations.[129] The snub was not intentional. In May Helene Weigel visited him at home. She was then appearing in the title role in the acclaimed first German production of *Mother Courage*, under the direction of the play's author, her husband Bert Brecht. With the welfare of his Rostock friends in mind, Grossman found out that Weigel would be happy to take gifts to Berlin so the Braeuers could pick them up there.[130]

In this period of political tension in Germany and internationally, the east German authorities sought to mobilize the population around its policies. Grossman might complain that "there are always new rallies, meetings, functions, and visits by journalists etc. which rob me of time," but he regarded them as important and was committed to the politics behind them.[131] Having joined the Victims of Fascism organization shortly after his arrival in Germany, he was officially recognized as a "victim of fascism" and a "fighter against fascism." He signed up for the Society for German-Soviet Friendship on May Day and became a member of the Socialist Unity (i.e., Communist) Party (Sozialistische Einheitspartei Deutschlands, SED) on June 9. He joined the Society for the Study of the Culture of the Soviet Union and the Cultural League for the Democratic Renewal of Germany too.[132] Previously Grossman had always described himself, for official purposes, as Jewish. Now, unable to conceive that anti-Semitism would be tolerated in "socialist" east Germany, he revealed his beliefs rather than his sense of solidarity by adopting the label "without religion."[133]

His personal experience of east Germany confirmed Grossman's political convictions and sustained his loyalty to the communist regime. When the official Soviet line in economics shifted and Jenö Varga fell out of favor for a period, it seemed to be a hopeful sign. In June 1949, Grossman had the opportunity to give a lecture on the "Varga discussion." He took the preparations for this very seriously. Here was an opportunity to settle some theoretical scores with Varga, who had savagely criticized *The Law of Accumulation* in 1930, and perhaps prepare the way for a wider acceptance in communist circles of his own analysis of capitalist crises.[134] Stalinist economic orthodoxy did swing away from the reformist underconsumptionism that Varga had articulated in 1946 but the line reverted to a radical underconsumptionist position like that Varga had defended in the early 1930s. An analysis closer to Henryk Grossman's concern with the relations of production and the accumulation process might have been embarrassing, as it could potentially be applied to the economies of eastern Europe.

Despite his enthusiasm for socialist construction in east Germany and the German Democratic Republic (Deutsche Demokratische Republik, DDR), established on October 7, 1949, when it came to his own Bundist past, he exercised some discretion. Previous involvement with the Bund had been fatal for many Russian Communists during the 1930s. Although he mentioned his membership of the Polish Communist Party and role in the People's University in curriculum vitaes prepared for the university and the authorities in Leipzig, Grossman did not refer to his political activities before World War I.[135]

During the summer semester, he taught four hours a week: a course on the "History of economic thought," for fourth-semester students, and another on "Economic history."[136] Because of his reputation, Grossman's first lectures on political economy were very well attended. But former students remembered that "as, however, Großmann [sic] was really already very ill, he spoke very softly and was difficult to understand, so that the number who came to the lectures quickly declined."[137] As only the first rows of students could hear his voice, a microphone was installed especially for him. But "because he trembled, his lecture notes continuously bumped the microphone, so that there was still only little that could be understood."[138] As well as creating problems for his teaching, Grossman's declining health also meant that he did not play a major role on the Committee of the Faculty or in other Faculty activities.[139] To the head of the east German educational authorities Schreiner wrote, in September 1949, that Grossman was in "a physical condition in which, but for the care of friends, he would be lost."[140]

There was another reason that the number of students attending lectures quickly dropped off. Grossman's concern to provide them with a thorough education in the fundamentals of political economy collided with the shortcomings of the education many students had received at school. "He shocked those present at the first lecture by reading out a seemingly unending list of materials, mainly in English and French, which should definitely be read, and that in the original (he spoke 7 languages himself). Those in front of him, however, were predominantly worker-students who had attained university entry through short courses, in which they also learned a bit of very faulty Russian."[141]

But Grossman was keen to establish personal contact with young people. In October 1949, committed Communists among the first intake of students with working-class or peasant backgrounds celebrated their graduation. Unlike many other members of staff and despite problems in getting to the tavern on the outskirts of Leipzig, Grossman attended the event. He had a great time and sought further contact with the graduates. When Karl Heinz Lange sent Grossman the poem he had recited at the party, the old professor replied,

> It was a delightful surprise for me that you sent me not only your poem "The note" but also your ballad about Fridolin the student, with a commentary. I was particularly moved by your friendly and benevolent affection. It will all be a lovely reminder of the celebration of the end of studies by the Socialist Student Activist Group of the first worker and peasant students at the University of Leipzig. For this, I am particularly in your debt and that of your comrades.
>
> I suffered frightful personal losses in the Second World War and lost my wife and son. In your midst I felt, all the more, as if [I was] in a new family.
>
> At the same time I would like to make the proposal that we could meet more often to discuss important current or theoretical problems. No supper needs to have been prepared [as in the case of the party]. It will be enough if we could meet over a glass of soda water or beer in a bar here, nearer the centre of town, rather than lose 3/4 of an hour just traveling.[142]

During winter semester 1949–50, Grossman conducted a seminar for senior undergraduate (fifth-semester) students on "Special problems in Marxism." The course dealt with a topic he regarded as very important, Marx's theory of simple reproduction.[143] In 1947 he had even written to Stead and Blake that the theory of crisis under conditions of simple reproduction was "my chief contribution to Marxist theory."[144]

Late in 1949 Grossman invited Bill Blake to visit him and stay in his apartment, at the same time sponsoring him for a post teaching U.S. literature at the university. In March 1950 Bill arrived. He found Henryk seriously ill in hospital, after an operation for a prostate growth and a further minor stroke. The doctors concluded that he had less than a year to live. Oskar Kurz soon came from Vienna to see his ailing cousin.[145] Henryk's otherwise poor physical shape, Parkinson's disease, arthritis, weakened kidneys and heart meant the surgery had an even more serious effect.

Christina had been right in her assessment, in New York, that he might work himself to death.[146] In Leipzig, his passion for teaching, university life, and politics seems to have prevented much restraint in his activity. Nevertheless, not long after the operation, Blake found "Despite his illness the clarity of his mind is simply astonishing: it was beautiful to hear his low voice following a train of reasoning and humanity."[147]

In Saxony at least, according to Blake, "the Party regards him as its great man in theory (they speak of him plainly as the first Marxian of Germany) and in the corridors heads of the State here, ministers, etc. glide in and out for news of his recovery." They ensured he had the best therapy available.[148] At the end of December 1949, for example, a welfare agency sponsored the supply of "2 bottles of red wine to Mr Großmann, who is recognized by us as a fighter against fascism, as he is currently in hospital and urgently needs this drink for the reestablishment of his health."[149]

This esteem was confirmed when the city of Leipzig nominated him for the National Prize in March 1950, "for the totality of his scientific achievements in the area of scientific socialism. One of his principal works, *The law of accumulation and collapse of the capitalist system* received the greatest attention around the world."[150] But Grossman did not win the prize, whose award had to be approved by Berlin authorities, schooled by their Russian exile in the importance of doctrinal purity. This bureaucratic mindset combined with anti-U.S. paranoia also meant that Blake failed to secure a post in east Germany.[151] Grossman was, however, successful in arranging for his friend in Paris, the historian Auguste Cornu, to teach in Leipzig.[152]

After the initial shock of the surgery, Grossman's condition improved. His concern for politics and sense of humor returned. "'Christina, Christina, she has to use her genius to portray resistance, in the human sense, against fascism,'" Blake reported him as saying. "I asked him 'And imagination?' His eyes opened and he said mockingly 'That is only for economics.'"[153] Fond memories of the institute under Horkheimer also animated him. "Of course he was in form for he proved, joyfully, that twenty people were *auswürfen* [rejects], *taugenichten* [ne'er-do-wells], *gesindel* [riff-raff], *chalatanen* [charlatans], etc. and as a result his health improved from minute to minute. He discussed the Institut, that really made him sprightly. I learned the entire German thesaurus for villainy, outright deceit, fraud, persecution, etc. Sounds like the days of the Marx-Engels correspondence studded with pediculi."[154]

A few days later Henryk came home, with a nurse and Dr Kurz to look after him. Not only senior government officials were concerned about his well-being. Felix Boenheim, who he had known in New York, was the head of Leipzig's Polyclinic in Härtelstrasse, one of the largest hospitals in east Germany; responsible for the city's communal health; and in ultimate, personal charge of Grossman's treatment.[155] Bill wanted to give his room in the apartment to Oskar Kurz, who, with "Viennese grandeur," refused. Grossman's equally developed sense of honor was complemented by his grasp of practicalities. "I go to Henryk and say (I know him) 'Situation has changed. My conduct must conform.' The hieroglyphics met this answer. 'Zees is fact. When I invited you to live with me I was healthy and alone. Now I have two beds only for Doctor and Nurse. Zank, you Beel.'"[156] Back at home, he lectured Bill,

> Henryk got a mania the first time I saw him after the awful greeting when I came (awful for me, he was angelic). I must write an article on the financial difficulties facing the British cabinet for Berlin papers, one especially with whom he is in verbindung [contact]. Good. I, against my will, wrote out a long summary and when in Berlin spoke to the editors. They said, (of course) that they never, never accept unsolicited articles, these must all come from some designated authority. I told this to Henryk. He said I ruined everything. I should have sent in a finished article, and at the sight of my genius, healthy editors would spring epilepsy, foam at the mouth, take a special train to Leipzig and crave my pardon for ever having been born in a world where they were so unfit to live compared to one like myself, or words to that effect. As it was I gave them the chance to be editors. Everyone, including myself, am terribly happy (really we are) at this development. It is the old "Professor" back in the saddle.[157]

Soon the Dietz publishing house of the Socialist Unity Party in Berlin sent cheering news: it would publish a long version of Grossman's Playfair essay. Because of the shortage of paper in England after the war, he had had to prune it severely for publication in the *Economic History Review*. Fritz Schälike, the thoroughly reliable Stalinist boss of Dietz, who reported to the SED Central Committee and Soviet censorship authorities, made publication dependent on greater emphasis being given to the differences between Playfair's and Lenin's positions on, for example, the export of capital. This presented no difficulties. But Grossman sought Albert Schreiner's advice in finding someone to subedit the essay, as Schälike thought its German was "insufficiently pure and [that it] contained many Americanisms." This preoccupation with linguistic purity reflected the concern of the DDR to demonstrate the legitimacy of their separate German state, unsullied by the influence of the United States. It also provided an excuse for at least delaying a publication by someone who did not express the party's line in economic theory. Later the concern for political orthodoxy at Dietz was formulated as the axiom that "any false comma" could be a political error.[158]

Within two months of returning home from hospital Grossman also sent Schälike the manuscript of a collection of his essays originally published in 1929 and 1932, with a new introduction "On Essence and appearance."[159] He had reworked the essays very lightly. In the study of Marx's plans for *Capital*, for example, he added some footnotes, deleted a favorable reference to Lukács, and inserted a sentence acknowledging that Lenin's *Imperialism* and Stalin's *The Foundations of Leninism* had applied Marxism to the period of monopoly capitalism.[160] Grossman did not, however, modify any of his arguments.

After his operation, Grossman still suffered from severe arthritic pain. In August, the University Rector Georg Mayer nevertheless noted that, although bed-ridden, his sick colleague was still working when he paid Grossman a visit. The Social Science Faculty decided to relieve him of all teaching responsibilities so that, in future, he could devote himself entirely to research.[161] Later in the month, an officer of the City Council attended Grossman's bedside to establish his status as a "victim of the Nazi regime" entitled to an additional pension. The official reported: "During the interview I found the above named confined to bed. He was fully aware during the interview and interested in current political events. By the bed I found the latest newspapers, this shows that he supports our reconstruction. The discussion was often disrupted, as G. had severe coughing fits."[162]

At the start of October Grossman had to return to the Polyclinic, where Boenheim visited him twice a week, organized a nurse to be permanently on hand, and obtained, through Bill Blake, medicine from England to treat his Parkinson's tremors.[163] Although he received the best care east Germany had to offer, Henryk Grossman soon died.

The university announced that "Professor Dr. jur. Henryk Großmann, Professor with the Chair of Political Economy and Director of the Institute for Political Economy died on November 24 1950 after long and severe suffering. With Prof. Dr. Großmann the University of Leipzig loses a scholar with a world wide reputation who also remained true to his scientific calling during the period of fascist dictatorship in Germany."[164]

In a fictionalized manuscript, Christina Stead wrote that Gerardus (Grossman) "died about November 23, we gather, after two months in the hospital, and 'as his working capacity was no more, his death was a release.'"[165]

* * *

Since his youth, Grossman had held fast to the fundamental Marxist idea that socialism means the revolutionary self-emancipation of the working class. Within this framework his views about some issues had certainly changed. He formulated the Jewish Social Democratic Party of Galicia's Bundist commitment to national cultural autonomy and federal structures within the Austrian social democratic movement; later, as a Communist, he believed that national oppression could be more effectively combated by a party organized along democratic centralist lines. Having embraced the Bolshevik revolution, Grossman did not identify the creeping counter-revolution in Russia during the 1920s, which took a form that no one had anticipated. But in 1933, his position had affinities with Trotsky's critique of Stalinism in Russia as a degeneration of socialism, but not the restoration of a form of capitalism. From late 1935 or 1936, Grossman again insisted that the USSR was socialist, without any qualifications.

Although they transgressed Stalinist dogmas, Grossman continued to defend his earlier contributions to the recovery of Marxism and developed them further. He had stressed the importance of the use value aspect of commodities in his lecture to the Academy of Sciences in 1919, and it underpinned his 1941 discussion of capitalist dynamics. Work on Descartes during the 1940s employed his account of the scientific process of abstraction already apparent in his discussions of Marx's method in *Capital* and the origins of the scientific worldview. "The Evolutionist Revolt against Classical Economics" extended the argument in *The Law of Accumulation* about the relationship between capitalism's tendency to break down and the working class as an active revolutionary subject. At the end of his life Grossman was eager to republish essays from his period in Frankfurt am Main.

After the dislocations of multiple exiles (from Austria, Poland, and Germany), the murder of friends and family by the Nazis, and the experience of poverty in New York, Grossman had gone to Leipzig with high expectations and large illusions about the regime in east Germany. He seems to have died with those illusions intact. They concealed the distance between his Marxist belief in the capacity of working class to usher in a radically democratic socialist order and the realities of the dictatorial, state capitalist regime in east Germany under direct Russian rule and then the German Democratic Republic. The contradiction between the basic tenets of Marxism and the Stalinist legend that the DDR was socialist deepened during Grossman's illness and after his death. The regime's repressive measures affected all layers of east German society, including Henryk Grossman's friends and colleagues.

In September 1948, the SED leadership had already set up Party Control Commissions "to root out the heretics and doubting Thomases." Members who had past or present connections with the West were particularly suspect. In cracking down on dissent, the government denounced Zionist influences: a thinly veiled appeal to anti-Semitism. The Stalinist leadership was fearful of both espionage and ideological contamination.[166] Behrens and other academics in Leipzig were, in 1949, accused of being Trotskyists. To save his party card and career, Behrens engaged in a self-criticism and undertook to learn Russian.

He suspected Albert Schreiner of denouncing him. Soon after, Schreiner suffered from a nervous disorder and left Leipzig for Berlin.[167]

In February 1950, the secret police and intelligence apparatus of the east German state was transformed into a full Ministry for State Security. The communist youth organization directed students to boycott the lectures of Ernst Bloch, Georg Mayer, Hans Mayer, and Fritz Behrens during the summer semester, as a protest against their "objectivism" and "cosmopolitanism." This was code for failure to meticulously follow the party line in all matters of scholarship.[168] During the same period, elected student councils were abolished and the process of transforming the trade unions into organs of SED authority was largely completed.[169] Walter Braeuer, while remaining a Marxist, left the SED before fleeing the DDR for the West, in May.[170] The regime throttled all controversy over economic or any other serious questions, to which Behrens had looked forward at the time of Grossman's inaugural lecture.[171]

Grossman had brought his large library to east Germany as a contribution to the education of a new generation of socialist students. Oskar Kurz donated it, the most valuable part of Henryk's estate, to the Central Committee of the Socialist Unity Party. For forty years, only the top officials of an oppressive dictatorship had access to the books. Grossman himself became a posthumous pawn in the regime's campaign against former emigrants to the West and the 1950–51 purge of suspect SED members that terminated open debate in the party. No doubt concerned to demonstrate her own and her husband's political purity, Hanna Budzislawski denounced her former friend Felix Boenheim, like herself suspect because of his stay in the United States, for having neglected Grossman and contributed to his death. Boenheim fought this spurious charge for years, eventually with success.[172]

The German Democratic Republic never officially acknowledged Grossman's contribution to Marxism. The stone Oskar Kurz erected on Henryk Grossman's grave was the only visible memorial to him. Dietz did not issue his Playfair study or his collection of essays. The publication of any work by Grossman might have implied the validity of his ideas in general.[173] The collection, in particular, included coherent, persuasive, and therefore subversive arguments repeatedly rejected by the oracles and choruses of Stalinist economics. None of Grossman's work was ever published in east Germany, where textbooks condemned his analysis of crises, in accord with the orthodox Stalinist response to *The Law of Accumulation*.[174]

Grossman's Marxism was essentially dormant until the late 1960s, when a new generation—initially activists in the west German new left—discovered his recovery and development of Marx's insights.[175]

Notes

Preface

1. Anwar Shaikh, "An Introduction to the History of Crisis Theories," in Bruce Steinberg et al., *U.S. Capitalism in Crisis* (New York: Union for Radical Political Economics, 1978), pp. 219–41.

Chapter 1: Growing Up in Galicia

1. Katalog Klasy 1A 1893, GLJ 27, to Katalog Klasy IV 1896, GLJ 34, Archiwum Państwowe w Krakowie (APK); Fragebogen, "Henryk Grossmann," PA 40, pp. 100–101, Universitätsarchiv Leipzig (UAL); letter from Friedrich Pollock to Klaus Hennings, July 13, 1967, VI 9, p. 222, Max-Horkheimer-Archiv; Christina Stead, notes, Box 2, Folder 7; and notes, Box 6, Folder 45, Christina Stead Collection, MS4967, National Library of Australia (Stead Collection). Christina Stead's literary estate is the most important source of information on Henryk Grossman's personal life. I have corrected obvious typographic errors in Stead's texts.

2. I. Rudnitsky, "The Ukrainians in Galicia under Austrian Rule," *Austrian History Yearbook,* 3 (2), Houston, 1967, pp. 404–5. Brix also provides examples of falsification of census results in order to maintain Polish preponderance in Galicia, Emil Brix, *Die Umgangssprachen in Altösterreich zwischen Agitation und Assimilation: Die Sprachenstatistik in den zisleithanischen Volkszählungen 1880 bis 1910* Veröffentlichungen der Kommission für Neuere Geschichte Österreichs Band 72 (Graz: Herman Böhlaus, 1982), pp. 367–69.

3. "Jewish Records Indexing—Poland," database, www.jewishgen.org, accessed March 1, 2002.

4. *Księga obejmująca wpisy urodzin Izraelitów w okręgu metrykalnym Kraków Rok 1881*, M-26, APK, p. 85; Fragebogen, UAL, p. 100. His official name-change to Henryk, in July 1915, was noted in the birth register, *Gimnazjum* (academic high school) and

university records. Henryk Grossmann was the most common German rendition of his name, but Heinrich Grossmann and Heinrich Großmann also occurred. In Poland he was Henryk Grossman. This was also the way he always signed his name and the name he used in his English-language publications. In the following, the version of his name associated with a publication by him or a document that refers to him is used in the citation of that publication or document.

5. Stead, notes, Box 6, Folder 45, Stead Collection.

6. *Księga obejmująca 1881*, p. 85; *Księga obejmująca wpisy urodzin Izraelitów w okręgu metrykalnym Kraków Rok 1884*, M-26, APK, p. 174; and Spis Ludności z31.XII.1900r. Dzielnica VIII Tom XVII p. 576, APK.

7. The family lived at Ulica Starowislna 27 from the date of Bernard's birth at the latest, *Księga obejmująca 1884*, p. 231, no. 693.

8. "Jewish Records Indexing—Poland."

9. "Katalog Klasy 1A 1893," GLJ 27, to "Katalog Klasy VIII 1900," GLJ 34, APK; GLJ 78 Examin dojrzalosci, Grossmann, Chaskel, APK.

10. Deaths file 274/1986/IV/Śr, Urząd Stanu Cywilnego, Kraków.

11. On Henryk's school reports his mother, "Solomea," is described as a business-woman in 1897, from 1898 "Sara" is a co-owner or owner of real-estate, "Katalog Klasy V 1897," GLJ 31, to "Katalog Klasy VIII 1900," GLJ 34, APK. The 1900 census described "Sara" as a house owner, the 1907 *Kraków City Directory* as an owner of real estate, Dzielnica VIII, Tom XVII, p. 576, Spis Ludności z31.XII.1900r., APK; *Kraków City Directory* 1907 www.polishroots.com/databases/krakow_citydir_1907.htm, accessed June 5, 2006. Renting out apartments in the building would have provided a regular income.

12. Oscar Kurz, birth certificate, 385/1885, Israelitische Kultusgemeinde Wien, Matrikelamt; letter from Bill Blake to Christina Stead, March 7, 1950, Christina Stead and William J. Blake, *Dearest Munx: The letters of Christina Stead and William J. Blake* (Carlton: Miegunyah Press, 2005), p. 489.

13. Hauptgrundbuchblatt in k. u. k. Kreigsministerium 1916 1. Abt. 45–1/468, Öster-reichisches Staatsarchiv, Kriegsarchiv; Henryk Grossman, Alien Registration Form, Immigration and Naturalization Service, October 31, 1940. Memorandum from L. G. Healy Re: Henryk Grossman; International Research Institute, October 15, 1940, Henryk Grossman file, Federal Bureau of Investigation.

14. Letter from Stead to Blake, April 10, 1944, Stead and Blake, *Dearest Munx*, pp. 296–97. Unless otherwise indicated, emphasis in all quotations is that of the original author.

15. Stead, notes, Box 6, Folder 45, Stead Collection.

16. Stead, notes and "Jan Callowjan (Kalojan) Henryk Grossman," Box 6, Folder 45, Stead Collection.

17. Grossman's socialist activities while at the *Gimnazjum* were also reported by his cousin, Oscar Kurz, to Tadeusz Kowalik, "Henryk Grossman: polsko-niemiecki teore-tyk ekonomii marksistowskiej," *Zycie gospodarcze* 16, April 17, 1960, p. 2.

18. Stead, notes, Box 6, Folder 45, Stead Collection.

19. Stead, notes, Box 6, Folder 45, Stead Collection; Stead wrote, he "became editor of socialist paper (for college apparently) at 15," Stead, "QUESTIONS to ask the Tyl," Box 5 Folder 32, Stead Collection.

20. Stead, "Jan Callowjan (Kalojan) Henryk Grossman" and notes, Box 6, Folder 45, Stead Collection. In the former, Stead states that the Lemberg conference took place in 1900, in the latter, in 1899. Stead also mentions the episode in notes, Box 2, Folder 7.

21. The following account of Galicia's population and economy, unless otherwise indicated, draws on Józef Buszko, *Zum Wandel der Gesellschaftsstructur in Galizien und der Bukowina* Österreichische Akademie der Wissenschaften (Phil. hist. Klasse. Sitzungsberichte Bd. 343, Wien 1978), pp. 15–31.

22. In 1900, 11 percent of large landholdings were held by bank and industrial capitalists, most of them Jews; Henryk Batowski, "Die Polen," in Adam Wandruszka and Peter Urbanitsch (eds.), *Die Habsburger Monarchie 1848–1918* (Wien: Verlag der Österreichischen Akademie der Wissenschaften, 1993), pp. 541–42.

23. Kerstin Jobst, *Zwischen Nationalismus und Internationalismus: Die polnische und ukrainische Sozialdemokratie in Galizien von 1890 bis 1914. Ein Beitrag zur Nationalitätenfrage im Habsburgerreich* (Hamburg: Dölling und Galitz, 1996), p. 46.

24. Herman Diamand was elected to the *Reichsrat* in 1907; Emil Haecker became the senior editor of the party's organ, *Naprzód*, which eventually appeared daily; Max Zetterbaum was probably the party's most important theorist.

25. Isaac Deutscher, "Discovering *Das Kapital*," in Isaac Deutscher, *Marxism in Our Time* (London: Jonathan Cape, 1972), p. 257.

26. Robert Wistrich, *Socialism and the Jews: The Dilemmas of Assimilation in Germany and Austria-Hungary* (East Brunswick: Associated University Presses, 1982), p. 315.

27. Feliks Tych, "Die Sozialdemokratische Partei Galiziens innerhalb die österreichischen Gesamtpartei: Vom Hainfelder Parteitag bis zum Zerfall der Monarchie," in Erich Fröschl, Maria Mesner, and Helge Zoitl (eds.), *Die Bewegung: Hundert Jahre Sozialdemokratie in Österreich* (Vienna: Passagen, 1990), pp. 251–54; Jerzy Myslinski, "Ignaz Daszynski: Führer der Polnischen Sozialdemokratischen Partei Galiziens und Schlesiens und seine Haltung gegenüber dem Wiener Zentrum der österreichischen Sozialdemokratie," in Fröschl, *Die Bewegung*, pp. 242–49.

28. See Massimo Salvadori, *Karl Kautsky and the Socialist Revolution 1880–1938* (London: New Left Books, 1979); Carl Schorske, *German Social Democracy, 1905–1917: The Development of the Great Schism* (Cambridge, Mass.: Harvard University Press, 1983); Georges Haupt, *Socialism and the Great War: The Collapse of the Second International* (Oxford: Clarendon Press, 1972).

29. Karl Marx and Frederick Engels, *Manifesto of the Communist Party* (Moscow: Progress Publishers, 1971 [1848]), pp. 38, 41, 44; Friedrich Engels, *Anti-Dühring (Herr Eugen Dühring's Revolution in Science)* (Peking: Foreign Languages Press, 1976 [1878]), pp. 354–56; Karl Marx, *Capital*, vol. 1 (Harmonsworth: Penguin, 1976 [1867]), pp. 798, 929–30; Karl Marx, *Capital*, vol. 3 (Harmonsworth: Penguin, 1981 [1894]). These issues

are discussed at length below. Also see Rick Kuhn, "Economic Crisis and Socialist Revolution: Henryk Grossman's *Law of Accumulation*, Its First Critics and His Responses," in Paul Zarembka (ed.), *Neoliberalism in Crisis, Accumulation, and Rosa Luxemburg's Legacy: Research in Political Economy*, vol. 21 (Amsterdam: Elsevir, 2004), pp. 181–221.

30. Hans Mommsen, *Die Sozialdemokratie und die Nationalitätenfrage im habsburgischen Vielvolkerstadt* (Wien: Europa Verlag, 1963), pp. 181–210.

31. For the national question and the PPSD, with a focus on relations with Ukrainian social democracy in Galicia, see Jobst, *Zwischen Nationalismus und Internationalismus.*

32. *Naprzód* was underwritten by financial support not only from the German-Austrian Party but also the German Social Democratic Party; Jobst, *Zwischen Nationalismus und Internationalismus*, p. 49. In 1891, Daszyński had worked in Berlin as the editor of the German Party's Polish newspaper, *Gazeta Robotnicza;* Walentyna Najdus, *Ignacy Daszyński 1866–1936* (Warszawa: Czytelnik, 1988), pp. 78–79; Hans-Ulrich Wehler, *Sozialdemokratie und Nationalstaat: Die deutsche Sozialdemokratie und die Nationalitätenfragen in Deutschland von Karl Marx bis zum Ausbruch des Ersten Weltkriegs* (Würzburg: Holzener-Verlag, 1962), pp. 115–16.

33. Jobst, *Zwischen Nationalismus und Internationalismus*, pp. 98–101.

34. Mommsen, *Die Sozialdemokratie und die Nationalitätenfrage*, pp. 314–15, 336; for the text of the resolution, pp. 335–36.

35. Marian Dabrowa "Die Kultur in Galizien 1867 bis 1914," in Walter Leitsch and Maria Wawrykowa, *Polen Österreich* (Wien/Warszawa, Österreichischer Bundesverlag/ Wydawnictwa Szkolne i Pedagogiczne, 1988), p. 223.

36. Chaskel Grossmann winter semester, 1900–1901, to summer semester 1904, 503 to 510, S II, Archiwum Uniwersytetu Jagiellonskiego (AUJ).

37. Antonio Gramsci, *Selections from the Prison Notebooks* (New York: International Publishers, 1971), pp. 10, 15, 330, 340.

38. Stead, notes, Box 2, Folder 7, Stead Collection; notes and "Jan Callowjan (Kalojan) Henryk Grossman," Box 6, Folder 45, Stead Collection; "Jan Callowjan (and his Sister Mrs. Rock.)," Box 10, Folder 75, Stead Collection.

39. Chaskel Grossmann winter semester, 1900–1901 to summer semester 1904, 503 to 510, S II, AUJ.

40. See Gramsci, *Selections from the Prison Notebooks*, pp. 10, 15, 330, 340.

41. *Album Studiosorum Universitatis Cracoviensis ab anno 1892/3 usque ad annum 1910/11*, AUJ.

42. Jerzy Myśliński, *Grupy polityczne Królestwa Polskiego w Zachodniej Galicji (1895–1904)* (Warsaw: Książka i Wiedza, 1967), pp. 89, 106, 274; Mirosław Frančić, "Postępowe organizacje studenckie w Krakowie (1895–1914)," in Henryk Dobrowolski, Mirosław Frančić, and Stanisław Konarski (eds.), *Postępowe tradycje młodzieży akademickiej w Krakowie* (Kraków: Wydawnictwo Literackie, 1962), pp. 80–81, 88; Police report 1001 Relacja z zebrani m odzie y akademicki, Mat 283, Starostwo Grodzkie Krakowskie, Wojewódzkie Archiwum Państwowe w Krakowie.

43. Frančić, "Postępowe organizacje studenckie," p. 86; Myśliński, *Grupy polityczne*, p. 90.

44. Max Rosenfeld, *Die polnische Judenfrage* (Wien-Berlin: Löwit Verlag, 1918), p. 68.

45. Raphael Mahler, "The Economic Background of Jewish Emigration from Galicia to the United States," *YIVO Annual of Jewish social Science 7* (New York, 1952), p. 257.

46. Max Rosenfeld, "Die Jüdische Bevölkerung in den Städten Galiziens 1881–1910," *Zeitschrift für Demographie und Statistik der Juden* 9 (2) (February 1913): 20; Robert Wistrich, "Austrian Social Democracy and the Problem of Galician Jewry 1890–1914," in *Yearbook of the Leo Baeck Institute* (1981): 95.

47. Frank Golczewski, *Polnisch-jüdische Beziehungen, 1881–1922* (Wiesbaden: Steiner, 1981), pp. 60–84; Peter G. J. Pulzer, *The Rise of Political Anti-Semitism in Germany and Austria* (New York: Wiley, 1964), pp. 141–42.

48. Martha Rozenblit, *The Jews of Vienna, 1867–1914: Assimilation and Identity* (Albany: State University of New York Press, 1983), pp. 10–11; John Bunzl, *Klassenkampf in der Diaspora: Zur Geschichte der jüdischen Arbeiterbewegung* (Vienna: Europaverlag, 1975), p. 119.

49. Gerald Stourzh, "Galten die Juden als Nationalität Altösterreichs?" in Anna Drabek, Mordechai Eliav, and Gerald Stourzh, *Prag, Czernowitz, Jerusalem: der Österreichische Staat und die Juden von Zeitalter des Absolutismus bis zum Ende der Monarchie, Studia Judaica Austraica* 10 (Eisenstadt: Edition Toetzer, 1984), pp. 73–98; Gerald Stourzh, *Die Gleichberechtigung der Nationalitäten in der Verfassung und Verwaltung Österreichs 1848–1918* (Wien: Verlag der Österreichischen Akademie der Wissenschaften, 1985), pp. 74–80; Brix, *Die Umgangssprachen in Altösterreich,* pp. 353–87.

50. Piotr Wróbel, "The Jews of Galicia under Austrian-Polish rule, 1869–1918," *Austrian History Yearbook* 25 (1994): 103.

51. J. Rotter and K. Subecki, "Protokoł r wiecu ogólno-akadem. odbytego dniu 28 November 1901 w Coll. Novum w Krakowie", Wiece opolakademickie, SII 738, AUJ; Jobst *Zwischen Nationalismus und Internationalismus,* p. 109.

52. On Radek during this period, see Józef Buszko, *Ruch socjalistyczny w Krakowie 1890–1914: Na tle ruchu robotniczego w zachodniej Galicji* (Kraków: Wydawnictwo Literackie, 1961), p. 213; Frančić, "Postępowe organizacje studenckie," p. 81; Warren Lerner, *Karl Radek: The Last Internationalist* (Stanford: Stanford University Press, 1970), pp. 6–7.

53. Letter from Henryk Grossman to the Commission of Inquiry into Karl Radek, September 17, 1912, Alfred Henke Nachlaß, Archiv der Bundesvorstand der SPD, Friedrich-Ebert-Stiftung; Georg W. Strobel, *Die Partei Rosa Luxemburgs, Lenin und die SPD: der polnische "europäische" Internationalismus in der russischen Sozialdemokratie* (Wiesbaden, F. Steiner, 1974), p. 373.

54. Myśliński, *Grupy polityczne,* pp. 89, 106, 274; Frančić, "Postępowe organizacje studenckie," pp. 80–81, 88; Police report 1001, Relacja z zebrani młodzieży akademicki.

55. "Z ostatniego kongresu galicyjskiego," *Przedświt* 24 (10–12) (October–December 1904): 467.

56. Memorandum from the director of police in Kraków to the district president, December 16, 1902, C. K. Dyrekcja Policji w Krakowie, Mat 27, Starostwo Grodzkie Krakowskie, APK; Buszko, *Ruch socjalistyczny,* p. 214. Note that Frančić mistakenly

gives the date for the establishment of *Promień*'s branch editorial office in Kraków as December 1903, Frančić, "Postępowe organizacje studenckie," p. 85; Myśliński, *Grupy polityczne,* p. 106. On Feldman, see Jonas Shmuel Blum, "Der yidisher arbeter und di Poylishe Sotsial-Dem Partey in Galitsie," in A. Tsherikover et al. (eds.), *Di yidishe sotsialistishe bevegung biz der grindung fun Bund* (Vilno/Paris: YIVO, 1939), p. 521.

57. Buszko, *Ruch socjalistyczny,* pp. 215–16.

58. Jakob Bros, "Tsu der geshikhte fun der Y. S. D. P.," in Galitsien *Royter Pinkes* 2 (Warsaw: Verlag Kultur Lige, 1924), p. 41; F. Gutman, "An araynfir-vort in sheykhes mit der antshteyung un antviklung fun zshe. p. s. d. bizn yor 1911," typescript, pp. 16–17, MG2 F107, Bund Archive, Yidisher visnshaftlikher institut/Institute for Jewish Research Archive (Bund Archive); Wasilewski mentions a debate between Grosser and himself, representing the views of the Bund and PPS, at the meeting of *Zjednoczenie,* though this may well have been the same gathering, which Gutman specifically identifies as taking place under the auspices of Ruch; Leon Wasilewski, "Ze wspomnien (1899–1904)," *Z pola walki* 4 (68) (1974): 250–51. In any case there was considerable continuity between the personnel of Ruch and the *Zjednoczenie* group (on which more below).

59. Police reports 438 and 443, Relacja z zebrani młodzieży akademicki.

60. Feliks Dzierżyński letter, February 11, 1905, in "Listy F. Dzierżyńskiego," *Z pola walki* 11–12 (1931): 110; Jerzy Myśliński, *Grupy polityczne Królestwa Polskiego w Zachodniej Galicji (1895–1904)* (Warsaw: Książka i Wiedza, 1967), p. 125.

61. Stead, "The Exploits of Jan Callowjan," notes for a story, Box 11, Folder 79, Stead Collection.

62. Ignacy Daszyński, "Nationalität und Sozialismus," *Sozialistische Monatshefte* 6 (10) (October 1902): 734.

63. Buszko, *Ruch socjalistyczny,* p. 206.

64. *Naprzód,* November 1, 1904.

65. Walentyna Najdus, *Polska Partia Socjalno-Demokratyczna Galicji i śląska 1890–1919* (Warszawa: Państwowe Wydawnictwo Naukowe, 1983), p. 398; Jobst, *Zwischen Nationalismus und Internationalismus,* pp. 134–36.

66. "Z ostatniego kongresu galicyjskiego," pp. 465–69.

67. Ibid.

68. Letter from Henryk Grossman, February 15, 1905, Sprawa Grossmana, 305/V/11 podt. 3, Zespol akt PPS, Archiwum Akt Nowych (Sprawa Grossmana), item 4; Bogdan Nawroczynski, *Szkołę Polską 1901–1917,* Tom II (Warszawa: Książnica-Atlas, 1934), p. 481.

69. Walentyna Najdus, "Galicja" in Stanisław Kalabiński, *Polska Klasa Robotnicza: Zarys dziejów,* Tom I część 3 (Warsaw: Państwowe Wydawnictwo Naukowe, 1978), pp. 436, 474.

70. "Od redakcyi," *Zjednoczenie* 1, February 1905, pp. 1–3.

71. Ruch socyalistyczny i opozycyjny w caracie, *Zjednoczenie* 1 (February 1905): 16, which quotes from Vladimir Ilych Lenin, "The National Question in Our Programme," *Collected Works,* vol. 6, 4th ed. (Moscow: Progress Publishers, 1964 [1903]), p. 460.

72. Rewolucya w Rosji, *Zjednoczenie* 1 (February 1905): 25–28.

73. "Ostrzeżenie," *Naprzód*, February 2, 1905, Sprawa Grossmana, item 1; "Przestroga," *Naprzód*, February 5, 1905, Sprawa Grossmana, item 2.

74. Letter from Henryk Grossman, February 15, 1905, Sprawa Grossman, item 4a.

75. "Ostrzeżenie," *Naprzód*, February 17, 1905, Sprawa Grossmana, item 5a; "Zakapturzony anarchism," *Naprzód*, February 17, 1905, Sprawa Grossmana, item 5b.

76. Letter from Henryk Grossman, February 18, 1905, Sprawa Grossmana, item 6.

77. Zbigniew Ostrowiec, "*Naprzód*", organ Polskiej Partyi Socyalno-Demokratycznej o "*Zjednoczeniu*", organie Młodz. Socyalistycznej (Przyczynek do charakterystyki bagna galicyjsk.) (Kraków: Zjednoczenie, 1905), pp. 6–7, 10.

78. Najdus, *Polska Partia Socjalno-Demokratyczna*, pp. 435–36.

79. Henryk Piasecki, *Sekcja Żydowska PPSD i Żydowska Partia Socjalno-Demokratyczna* (Wrocław: Zakład Narodowy imienia Ossolińskich, 1982), p. 109.

80. Buszko, *Ruch socjalistyczny*, p. 234.

81. Executive Committee resolution, February 21, 1905, Sprawa Grossmana, item 9.

82. Letter from Henryk Grossman, February 22, 1905, Sprawa Grossmana, item 10.

83. "W sprawie ostrzeżeń," *Naprzód*, February 21, 1905, Sprawa Grossmana, item 8.

84. "Założenie i działalnść żydowskiej partii socjalno-demokratiycznej separatystów in Galicji w 1905 r.," Mat 80, items 177 and 304, Starostwo Grodzkie Krakowskie, Wojewódzkie Archiwum Państwowe w Krakowie; Buszko, *Ruch socjalistyczny*, p. 235.

85. "Sprawy partyjnie," *Naprzód*, February 26, 1905, Sprawa Grossmana, item 12.

86. Letter from Maurycy Papier, March 2, 1905, Sprawa Grossmana, item 17.

87. Jakob Thon, "Die Berufsgliederung der Juden in Galizien," *Zeitschrift für Demographie und Statistik der Juden* 3 (8–9) (August–September 1907): 114–16.

88. Max Rosenfeld, *Die polnische Judenfrage* (Wien-Berlin: Löwit Verlag, 1918), p. 81.

89. On the emergence of the Jewish labor movement in Galicia, see Henryk Grossman, *Bundizm in Galitsien* (Kraków: Publishing House of the *Social Democrat*, 1907 [cover has 1908, title page 1907]); Jakob Bross, "The Beginning of the Jewish Labor Movement in Galicia," *YIVO Annual of Jewish Social Science* 5 (1950); Yosef Kisman, "Di yidishe sotsial-demokratishe bevegung in Galitsie un Bukovine," in G. Aronson et al. (eds.), *Di geshikhte fun Bund drite band* (New York: Farlag Unzer Tsayt, 1966); Najdus, *Polska Partia Socjalno-Demokratyczna*; Piasecki, *Sekcja Żydowska*.

90. Bross dated the start of the problem period to 1899–1901, "The Beginning of the Jewish Labor Movement," p. 82; also see Bros, "Tsu der geshikhte," pp. 32, 43–44. According to Grossman, the decline occurred after 1897, Grossman, *Bundizm in Galitsien*, p. 25.

91. *Yidisher sotsial-demokrat* 2 (May 1905): 39.

92. Grossman argued that this opportunism was already apparent in the GPSD's approach to the 1892 Kolomea weavers strike; Grossman, *Bundizm in Galitsien*, pp. 19, 25, 29.

93. Jüdische sozial-demokratische Partei (JüSDP), *An die Sozialdemokraten in Oesterreich!* (Krakau: Der Sozialdemokrat, 1905), p. 1.

94. Sigmund Gliksman, "Etapen bis tsu der proklamirung fun der YSDP in Galitsie," *Sotsial-demokrat*, May 1, 1920, p. 3; Bros, "Tsu der geshikhte," p. 40.

95. *Yidisher sotsial-demokrat* 2 (May 1905): 39; Piasecki, *Sekcja Żydowska*, pp. 87–88, 91.

96. Stead, notes, Box 6, Folder 45, Stead Collection. Also see Henryk Grossman letter, July 13 (probably 1905), MG2 F107, Bund Archive; "Poylinklub, Yidenklub, un der zion-istisher sharlatanizmus," *Sotsial-demokrat*, September 28, 1906, pp. 1–2, signed H. G. in Roman letters; Leon Feyner, "Di bundishe prese in Kraków fun 1905 bis 1930," *Histor-isher samlbuch: materialn un dokumentn tsushtayer tsu der geshikhte fun algemayner yidishn arbeter-bund* (Warsaw: Farlag Ringen, 1948), p. 20.

97. Stead, "Notes from a visit to 'the Tyl,'" Box 5, Folder 32, Stead Collection.

98. Chaskel Grossmann "Rodowód" 1901/1902 and 1902, 505–6, S II, AUJ.

99. Stead, notes, Box 6, Folder 45, Stead Collection.

100. *Yidisher sotsial-demokrat* 2 (May 1905): 39; Piasecki, *Sekcja Żydowska*, pp. 87–88, 91.

101. Ostrowiec *"Naprzód" o "Zjednoczeniu"*, pp. 6–7.

102. Bros, "Tsu der geshikhte," p. 43.

103. David F. Good, *The Economic Rise of the Habsburg Empire 1750–1914* (Berkeley: University of California Press, 1984), p. 165.

104. Frančić, "Postępowe organizacje studenckie," p. 89; Piasecki, *Sekcja Żydowska*, p. 97.

105. Gramsci, *Selections*, pp. 15–16. For the relationship between Gramsci's concep-tion of intellectuals and the revolutionary party, see John Molyneux, *Marxism and the Party* (London: Pluto, 1978), pp. 148–54.

106. *Yidisher sotsial-demokrat* 2 (May 1905): 39.

107. Najdus, *Polska Partia Socjalno-Demokratyczna*, pp. 392–94.

108. Gliksman, "Etapen," p. 3.

109. The German-Austrian Party provided financial subventions for the Polish organization; Tych, "Die Sozialdemokratische Partei Galiziens," pp. 251–52. Adler also acted as an intermediary in Daszyński's efforts to obtain funds from the SPD to enable *Naprzód* to become a daily newspaper from January 1900; Jobst, *Zwischen Nationalis-mus und Internationalismus*, p. 49.

110. There are different accounts of the numbers at the conference and the numbers who voted for Diamand's motion. The figures given are from "Konferencya towarzyszy żydowskch we Lwowie," *Przedświt* 23 (6) (June 1903): 252–57, but also see Piasecki, *Sekcja Żydowska*, pp. 79–83; Gliksman, "Etapen," p. 3.

111. Piasecki, *Sekcja Żydowska*, p. 97.

112. Gliksman, "Etapen," p. 3.

113. Piasecki, *Sekcja Żydowska*, p. 86.

114. Feyner, "Di bundishe prese," p. 20.

115. *Yidisher sotsial-demokrat* 2 (May 1905): 39. M. Aleksandrovitsh, "Peysekh Dem-bitser," in Jakob S. Herts (ed.), *Doyres Bundisten*, vol. 2 (New York: Farlag Unzer Tsayt, 1956), pp. 200–201.

116. Piasecki, *Sekcja Żydowska*, pp. 86–87.

117. Gliksman pointed out that the party took disciplinary action against Eyneygler, Abraham Poch, and Yitskhok Blind for circulating Bundist material; "Etapen," p. 3. See David Salamander's criticisms of the distribution of non-PPSD material in Yiddish by Jewish workers' associations; *Naprzód*, November 3, 1904, p. 1. Salamander was a Jewish supporter of the party leadership.

118. Jakob Kener, *Kvershnit (1897–1947): fragmenten fun zikhrones, epizoden vegn umgekomene kedoyshim, martirer un kemfer* (New York: Tsentral komitet fun linke Poale-Tsion in di Fareynikte Shtotn un Kanade, 1947), pp. 23–24; Anshel Reiss, *Bereshit tenuot hapoelim hayehudim begalitsyah* (Tel Aviv: World Federation of Polish Jews, 1973), pp. 48–53.

119. Kener, *Kvershnit*, p. 23; Bunzl, *Klassenkampf in der Diaspora*, p. 124.

120. Buszko, *Ruch socjalistyczny*, p. 204.

121. Bros, "Tsu der geshikhte," p. 44.

122. Kisman, "Di yidishe sotsial-demokratishe bevegung," p. 365; Piasecki, *Sekcja Żydowska*, p. 90.

123. Karol Eyneygler, "Fun meyne notitsen," *Sotsial-demokrat*, May 1, 1920, p. 4.

124. For Daszyński's statements at meetings of the Kraków Committee of the PPSD on September 26 and October 24, 1904, see Piasecki, *Sekcja Żydowska*, pp. 88–90.

125. See K. S. Kazdan, "Der Bund biz dem finftn tsuzamenfor," in G. Aronson et al. (eds.), *Di geshikhte fun Bund: ershter band* (New York: Farlag Unzer Tsayt, 1960), pp. 238–40; on Lekert and the Bund's attitude to individual acts of violence, see Henry J. Tobias, *The Jewish Bund in Russia from its Origins to 1905* (Stanford: Stanford University Press, 1972), pp. 148–51; and Ezra Mendelsohn, *Class Struggle in the Pale: The Formative Years of the Jewish Workers Movement in Tsarist Russia* (Cambridge: Cambridge University Press, 1970), p. 103.

126. Gliksman, "Etapen," p. 3.

127. Bros, "Tsu der geshikhte," pp. 40–41. Kisman, "Di yidishe sotsial-demokratishe bevegung," p. 368. For the separatists' receipt of Bund literature, see a letter from Henryk Grossman to the Foreign Committee of the Bund, April 8, 1905, MG2 F107 Bund Archive.

128. Leon Wasilewski, "Ze wspomnień (1899–1904)," *Z pola walki* 4 (68) (1974): 250–51; letter from Henryk Grossman to the Foreign Committee of the Bund, April 8, 1905, MG2 F107 Bund Archive.

129. Letters from Henryk Grossman to the Foreign Committee of the Bund, April 8, 1905, MG2 F107, Bund Archive, and July 3, 1905, ibid.

130. *Jahrbuch der Sozialdemokratischen und Anarchistischen Bewegung des Jahres 1904* C 1021, Archiv der Bundespolizeidirektion Wien (SAB 1904), p. 28.

131. Quoted in Piasecki, *Sekcja Żydowska*, p. 90.

132. Bros, "Tsu der geshikhte," pp. 44–45; Kisman, "Di yidishe sotsial-demokratishe bevegung," pp. 365–66; Piasecki, *Sekcja Żydowska*, p. 58.

133. *Naprzód*, November 1, 1904.

134. SAB 1904, p. 29; *Naprzód*, November 3, 1904; Piasecki, *Sekcja Żydowska*, p. 93.

135. *Naprzód,* November 3, 1904.

136. Gliksman, "Etapen," p. 3; Feyner, "Di bundishe prese," p. 18. Gliksman states that the decision to publish the *Yidisher sotsial-demokrat* was made after the Galician Trade Union Congress of late March 1905. Feyner's observation that it was taken after the PPSD Congress in late 1904 is more probable.

137. Henryk Grossman, *Proletariat wobec kwestyi żydowskiej z powodu niedysku-towanej dyskusyi w Krytyce* (Kraków: Drukani Wladysława Teodorczuka, January 1905), p. 31.

138. Ibid., p. 14. Cf. M. Helvetius, *A treatise on Man his intellectual faculties and his education,* vol. II, (New York: Burt Franklin, 1969 [1810]), p. 90, with Benjamin Disraeli, *Sybil* (Ware: Wordsworth Classic, 1995), p. 58. Kelles-Krauz drew on Ernest Renan's account of nations. Grossman's attack on Kelles-Krauz's bourgeois standpoint accorded with Medem's critique of Renan; see Vinitski (Vladimir Medem), "Di sotsialdemokratie un di natsionale frage," *Yidishe arbeyter* 17 (1904): 29.

139. The quotation is from Wileński (Józefa Kwiatka), *Kwestia żydowska* (Kraków: Latarnia, 1904), distributed by the PPSD; see Piasecki, *Sekcja Żydowska,* p. 149.

140. Grossman, *Proletariat wobec kwestyi żydowskiej,* p. 17.

141. Ibid. p. 18.

142. Ibid.

143. Ibid., pp. 20–21.

144. Ibid., pp. 23–25, 37.

145. Ibid., p. 26.

146. Ibid., pp. 42–43.

147. Ibid., p. 42. For a description and defense of Lenin's predilection for this methodology, see Tony Cliff, *Lenin,* vol. 1: *Building the Party* (London: Pluto, 1975), pp. 66–68.

148. Grossman, *Proletariat wobec kwestyi żydowskiej,* pp. 28–30, 33, 43.

149. Ibid., p. 42.

150. Marx and Engels, The *Manifesto of the Communist Party,* p. 52. Kautsky had elaborated on the analysis and helped confirm it as a tenet of orthodox Marxism; "Die moderne Nationalität," *Neue Zeit* 5 (1887): 392–405, 442–51.

151. Medem "Di sotsialdemokratie un di natsionale frage," p. 30. The relevant passage is cited by Koppel S. Pinson, "Arkady Kremer, Vladimir Medem, and the Ideology of the Jewish Bund," *Jewish Social Studies* 7 (3) (1945): 251.

152. Grossman, *Proletariat wobec kwestyi żydowskiej,* p. 39.

153. Ibid., p. 40.

154. Ibid., p. 41.

155. Ibid., pp. 39, 44; Bros, "Tsu der geshikhte," p. 44.

156. *Di naie epokhe in der yidisher arbeter baevegung/ Povorotnyi punkt v istorii yevreiskago rabochago dvizheniia,* cited by Tobias, *The Jewish Bund,* pp. 55–56, and Israel Getzler, *Martov: A Political Biography of a Russian Social Democrat* (Melbourne: Melbourne University Press, 1967), pp. 25–26.

157. See Żydowska Partia Socjalno-Demokratyzna (ŻPSD), "Święto majowe," in ŻPSD, *Przed Kongresem,* (Kraków, June 2, 1905), p. 6.

158. Ostrowiec, *"Naprzód" o "Zjednoczenie"*, pp. 6–7.

159. Letter from Jakob Bross and Maurycy Papier to the Executive Committee of the PPSD, received by hand, February 21, 1905, Sprawa Grossmana, item 7.

160. Buszko, citing the report of a police informer on the party Executive meeting of February 26, 1905, *Ruch socjalistyczny*, p. 236.

161. "Sprawy partyjnie," *Naprzód*, March 5, 1905, Sprawa Grossmana, item 18; *Głos Robotniczy*, March 11, 1905, p. 6; Buszko, *Ruch socjalistyczny*, p. 236.

162. For a more detailed discussion of the issues, see Rick Kuhn, "Jewish Socialists in Galicia and Marxist Debates over the National Question before World War I," paper presented to the Political Thought and Capitalism Seminar, University of Newcastle, February 17–19, 1998, http://eprints.anu.edu.au/archive/00002598/01/Jewish_socialists_ and_national_question.pdf, accessed June 5, 2006.

163. Karl Renner, "State and Nation," in Ephraim Nimni (ed.), *National Cultural Autonomy and Its Contemporary Critics* (Abingdon: Routledge, 2005 [1899]), pp. 15–47; Norbert Leser, *Zwischen Reformismus und Bolschewismus: Der Austromarxismus als Theorie und Praxis* (Vienna: Europa Verlag, 1968), p. 250.

164. Roman Rosdolsky, *Engels and the Nonhistoric Peoples: The National Question in the Revolution of 1848* (Glasgow: Critique Books, 1987), p. 184.

165. "Ruch socyalistyczny i opozycyjny w caracie," *Zjednoczenie* 1, February 1905, p. 16.

166. Vladimir Ilych Lenin, "Does the Jewish Proletariat Need an Independent Political Party (1903)," *Lenin on the Jewish Question* (New York: International Publishers, 1974), p. 24. The most systematic statement of the *Iskraist* position is Vladimir Ilych Lenin, *What is to be Done?*, *Collected Works*, vol. 5, 4th ed. (Moscow: Progress Publishers, 1986 [1902]), pp. 382–91.

167. Raimund Löw, "Theorie und Praxis des Austromarxismus," in Raimund Löw, Siegfried Mattl, and Alfred Pfabigan, *Der Austromarxismus—eine Autopsie: Drei Studien* (Frankfurt am Main: ISP-Verlag, 1986), p. 14.

168. Lenin, "The National Question in our Programme," p. 463.

169. Lenin, *What is to be Done?* p. 412. Also see Lenin, "The National Question in our Programme," p. 461.

170. "Sprawy partyjnie," *Naprzód*, March 5, 1905, Sprawa Grossmana, item 18; *Głos Robotniczy*, March 11, 1905, p. 6; Buszko, *Ruch socjalistyczny*, p. 236.

171. "Wyjaśneinie," *Naprzód*, March 12, 1905, item 20; "Sprawy partyjnie," *Naprzód*, March 18, 1905, Sprawa Grossmana, item 21.

172. Vladimir Ilych Lenin, "The Position of the Bund in the Party," *Lenin on the Jewish Question* (1903), pp. 48–49.

173. "Posiednzienie Zarzadu", *Naprzód*, March 25, 1905, Sprawa Grossmana, item 22; Piasecki, *Sekcja Żydowska*, pp. 111–12.

174. Buszko, *Ruch socjalistyczny*, p. 237.

175. Buszko, citing the report of a police informer on the party Executive meeting of March 5, 1905, *Ruch socjalistyczny*, p. 237.

176. Buszko, *Ruch socjalistyczny*, pp. 242–43.

177. SAB 1905, p. 50. For statistics on the Austrian, including the Galician trade union movement, see *Die Gewerkschaft* neue Folge 7 (12), June 23, 1905, p. 184.

178. Najdus, *Polska Partia Socjalno-Demokratyczna*, p. 392.

179. *Yidisher sotsial-demokrat* 1 (April 1905): 29–30, the previously withheld April issue was bound together with the May issue of the *Yidisher sotsial-demokrat*; Kisman, "Di yidishe sotsial-demokratishe bevegung," pp. 366–67.

180. Piasecki, *Sekcja Żydowska*, p. 113; Najdus, *Polska Partia Socjalno-Demokratyczna*, p. 437.

181. Tobias, *The Jewish Bund*, pp. 296, 299.

182. "Fun shtedt un shtedtlikh," *Yidisher sotsial-demokrat* 1 (April 1905): 26–29.

183. "Fun shtedt un shtedtlikh," *Yidisher sotsial-demokrat* 2 (May 1905): 40.

184. Eyneygler, "Fun meyne notitsen," p. 4.

185. ŻPSD, "Święto majowe," p. 6; Piasecki, *Sekcja Żydowska*, p. 113.

186. Eyneygler, "Fun meyne notitsen," p. 4.

187. Ibid.; Bros, "Tsu der geshikhte," p. 45; L. Feyner, "Di bundishe prese," pp. 18–23; Kisman, "Di yidishe sotsial-demokratishe bevegung," pp. 366–67. The precise sequence of events in the preparation of the split between late 1904 and May 1905 is not entirely clear.

188. Buszko, *Ruch socjalistyczny*, p. 237, citing a police report of April 3, 1905.

189. Letter from Henryk Grossman to the Foreign Committee of the Bund, Kraków, April 8, 1905, MG2 F107, Bund Archive. Grossman refers to Bronisław Grosser, one of whose pseudonyms was Sławek, as Sławka Gr .

190. Henryk Schreiber, "Erb der prokamirung," *Sotsial-demokrat*, May 1, 1920, p. 4.

191. ŻPSD, "Agitacya w kraju" in ŻPSD, *Przed Kongresem*, p. 9.

192. Letter from Henryk Grossman to the Foreign Committee of the Bund, Kraków, April 8, 1905, MG2 F107, Bund Archive, YIVO Institute for Jewish Research Archive, New York; Yehushe Loubshteyn, "Dr. Leyb Landau," in Jakob S. Herts (ed.), *Doyres Bundisten,* vol. 3 (New York: Farlag Unzer Tsayt, 1968), p. 93.

193. *Yidisher sotsial-demokrat*, 2 (May 1905): 37–38.

194. Cited by Jack Jacobs, *On Socialists and the Jewish Question after Marx* (New York: New York University Press, 1992), pp. 92, 214.

195. Buszko, *Ruch socjalistyczny*, p. 237.

Chapter 2: Leading the Jewish Social Democratic Party

1. Walentyna Najdus, *Polska Partia Socjalno-Demokratyczna Galicji i śląska 1890–1919* (Warszawa: Państwowe Wydawnictwo Naukowe, 1983), p. 437. In Yiddish the new party was the *Yidishe sotsial-demokratishe partey in Galitsien;* and in Polish Żydowska Partya Socyalno-Demokratyczna Galicyi, or the ŻPS.

2. Komitet Organizacyjny Żydowskiej partyi Socyalno-Demokraticyczney w Galicyi, *Czego chcemy?* (Kraków, 1905); Yidishe sotsial-demokratishe partey in Galitsien, "Vos Viln Mir?," *Yidisher sotsial-demokrat* 2 (May 1905): 1–9. There are some significant differences in expression between the Polish and Yiddish versions.

3. Żydowska Partia Socjalno-Demokratyzna (ŻPSD), "Święto majowe," in ŻPSD, *Przed Kongresem*, (Kraków: June 2, 1905), p. 7; Najdus, *Polska Partia Socjalno-Demokratyczna*, p. 437.

4. ŻPSD, "Święto majowe," pp. 6–7.

5. Ibid., p. 7.

6. Najdus, *Polska Partia Socjalno-Demokratyczna*, p. 440; *Sotsial-demokrat*, October 27, 1905; Henryk Piasecki, *Sekcja Żydowska PPSD i Żydowska Partia Socjalno-Demokratyczna* (Wrocław: Zakład Narodowy imienia Ossolińskich, 1982), p. 47.

7. Leon Feyner, "Di bundishe prese in Kraków fun 1905 bis 1930," in *Historisher samlbuch: materialn un dokumentn tsushtayer tsu der geshikhte fun algemayner yidishn arbeter-bund* (Warsaw: Farlag Ringen, 1948), p. 18. Solomon Reyzen indicated Grossman "published" the manifesto; *Leksikon fun der yidisher literatur, prese un filologie*, vol. 1, 2nd ed. (Vilno: Vilner Farlag fun B. Kletskin, 1926), column 616.

8. Komitet organizacyjny, *Czego chcemy?* p. 2.

9. Ibid., p. 4.

10. Ibid., pp. 5, 7–8.

11. Ibid., p. 7; Henryk Grossman, *Proletariat wobec kwestyi żydowskiej z powodu niedyskutowanej dyskusyi w "Krytyce"* (Kraków, 1905), p. 11; *Yidisher sotsial-demokrat* 1 (April 1905): 3.

12. Yosef Kisman, "Di yidishe sotsial-demokratishe bevegung in Galitsie un Bukovine," in G. Aronson et al. (eds.), *Di geshikhte fun Bund drite band* (New York: Farlag Unzer Tsayt, 1966), p. 376.

13. Daszyński cited in "Eine jüdische Gründung," *Arbeiter-Zeitung*, Thursday, May, 4, 1905, no. 122, p. 4. Also see the review of Grossman's *Proletariat wobec kwestyi żydowskiej* by "R." in *Promien* 7 (5–6), May–June 1905, pp. 262–64.

14. ŻPSD, "Agitacya w kraju," in ŻPSD, *Przed Kongresem*, pp. 9–10.

15. Rosa Luxemburg, "Foreword to the Anthology The Polish Question and the Socialist Movement", *The National Question: Selected Writings by Rosa Luxemburg* (New York: Monthly Review Press, 1976 [Kraków, 1905]), p. 90. See Henryk Grossman's reference to Daszyński's support for the split by the PPS in German-occupied Poland from the German Social Democratic Party; ŻPSD, "Odpowiedzi Polskiej Partyi Soc.-Dem. Galicyi," in ŻPSD, *Przed Kongresem*, p. 4.

16. "Die Gesamtexekutive und die jüdischen Separatisten in Galizien," *Arbeiter-Zeitung*, 135, Wednesday, May 17, 1905, p. 7.

17. "Eine jüdische Gründung," *Arbeiter-Zeitung* 122, Thursday, May 4, 1905, p. 4.

18. Minutes of sitting of May 12, 1905, Parteivertretung, "Exekutive Handprotokolle 12.1.1905 bis 16.8.1905," Heft 3, Sitzungsprotokolle, Alte partei Archiv, Verein für Geschichte der Arbeiterbewegung, Wien.

19. "Die Gesamtexekutive und die jüdischen Separatisten in Galizien," *Arbeiter-Zeitung*, 135, Wednesday, May 17, 1905, p. 8. Also see Raimund Löw, *Der Zerfall der "Kleinen Internationale": Nationalitätenkronflikte in der Arbeiterbewegung des alten Österreich (1889–1914)* (Wien: Europaverlag, 1984), pp. 63–64; and "Bericht der Gesamtparteivertretung der Sozialdemokratie in Oesterreich an den Parteitag 1905 in Wien," in

Sozialdemokratische Arbeiter Partei Österreich, *Protokoll über die Verhandlungen des Gesamtparteitages der Sozialdemokratischen Arbeiterpartei in Österreich 30 October-2 November 1905* (Wien, 1905), p. 16.

20. *Yidisher sotsial-demokrat* 3 (June 1905): 4–5.

21. ŻPSD, "Agitacya w kraju," pp. 10–11.

22. Jüdische sozial-demokratische Partei (JüSDP), *Bericht zum Gesamt-Parteitage der Oesterreichischen Sozialdemokratie in Wien 1905 (1 Mai-23 Oktober 1905)*, "Der Sozialdemokrat," Krakau, 1905, p. 2.

23. ŻPSD, "Odpowiedz Polskiej Partyi soc. dem. Galicyi," in ŻPSD, *Przed Kongresem*, pp. 1–6. For Grossman's authorship, see Piasecki, *Sekcja Żydowska*, p. 126.

24. ŻPSD, "Odpowiedz," p. 6. Grossman's quotation from Ignacy Daszyński "Nationalität und Sozialismus," *Sozialistische Monatshefte* 6 (10) (October 1902): 735 is truncated.

25. *Yidisher sotsial-demokrat* 3 (June 1905): 20.

26. Letter from Henryk Grossman to the Foreign Committee of the Bund, July 27, 1905, MG2 F107, Bund Archive, Yidisher visnshaftlikher institut/YIVO Institute for Jewish Research Archive, New York.

27. *Yidisher sotsial-demokrat* 3 (June 1905): 25.

28. Ibid., p. 22; also see Grossman, *Proletariat wobec kwestyi żydowskiej;* ŻPSD, "Odpowiedz."

29. *Yidisher sotsial-demokrat* 3 (June 1905): 23–24.

30. Letter from Henryk Grossman to the Bund, July 27, 1905, MG2 F107, Bund Archive.

31. *Yidisher sotsial-demokrat* 3 (June 1905): 27. The photograph is item PO 2195, YIVO Institute for Jewish Research Archive, New York.

32. JüSDP, *Bericht zum Gesamt-Parteitag*, pp. 1–2. Also see Jakob Bros, "Tsu der geshikhte fun der Y. S. D. P.," in *Galitsien* Royter Pinkes 2 (Warsaw: Verlag Kultur Lige, 1924), p. 44.

33. JüSDP, *Bericht zum Gesamt-Parteitag*, p. 1.

34. *Yidisher sotsial-demokrat* 3 (June 1905): back cover.

35. Letter from Henryk Grossman, July 3, 1905, MG2 F107, Bund Archive; letter from Henryk Grossman, July 13 (1905), MG2 F107, Bund Archive.

36. *Sotsial-demokrat*, October 20, 1905, p. 2.

37. David F. Good, *The Economic Rise of the Habsburg Empire 1750–1914* (Berkeley: University of California Press, 1984), pp. 122–23, citing Michael Mesch, "Die Einkommenssituation der österreichischen Arbeiterschaft in der Spätgrunderzeit, 1890–1914" (unpublished Ph.D. thesis, University of Vienna, 1982).

38. Walentyna Najdus, "Galicja," in Stanisław Kalabiński, *Polska Klasa Robotnicza: Zarys dziejów*, Tom I, część 3 (Warsaw: Państwowe Wydawnictwo Naukowe, 1978), p. 436.

39. JüSDP, *Bericht zum Gesamt-Parteitag*, p. 2.

40. *Yidisher sotsial-demokrat* 4–5 (July–August 1905): 38–39.

41. Letter from Henryk Grossman to the Bund, July 27, 1905, MG2 F107, Bund Archive.

42. JüSDP, *Bericht zum Gesamt-Parteitag*, p. 1.

43. The request to the Bund for an editor is in a letter from Henryk Grossman, July 27, 1905, Bund MG2 F107, Bund Archive; Feyner, "Di bundishe prese," p. 20. *Sotsial-demokrat*, October 6, 1905, p. 3.

44. *Sotsial-demokrat*, November 3, 1905, p. 3.

45. Letter from Henryk Grossman to Victor Adler, October 23, 1905, Mappe 176, Adler-Archiv, Verein für Geschichte der Arbeiterbewegung. This matter was also highlighted in *Sotsial-demokrat*, October 27, 1905, p. 3.

46. JüSDP, *Bericht zum Gesamt-Parteitage*; JüSDP, *An die Sozialdemokraten in Oesterreich!* "Der Sozialdemokrat," Krakau, 1905. Grossman wrote this address, according to Feyner, "Di bundishe prese," p. 19. It is likely that he, as Jewish Social Democratic Party (JSDP) secretary, also wrote the *Report*.

47. JüSDP, *An die Sozialdemokraten in Oesterreich*, p. 1.

48. Ibid., p. 2.

49. JüSDP, *Bericht zum Gesamt-Parteitage*, p. 1.

50. Ibid.

51. Ibid., pp. 1–2.

52. *Sotsial-demokrat*, November 3, 1905, p. 3; November 10, p. 2. Also see Sozialdemokratische Arbeiter Partei Österreich, *Protokoll über die Verhandlungen*, p. 70.

53. Maria Sporrer, "Aspekte zur Frauenwahlrechtsbewegung bis 1918 in der Österreichischen Sozialdemokratie," in Helmut Konrad, *Imperialismus und Arbeiterbewegung in Deutschland und Österreich Bilaterales Symposium DDR-Österreich zur Geschichte der Arbeiterbewegung* (Wien: Europaverlag, 1985), pp. 107–8.

54. William Alexander Jenks, *The Austrian Electoral Reform of 1907* (New York: Columbia University Press, 1950), p. 41.

55. Hans Mommsen, *Die Sozialdemokratie und die Nationalitätenfrage im habsburgischen Vielvolkerstadt* (Wien: Europa Verlag, 1963), pp. 366, 370–71.

56. Jósef Buszko and Henryk Dobrowolski, *Udział Galicji w rewolucji 1905–1907* (Kraków: Wydawnictwo Literackie, 1957), p. 92.

57. *Jahrbuch der Sozialdemokratischen und Anarchistischen Bewegung des Jahres 1905* C 1021, Archiv der Bundespolizeidirektion Wien (SAB 1905), 1905, p. 41.

58. *Sotsial-demokrat*, November 10, 1905, p. 3.

59. Ibid., pp. 3–4; November 17, 1905, p. 4; November 24, 1905, p. 1.

60. Jenks, *The Austrian Electoral Reform of 1907*, p. 44; Mommsen, *Die Sozialdemokratie und die Nationalitätenfrage*, p. 372.

61. "Der vahlkampf," *Sotsial-demokrat*, December 1, 1905, pp. 1–2; *Arbeiter-Zeitung*, November 29, 1905, p. 5; Najdus, "Galicja," p. 456. Najdus reports that the police estimated the size of the Kraków demonstration as only 10,000.

62. Mommsen, *Die Sozialdemokratie und die Nationalitätenfrage*, pp. 370–81.

63. Jindřich [sic] Grossmann, "Židovská Strana Sociálně Demokratická v Haliči," *Akademie: Socialistická Revue* 1906. German translation "Die Jüdische Sozialdemokratische Partei in Galizien," in Löw, *Der Zerfall der "Kleinen Internationale,"* pp. 220–27. On Czech social democracy during this period, see Bernard Wheaton, *Radical Socialism in Czechoslovakia: Bohumir Smeral, the Czech Road to Socialism and the Origins of the Czechoslovak Communist Party (1917–1291)*, East European Monographs (Boulder, 1986), pp. 3–12, 174.

64. Najdus, *Ignacy Daszyński*, p. 241; Kerstin Jobst, *Zwischen Nationalismus und Internationalismus: Die polnische und ukrainische Sozialdemokratie in Galizien von 1890 bis 1914. Ein Beitrag zur Nationalitätenfrage im Habsburgerreich* (Hamburg: Dölling und Galitz, 1996), pp. 193, 223.

65. "Die Stärke der Gewerkschaften nach Kronländern geordnet," *Die Gewerkschaft* new series 7 (12) (June 23, 1905): 184; Heinrich Beer, "Die Gewerkschaftsbewegung in Österreich," *Neue Zeit* 24 (2) no. 45 (August 1, 1906): 628–29; "Die Stärke und Leistungsfähigkeit der Gewerkschaften Österreichs im Jahre 1906," *Die Gewerkschaft* new series 9 (11) (June 14, 1907): 191–92; "Sozialpolitische Chronik: Die österreichische Gewerkschaftsbewegung im Jahre 1910," *Archiv für Sozialwissenschaft und Sozialpolitik* 32 (1911): 924.

66. *Sotsial-demokrat*, March 2, 1906, p. 3; "Dos 40 yohriger yubileum fun 'Kapital,'" ibid., July 19, 1907, p. 1.

67. Jenks, *The Austrian Electoral Reform*, pp. 57, 145.

68. "Der II oyserordentlikher kongres fun der Yud. Sots. Dem. Partey," *Sotsial-demokrat*, June 8, 1906, p. 3; "Nakhn tsuzamenfahr," *Sotsial-demokrat*, June 8, 1906, p. 1.

69. "Der II oyserordentlikher kongres fun der Yud. Sots. Dem. Partey," *Sotsial-demokrat*, June 8, 1906, p. 2.

70. "Nakhn tsuzamenfahr," *Sotsial-demokrat*, June 8, 1906, p. 1.

71. "Der II oyserordentlikher kongres fun der Yud. Sots. Dem. Partey, II fortsetsung," *Sotsial-demokrat*, June 15, 1906, p. 2.

72. Ibid.

73. See, for example, on the relationship between periods of "peaceful" development and those of revolutionary struggle, Vladimir Ilych Lenin, "Karl Marx: A Brief Biographical Sketch with an Exposition of Marxism," "Karl Marx and His Teachings," *Collected Works*, vol. 21, 4th ed. (Moscow: Progress Publishers, 1980 [1918, written 1914]), p. 75; also Paul Frölich, *Rosa Luxemburg* (London: Pluto, 1972), pp. 110–11.

74. *Arbeiter-Zeitung*, June 10, 1906, p. 1.

75. Jenks, *The Austrian Electoral Reform*, pp. 68, 94–95, 100, 104, 118, 127.

76. "Der II oyserordentlikher kongres, II fortsetsung," p. 3.

77. Ibid.

78. *Sotsial-demokrat*, December 29, 1905 p. 3; January 5, 1906, p. 4. In the first report, the talk is entitled "The National Question in Relation to the Political Situation in Austria," in the second "The Jews and the Political Situation in Austria." Also see Y. A., "The Z.P.S. (later, the Bund) in Przemysl," in Arie Menczer (ed.), *Sefer Przemysl* Irgun Yotzei

Przemysl, Tel Aviv 1964 translation at www.jewishgen.org/yizkor/przemysl/prz286 .html#Page288, accessed June 5, 2006.

79. Henry J. Tobias, *The Jewish Bund in Russia from its Origins to 1905* (Stanford: Stanford University Press, 1972), pp. 331–32; J. S. Herts, "Di ershte ruslender revolutsie," in G. Aronson et al. (eds.), *Di geshikhte fun Bund: tsveyter band* (New York: Farlag Unzer Tsayt, 1962), p. 375; Nora Levin, *Jewish Socialist Movements, 1871–1917: While the Messiah Tarried* (London: Routledge & Kegan Paul, 1978), pp. 303, 319, 324; Julius Martow, *Geschichte der russischen Sozialdemokratie* (Erlangen: Politladen, 1973 [1926]), p. 190. The reunification of the Bund and the RSDLP was reported in "Di fereynigung fun dem Bund mit der Rus. Sots. Dem. Arbeyter Partey," *Sotsial-demokrat,* May 25, 1906, p. 2. The Bolsheviks at the unification Congress were bound by factional discipline to vote in favor of readmitting the Bund, while more than two-thirds of the Mensheviks voted against. During the revolution the tactical positions of the Bund were closer to those of the Bolsheviks than the Mensheviks; Jonathan Frankel, *Prophecy and Politics: Socialism, Nationalism, and the Russian Jews* (Cambridge: Cambridge University Press, 1981), p. 247.

80. *Sotsial-demokrat,* June 8, 1905, p. 4.

81. Ibid., p. 4.

82. For this weakness in Renner's position, see Hans Mommsen, *Arbeiterbewegung und Nationale Frage* (Göttingen: Vandehoeck & Ruprecht, 1979), pp. 206–7; Peter Kulemann, *Am Beispiel des Austromarximus: Sozialdemokratische Arbeiterbewegung in Österreich von Hainfeld bis zur Dollfuss-Diktatur* (Hamburg: Junius, 1979), p. 131.

83. For a critique of the demand for national cultural autonomy, see Vladimir Ilych Lenin, "Theses on the National Question," *Lenin on the Jewish Question* (New York: International Publishers, 1974 [1925, written 1913]), p. 79; "Critical Remarks on the National Question", *Collected Works,* vol. 20, 4th ed. (Moscow: Progress Publishers, 1972 [1913]), p. 36; Karl Kautsky, "Nationalität und Internationalität," *Neue Zeit,* Ergänzungsheft, January 18, 1908, pp. 29–31.

84. *Sotsial-demokrat,* June 22, 1906, p. 3; Kisman, "Di yidishe sotsial-demokratishe bevegung," p. 414; *Sotsial-demokrat,* June 15, 1906, pp. 3–4; "Der 'Allgemeine Jüdische Arbeiterbund' zur Zeit der russischen Revolution," p. 243. Also see Bros, "Tsu der geshikhte," p. 46; Piasecki, *Sekcja Żydowska,* p. 143; Najdus, *Polska Partia Socjalno-Demokratyczna,* p. 440.

85. *Sotsial-demokrat,* June 8, 1906, p. 4; M. Aleksandrovitsh, "Dr. Henryk Shrayber," in Herts, *Doyres Bundisten,* vol. 2, pp. 192–93. Like Grossman, Hirsch Shrayber Polonized his Yiddish given name.

86. Abraham Spanlang took over from Grossman as publisher and responsible editor; *Sotsial-demokrat,* October 19, 1906, p. 4; October 26, 1906, p. 4.

87. "Korespondenzies," *Sotsial-demokrat,* August 24, 1906, p. 4; Henryk Grossman, "Vegn unzere agitatsie un propaganda," *Sotsial-demokrat,* August 24, 1906, p. 2.

88. Grossman, "Vegn unzere agitatsie un propaganda," p. 2.

89. Ibid., pp. 2–3.

90. Grossman, "Vegn unzere agitatsie un propaganda," *Sotsial-demokrat,* September 14, 1906, pp. 2–3.

91. Ibid., p. 3.

92. Karol Eyneygler, "Vegn unzere agitatsie un propaganda," *Sotsial-demokrat,* September 28, 1906, pp. 2–3.

93. Ibid., p. 3.

94. "Sozialpolitische Chronik," p. 924.

95. Jakob Grobler and Henryk Shrayber, "Berikht fun der eksekutiv-komitet tsum III partey-tag in Lemberg 1908," *Sotsial-demokrat,* October 9, 1908 (Shrayber "Berikht 2"), p. 2; "Tetigkeytsberikht fun der YSDP in Galitsien fun Oktober 1908 biz November 1910," *Sotsial-demokrat,* October 21, 1910, p. 3.

96. *Sotsial-demokrat,* June 22, 1906.

97. "Chryzanow," in *Encyclopaedia Judaica vol. 5: C-Dh* (Jerusalem: Keter, 1971), p. 534.

98. *Sotsial-demokrat,* June 8, 1906, p. 4.

99. *Sotsial-demokrat,* July 13, 1906, p. 3.

100. Christina Stead, "The Azhdnov Tailors," in Christina Stead, *The Ocean of Story* (Ringwood: Penguin, 1986 [1971]), p. 121. This passage closely matches Stead's notes based on conversations with Grossman and her husband Bill Blake; Christina Stead, notes, Box 4, Folder 32, Christina Stead Collection MS4967, National Library of Australia (Stead Collection).

101. Leaflet, "Khaveyrim! Yidishe arbeter!" MG7 F29, Bund Archive. The print run is given in Henryk Shrayber, "Berikht fun der eksekutiv-komitet tsum III partey-tag in Lemberg 1908," *Sotsial-demokrat,* October 16, 1908 (Shrayber "Berikht 3") p. 2.

102. Leaflet, "Khaveyrim! Yidishe arbeter!" MG7 F29, Bund Archive; *Sotsial-demokrat,* May 17, 1907; Kisman, "Di yidishe sotsial-demokratishe bevegung," p. 383.

103. *Sotsial-demokrat,* September 28, 1906, pp. 1, 4; October 10, 1906, p. 4.

104. "Partey eninim," *Sotsial-demokrat,* October 19, 1906, p. 2; *Sotsial-demokrat,* October 26, 1906, p. 4.

105. "Heinrich Grossmann," Sig 45^2 Abt 150 Nr 376, p. 198, Akten der WiSo Fakultät, Archiv der Johann Wolfgang Goethe Universität, Frankfurt am Main.

106. Józef Modrzejewski, "Rafał Taubenschlag: 1881–1958," *Altertum* 4 (4) (1958): 248, 251.

107. "Khronik," *Sotsial-demokrat,* July 12, 1907, p. 3; Mariusz Kulczykowski, *Żydzi-studenci Uniwersytetu Jagiellonskiego w dobie autonomicznej Galicji 1867–1918* (Kraków: Instytut Historii Uniwersytetu Jagiellonskiego, 1995), p. 364.

108. Grossman, *Proletariat wobec kwestyi żydowskie,* pp. 27–30; JüSDP, *Bericht zum Gesamt-Parteitag,* p. 1; Henryk Grossman, "Vegn unzere agitatsie un propaganda," *Sotsial-demokrat,* August 24, 1906, p. 2.

109. Letters from Stead to Blake, April 10, 1944, Christina Stead and William J. Blake, *Dearest Munx: The letters of Christina Stead and William J. Blake* (Carlton: Miegunyah Press, 2005), p. 297; April 11, 1944, ibid., p. 299; Stead, "The Exploits of Jan Callowjan," notes for a story, Box 11, Folder 79, Stead Collection.

110. Marriage certificate, 341/I/1908, Israelitische Kultusgemeinde Wien, Matrikelamt.

111. She did not attend the Kraków Academy of Fine Arts. Kraków's private art institutions included Leonard Stroynowski's school and Maria Niedzielska's Fine Arts

School for Women; Danuta Batorska, "Zofia Stryjeńska: Princess of Polish Painting," *Women's Art Journal* 19 (2) (Fall 1998–Winter 1999): 24–29.

112. Janina Grossman, "Portret Własny," in Edward Reicher, *Katalog Zbiorów Edwarda Rejchera* (Vienna, 1918).

113. For Edward Reicher's collection, see *Zbiory polskie: archiwa, bibljoteki, gabinety, galerje, muzea i inne zbiory pamiątek przeszłości w ojczyźnie i na obczyznie, w porządku alfabetycznym według miejscowości ułożone*, vol. 1 (Warszawa and Kraków: A-M, J. Mortkowicz, 1926), p. 12.

114. Letter from Blake to Stead, March 17, 1950, Stead and Blake, *Dearest Munx*, p. 496.

115. W. Czernic-Żalińska, "Salon sztuki 'Skarbiec' in Warszawie," *Rocznik Muzeum Narodowego w Warszawie* 10 (1966): 476; Jolanta Maurin-Bialostocka et al. (eds.), "Grossman, Janina," *Slownik Artystow Polskich i Obcych w Polsce Dzialajacych Malarze, Rzeźbiarze, Graficy,* Tom II: *D-G* (Wrocław: Polska Akademia Nauk, Instytut Sztuki, Zaklad Narodowy imienia Ossolińskich, 1975), p. 485.

116. Leon Trotsky, *The War and the International* (London: Young Socialist Publishers, 1971 [1914]) p. 64. Trotsky lived in Vienna from October 1907 until August 3, 1914, and was from 1909 critical of the chauvinism of the Austrian Party; Leon Trotsky, *My Life: An Attempt at an Autobiography* (New York: Pathfinder, 1970), pp. 205, 211, 235–36.

117. SAB, 1908, p. 17; SAB, 1909, p. 25.

118. Jakob Grobler and Henryk Shrayber, "Berikht fun der eksekutiv-komitet tsum III partey-tag in Lemberg 1908," *Sotsial-demokrat,* October 2, 1908, p. 2; "Di resolutsie un motiven," *Sotsial-demokrat,* March 22, 1907, p. 1.

119. For an example of the JSDP's critique of Zionism, see "Der bankrot fun'm tsionizm," *Sotsial-demokrat,* July 13, 1906, p. 1; "H. G." (presumably Henryk Grossman), "Poylenklub, Yidenklub un der Tsionistisher sharlotanizmus," *Sotsial-demokrat,* September 28, 1906, pp. 1–2.

120. *Sotsial-demokrat,* March 22, 1907, p. 4.

121. *Sotsial-demokrat,* April 12, 1907, p. 1.

122. Ibid.

123. *Sotsial-demokrat,* April 1, 1907, p. 4; Jobst, *Zwischen Nationalismus und Internationalismus,* p. 174.

124. *Sotsial-demokrat,* April 1, 1907, p. 4.

125. Ibid.

126. "Der 1. Mai 1907," *Sotsial-demokrat,* May 10, 1907, p. 2.

127. Feliks Gutman, "Vegn der grindung un tetikeyt fun Galitsyaner Bund," *Unzer Tsayt,* September 1955, pp. 30–32.

128. *Sotsial-demokrat,* June 19, 1908, p. 3; June 26, 1908, p. 4.

129. Trotsky, *The War and the International,* p. 64.

130. *Liber Rigorosum Ç. R. Facultatis Juridico Politicae X,* WP II 524, Archiwum Uniwersytetu Jagiellonskiego (*Liber Rigorosum*).

131. Henryk Grossman, *Bundizm in Galitsien* Publishing House of the *Social Democrat* (Kraków, 1907 [cover has 1908, title page 1907]), serialized in *Sotsial-demokrat* between September 13, 1907, and November 29, 1907.

132. Otto Bauer, *The Question of Nationalities* (Minneapolis: University of Minnesota Press, 2000 [1907]), p. 31.

133. Ibid., pp. 291–92. McCagg claims that Adler explicitly asked Bauer "to come up with a well thought-out explanation of the party position," but provides no evidence to back this up; William McCagg, "The Assimilation of Jews in Austria," in Bela Vago (ed.), *The Assimilation of Jews in Modern Times* (Boulder: Westview, 1981), pp. 139–40.

134. Vladimir Ilych Lenin, "'Cultural-national' autonomy," *Lenin on the Jewish Question* (1913), p. 91.

135. Grossman, *Bundizm in Galitsien*, pp. 5–7.

136. Ibid., pp. 7–9, 13.

137. Ibid., pp. 10–12.

138. Ibid., p. 12.

139. Ibid., pp. 14–15.

140. ibid pp. 13–14, 16–17, 22, 24–25.

141. Ibid., pp. 25–26.

142. Grossman, *Bundizm in Galitsien*, p. 24. Letter from Henryk Grossman to the Bund, July 27, 1905, MG2 F107, Bund Archive.

143. Cited by Grossman from the 1903 report of the General Party, *Bundizm in Galitsien*, p. 19.

144. Ibid., pp. 23, 27.

145. Ibid., pp. 30–32.

146. Ibid., pp. 33, 37.

147. Ibid., pp. 33–34.

148. Ibid., pp. 34–35.

149. Ibid., pp. 37, 39.

150. Ibid., p. 41.

151. Ibid.

152. See, for example, Vladimir Ilych Lenin, *What is to be Done?*, *Collected Works*, vol. 15, 4th ed. (Moscow: Progress Publishers, 1986 [1902]), pp. 389–90, 412–13; Vladimir Ilych Lenin, *Two Tactics of Social-Democracy in the Democratic Revolution*, *Collected Works*, vol. 9, 4th ed. (Moscow: Progress Publishers, 1977 [1906]), pp. 17–18, 136–38; the discussion of Lenin's organizational response to the 1905 revolution in Cliff, *Lenin*, pp. 171–83; Georg Lukács, *History and Class Consciousness* (London: Merlin, 1971 [1923]), pp. 46–82, 149–222; *Lenin* (London: NLB, 1970 [1924]), pp. 24–38, 49–50; Antonio Gramsci, *Selections from the Prison Notebooks* (New York: International Publishers, 1971), pp. 10, 330, 340.

153. Grossman, *Bundizm in Galitsien*, pp. 42–43.

154. Ibid., p. 46.

155. "The Irish working class must emancipate itself, and in emancipating itself, must, perforce, free its country . . . The freedom of the working class must be the work of the working class." James Connolly, *Erin's Hope*, 1902 edition cited by David Howell, *A Lost Left: Three Studies in Socialism and Nationalism* (Manchester: Manchester University Press, 1986), p. 42.

156. Grossman, *Bundizm in Galitsien*, p. 47.

157. Ośrodek Myśli Politycznej, "Wladyslaw Leopold Jaworski," www.omp.org.pl/jaworski_ang.php, Kraków, 1998, accessed June 4, 2006; Buszko and Dobrowolski, *Udział Galicji*, pp. 122, 196.

158. *Liber Rigorosum.*

159. Piasecki, *Sekcja Żydowska*, p. 308.

160. "Nakh dem XI kongres fun der PPSD," *Sotsial-demokrat*, June 12, 1908, pp. 1–2; "Di yidishe debate auf dem XXI kongres fun der PPSD," *Sotsial-demokrat*, June 12, 1908, pp. 3–4; "Sprawa organizacyi żydowskiej," *Naprzód*, June 11, 1908, pp. 1–2; "Sprawa organizacyi żydowskiej," *Naprzód*, June 12, 1908, pp. 1–2; Kisman, "Di yidishe sotsial-demokratishe bevegung," pp. 429–32.

161. For the discussion of the issue by the Jewish carpenters in Lwów, see *Sotsial-demokrat*, June 26, 1908, p. 4.

162. *Sotsial-demokrat*, June 19, 1908, pp. 3–4.

163. *Sotsial-demokrat*, June 26, 1908, p. 4.

164. "Di ershte mapl fun der neye Sektsie in Stri," *Sotsial-demokrat*, June 19, 1908, p. 4.

165. Yehushe Ehrenman, "Der gurl fun a PPSisher resolutsie in der Yidisher organizatsions-frage," *Sotsial-demokrat*, October 2, 1908, p. 2.

166. The party had on-going contact with a further nine towns; Shrayber, "Berikht 3," p. 2. Also see Shrayber, "Berikht 2," p. 2. For a list of JSDP points of contact in thirty-eight towns in 1907, see *Sotsial-demokrat*, September 27, 1907, p. 4.

167. Piasecki, *Sekcja Żydowska*, pp. 216–17.

168. Calculation based on the 16,079 members of social democratic unions in Galicia, who constituted the vast bulk of the membership of the PPSD and JSDP; SAB, 1908, p. 17.

169. Shrayber, "Berikht 2," p. 2; the ironic report about the PZ congress in the JSDP's newspaper was very skeptical about the number of members the Labor Zionists claimed; "Der kongres fun di 'Alveltlikhe Poale-Tsion' fin Esterreykh," *Sotsial-demokrat*, June 19, 1908, p. 3; Kener, *Kvershnit*, p. 106.

170. Najdus, *Ignacy Daszyński*, pp. 240–41.

171. "Mir senen di balebotim," *Sotsial-demokrat*, June 22, 1906, p. 1; "An den Verbandsvorstand der Schneidergewerkschaft in Wien," *Sotsial-demokrat*, August 14, 1908, pp. 1–3; *Sotsial-demokrat*, October 16, 1908, p. 1; Bros, "Tsu der geshikhte," p. 28.

172. "An den Verbandsvorstand der Schneidergewerkschaft in Wien," *Sotsial-demokrat*, August 14, 1908, pp. 1–3; Papier, "Di profesionele bevegung," p. 6; also Papier's speech reported in "Partey-kampf oder antisemitizmus," *Sotsial-demokrat*, August 14, 1908, p. 4.

173. "An den Verbandsvorstand der Schneidergewerkschaft in Wien," *Sotsial-demokrat*, August 14, 1908, pp. 1–3.

174. "Partey-kampf oder antisemitizmus," *Sotsial-demokrat*, August 14, 1908, p. 4.

175. "Von dem Schneiderverbande Oesterreich" and "Di gesamt-forstands-sitsung fun'm Shneyder Ferband," *Sotsial-demokrat*, September 4, 1908, pp. 1–2, 3; Shrayber, "Berikht 2," p. 2; Papier, "Di profesionele bevegung," p. 6.

176. "Der III. kongres fun der YSDP," *Sotsial-demokrat*, October 30, 1908 ("Der III. kongres 2"), pp. 2–3.

177. Ibid., p. 2.

178. Ibid.

179. Gutman lists the intellectuals in the party in Kraków and Lemberg; "On oreyn-fir-vort," p. 31.

180. "Der III. kongres fun der YSDP in Galitsien," *Sotsial-demokrat*, October 23, 1908 ("Der III. kongres 1"), p. 2.

181. Duncan Hallas, *The Comintern* (London: Bookmarks, 1985), pp. 64–69.

182. "Der III. kongres 1," p. 3; "Der III. kongres 2," pp. 2–3.

183. "Der III. kongres 2," p. 3.

184. *Liber Rigorosum; Liber Promotionum Universitas Jagellonicae Ab Anno 1893* Signatur S II 520, Archiwum Uniwersytetu Jagiellonskiego (AUJ).

185. Marriage certificate, 341/I/1908, Israelitische Kultusgemeinde Wien, Matrikelamt.

186. *Sotsial-demokrat*, December 4, 1908, p. 7.

Chapter 3: Respectable Careers

1. Solomon Reyzen, *Leksikon fun der Yidisher literatur, prese un filologye*, vol. 1, 2nd ed., (Vilno: Vilner Farlag fun B. Kletskin, 1926), column 616. Reyzen seems to be the source of this mistake in Isaac Landman (ed.), *The Universal Jewish Encyclopedia*, vol. 5 (New York: Universal Jewish Encyclopedia Company, 1948), p. 107; and *Leksikon fun der nayer Yidisher literatur* (New York: Congress for Jewish Culture, 1958), pp. 354–55.

2. "Personalnachweis: Oskar Kurz," Grundbuchsblätter Wien 1885, Österreichisches Staatsarchiv, Kriegsarchiv (ÖSK); "Kurz, Oskar," in H. A. Strauss and W. Röder (general eds.), *International Biographical Dictionary of Central European Emigrés 1933–1945*, vol. 2, part 1: *The Arts, Sciences and Literature* (New York: K. G. Saur, 1980–83), p. 406.

3. Jakub Forst-Battaglia, "Polnische Kulturleistungen in Wien," in Walter Leitsch and Stanislaw Trakowski (eds.), *Polen im alten Österreich: Kultur und Politik* (Wien: Böhlau, 1993), pp. 259–60.

4. Carl Schorske, *Fin-de-siècle Vienna: Politics and Culture* (New York: Vintage Books, 1981), pp. 8–9.

5. Marriage certificate, 341/I/1908, Israelitische Kultusgemeinde Wien, Matrikelamt.

6. Henryk Grossmann, *Österreichs Handelspolitik mit Bezug auf Galizien in der Reformperiode 1772–1790*, series *Studien zur Soziale-, Wirtschafts- und Verwaltungsgeschichte*, edited by Carl Grünberg, number 10 (Vienna: Konegen, 1914), pp. vii, xi.

7. No comprehensive biography of Carl Grünberg has been written. Günther Nenning, "Biographie C. Grünberg," in *Indexband zu Archiv für die Geschichte des Sozialismus und der Arbeiterbewegung (C. Grünberg)* (Zürich: Limmat-Verlag, 1973), pp. 1–224, comes closest but is short on personal details and focuses on a limited number of his writings. Also see Ulrike Migdal, *Die Frühgeschichte des Frankfurter Instituts für Sozialforschung* (Frankfurt: Campus Verlag, 1981), pp. 56–72; Rolf Wiggershaus, *The Frankfurt School: Its History, Theories and Political Significance* (Cambridge, Mass.: Polity, 1995),

pp. 21–22; and Günther Nenning, "Einleitung" to *Archiv für die Geschichte des Sozialismus und der Arbeiterbewegung* Band 1 (Graz: Akademische Druck- u. Verlagsanstalt, reprint 1966), p. viii.

8. "Personalbogen," "Grossmann, Heinrich 1927–1967," Akten des Rektors Abt 1 Nr 15, Archiv der Johann Wolfgang Goethe Universität, Frankfurt am Main (Personalbogen); also Henryk Grossman, curriculum vitae in "Akta osobowe Henryka Grossmana," Glowny Urzad Statystyczny, Centralna Biblioteka Statystyczna, Warsaw (curriculum vitae GUS), folio 1; and curriculum vitae by Henryk Grossman, "Grossmann, Heinrich," Akten der WiSo Fakultät," Sig 452 Abt 150 Nr 376, p. 198 (curriculum vitae UFM).

9. *Werdegang und Schriften der Mitglieder der Vereinigung der Sozial- und Wirtschaftlichen Hochschullehrer,* August 1931, cited by Klaus Hennings in a letter to the dean of the Economics and Social Science Faculty, University of Frankfurt am Main, October 11, 1967, UFM, pp. 239–40. The official records of Grossman's legal activities were presumably burned in the fire that destroyed the Palace of Justice in Vienna in 1927.

10. The evidence of this change is amendments to the records of Grossman's birth, academic qualifications, and marriage: *Ursde IV 1881–1885 IV Mjz,* M-60, Archiwum Państwowe w Krakowie, p. 69; *Album Studiosorum Universitatis Cracoviensis ab anno 1892/3 usqu ad annum 1910/11;* marriage certificate, 341/I/1908, Israelitische Kultusgemeinde Wien, Matrikelamt.

11. Curriculum vitae UFM; curriculum vitae GUS. Eugen von Böhm-Bawerk, *Karl Marx and the Close of his System,* in Paul Sweezy (ed.), *Karl Marx and the Close of his System by Eugen von Böhm-Bawerk & Böhm-Bawerk's Criticism of Marx by Rudolf Hilferding* (London: Merlin, 1975 [1896]), pp. 1–118.

12. "Personalblatt Dr Heinrich Großmann," K. u. K. Kreigsministerium, Abt 10KW, ÖSK (Personalblatt).

13. Grossmann, *Österreichs Handelspolitik,* p. x.

14. Curriculum vitae GUS.

15. Grossmann, *Österreichs Handelspolitik,* pp. x–xi.

16. Personalbogen.

17. Leaflet advertising talks at the Jüd Arb.-Bildiungs Verein "Ferdinand Lassalle," MG2 Folder 130, Bund Archive, Yidisher visnshaftlikher institut/YIVO Institute for Jewish Research Archive, New York; also see Jack Jacobs, "Written out of History: Bundists in Vienna and the Varieties of Jewish Experience in the Austrian First Republic," in Michael Genner and Derek J. Penslar (eds.), *In Search of Jewish community: Jewish Identities in Germany and Austria, 1918–1933* (Bloomington: Indiana University Press, 1998), pp. 115–33.

18. Personalblatt, A decade after writing this document, Grossman noted that he had visited Paris in 1909–10; curriculum vitae UFM. Given his seminar attendance in Vienna and the advisability of undertaking considerable preliminary research among the more extensive sources in Vienna before the trip, as well as its closeness to the event, the dates indicated on his army personnel sheet are more plausible. What is more, one of his publications in 1911 indicated that he was then living in Paris, "Eine Wiener Volkszählung im Jahre 1777," in *Statistische Monatschrift,* new series 16, 1911, Brünn, p. 58.

19. H. Bartnicka and J. Szczepińska, *Katalog prac artystów Polskich, wystawiających w Paryzu na: Salon des Indépendants, Salon d'Automne, Salon de Tuilleries* (Warszawa: Maszynopis, 1960), pp. 288, 290. One of the portraits shown may have been the painting of her son reproduced in a 1918 catalogue of her father's collection, titled "Portret synka" and dated 1912; Edward Reicher, *Katalog Zbiorów Edwarda Rejchera* (Vienna, 1918). It is unlikely that Janina lived in Paris in 1912: her address for the Salons was only care of M. Marcel, 8 Impasse Rousin.

20. Paul Fröhlich, *Rosa Luxemburg* (London: Pluto, 1983), pp. 75–76.

21. Christina Stead, "29.II.45?" Box 5, Folder 32, Christina Stead Collection MS4967, National Library of Australia.

22. Henryk Grossmann, "Jean Jaurès," in Ludwig Elster (ed.), *Wörterbuch der Volkswirtschaft*, vol. 2, 4th ed. (Jena: Fischer, 1932), pp. 382–83.

23. Henryk Großmann, "Eine Wiener Volkszählung im Jahre 1777," *Statistische Monatschrift* (37), new series 15 (1911): 56–58.

24. *Sotsial-demokrat*, November 11, 1910, pp. 2, 7.

25. Yosef Kisman, "Di yidishe sotsial-demokratishe bevegung in Galitsie un Bukovine," in G. Aronson et al. (eds.), *Di geshikhte fun Bund 3* (New York: Farlag Unser Tsait, 1966), pp. 432–35, 442–44.

26. Hans Hautmann, *Die Anfänge der Linksradikalen Bewegung und der Kommunistische Partei Deutschösereichs* (Wien: Europa Verlag, 1970), p. 1; Josef Strasser, *Der Arbeiter und die Nation* (Wien: Junius Verlag, 1982 [1912]).

27. Georg W. Strobel, *Die Partei Rosa Luxemburgs, Lenin und die SPD: der polnische "europäische" Internationalismus in der russischen Sozialdemokratie* (Wiesbaden: F. Steiner, 1974) is a magnificent and very detailed study of Polish social democracy, and constitutes the main source for the account here; for the specifics of the Radek Affair; see pp. 372–77. Also see Jim Tuck's lively *Engine of Mischief: An Analytical Biography of Karl Radek* (New York: Greenwood Press, 1988).

28. Declaration by Henryk Grossman on the Radek Affair, September 17, 1912, Alfred Henke Nachlaß, Archiv der sozialen Demokratie der Friedrich-Ebert-Stiftung.

29. He is similarly described as a "writer" in the forerunner of the telephone book, *Lehrmanns Allgemeiner Wohnungs-Anzeiger nebst Handels- und Gewerbe-Adreßbuch für die K. K. Reichs- Haupt und Residenzstadt Wien (Lehrmann)*, vols. 54–60 (Wien: Alfred Hölder, 1912–18).

30. The translations are in Carl Grünberg, "Die Internationale und der Weltkrieg: 6. Die polnische Sozialdemokratie," *Archiv für die Geschichte des Sozialismus und der Arbeiterbewegung*, 6 (1916): 479–87; for Grünberg's acknowledgment of "Dr. Henryk Grossmann–Wien," see p. 376. The materials Grünberg brought together in the journal were also published as a monograph: Carl Grünberg (ed.), *Die Internationale und der Weltkrieg, materialien gesammelt von Carl Grunberg* (Leipzig: C. L. Hirschfeld, 1916 [reprinted Minkoff Reprint, 1976]).

31. Martha Rozenblit, *The Jews of Vienna, 1867–1914: Assimilation and Identity* (Albany: State University of New York Press, 1983), pp. 17, 22, 78.

32. Henryk Grossman, "Rozległość Galicyi po zajęciu jej przez Austrę," in *Kwartalnik Historyczny* 25 (3/4) (1911): 472–78.

33. "Polityka przemysłowa i handlowa rządu Terezynansko-Józefińskiego w Galicyi 1772–1790: Referat na V. Zjazd prawników i ekonomistów polskich," *Przegląd prawa i administracyi* (Lwow, 1912), pp. 37–38.

34. Ibid., p. 41.

35. Henryk Grossman, "Polityka przemysłowa i handlowa rządu Terezynansko-Józefińskiego w Galicyi 1772–1790: Referat na V. Zjazd prawników i ekonomistów polskich," *Przegląd prawa i administracyi* (Lwów, 1912 offprint), pp. 1–8, 13–19.

36. Ibid., pp. 41–42.

37. Henryk Grossman, "Vegn unzere agitatsie un propaganda," *Sotsial-demokrat,* August 24, 1906, p. 2.

38. Curriculum vitae GUS; curriculum vitae UFM indicates that the prize was awarded in 1910.

39. Henryk Großmann, "Die amtliche Statistik des galizischen Aussenhandels 1772–1792," *Statistische Monatschrift* new series 18 (Brünn, 1913): 222–33.

40. Ibid., pp. 224–28.

41. Ibid., pp. 225, 231, 232–33.

42. Ibid., pp. 224, 232.

43. Ibid., p. 222.

44. Carl Grünberg, "Gutachtlicher Bericht. Betr. Habilitation des Dr Henryk Grossmann. 27 January 1927," UFM, pp. 212–15.

45. Grossmann, *Österreichs Handelspolitik,* pp. vii–viii; also see pp. 404, 478 for references to the second volume.

46. Ibid., pp. ix–x, 3–10. Henryk Grossman, *Proletariat wobec kwestyi żydowskiej z powodu niedyskutowanej dyskusyi w "Krytyce"* (Kraków, Drukani Wladysława Teodorczuka, January 1905), p. 42.

47. Grossmann, *Österreichs Handelspolitik,* pp. 63, 476–88.

48. Ibid., pp. 226–27, 291–97, 488–90; quotation p. 483.

49. Jakob Pistiner review of Grossmann's *Österreichs Handelspolitik* in *Der Kampf* 8 (6), June 1, 1915, p. 24.

50. Kisman, "Di yidishe sotsial-demokratishe bevegung," pp. 447–56, 460, 463–64.

51. Grossmann, *Österreichs Handelspolitik,* p. 383.

52. Pistiner review, p. 224.

53. Henryk Grossmann, "Lebenslauf," "Henryk Grossmann," PA 40, Universitätsarchiv Leipzig (UAL) pp. 64–66; also see "Beurteilung," August 14, 1950, UAL, p. 57. Roman Rozdolski independently interpreted Grossman's argument as a Marxist one in *Die grosse Steuer- und Agrarreform Josefs II. Ein Kapitel zur österreichischen Wirtschaftsgeschichte* (Warsaw: Państwowe Wydawnicto Naukowe, 1961), p. 90.

54. Grossmann, *Österreichs Handelspolitik,* p. 475.

55. Roman Rosdolsky, *Untertan und Staat in Galizien: die Reformen unter Maria Theresia und Joseph II.* (Mainz: Verlag Philipp von Zabern, 1992 [1962]), pp. 12, 21, 33.

56. Reviews of Henryk Grossmann, *Österreichs Handelspolitik* by Heinrich Ritter von Srbik, *Historische Zeitschrift* 115 (1916): 419–23; Hugo Rachel, *Deutsche Literaturzeitung*, 46/47 (November 14–21, 1914): 2522–23; Mario Alberti, *Giornale degli Economisti*, (November 1914): 343–44; Karl Pribram, *Archiv für Sozialwissenschaft und Sozialpolitik* 42 (2) (1916): 623–25; Rudolf Leonhard, "Polnische Perspektiven," *Schmollers Jahrbuch für Gesetzgebung, Verwaltung und Volkswirtschaft im Deutschen Reiche* 41 (1) (1917): 430–33.

57. Personalbogen; birth certificate, Stanislaus Eugen Grossmann 691/1914, Israelitische Kultusgemeinde Wien, Matrikelamt.

58. Hauptgrundbuchblatt in k. u. k. Kreigsministerium 1916 1. Abt. 45–1/468 ÖSK (Hauptgrundbuchblatt). In March 1916 the 5th Field Artillery Regiment was redesignated the 4th Field Artillery Regiment.

59. Hauptgrundbuchblatt.

60. The proposal that Grossman be promoted stated that he had only spent a month in the field; Wissenschaftliche Komitee für Kriegswirtschaft zu 1 Abteilung des k. u. k. KMs, September 24, 1916, k. u. k. Kreigsministerium, 1916, 1. Abt. 45–1/468, ÖSK. A later, unsuccessful suggestion that he receive a decoration indicated that he was a noncommissioned instructor in the field from May 10 to July 17, 1916; Henryk Großmann, "Belohnungsantrag" k. u. k. Kreigsministerium Präsidialbüro, 1918, 5–16/12–2, ÖSK.

61. Henryk Grossmann, "Die Anfänge und geschichtliche Entwicklung der amtlichen Statistik in Österreich," *Statistische Monatschrift* new series 21 (June–July 1916): 331–423; "Erwiderung zu einer Kritik von Alfred Gürtler," *Statistische Monatschrift* new series 21 (1916): 676–77.

62. Curriculum vitae GUS; Grünberg, "Gutachtlicher Bericht". For the activities of the military formations that Grossman belonged to, see Edmund Glaise-Horstenau et al., *Österreich-Ungarns letzter Krieg Band 4 Das Kriegsjahr 1916 erster Teil* (Wien: Verlag der Militärwissenschaflichen Mitteilungen, 1933), pp. 377, 391, 399, 401–6, 409–10, and Beilage, pp. 2, 18, 20.

63. The painting was part of an exhibition at the Towarzystwo Przyjaciol Sztuk Pięknych (Society of the Friends of the Fine Arts), "Grossman, Janina," in Jolanta Maurin-Bialostocka et al. (eds.), *Słownik Artystów Polskich i Obcych w Polsce Działających Malarze, Rzeźbiarze, Graficy*, Tom II: *D-G* (Wrocław: Polska Akademia Nauk, Instytut Sztuki, Zakład Narodowy imienia Ossolińskich-Wydawnictwo, 1975), p. 485.

64. Janina started advertising under the "academic painter" category in the business section of the *Address book* in 1915, *Lehrmann* volumes 57 to 61, 1915 to 1919.

65. Ibid., p. 334. I am grateful to Anton Tantner for pointing out that Grossman's study provided insights into archival material that has been lost.

66. Grossmann, "Die Anfänge und geschichtliche Entwicklung," pp. 331–423.

67. Pribram review of Henryk Grossman's *Österreichs Handelspolitik*.

68. Grossmann, "Die Anfänge und geschichtliche Entwicklung," pp. 343–45.

69. Ibid., p. 345.

70. Ibid., pp. 410–11, 413–16.

71. Henryk Grossmann, "Lebenslauf" UAL, pp. 64–66.

72. Grossmann, "Die Anfänge und geschichtliche Entwicklung," p. 332.

73. Ibid.

74. "Österreich über alles, wann es nur will," ibid., p. 421.

75. Ibid., pp. 333.

76. Alfred Gürtler, "Die Anfänge und geschichtliche Entwicklung der amtlichen Statistik in Österreich," *Statistische Monatsschrift* 21 (1916): 673–75; Henryk Großmann, "Erwiderung," pp. 676–77.

77. Letter from Henryk Grossman to Max Horkheimer, July 20, 1935, Max Horkheimer, *Gesammelte Schiften,* Band 15: *Briefwechsel 1913–1936* (Frankfurt am Main: Fischer, 1995), p. 376.

78. For the Austrian military administration of the Kingdom of Poland, see Rudolf Mitzka, "Die k. u. k. Militärverwaltung in Russisch Polen," in Hugo Kerchnawe et al., *Die Militärverwaltung in den von den österreichisch-ungarischen Truppen besetzten Gebieten* (Wien: Hölder-Pichler-Tempsky, and New Haven: Yale University Press, 1928), pp. 8–52.

79. Heinrich Grossmann, k. u. k. Kreigsministerium, 1916, 1. Abt. 45–1/468, ÖSK.

80. Rainer Egger, "Rüstungsindustrie in Niederösterreich und Heeresverwaltung während des Ersten Weltkrieges," in *Bericht über den 16. österreichischen Historikertag in Krems/Donau,* September 3–7, 1985, publication 25/1985 of the Verband österreichischer Geschichtsvereine, pp. 412–14.

81. Workbook dated 1916–17, "Henryk Grossman," III-155, Archiwum Polskiej Akademii Nauk (APAN), cited in Jürgen Scheele, *Zwischen Zusammenbruchsprognose und Positivismusverdikt: Studien zur politischen und intellektuellen Biographie Henryk Grossmanns (1881–1950)* (Frankfurt am Main: Lang, 1999), pp. 22–23. Cf. curriculum vitae UFM.

82. On the origins of the paper and Pribram's assessment, see Henryk Grossman, "Majątek Społeczny Królestwa Poskiego," *Miesięcznik Statystyczny* 5 (Warsaw, 1922), pp. 255–56 and 277. On the originality of Grossman's work, see Joseph Marcus, *Social and Political History of the Jews in Poland, 1919–1938* (New York: Mouton, 1983), p. 250.

83. Hence, for example, a letter from a subordinate to Grossman in Vienna, concerning instructions Grossman had given and his anticipated return, September 22, 1917, APAN.

84. Henryk Großmann, "Die Kreditorganisation des Königreiches Polen vor dem Kriege," in Ludwig Ćwikliński (ed.), *Das Königreich Polen vor dem Kriege (1815–1914)* (Leipzig and Vienna: Deuticke, 1917), pp. 180–209.

85. Ibid., pp. 189, 204.

86. Feliks Gutman, "Vegn der grindung un tetikeyt fun 'Galitsianer Bund,'" *Unzer Tsait* (September 1955): 30.

87. Letter from the Wissenschaftliche Komitee der Kriegswirtschaft, April 21, 1917, k. u. k. Kreigsministerium 1917 1.Abt. 92–1026; Heinrich Grossmann, "Vermerkblatt für Qualifikationsbeschreibung," Quall. Kart. 874, September 30, 1918, k. u. k. Kreigsministerium Präsidialbüro, 1918, 5–16/12–2 ÖSK. Grossman claimed fluency in Russian in 1918, but not 1916; cf. the 1916 Hauptgrundbuchblatt with the 1918 Personalblatt.

88. Otto Bauer, *Die österreichische Revolution* (Wien: Verlag der Wiener Volksbuchhandlung, 1965), p. 77.

89. Curriculum vitae GUS.

90. Ibid.

91. Plaschka *Innere Front,* pp. 278–79.

92. Personalblatt.

93. Heinrich Grossmann, "Vermerkblatt für Qualifikationsbeschreibung," Quall. Kart. 874, September 30, 1918, k. u. k. Kreigsministerium Präsidialbüro, 1918, 5–16/12–2 ÖSK.

94. Curriculum vitae GUS.

95. *Katalog Zbiorów Edwarda Rejchera* (Wien, 1918).

96. Maurin-Bialostocka, "Grossman, Janina," p. 485; file note on the 1917 exhibition provided by the Polska Akademia Nauk, Instytut Sztuki; *Lehrmanns* vols. 61 to 65, 1919 to 1924.

97. Grünberg, "Gutachtlicher Bericht;" curriculum vitae UFM.

98. On Pribram, see author's preface and biographical introduction to Karl Pribram, *A History of Economic Reasoning* (Baltimore: Johns Hopkins University Press, 1983), pp. xvii–xxxiii. Also see Wilhelm Zeller, "Geschichte der zentralen amtlichen Statistik in Österreich," in *Geschichte und Ergebnisse der zentralen amtlichen Statistik in Österreich 1829–1979 Beiträge zur österreichischen Statistik,* vol. 500 (Wien, 1979), p. 103.

99. See the sustained apologetic for this position in Bauer, *Die österreichische Revolution.*

100. See Hautmann, *Die Anfänge der Linksradikalen Bewegung,* pp. 81–83.

101. Piotr Wróbel, "The Jews of Galicia under Austrian-Polish rule, 1869–1918," *Austrian History Yearbook* 25 (1994): 135.

102. Margarete Grandner, "Staatsbürger und Ausländer: Zum Umgang Österreichs mit den jüdischen Flüchtlingen nach 1918," in Gernot Heiss and Oliver Rathkolb (eds.), *Asylland Wider Willen, Flüchtlinge in Österreich im europäischen Kontext seit 1914* (Vienna: Verlag Jugend und Volk, 1995), p. 63. Also see F. L. Carsten, *The First Austrian Republic 1918–1938: A Study Based on British and Austrian Documents* (Aldershot: Gower, 1986), p. 30.

103. Grandner, "Staatsbürger und Ausländer," pp. 65–67, and Rudolf Thienel, *Österreichische Staatsbürgerschaft I: Historische Entwicklung und Völkerrechtliche Gundlagen* (Wien: Österreichische Staatsdruckerei, 1989), p. 50.

104. Wilhelm Zeller, "Geschichte der zentralen amtlichen Statistik in Österreich," p. 104; also see Österreichisches Statistisches Zentralamt (ed.), *Von der direction der administrativen Statistik zum Österreichischen Statistischen Zentralamt 1840–1990* (Wien: Österreichisches Statistisches Zentralamt, 1990), pp. 22, 24.

105. For Grossman's registration in Kraków, see Personalblatt and Hauptgrundbuchblatt.

106. Grünberg, "Gutachtlicher Bericht."

Chapter 4: A Communist Academic

1. Christina Stead, notes, Box 6, Folder 45, Christina Stead Collection, MS4967, National Library of Australia (Stead Collection). Grossman's presence in Kraków is also suggested by the delivery of his paper to the Academy of Sciences, not to mention the fact that his mother still lived there.

2. Henryk Grossman, "The Theory of Economic Crises," in *Bulletin International de l'Académie Polonaise des Sciences et des Lettres. Classe de Philologie, Classe d'Histoire et de Philosophie. Les Années 1919, 1920* (presented June 16, 1919), 1922, pp. 285–86, reprinted in Paul Zarembka (ed.), *Value, Capitalist Dynamics and Money: Research in Political Economy* 18 (New York: Elsevier Science, 2000), pp. 171–80.

3. Otto Bauer, "The Accumulation of Capital," *History of Political Economy* 18 (1) (1986): 88–110.

4. The article on the fortieth anniversary of the publication of *Capital* in the JSDP's *Sotsial-demokrat*, for example, did not mention use value, in its summary of the book's key discoveries, "Dos 40 johrige jubileum fun *Kapital*," *Sotsial-demokrat*, July 19, 1907, p. 1. Authoritative Marxist economists such as Hilferding and Boudin explicitly excluded use values from the scope of their principal economic analyses; Louis Boudin, *The Theoretical System of Karl Marx* (Chicago: Kerr, 1915), p. 55; Rudolf Hilferding, *Böhm-Bawerk's Criticism of Marx*, in Paul. M. Sweezy (ed.), *Karl Marx and the Close of his System* (London: Merlin, 1975 [1904]), p. 130. Roman Rosdolsky identified I. I. Rubin and Grossman as undertaking pioneering work on the economic significance of use value; *The Making of Marx's 'Capital'* (London: Pluto, 1977), pp. 73–74, 87–88; Rosdolsky, however, cited *Marx, die klassische Nationalökonomie und das Problem der Dynamik* (Institut für Sozialforschung, duplicated, New York 1941), which appeared twenty years after Grossman first addressed the issue.

5. Rudolf Hilferding, *Finance Capital: A Study of the Latest Phase of Capitalist Development* (London: Routledge & Kegan Paul, 1981 [1910]), pp. 284–85.

6. Henryk Grossman, "Marx und die Klassische Oekonomie oder Die Lehre vom Wertfetisch," original Folder 18, in 1997 Folder 68, pp. 111–12, "Henryk Grossman," III-155, Archiwum Polskiej Akademii Nauk (APAN).

7. Vladimir Ilych Lenin, *State and Revolution, Collected Works*, vol. 25, 4th ed. (Moscow: Progress Publishers, 1980 [1918, written 1917]), pp. 385–497.

8. Georg Lukács, *History and Class Consciousness* (London: Merlin, 1971 [1923]), pp. 105–6.

9. Henryk Grossman, curriculum vitae, in "Akta osobowe Henryka Grossmana," Glowny Urzad Statystyczny, Centralna Biblioteka Statystyczna, Warsaw (curriculum vitae GUS), folio 1.

10. Stanisław Tołwiński, *Wspomnienia 1895–1939* (Warsaw: Państwowe Wydnawnictwo Naukowe, 1971), pp. 172–73.

11. Ludwig Ćwikliński (ed.), *Das Königreich Polen vor dem Kriege (1815–1914)* (Leipzig and Vienna: Deuticke, 1917).

12. GUS, folios 4 and 5.

13. Henryk Grossman, "Znaczemie i zadania pierwszego proszechnego ludności w Polsce," *Miesięcznik Statystyczny* 1 (Warsaw, 1920), pp. 88, 89, 96.

14. Ibid., p. 100; Rick Kuhn, "Organizing Yiddish-speaking Workers in pre-World War I Galicia: The Jewish Social Democratic Party," in Leonard Greenspoon (ed.), *Yiddish Language & Culture: Then & Now* (Omaha: Creighton University Press, 1998), p. 56.

15. Gabriel Simoncini, *The Communist Party of Poland* (Lewiston: Mellen Press 1993), p. 30; Tadeusz Szafar, "The Origins of the Communist Party in Poland," in I. Banac, *War and Society in East Central Europe* (New York: Atlantic Studies, 1983), p. 13, note 23, p. 41; Ministry for Internal Affairs reported in Józef Ławnik, "Represje policyjne wobec ruchu komunistycznego w Polsce 1918–1939," *Z pola walki* 83 (3) (1978): 54.

16. *Sotsial-demokrat,* May 1, 1920.

17. Henryk Grossman, "Lebenslauf von Professor Dr. Henryk Grossman," August 3, 1949, "Henryk Grossmann," Universitätsarchiv Leipzig, PA 40 (UAL), pp. 61–63; Henryk Grossmann, "Lebenslauf" UAL, pp. 64–66; "Btr.: Großman, Henryk, geb.: 14.4.81–9053 (Anerkennung)," September 12, 1950, VdN-Akte von Henryk Großmann 13630, Bezirksrat Leipzig 20237, Sächsisches Staatsarchiv Leipzig (SSAL). On splits from the Bund, see M. K. Dziewanowski, *The Communist Party of Poland: An Outline History* (Cambridge, Mass.: Harvard University Press, 1976), p. 98; Jaff Schatz, *The Generation: The Rise and Fall of the Jewish Communists of Poland* (Berkeley: University of California Press, 1991), p. 95; Simoncini, *The Communist Party of Poland,* pp. 38–39, 84–86, 98; Gertrud Pickhan, *"Gegen den Strom" der Allgemeine Jüdische Arbeiterbund "Bund" in Polen 1918–1939* (Stuttgart: Deutsche Verlags-Anstalt, 2001), p. 87. On Jewish Social Democratic Party members who became Communists, see Janusz Radziejowski, *The Communist Party of Western Ukraine 1919–1929* (Edmonton: Canadian Institute of Ukrainian Studies, 1983), p. 8; Feliks Gutman, "Vegn der grindung un tetikeyt fun 'Galitsyaner Bund,'" *Unzer Tsayt,* September 1955, p. 32; Yosef Kisman, "Di yidishe sotsial-demokratishe bevegung in Galitsie un Bukovine," in G. Aronson et al. (eds.), *Di geshikhte fun Bund drite band* (New York: Farlag Unzer Tsayt, 1966), pp. 473–74.

18. Szafar, "The Origins of the Communist Party in Poland," p. 50; Simoncini, *The Communist Party of Poland,* pp. 58, 71–72.

19. Stead, notes, Box 6, Folder 45, Stead Collection.

20. See E. H. Carr, *The Bolshevik Revolution 1917–1923,* vol. 3 (Harmondsworth: Penguin, 1977), pp. 167–69, and, a less disinterested but more detailed, Polish account, Adam Zamoyski, *The Battle for the Marchlands* (Boulder and New York: East European Monographs/Columbia University Press, 1981).

21. GUS, folio 11,.

22. Stead, notes, Box 2, Folder 7, Stead Collection; notes, Box 6, Folder 45, ibid.

23. GUS, folios 14–18, 22, 24.

24. *Lehrmanns Allgemeiner Wohnungs-Anzeiger nebst Handels- und Gewerbe-Adreßbuch für Wien Band II* (Wien: Alfred Hölder, 1919–24); "Grossman, Janina," in Jolanta Maurin-Bialostocka et al. (eds.), *Słownik Artystów Polskich i Obcych w Polsce Działających Malarze, Rzeźbiarze, Graficy: Tom: II D-G* (Wrocław: Polska Akademia Nauk. Instytut Sztuki, Zakład Narodowy im. Ossolińskich, 1975), p. 485.

25. Antony Polonsky, *Politics in Independent Poland 1921–1939: The Crisis of Constitutional Government* (Oxford: Oxford University Press, 1972), p. 106; Henryk Grossman, "Statystyka ruchu towaronego na kolejach zelaznych," *Miesięcznik Statysticzny* 3 (1921): 1–28

26. Carl Grünberg, "Gutachtlicher Bericht. Betr. Habilitation des Dr Heinrich Grossmann. 27 January 1927," "Heinrich Grossmann," Akten der WiSo Fakultät, Sig 45² Abt 150 Nr 376, Archiv der Johann Wolfgang Goethe Universität, Frankfurt am Main (UFM), pp. 212–15.

27. GUS, folio 21; curriculum vitae by Henryk Grossmann in "Grossmann, Heinrich," January 1927, UFM, p. 198 (curriculum vitae UFM); Grünberg, "Gutachtlicher Bericht." Grossman's departure from GUS gives weight to other criticisms of the census; see Stephan M. Horak, *Poland and her National Minorities, 1919–1939* (New York: Vantage, 1961), pp. 80–83; Kenneth C. Farmer, "National Minorities in Poland, 1919–1980," in Stephan M. Horak, *Eastern European National Minorities 1919–1980* (Littleton, Colo.: Libraries Unlimited, 1985), p. 37.

28. Henryk Grossman, "Majątek Społeczny Królestwa Poskiego," *Miesięcznik Statysticzny* 5, Warsaw, 1922, pp. 255–77. Joseph Marcus, *Social and Political History of the Jews in Poland, 1919–1938* (Berlin, New York, and Amsterdam: Mouton, 1983), p. 250.

29. Henryk Grossman, "Struktura społeczna i gospodarcza Księstwa Warszawskiego na podstawie spisów ludności 1808–1810 roku," *Kwartal Statystyczny* 2 (1), Warsaw, 1925, pp. 1–108.

30. Zofia Skubała-Tokarska, *Społeczna Role Wolnej Wszechnicy Polskiej* (Wrocław: Polska Akademia Nauk, 1967), pp. 247–49; curriculum vitae UFM; Grünberg, "Gutachtlicher Bericht;" Zygmunt Zagórowski, (ed.), *Spis nauczycieli: szkół wyższych, średnich, zawodowych, seminarjów nauczycielskich oraz wykaz zakładów naukowych i władz szkolnych* (Lwów-Warszawa: Książnica Polska, 1924), p. 108.

31. Henryk Piasecki, *Sekcja Żydowska PPSD i Żydowska Partia Socjalno-Demokratyczna* (Wrocław: Zakład Narodowy imienia Ossolińskich, 1982), p. 173; Georg Waldemar Strobel, *Die Partei Rosa Luxemburgs, Lenin und die SPD: der polnische "europaische" Internationalismus in der russischen Sozialdemokratie* (Wiesbaden: F. Steiner, 1974), pp. 63, 124, 468; Maria Meglicka, *Prasa Komunistycznej Partii Robotniczej Polski 1918–1923* (Warszawa: Zakład Historii Partii przy KC PZPR, Książka i Wiedza, 1968), p. 278; Tołwiński, *Wspomnienia*, p. 172.

32. Wolna Wszechnica Polska, *Skład osobowy i spis wykładów: na rok akademicki 1924/1925* (Warsaw, 1924), p. 9; curriculum vitae UFM; Grünberg, "Gutachtlicher Bericht"; Roman Jabłonowski, *Wspomnienia (1905–1928)* (Warszawa: Państwowe Wydawnictwo Naukowe, 1962), pp. 243–44; Franciszka Świetlikowa, "Centralne instancje partyjne KPP w latach 1918–1938," *Z pola walki* 4 (1969): 141.

33. Simoncini, *The Communist Party of Poland*, pp. 77, 81.

34. Aleksander Kochański, "Rudniański, Stefan," in Instytut Historii, Polska Akademia Nauk *Polski Słownik Biograficzny*, vol. 32 (Wrocław: Zakład Narodowy im. Ossolińskich, 1989–91), p. 607.

35. Henryk Cimek and Lucjan Kieszczynski, *Komunistyczna Partia Polski 1918–1938* (Warsaw: Książka i Wiedza, 1984), p. 47; Edward Kołodziej, *Komunistyczna Partia Robotnicza Polski w Ruch Zawodowym 1918–1923* (Warsaw: Ksiąåka i Wiedza, 1978), p. 154; Francizka Świetlikowa, *Kommunistyczna Partia Robotnicza Polski 1918–1923* (Warsaw: Książka i Wiedza, 1968), p. 215; Meglicka, *Prasa Komunistycznej Partii Robotniczej Polski,* p. 278; Roman Loth, "'Kultura Robotnicza'—'Nowa Kultura,'" *Przegląd Humanistyczny* 1 (1965): 96–97. Grossman also provided a brief description of the activities of the People's University; Grossmann, "Lebenslauf" UAL, pp. 64–66. A note, based on testimony from Grossman, indicated that he was "president" of the People's University from 1922 to 1925; "Btr.: Großman, Henryk, geb.: 14.4.81–9053 (Anerkennung)," September 12 1950, SSAL.

36. Tołwiński, *Wspomnienia,* pp. 178–79.

37. Jabłonowski, *Wspomnienia,* p. 243.

38. "Khronik," *Sotsial-demokrat,* March 2, 1906, p. 3.

39. Wolna Wszechnica Polska w Warszawie, *Skład osobowy i spis wykładów na rok Adademicki 1922/23* (Warszaw, 1922), p. 34.

40. Tołwiński, *Wspomnienia,* pp. 175–76.

41. Karl Marx, *Niewydane Pisma* translated and with an introduction, "Przycznek do historji socjalizmu w Polsce przed laty czterdziestu," by Henryk Grossman, (Warszawa: Książka, 1923). On the relationship between Book and the People's University, see Krystyna Dolindowska, *"Książka" i "Tom": Z dzijow legalnych widawnictw KPP 1918–1937* (Warszawa: Centralne Archiwum KC PZPR, 1977), p. 34.

42. For Grossman's involvement with the translation of the first part of the first volume of Marx's *Capital* into Polish, published in 1926, see Dolindowska, *"Książka" i "Tom,"* pp. 32, 80.

43. For a more recent survey of how Marx was received in Poland before 1883, see Andrzej Grodek, *Wybór pism,* vol. 1: *Studia z historii myśli ekonomicznej* (Warsaw: Państwowe Wydawnictwo Naukowe, 1963), pp. 433–62; Grossman's contribution on Pawlicki is at p. 455.

44. Grossman, "Przycznek do historji socjalizmu w Polsce przed laty czterdziestu," p. vii.

45. Kołodziej, *Komunistyczna Partia Robotnicz Polski,* p. 154; Meglicka, *Prasa Komunistycznej Partii Robotniczej Polski,* pp. 277, 281, 288, 337; Loth, "'Kultura Robotnicza'—'Nowa Kultura,'" p. 96.

46. Henryk Grossman, "Ekonomiczny system Karola Marksa," *Kultura Robotnicza* 2 (10), no. 32 (March 17 1923): 295.

47. Ibid., p. 298.

48. Ibid., pp. 298–99.

49. See Rick Kuhn, "Henryk Grossman and the Recovery of Marxism," *Historical Materialism* 13 (3) (2005): 59–62.

50. Henryk Grossman, "Inhalt," December 6, 1924, in 1997 Folder 39 "Zur Dynamik des kapitalistischen Wirtschaftsmechanismus 1924–1926," APAN.

51. Curriculum vitae UFM; Grünberg, "Gutachtlicher Bericht," The title of the early version of Grossman's manuscript study was in Polish, "Tendencje rozwojowe współczesnego kapitalizmu," the later title in German, "Die Entwicklungstendenzen des "reinen" und empirischen Kapitalismus," original Folder 41, in 1997 Folders 40–45, APAN. The preface to "Die Entwicklungstendenzen" was dated November 1926. Grossman made numerous handwritten additions to these typed manuscripts.

52. Grossman, "Die Entwicklungstendenzen."

53. Henryk Grossman, *Simonde de Sismondi et ses théories économiques. Une nouvelle interprétation de sa pensée* appeared in the Bibliotheca Universitatis Liberae Polniae, fasc. 11, Warsaw, 1924.

54. International Institute of Social Research, American Branch, *International Institute of Social Research: A Short Description of its History and Aims*, New York, probably 1934, Columbia University Archives, p. 14.

55. Charles Gide and Charles Rist, *Histoire des doctrines économiques: depuis les physiocrates jusqu'a nos jours* (L. Larose et L. Tenin: Paris, 1909). The book went through multiple editions in French and also in English and German translations over the following forty years.

56. Grossman, *Simonde de Sismondi*, pp. 2–3, 17, 39, 60.

57. Henryk Grossmann, "Recensionen [sic] der Pressarbeiten (Prof. Dr. Henryk Großman)," UAL, p. 69.

58. Grossman, *Simonde de Sismondi*, pp. 9–10, 13, 15–17.

59. Ibid., p. 11, the ellipsis in the quotation from Sismondi is Grossman's.

60. Ibid., pp. 27–29.

61. Ibid., pp. 30–31.

62. Ibid., p. 50.

63. See Lukács, *History and Class Consciousness*, p. 49.

64. Ibid., pp. 12, 35, 152.

65. Grossman, *Simonde de Sismondi*, pp. 33–38.

66. Ibid., pp. 38–39, 42–45, 48–50, the quotation is from p. 49; Grossman, "The Theory of Economic Crises."

67. Grossman, *Simonde de Sismondi*, pp. 27, 38, 44–45, 52–53, 56–58, 59.

68. Ibid., pp. 64–75; Lukács, *History and class consciousness*, p. 243. The translation of the Marx quotation is from Karl Marx, *Theories of Surplus Value*, vol. 3 (Moscow: Progress Publishing, 1975), p. 56.

69. Grossman, *Simonde de Sismondi*, p. 77.

70. Jan Dmochowski (ed.), *Mikołaju Kopernika Rozprawny o moncie i inne pisma ekonomiczne oraz J. L. Decjusza Traktat o biciu monety* (Warsaw: Nakład Gebethnera i Wolffa, 1923), APAN.

71. A handwritten manuscript in Polish, "Historia niewoli u ludów Chrześcijańskich od czsów Chrystusa do koca XIX wieku"(The History of Slavery amongst Christian Peoples from the Time of Christ to the end of the 19th Century), was completed no earlier than 1922; in 1997 Folder 1, APAN. Grossman mentioned a manuscript "critical history of slavery" in his correspondence in 1933 and 1935; letter from Grossman to the

Dekan der Wirtschafts- und Sozialiwssenschaftlichen Fakultät, April 22, 1933, UFM, pp. 224–25; letter from Henryk Grossman to Leo Löwenthal, December 10, 1933, File A 325, Leo-Löwenthal-Archiv, Universitäts- und Stadtarchiv Frankfurt am Main, p. 76; letter from Grossman to Max Beer, January 19, 1935, Box 1, Max Beer Nachlaß, Archiv der sozialen Demokratie der Friedrich-Ebert-Stiftung. Grossman included the manuscript on a much later list of unpublished works, "History of slavery during the Christian period consisting of three chapters: I. Agrarian slavery in antiquity and the early middle ages; II. The rise of galley slavery during the period of exploration; III. The period of plantation slavery during the 19th century;" "Aufzählung der nicht veröffentlichten und nicht registrierten Arbeiten von Prof. Dr. Henryk Grossman," UAL, p. 68.

72. On economic and political conditions in this period, see R. F. Leslie, Antony Polonsky, Jan Ciechanowski, and Z. Pelczynski *The History of Poland Since 1863* (Cambridge: Cambridge University Press, 1980), p. 149; Antony Polonsky, *Politics in Independent Poland 1921–1939: The Crisis of Constitutional Government* (Oxford: Oxford University Press, 1972), pp. 100–126.

73. On political developments in late 1922 and early 1923, see Polonsky, *Politics in Independent Poland*, pp. 112–13.

74. Tołwiński, *Wspomnienia*, pp. 183–84; Loth, "'Kultura Robotnicza'—'Nowa Kultura,'" p. 114.

75. Simoncini, *The Communist Party of Poland*, pp. 103–4, 107; Polonsky, *Politics in independent Poland*, pp. 114–15, 117–18; Dziewanowski, *The Communist Party of Poland*, p. 106.

76. Simoncini, *The Communist Party of Poland*, pp. 89–92, 94–95, 121.

77. Grossmann, "Lebenslauf" UAL, pp. 64–66; Rat der Stadt Leipzig, Kommunalabteilung für die "Opfer des Faschismus," Fragebogen, March 15, 1949, SSAL; Karl August Wittfogel, "Aus der Gründungszeit des Instituts für Sozialforschung," in Bertram Schefold (ed.), *Wirtschafts- und Sozialwissenschaftler in Frankfurt am Main* (Marburg: Metropolis, 1989), p. 53.

78. Polonsky, *Politics in Independent Poland*, pp. 119–21; Radziejowski, *The Communist Party of Western Ukraine*, p. 5.

79. "Walka z komunizmem," *Gazeta Administracji I Policja Państwowej*, August 9, 1924, pp. 679–80; Jabłonowski, *Wspomnienia*, p. 243; Kommunalabteilung für die "Opfer des Faschismus," Fragebogen; Loth, "'Kultura Robotnicza'—'Nowa Kultura,'" p. 97; Meglicka, *Prasa Komunistycznej Partii Robotniczej Polski*, p. 290; Ławnik, "Represje policyjne," pp. 38, 55–56. P. Minc, who had come over to the KPRP from the Bund also recalled the arrests in the summer of 1925 but mistakenly described Professor Grossman as a member of the party's Central Editorial Group, which used the apartment; *Di geshikhte fun a falsher iluzie* (Buenos Aires: Tsentral-farband fun Poylishe Yidn in Argentina, 1954), p. 142.

80. The classic account of the degeneration of the Russian revolution is Leon Trotsky, *The Revolution Betrayed: What is the Soviet Union and Where is it Going?* (New York: Pathfinder, 1991 [1937]). A more recent, scholarly study is Michal Reiman, *The Birth of Stalinism: The USSR on the Eve of the "Second Revolution"* (Bloomington: Indiana University Press, 1987). Tony Cliff, *State Capitalism in Russia* (London: Pluto, 1974 [1955]) provided a path-breaking analysis account of the Stalinist regime as "state capitalist."

81. J. V. Stalin, "The Communist Party of Poland," speech delivered at a meeting of the Polish Commission of the Comintern, July 3, 1924, in J. V. Stalin, *Works*, vol. 6 (Moscow: Foreign Languages Publishing House, 1953 [1924]), pp. 276–84; Simoncini, *The Communist Party of Poland*, pp. 127–32.

82. See Duncan Hallas, *The Comintern* (London: Bookmarks, 1985), pp. 86–89.

83. Isaac Deutscher, "The Tragedy of the Polish Communist Party," *The Socialist Register* (London: Merlin, 1982), pp. 135, 144–45; Simoncini, *The Communist Party of Poland*, pp. 126–28; J. P. Nettl, *Rosa Luxemburg* (London: Oxford University Press, 1966), pp. 800, 806.

84. Loth, "'Kultura Robotnicza'—'Nowa Kultura,'" p. 112, and. Meglicka, *Prasa Komunistycznej Partii Robotniczej Polski*, p. 290.

85. Stead, notes, Box 6, Folder 45, Stead Collection; Jabłonowski, *Wspomnienia*, p. 243. On Grossman's arrival in Germany, see Reichssicherheitshauptamt, R59 St 3/443 I, documents of the Arbeitsgemeinschaft zum Studium sowjet-russischer Plan- wirtschaft ("Arplan") for 1942–43, IV A 1 b 4764/42 Berlin 30.12.42, Bundesarchiv, Abteilung Potsdam; Wittfogel, "Aus der Gründungszeit," p. 53.

86. Grossman's personnel form from the University of Frankfurt in 1930 states that he was married; "Personalbogen," "Grossmann, Heinrich 1927–1967," Abt 1 Nr 15, Akten des Rektors, Archiv der Johann Wolfgang Goethe Universität, Frankfurt am Main. By 1940 he was divorced; Henryk Grossman, Alien Registration Form, Immigration and Naturalization Service, October 31, 1940; R. W. Meadows report, October 15, 1941, Hen- ryk Grossman file, Federal Bureau of Investigation.

87. Stead, notes, Box 6, Folder 45, Stead Collection. Contrast Friedrich Pollock's assertion that "the marriage seems to have broken down because Grossman's life was more and more exclusively occupied with his scientific work;" letter from Friedrich Pollock to Klaus Hennings, July 13, 1967, IV 10.1–94, p. 222, Max-Horkheimer-Archiv, Universitäts- und Stadtarchiv Frankfurt am Main. The implication that Henryk's research meant he had no time for relationships cannot be taken seriously, in light of other limited but more reliable information about his private life.

88. Letter from Christina Stead to Bill Blake, April 11, 1944, Christina Stead and William J. Blake, *Dearest Munx: The letters of Christina Stead and William J. Blake* (Carl- ton: Miegunyah Press, 2005), pp. 300–301.

89. Ellipsis in the original; the destruction of Grossman's papers is mentioned in two documents in Box 6, Folder 45, Stead Collection. For Grossman's awareness of the importance of even the ephemeral pamphlets and leaflets for understanding the labor movement's history, see letters from Henryk Grossman to Paul Mattick, September 16, 1931, Mattick Collection, Internationaal Instituut voor Sociale Geschiedenis and April 14, 1931, ibid.

Chapter 5: Marxist Economics and the Institute for Social Research

1. Bertolt Brecht, *Journals 1934–1955* (London: Methuen, 1993), pp. 230–31.

2. Rolf Wiggershaus, *The Frankfurt School: Its History, Theories and Political Signifi- cance* (Cambridge: Polity, 1995), p. 44.

3. The quotation refers specifically to Horkheimer and Adorno, but applies equally to Pollock and Weil; Wolfgang Abendroth, *Ein Leben in der Arbeiterbewegung* (Frankfurt am Main: Suhrkamp, 1976), p. 70. Also see Wiggershaus, *The Frankfurt School*, pp. 7–11, 41–45.

4. On Felix Weil and Malik Verlag, see John Willett, *The New Sobriety 1917–1933: Art and Politics in the Weimar Period* (London: Thames and Hudson, 1978), p. 82.

5. Karl Korsch, "Marxism and Philosophy," in *Marxism and Philosophy* (London: NLB, 1970 [1925 but appeared as an off-print in 1923]), pp. 29–85.

6. Georg Lukács, *History and Class Consciousness* (London: Merlin, 1971 [1923]), pp. 2–3, 8, 149 et seq. John Rees provides a valuable and accessible account of Lukács's contribution, *The Algebra of Revolution: The Dialectic and the Classical Marxist Tradition* (London: Routledge, 1998), pp. 202–61.

7. Wiggershaus, *The Frankfurt School*, pp. 13–21.

8. Ibid., pp. 21–23; Franz Schiller, "Das Marx-Engels-Institut in Moskau," *Archiv für die Geschichte des Sozialismus und der Arbeiterbewegung* 15 (1930): 418–20; D. J. Struik, "David Ryazanov," in John Eatwell, Murray Milgate, and Peter Newman (eds.), *The New Palgrave: Marxian Economics* (New York: Norton, 1990), pp. 336–37.

9. Ulrike Migdal, *Die Frühgeschichte des Frankfurter Instituts für Sozialforschung* (Frankfurt: Campus Verlag, 1981), pp. 68–69.

10. Letter from Henryk Grossman to Max Horkheimer, December 19, 1936, Max Horkheimer, *Gesammelte Schiften*, Band 15: *Briefwechsel 1913–1936* (Frankfurt am Main: Fischer, 1995) (MHGS15), p. 796; Karl August Wittfogel, "Aus der Gründungszeit des Instituts für Sozialforschung," in Bertram Schefold (ed.), *Wirtschafts- und Sozialwissenschaftler in Frankfurt am Main* (Marburg: Metropolis, 1989), p. 53. On Sorge and Wittfogel, see Migdal, *Frühgeschichte*, pp. 83–94; Gary L. Ulmen, *The Science of Society: Toward an Understanding of the Life and Work of Karl August Wittfogel* (The Hague: Mouton, 1978).

11. Wiggershaus, *The Frankfurt School*, pp. 30–34.

12. Fernando Claudin, *The Communist Movement* (Harmondsworth: Penguin, 1975), p. 77. Also see Ossip K. Flechtheim, *Die KPD in der Weimarer Republik* (Frankfurt am Main: Europäische Verlagsanstalt, 1969), p. 217.

13. "Lebenslauf von Professor Dr. Henryk Grossman," August 3, 1949, pp. 61–63, "Henryk Grossmann," Universitätsarchiv Leipzig, PA 40 (UAL). Grossman made a trip out of Germany in April 1930, for example; letter from Henryk Grossman to the rector, April 24, 1930, "Grossmann, Heinrich 1927–1967," Akten des Rektors, Abt 1 Nr 15, Archiv der Johann Wolfgang Goethe Universität, Frankfurt am Main.

14. Judit Pákh (ed.), *Frankfurter Arbeiterbewegung in Dokumente 1832–1933 Band 2 1914–1933: Von Ersten Weltkrieg bis zur faschistischen Diktatur* (Frankfurt am Main: Verein für Frankfurter Arbeitergeschichte, Union-Druckerei und Verlagsanstalt, 1997), p. 1144.

15. Grossman's status at the WWP is indicated by *Skład osobowy i spis wykładów na rok Akademicki 1925/26* (Warszawa, 1925), p. 9; ibid., *1926/27* (Warszawa 1926), p. 29; *Minerva: Jahrbuch der Gelehrten Welt*, 28, part 2 (1926): 2191; and a curriculum vitae by

Henryk Grossman in "Heinrich Grossmann," January 1927, Akten der WiSo Fakultät, Sig 45² Abt 150 Nr 376, Archiv der Johann Wolfgang Goethe Universität, Frankfurt am Main, (curriculum vitae UFM), p. 198.

16. Henryk Grossmann, *Das Akkumulations- und Zusammenbruchsgetz des kapitalistischen Systems (zugleich eine Krisentheorie)* (Leipzig: Hirschfeld, 1929), p. xi.

17. Christina Stead, "The Exploits of Jan Callowjan," Box 11, Folder 79, Christina Stead Collection MS4967, National Library of Australia (Stead Collection).

18. Letter from Henryk Grossman to Max Beer, January 19, 1935, Box 1, Max Beer Nachlaß, Archiv der sozialen Demokratie der Friedrich-Ebert-Stiftung (Beer Collection).

19. Stead, notes, Box 6, Folder 45, Stead Collection; *Werdegang und Schriften der Mitglieder der Vereinigung der Sozial- und Wirtschaftswissenschaftlichen Hochschullehrer* Supplement 1931, pp. 19–20; *Adreßbuch Frankfurt* 1933.

20. Letter from Grossman to Horkheimer, November 6, 1936, MHGS15, p. 715.

21. Albert Mohr, *Das Frankfurter Schauspiel: 1929–1944* (Frankfurt am Main: Waldemar Kramer, 1974), pp. 13, 44; Stead, notes, after a visit by Grossman in 1945, Box 5, Folder 32, Stead Collection.

22. Stead, notes, Box 11, Folder 79, Stead Collection. On Zur Mühlen, see Manfred Altner, *Hermynia Zur Mühlen Eine Biographie* (Bern: Lang, 1997).

23. For Prussian university policy under the Empire, see Bernt Engelmann, *Trotz alledem: Deutsche Radikale 1777–1977* (München: Bertelsmann, 1977), pp. 300–308.

24. Carl Grünberg, "Gutachtlicher Bericht. Betr. Habilitation des Dr Heinrich Grossmann. 27 January 1927," UFM, pp. 212–15; letter from the Prussian Ministry of Education to the dean of the Faculty of Economics and Social Sciences, Professor Dr. Gerloff, May 21, 1926, ibid., p. 195. For attempts by the provincial authorities and police to discredit the institute, see Migdal, *Die Frühgeschichte*, pp. 102–5.

25. Letter from Carl Grünberg to the provincial president Rudolf Schwander, February 27, 1926; cited by Migdal, *Die Frühgeschichte*, p. 103.

26. Faculty meeting of June 2, 1926, UFM, p. 201. Also see Dean Gerloff to the University Kuratorium, June 26, 1926, ibid., pp. 202–3.

27. Rector of the University of Frankfurt am Main to Ministerrat Dr. Windelband, December 15, 1926, ibid., pp. 204–7.

28. Stefan Bauer (Basel) review of Henryk Grossman's *Simonde de Sismondi et ses théories économiques, Archiv für die Geschichte des Sozialismus und der Arbeiterbewegung* 12 (1927): 428–32.

29. On Oppenheimer's ideas, see Erich Preiser, "Franz Oppenheimer: Gedenkrede zur 100. Wiederkehr seines Geburtstages," in *Franz Oppenheimer zum Gedächtnis* (Frankfurt am Main: Frankfurter Universitätsreden 35, 1964), pp. 11–25. Oppenheimer's assessment of Grossman's work is in Franz Oppenheimer, "Gutachten," January 26, 1927, UFM, p. 207.

30. Carl Grünberg, "Gutachtlicher Bericht."

31. "Personalbogen," "Grossmann, Heinrich 1927–1967," Abt 1 Nr 15, Akten des Rektors, Archive der Johann Wolfgang Goethe University of Frankfurt am Main; letter

from Kalvermann, dean of the Faculty of Economics and Social Science, to the Ministry, rector, and Kuratorium, June 29, 1927, UFM, p. 219.

32. An annotation on curriculum vitae UFM, dated July 6, 1929, stated "In 1928 Grossman resigned his position in Warsaw"; Sara Grossman, death certificate, Urzad Stanu Cywilnego w Krakowie.

33. Grossman's status at the WWP is indicated by *Skład osobowy i spis wykładów na rok Akademicki 1925/26* (Warszawa, 1925), p. 9 and ibid., *1926/27* (Warszawa, 1926), p. 29.

34. Letter from the dean of the Faculty of Economics and Social Science to the Prussian minister for science, art and education, July 6, 1929, UFM, pp. 221–22; letter from the Prussian minister for science, art and education to Grossmann, March 26, 1930, ibid., p. 223; Johann Wolfgang Goethe-Universität Frankfurt am Main *Verzeichnis der Vorlesungen Winter-Halbjahr 1929–30 und Personalverzeichnis* (Frankfurt am Main: Verlag Universitätsbuchhandlung Blazek u. Bergmann, 1929) (*Verzeichnis*), p. 4.

35. Henryk Grossman, "Curriculum vitae" in "Akta osobowe Henryka Grossmana," p. 1, Glowny Urzad Statystyczny, Centralna Biblioteka Statystyczna, Warsaw.

36. Curriculum vitae UFM; Grossmann, *Das Akkumulations- und Zusammenbruchsgetz*, p. v; Henryk Grossman, "Die Entwicklungstendenzen des 'reinen' und empirischen Kapitalismus," original Folder 41, in 1997 Folders 40–45, "Henryk Grossman," III-155, Archiwum Polskiej Akademii Nauk (APAN). Grünberg, "Gutachtlicher Bericht."

37. *Verzeichnis*, winter semester 1927–28, p. 32; *Verzeichnis*, winter semester 1928–29, p. 55; in summer semester 1924, Grossman had taught "The Theory of Commercial Policy," Wolna Wszechnica Polska, *Skład osobowy i spis wykładów: na rok akademicki 1924/1925*, (Warszawa: Wolna Wrzechnica Polska, 1924), p. 64.

38. Tsing-i Yu, *Das Problem der ausländischen Kapitalanlage in China (als Beitrag zur Theorie des Kapitalexports)* (Frankfurt: Wirtschafts- und sozialwissenschafliche Dissertationen, vol. 15, 1935 [originally submitted 1932]). Grossman's role as a supervisor is indicated in *Abgeschlossene Promotionen der Wirtschafts- und Sozialwissenschaftlichen Fakultät und des Fachbereichs Wirschaftswissenschaft in den Jahren 1916 bis 1995*, University of Frankfurt am Main, p. 100. The latter publication designates the author of the thesis as "Yu, Tsi-I S. y.," while he is "Tsing-Y-U" in *International Institute of Social Research: A Short Description of its History and Aims* (New York, n.d [1934 or 1935]), p. 15, held by Columbia University Archives. For Grossman's relationship with the other students, see a fragment of a letter from Henryk Grossman to Leo Löwenthal, no date but located in the archive between correspondence on August 18 and October 26, 1934, A 325, Leo-Löwenthal-Archiv Universitäts- und Stadtarchiv Frankfurt am Main (LLA), p. 87.

39. Ilse or Heinz Langerhans reported this to Ilse Mattick; Ilse Mattick interviewed by Rick Kuhn, November 24, 1993, notes confirmed in subsequent correspondence (Ilse Mattick interview).

40. For the institute's support for Sternberg's study, see Manfred Gangl, *Politische Ökonomie und Kritische Theorie: Ein Beitrag zur theoretischen Entwicklung der Frankfurter Schule* (Frankfurt and New York, 1987), p. 91.

41. For an overview of Sternberg's political development, his positions, and the debate over them, see Helga Grebing, *Der Revisionismus von Bernstein bis zum "Prager Frühling"* (München: Beck, 1977), pp. 121–36. Fritz Sternberg, *Der Imperialismus* (Frankfurt: Verlag Neue Kritik, 1971 [1926]), pp. 7–10.

42. Henryk Grossmann, "Eine neue Theorie über Imperialismus und die soziale Revolution," *Archiv für die Geschichte des Sozialismus und der Arbeiterbewegung* 13 (1928): 142. The essay was republished in Henryk Grossmann, *Aufsätze zur Krisentheorie* (Frankfurt am Main: Verlag Neue Kritik, 1971), pp. 113–64.

43. Grossmann, "Eine neue Theorie," pp. 145, 149–150, 173, 183.

44. Vladimir Ilych Lenin, "Conspectus of Hegel's book *The Science of Logic*," *Collected Works*, vol. 38, 4th ed. (Moscow: Progress Publishers, 1981 [1929]), pp. 114, 130, 180, 182, 208. Also see Lenin's later "On the Significance of Militant Materialism," *Collected Works*, vol. 33, 4th ed. (Moscow: Progress Publishers, 1980 [1922]), pp. 233–34; and Rees, *The Algebra of Revolution*, pp. 184–94.

45. Grossmann, "Eine neue Theorie," pp. 158–60.

46. Ibid., pp. 161–62, emphasis and ellipsis in the original. The Lenin quotations are from Vladimir Ilych Lenin, "The Collapse of the Second International," *Collected Works*, vol. 21, 4th ed. (Moscow: Progress Publishers, 1980 [1915]), pp. 213–14, 228, 240. Lenin restated his position in *Leftwing Communism—an Infantile Disorder, Collected Works*, vol. 31, 4th ed. (Moscow: Progress Publishers, 1966 [1920]), pp. 84–85, also see p. 94.

47. Georg Lukács, *Lenin* (London: NLB, 1970 [1924]), pp. 31–34.

48. Grossmann, "Eine neue Theorie," p. 156.

49. Ibid., pp. 164–68, 180.

50. Ibid., pp. 169–79; *Verzeichnis*, summer semester 1928, p. 51.

51. Grossmann, "Eine neue Theorie," p. 185.

52. Henryk Grossmann review of Maurice Bourgin's *Les systemes socialistes et l'évolution économique*, 3rd ed. (Paris, 1925), *Archiv für die Geschichte des Sozialismus und der Arbeiterbewegung* 13 (1928): 344–45.

53. Henryk Grossmann review of Othmar Spann's, *Die Haupttheorien der Volkswirtschaftslehre. 12. bis 15. Auflage* (Leipzig, 1923), *Archiv für die Geschichte des Sozialismus und der Arbeiterbewegung* 13 (1928): 341–44.

54. Georg Lukács review of Othmar Spann's *Kategorienlehre* (Jena: Fischer, 1927), *Archiv für die Geschichte des Sozialismus und der Arbeiterbewegung* 13 (1928): 302–6.

55. Curriculum vitae UFM; Grünberg, "Gutachtlicher Bericht"; Henryk Grossmann, *Das Akkumulations- und Zusammenbruchsgetz des kapitalistischen Systems (zugleich eine Krisentheorie)* (Leipzig: Hirschfeld, 1929), p. v. The abridged English translation is Henryk Grossmann, *The Law of Accumulation and Breakdown of the Capitalist System: Being also a Theory of Crises* (London: Pluto, 1992).

56. Grossmann, *The Law of Accumulation*, p. 39.

57. Ibid., pp. 56–57.

58. Ibid., p. 33.

59. Henryk Grossman, *Proletariat wobec kwestyi żydowskiej z powodu niedyskutowanej dyskusyi w "Krytyce"* (Kraków: Drukani Władysława Teodorczuka, January 1905), p. 42;

Österreichs Handelspolitik mit Bezug auf Galizien in der Reformperiode 1772–1790 (Wien: Konegen, 1914), pp. ix–x. On Lenin's "stick bending," see Vladimir Ilych Lenin, "Speech on the Party Programme" at the Second Congress of the RSDLP July 17 (30)-August 10 (23) 1903, *Collected Works*, vol. 6, 4th ed. (Moscow: Progress Publishers, 1964), p. 489; and Tony Cliff, *Lenin*, vol. 1: *Building the Party* (London: Pluto, 1975), pp. 66–68.

60. Henryk Grossmann, "Die Fortentwicklung des Marxismus bis zur Gegenwart," in Henryk Grossmann and Carl Grünberg, *Anarchismus, Bolschewismus, Sozialismus* (Frankfurt am Main: Europäische Verlagsanstalt, 1971 [originally published in Ludwig Elster (ed.), *Wörterbuch der Volkswirtschaft*, vol. 3, 4th ed. (Jena: Fischer, 1933), pp. 313–41, an offprint appeared in 1932, titled *Fünfzig Jahre Kampf um den Marxismus 1883–1932* (Jena: Fischer, 1932), p. 336.

61. Grossmann, *The Law of Accumulation*, pp. 40–41, 51.

62. Rosa Luxemburg, *Reform or Revolution* (London: Bookmarks, 1989 [1898–99]), pp. 26–27; *The Accumulation of Capital* (London: Routledge, 1963 [1913]), p. 325.

63. Grossmann, *The Law of Accumulation*, pp. 41–42, 125–26.

64. Georg Lukács, "The Marxism of Rosa Luxemburg," in Lukács, *History and Class Consciousness*, pp. 30–40; Lukács, *Lenin*, p. 47.

65. See Grossmann, "Eine neue Theorie."

66. Grossmann, *Das Akkumulations- und Zusammenbruchsgesetz*, p. 22. The emphasis is Grossman's, rather than Vladimir Ilych Lenin's, in "Report on the International Situation and the Fundamental Tasks of the Communist International," delivered to the Second Congress of the Communist International, July 19, 1920, *Collected Works*, vol. 31, 4th ed. (Moscow: Progress Publishers, 1982), pp. 226–27. This passage is much abbreviated in Grossmann, *The Law of Accumulation*, p. 42.

67. For Marx's method in *Capital*, see Grossmann, *The Law of Accumulation*, pp. 29–33, 63–67, 83–86, 130.

68. Henryk Grossman, "The Theory of Economic Crises," in *Bulletin International de l'Académie Polonaise des Sciences et des Lettres. Classe de Philologie, Classe d'Histoire et de Philosophie. Les Années 1919, 1920* (presented June 16 1919) (1922): 285–90; and Henryk Grossman, *Simonde de Sismondi et ses théories économiques. Une nouvelle interprétation de sa pensée* (Warsaw: Bibliotheca Universitatis Liberae Polniae, fasc. 11, 1924), p. 59. Grossman's critique of the neglect of the use value side of the organic composition of capital by the "epigones of Marx," in a page-long footnote, is missing from the English translation; Grossmann, *Das Akkumulations- und Zusammenbruchsgetz*, pp. 326–27, also p. 330.

69. Grossmann, *The Law of Accumulation*, pp. 61, 144–47.

70. Ibid., pp. 119, 123–24.

71. Otto Bauer, "The Accumulation of Capital," *History of Political Economy* 18 (1) (Spring 1986 [1913]): 88–110.

72. Grossmann, *The Law of Accumulation*, pp. 74–77, 168.

73. Ibid., p. 189.

74. Grossmann, *Das Akkumulations- und Zusammenbruchsgesetz*, pp. 136–37. The passage is abbreviated in the published English translation, Grossmann, *The Law of Accumulation*, p. 82.

75. Grossmann, *The Law of Accumulation*, p. 103; also see Grossmann, "Die Fortentwicklung des Marxismus," pp. 331–32.

76. Grossmann, *The Law of Accumulation*, p. 83.

77. Ibid., pp. 189–90.

78. Ibid., pp. 96–101. Sam Pietsch pointed out to me that two steps in the derivation of Grossman's formula are misspecified in the translation of his book; ibid., p. 97; cf. Grossmann, *Das Akkumulations- und Zusammenbruchsgesetz*, pp. 184–85.

79. Grossmann, *The Law of Accumulation*, pp. 95–96.

80. Lenin, "Report on the International Situation and the Fundamental Tasks of the Communist International," p. 227.

81. Grossmann, *The Law of Accumulation*, p. 85.

82. Ibid., p. 99.

83. Ibid., pp. 112–17.

84. Ibid., p. 128.

85. Henryk Grossman, "Tendencje rozwojowe współczesnego kapitalizmu," original Folder 41, APAN.

86. Grossmann, *The Law of Accumulation*, p. 119.

87. Ibid., p. 133.

88. Ibid., pp. 137–38. The German original makes an explicit reference to the 1919 presentation; Grossmann, *Das Akkumulations- und Zusammenbruchsgetz*, p. 311; Grossman, "The Theory of Economic Crises," pp. 288–89.

89. Grossmann, *Das Akkumulations- und Zusammenbruchsgetz*, p. 329.

90. Ibid., p. 316.

91. Grossmann, *The Law of Accumulation*, p. 140.

92. Ibid., pp. 140–44.

93. Ibid., pp. 147–49.

94. Ibid., pp. 154–55.

95. Ibid., pp. 149–52, 199–200.

96. Ibid., pp. 153–54.

97. Ibid., p. 158.

98. Grossmann, *Das Akkumulations- und Zusammenbruchsgetz*, pp. 414–15.

99. Grossmann, *The Law of Accumulation*, pp. 161–64; Grossmann, *Das Akkumulations- und Zusammenbruchsgetz*, p. 395.

100. This section of Grossman's book is entirely missing from the English translation; Grossmann, *Das Akkumulations- und Zusammenbruchsgetz*, pp. 396–415.

101. Henryk Grossman, "Historia niewoli u ludów Chrzścijańskich od czsów Chrystusa do koca XIX wieku," in 1997 Folder 1, APAN.

102. Grossmann, *Das Akkumulations- und Zusammenbruchsgetz*, pp. 296–97, 300.

103. Grossmann, *The Law of Accumulation*, pp. 166–68.

104. Ibid., p. 172. Grossmann, *Das Akkumulations- und Zusammenbruchsgetz*, p. 430, acknowledged that Otto Bauer had identified this mechanism, without linking it to capitalism's crisis tendency; see Bauer *The Question of Nationalities* (Minneapolis: University of Minnesota Press, 2000 [1907]), p. 200. Also see Henryk Grossmann, "Die Änderung des ursprünglichen Aufbauplans des Marxschen 'Kapital' und ihre

Ursachen," *Archiv für die Geschichte des Sozialismus und der Arbeiterbewegung* 14 (1929): 305–38; Henryk Grossman, "'Das Problem der Durchschnittsprofitrate in der modernen volkswirtschaftlichen Theorie,' von: Professor Henryk Grossmann," original Folder 37, in 1997 Folder 62, APAN, pp. 34–35.

105. Grossmann, *The Law of Accumulation*, p. 172.

106. Ibid., pp. 174–79; most of the empirical material is not in the English translation; see Grossmann, *Das Akkumulations- und Zusammenbruchsgetz*, pp. 450–70.

107. Grossmann, *Das Akkumulations- und Zusammenbruchsgetz*, pp. 527–28.

108. Ibid., pp. 498–99; Grossmann, *The Law of Accumulation*, pp. 180–81, 193.

109. Grossmann, *Das Akkumulations- und Zusammenbruchsgetz*, pp. 519–20. A compressed version of Grossman's critique of the literature is in Grossmann, *The Law of Accumulation*, pp. 179–85.

110. Grossmann, *Das Akkumulations- und Zusammenbruchsgetz*, pp. 527–29; Grossmann, *The Law of Accumulation*, pp. 180, 187–88.

111. Grossmann, *The Law of Accumulation*, p. 192.

112. Ibid., p. 194.

113. Grossmann, *Das Akkumulations- und Zusammenbruchsgetz*, p. 572; an abbreviated discussion of the issue is in the English edition, *The Law of Accumulation*, p. 197.

114. Grossmann, *Das Akkumulations- und Zusammenbruchsgetz*, pp. 590–91, 595–99. For an illuminating account of Grossman's position that includes a translation of a section not included in *The Law of Accumulation*, see Kenneth Lapides, "Henryk Grossmann on Marx's Wage Theory and the 'Increasing Misery' Controversy," *History of Political Economy* 26 (2) (Summer 1994): 239–46.

115. Grossmann, *Das Akkumulations- und Zusammenbruchsgetz*, p. 600.

116. Ibid., pp. 601–3.

117. Henryk Grossman, *Der Bundizm in Galitsien* Ferlag der *Sotsial-democrat* (Kraków, 1907), pp. 35, 41, 45–46.

118. See Rudolf Hilferding, "Die Aufgaben der Sozialdemokratie in der Republik," *Zwischen den Stühlen oder über die Unvereinbarkeit von Theorie und Praxis: Schriften Rudolf Hilferdings 1904 bis 1940* (Bonn: J. H. W. Dietz, 1982 [1927]), pp. 214–36.

119. Grossmann, *Das Akkumulations- und Zusammenbruchsgetz*, p. 606.

120. Ibid., pp. 610–19.

121. Ibid., pp. 619–20.

122. Ibid., pp. 621, 622.

123. Lukács, *History and Class Consciousness*, pp. 83–84.

124. Giacomo Marramao, "Political Economy and Critical Theory," *Telos* 24 (Summer 1975): 64. Also see Giacomo Marramao, "Theory of the Crisis and the Problem of Constitution," *Telos* 26 (Winter 1975–76): 162–63; and Rick Kuhn, "Henryk Grossman and the Recovery of Marxism," *Historical Materialism* 13 (3) (2005): 57–100.

125. An interpretation of Grossman's work, originating with Martin Jay, misunderstands his perspective. In his influential and path-breaking account of the Frankfurt School, Jay argued that Grossman "had, however, absorbed his Marxism in the years when Engels's and Kautsky's monistic materialistic views prevailed. He remained

firmly committed to this interpretation and thus largely unsympathetic to the dialectical, neo-Hegelian materialism of the younger Institut members"; Martin Jay, *The Dialectical Imagination* (Berkeley: University of California Press, 1996 [1973]), p. 17.

126. Bourgeois reviews of Grossman's book: Theodor Brauer *Literarischer Handweiser: Kritische Monatsschrift* 65 (July 1929): columns 766–67; Leonhard Miksch, "Zusammenbruch des kapitalistischen Systems?" *Frankfurter Zeitung* 75 (610), Sunday, August 17, 1930, p. 7; Adolf Caspary *Weltwirtschaftliches Archiv* 32 (2) (1930): 81; Franz Oppenheimer *Archiv für Rechts- und Wirtschaftsphilosophie* 24 (1930–31): 402–6; Emanuel Hugo Vogel *Vierteljahresschrift für Sozial und Wirtschaftschaftsgeschichte* 23 (1931): 389–91; Karl Muhs, "Das Gesetz der fallenden Profitrate und die Zusammenbruchstendenz des Kapitalismus," *Jahrbuch für Nationalökonomie und Statistik* 135 (1) (July 1931): 9, 13–14.

Social democratic reviews: Alfred Braunthal, "Der Zusammenbruch der Zusammenbruchstheorie," *Die Gesellschaft: Internationale Revue für Sozialismus und Politik* 6, 2 (10) (1929): 280–304; Helene Bauer, "Ein neuer Zusammenbruchstheoretiker," *Der Kampf* 22 (6) (June 1929): 270–80; Conrad Schmidt, "Zusammenbruchstheorie," *Sozialistische Monatshefte* 35 (1929): 638–41; Hans Otto, "Zusammenbruch des Kapitalismus?" *Rote Revue: Sozialistische Monatsschrift* 8 (12) (August 1929): 388–92; Arkadij Gurland, "Absatz und Verwertung im Kapitalismus: Zur neueren Diskussion des Zusammenbruchsproblems," *Der Klassenkampf* 4 (3) (February 1, 1930): 75–83; Fritz Sternberg, *Eine Unwältzung der Wissenschaft? Kritik des Buches von Henryk Grossmann "Das Akkumulations- und Zusammenbruchsgesetz des kapitalistischen System". Zugleich eine positive Analyse des Imperialismus* (Berlin: Prager, 1930); Hans Neisser, "Das Gesetz der fallenden Profitrate als Krisen- und Zusammenbruchsgesetz," *Die Gesellschaft* 8 (1) (1931): 72–85.

Communist reviews: Otto Benedikt, "Die Akkumulation des Kapitals bei wachsender organische Zusammensetzung," *Unter dem Banner des Marxismus* 3 (6) (1929): 869–911; Kraus, "Die marxistische Zusammenbruchstheorie," *Die Internationale* 13 (1/2) (1930): 53–59, 13 (3) (1930): 89–96 and 13 (4) (1930): 122–25; BL (Boris Livshits), *Vestnik Kommunisticheskaia akademiia* Moscow 35–36 (1929): 351–66; E. Varga "Nakoplenie i krakh kapitalizma" *Problemi ekonomiki* 3 (1930): 31–62; Eugen Varga, "Akkumulation und Zusammenbruch des Kapitalismus," *Unter dem Banner des Marxismus* 4 (1) (1930): 60–95, this German and the preceding Russian version are virtually identical; M. Ragol'sky "Protiv novogo izvrashcheniya Marksovoi teorii nakopleniya," *Bol'shevik* 7 (7–8) (April 30, 1930): 36–47 and 7 (10) (May 31, 1930): 88–101.

Council communist reviews and debates: Karl Korsch, "Über einige grundsätzliche Voraussetzungen für eine materialistische Diskussion der Krisentheorie," in Karl Korsch, Paul Mattick, and Anton Pannekoek, *Zusammenbruchstheorie des Kapitalismus oder Revolutionäres Subjekt* (Berlin: Karin Kramer Verlag, 1973 [1933]), pp. 97–98. There is a very weak English translation, "Some Fundamental Presuppositions for a Materialist Discussion of Crisis Theory," in *Karl Korsch: Revolutionary Theory* (Austin: University of Texas Press, 1977), pp. 171–86. "Die Grundlagen einer revolutionären Krisentheorie," *Proletarier: Zeitschrift für theorie und Praxis des Rätekommunismus* 1 (1) (February 1933), republished in Karl Korsch, Paul Mattick, and Anton Pannekoek,

Zusammenbruchstheorie des Kapitalismus oder revolutionäres Subjekt (Berlin: Karin Kramer, 1973), pp. 71–90. Anton Pannekoek, "The Theory of the Collapse of Capitalism," *Capital and Class* 1 (1977 [1934]): 59–81. In addition to repeating Korsch's quotations and arguments about Grossman's position on class struggle, Pannekoek reiterated, also without acknowledgment, Varga's arguments and quotations from Grossman and Marx on imperialism.

127. Paul Mattick's review of *Das Akkumulations- und Zusammenbruchsgetz* in *Chicagoer Arbeiter Zeitung* 5 (1931) was mentioned in a letter from Henryk Grossman to Paul Mattick, June 21, 1931, in Henryk Grossmann, *Marx, die klassische Nationalökonomie und das Problem der Dynamik* (Frankfurt am Main: Europäische Verlagsanstalt, 1969) (*Dynamik*), p. 89. Mattick soon reviewed Grossman's essays on Marx's plan for *Capital, Chicagoer Arbeiter-Zeitung* 1 (10) (December 1931): 3; and then Grossman's 1932 essay on Marx's and Luxemburg's different accounts of the significance of gold production, Paul Mattick, *Der Freidenker* 62 (24) (June 12, 1932): 5. This was republished in another atheist journal, in Vienna, *Der Atheist* 7 (January 1, 1933). Grossman mentioned a favorable article in *Modern Monthly* that Mattick had sent (and either written or inspired), letter from Grossman to Mattick, May 7, 1933, *Dynamik*, p. 98. Mattick offered longer expositions of Grossman's approach as part of the *Program of the Industrial Workers of the World* (Chicago, 1933), republished as "Die Todeskrise des Kapitalismus," in Korsch, Mattick, and Pannekoek, *Zusammenbruchstheorie des Kapitalismus oder Revolutionäres Subjekt,* pp. 100–112; and "Zur Marx'schen Akkumulations- und Zusammenbruchstheorie," *Rätekorrespondenz* 4 (1934), republished in Korsch, Mattick, and Pannekoek, *Zusammenbruchstheorie,* pp. 47–70. Soon Mattick produced a substantial discussion in English, "The Permanent Crisis: Henryk Grossmann's Interpretation of Marx' Theory of Capitalist Accumulation," *International Council Correspondence* 1 (2) (November 1934): 1–20. He went over Grossman's account of the reproduction schemes of Marx, Luxemburg and Bauer in "Luxemburg versus Lenin" in Paul Mattick, *Anti-Bolshevik Communism* (London: Merlin, 1978 [1935–36]), pp. 19–48. Mattick's best known economic analysis is *Marx and Keynes* (London: Merlin, 1974 [1969]).

128. Mohan Tazerout, "Théorie économique et sociologie économique," *Revue internationale de sociologie* 40 (5–6) (May–June 1932): 308. Tazerout also referred to *The Law of Accumulation* as a "fundamental book" in a review of two works by Arthur Salz, "Politique ou économique," *Revue internationale de sociologie* 40 (5–6) (May–June 1932): 616. No French translation of *The Law of Accumulation* was published. Jean Duret, *Le Marxisme et les crises* (Paris: Éditions d'aujourd'hui, 1977 [1933]), pp. 62–71.

129. Henryk Grossman, *Shihon no chikuseki narabi ni hokai no riron,* translated by Hiromi Arisawa and Katsumi Moritani (Tokyo: Kaizosha, 1932).

130. On Hirano, see Shobei Shiota (ed.), *Dictionnaire biographique du mouvement ouvrier international II, Japon* Tome 1 (Paris: Les Editions Ouvrières, 1978), pp. 172–73; Yoshitaro Hirano review of K. Fukimoto's *Zur Methodologie der Kritik der Politischen Ökonomie* (Tokyo, 1926), *Archiv für die Geschichte des Sozialismus und der Arbeiterbewegung* 14 (1929): 157–59; Germaine A. Hoston, "Hirano, Yoshitaro," in Robert A. Gorman, *Biographical Dictionary of Marxism* (Westport: Greenwood, 1986), pp. 137–38; Yoshitaro

Hirano, Preface to Henryk Grossman, *Maruki shizumu notameno toso gojunen* from *Chuo Koron* 48 (543) (1933); Germaine A. Hoston, *Marxism and the Crisis of Development in Prewar Japan* (Princeton: Princeton University Press, 1986), pp. 176, 332.

131. Grossmann, *The Law of Accumulation*, pp. 93–94; "This method of criticising Marx only shows the unparalleled 'thoughtlessness and superficiality' of Muhs himself," Grossmann, *Das Akkumulations- und Zusammenbruchsgetz*, p. 158; "There is not the least trace of any theory in Muhs," Grossmann, *The Law of Accumulation*, p. 94.

132. Grossmann, *The Law of Accumulation*, pp. 48, 88, 127, 165; Grossmann, *Das Akkumulations- und Zusammenbruchsgetz*, pp. 200–201, 500, 583.

133. Grossmann, *Das Akkumulations- und Zusammenbruchsgetz*, p. 517. Grossman also mocked Varga for reproducing Böhm-Bawerk's fable that Marx skipped over the influence of competition on prices; ibid., p. 438.

134. Karl Muhs, *Spengler und der wirtschaftliche Untergang Europas* (Berlin: Junker und Dunnhaupt, 1934), p. 2.

135. Franz Oppenheimer review of Grossmann's *Das Akkumulations- und Zusammenbruchsgetz*.

136. Richard Day, *The "Crisis" and the "Crash": Soviet Studies of the West (1917–1939)* (London: NLB, 1981), pp. 133, 152–53.

137. Nikolai Dmitrievich Kondratiev, *Problemy ekonomicheskoi dinamiki* (Moscow: Ekonomika, 1989), p. 473; George D. Jackson, *Comintern and Peasant in East Europe, 1919–1930* (New York: Columbia University Press, 1966), pp. 73, 295.

138. Grossmann, *The Law of Accumulation*, pp. 199–200; Grossmann, *Das Akkumulations- und Zusammenbruchsgesetz*, pp. 309, 437–38, 576.

139. Day, *The "Crisis" and the "Crash,"* pp. 148–51, 187, 202–11.

140. "Grossman (Grossmann), Genrik," in *Bol'shaia sovetskaia entsiklopediia*, vol. 19 (Moskva, 1930), p. 450; Henryk Grossman, "Lebenslauf" UAL, pp. 64–66; letters from Grossman to Walter Braeuer, January 13, 1948, Braeuer Nachlaß, Johann-Heinrich von Thünen Museum, Tellow (Braeuer Collection); June 25, 1948, ibid. Grossman's correspondence with Braeuer is published in Jürgen Scheele, *Zwischen Zusammenbruchsprognose und Positivismusverdikt: Studien zur politischen und intellektuellen Biographie Henryk Grossmanns (1881–1950)* (Frankfurt: Lang, 1999), pp. 244–65.

141. Day, *The "Crisis" and the "Crash,"* p. 221.

142. Stead, notes, Box 6, Folder 45, Stead Collection; letter from Grossman to Mattick, March 6, 1933, Mattick Collection, Internationaal Instituut voor Sociale Geschiedenis (IISG).

143. Henryk Grossman manuscript starting "Die Entwertung sollen die Zusammenbruchstendenz aufheben . . . " in original Folder 45 "Stellungnahme zur Kritik am Hauptwerk', APAN (Entwertung). The emphasis is Grossman's rather than Bauer's. Longer extracts from Grossman's manuscripts quoted in this section can be found in Rick Kuhn, "Economic Crisis and Socialist Revolution: Henryk Grossman's *Law of Accumulation*, its First Critics and His Responses," *Research in Political Economy* 21 (2004): 181–221, preprint version at http://eprints.anu.edu.au/archive/00002400/01/Economic_crisis_and_socialist_revolution_eprint_secure.pdf, accessed June 5, 2006.

144. Grossmann, *Das Akkumulations- und Zusammenbruchsgetz*, pp. 289, 453.

145. Grossman, Entwertung.

146. Ibid.

147. Ibid., cf. Grossman, "The Theory of Economic Crises," and Henryk Grossman, *Simonde de Sismondi.*

148. Henryk Grossman, manuscript starting "Nach Braunthal, ging Marx von der Beobachtung aus . . . " in original Folder 45 "Stellungnahme zur Kritik am Hauptwerk," APAN.

149. Henryk Grossman, manuscript starting "Br. verweist . . . ' in original Folder 45 "Stellungnahme zur Kritik am Hauptwerk," APAN.

150. Letter from Grossman to Mattick, June 21, 1931, *Dynamik,* pp. 86–87.

151. From the sense of this paragraph (and consistency with his argument elsewhere), Grossman seems to have left out a negative particle from this sentence.

152. Letter from Grossman to Mattick, June 21, 1931, *Dynamik,* p. 88.

153. Letter from Grossman to Mattick, May 7, 1933, *Dynamik,* pp. 98–99. Grossman was commenting on Korsch, "Die Grundlagen einer revolutionären Krisentheorie."

154. Letter from Grossman to Mattick, November 1, 1933, *Dynamik,* pp. 105–6.

155. Grossman, "Das Problem der Durchschnittsprofitrate in der modernen volks-swirtschaftlichen Theorie," pp. 38–47.

156. Original Folder 32, APAN, cited in Scheele, *Zwischen Zusammenbruchsprognose und Positivismusverdikt,* pp. 66–67.

157. See Michael Löwy, *Georg Lukács: from Romanticism to Bolshevism* (London: NLB, 1979), pp. 193–205; and Andrew Arato and Paul Breines, *The Young Lukács and the Origins of Western Marxism* (London: Pluto, 1979), pp. 190–200.

158. Duncan Hallas, *The Comintern* (London: Bookmarks, 1985), pp. 126–38.

159. Karl August Wittfogel, "Aus der Gründungszeit des Instituts für Sozial-forschung," in Bertram Schefold (ed.), *Wirtschafts- und Sozialwissenschaftler in Frankfurt am Main* (Marburg: Metropolis, 1989), p. 53. Wittfogel subsequently became a right-wing anticommunist.

160. Letter from Karl Korsch to Paul Mattick, October 30, 1938, Karl Korsch, "Briefe an Paul Partos, Paul Mattick und Bert Brecht 1934–1939," in Claudio Pozzoli (ed.), *Jahrbuch Arbeiterbewegung Band 2: Marxistische Revolutionstheorien* (Frankfurt am main: Fischer, 1974), p. 186. Ilse Mattick knew Grossman in New York, during the late 1930s and early 1940s; Ilse Mattick interview.

161. Grossmann, *Das Akkumulations- und Zusammenbruchsgetz,* p. 326.

162. Letter from Grossman to Mattick, June 21, 1931, *Dynamik,* p. 92.

163. For recognition of the dangers of being identified as a heretic by the communist movement, see letter from Grossman to Blake, July 10, 1947, Box 17, Folder 125, Stead Collection.

164. Letter from Grossman to Mattick, June 21, 1931, *Dynamik,* p. 86.

165. Henryk Grossmann, "Die Änderung des ursprünglichen Aufbauplans des Marxschen 'Kapital' und ihre Ursachen," *Archiv für die Geschichte des Sozialismus und der Arbeiterbewegung* 14 (1929): 305–38; *Verzeichnis,* summer semester 1929, p. 50. There

is a translation of an important section of Grossman's essay in Kenneth Lapides, "Henryk Grossmann and the Debate on the Theoretical status of Marx's *Capital*," *Science & Society* 56 (2) (Summer 1992): 133–62.

166. Grossmann, "Die Änderung des ursprünglichen Aufbauplans," p. 311.

167. Ibid., pp. 312–14, 327. Also see pp. 105, above.

168. Grossmann, "Die Änderung des ursprünglichen Aufbauplans," pp. 312–21.

169. Ibid., pp. 336, n. 40, 338; Lukács *History and Class Consciousness*, p. 31.

170. Grossmann, "Die Änderung des ursprünglichen Aufbauplans," p. 336.

171. See the excellent survey of the debate on the completeness of *Capital*, Marx's modifications of its structure, their implications, and Grossman's contribution by Lapides, "Henryk Grossmann and the Debate on the Theoretical Status of Marx's *Capital*."

172. Letter from the Prussian Ministry of Science and Culture to Carl Grünberg, December 17, 1928, in "Grünberg, Carl," WiSo FAK, Signatur Abt.150 Nr. 376, Archiv der Johann Wolfgang Goethe University of Frankfurt am Main, p. 173.

173. Wiggershaus, *The Frankfurt School*, pp. 33–35, 37–38.

174. Ibid., p. 104.

175. Ibid., p. 39.

176. Letter from Grossman to Mattick, June 30, 1932, IISG.

177. Joseph Dunner, *Zu Protokoll gegeben: Mein Leben als Deutscher und Jude* (München: Kurt Desch, 1971), p. 66. Abendroth, *Ein Leben in der Arbeiterbewegung*, p. 129; Wiggershaus, *The Frankfurt School*, pp. 112–13.

178. *Verzeichnis*, summer semester 1929, p. 50; *Verzeichnis*, winter semester 1929–30, p. 51; "Changes in the Concept of Labor in Economics," *Verzeichnis*, summer semester 1930, p. 54; *Verzeichnis*, winter semester 1931–32, p. 56; *Verzeichnis*, winter semester 1932–33, p. 56.

179. *Verzeichnis*, summer semester 1930, p. 54; *Verzeichnis*, summer semester 1931, p. 55.

180. Work for the second volume, confiscated by the Nazis in 1933, is mentioned in a letter from Grossman to the dean, April 22, 1933, UFM, pp. 224–25.

181. Henryk Grossmann, "Die Goldproduktion im Reproduktionsschema von Marx und Rosa Luxemburg," in *Festschrift für Carl Grünberg zum 70. Geburtstag* (Leipzig: Hirschfeld, 1932), pp. 152–84; "Die Wert-Preis-Transformation bei Marx und das Krisenproblem," *Zeitschrift für Sozialforschung (ZfS)* 1 (1/2) (1932): 55–84.

182. Günther Nenning, "Biographie C. Grünberg," in *Indexband zu Archiv für die Geschichte des Sozialismus und der Arbeiterbewegung (C. Grünberg)* (Zürich: Limmat-Verlag, 1973), p. 17.

183. Grossmann, "Die Goldproduktion im Reproduktionsschema," pp. 154–60; Luxemburg, *The Accumulation of Capital*, p. 79.

184. Henryk Grossman, "Inhalt," December 6, 1924, original folder 39, APAN; Grossmann, "Die Goldproduktion im Reproduktionsschema," pp. 167–84.

185. Day, *The "Crisis" and the "Crash,"* pp. 148–51, 187, 202–11.

186. Nettl, *Rosa Luxemburg*, pp. 811–20. It may not be a coincidence that Varga's debut performance as an economist in *Neue Zeit* was a contribution on gold production and

inflation; Eugen Varga, "Goldproduktion und Teuerung," *Neue Zeit* 30, 1 (7), November 17, 1911, pp. 212–20.

187. Letter from Grossman to Mattick, September 16, 1931, *Dynamik* pp. 93–95; *Verzeichnis,* summer semester 1932, p. 56; Henryk Grossmann, "Die Wert-Preis-Transformation bei Marx und das Krisenproblem," *ZfS* 1 (1) (1932): 55–84; Grossman, "Das Problem der Durchschnittsprofitrate;" Henryk Grossman, "Zum Abschluss des Streites um die Wert-Preisrechnung im Marxschen System" (a typed-up version of a student's notes) original Folder 40, in 1997 Folder 63, pp. 36–44, APAN.

188. Grossmann, "Die Wert-Preis-Transformation," p. 60.

189. Karl Marx, *Capital,* vol. 3 (Harmondsworth: Penguin, 1981 [1894]), pp. 241–313.

190. Grossmann, "Die Wert-Preis-Transformation," pp. 55–63.

191. Ibid., footnote, pp. 63–64. The first location Grossman refers to in *Das Akkumulations- und Zusammenbruchsgesetz,* from which he quoted, is missing from the English translation, the second has been edited down; Grossmann, *Das Akkumulations- und Zusammenbruchsgesetz,* pp. 107, 211; Grossmann, *The Law of Accumulation,* p. 129. M. C. Howard and J. E. King apparently overlooked or did not understand the significance of this argument both in Grossman's book and this essay when, following Neisser, they suggested that he should have conducted his own analysis of crises in terms of prices of production, *A History of Marxian Economics,* vol. 1: *1883–1929* (Basingstroke: Macmillan, 1989), p. 330.

192. Gurland, "Absatz und Verwertung im Kapitalismus," p. 79; Neisser, "Das Gesetz der fallenden Profitrate," p. 74.

193. Grossmann, "Die Wert-Preis-Transformation bei Marx," footnote, pp. 63–64.

194. Ibid., pp. 64–71.

195. Ibid., p. 82.

196. Ibid., pp. 72–80.

197. Ibid., pp. 80–84.

198. Grossman, "Zum Abschluss des Streites um die Wert-Preisrechnung," pp. 36–44, APAN; Grossman, "Das Problem der Durchschnittsprofitrate," pp. 25–33. Longer summaries of these manuscripts can be found in Scheele, *Zwischen Zusammenbruchsprognose und Positivismusverdikt,* pp. 85–96.

199. Grossman, "Das Problem der Durchschnittsprofitrate," pp. 33–34.

200. Ibid., pp. 34–35.

201. On Grossman's support for the KPD line, see Willy Strzelewicz, "Diskurse im Institut für Sozialforschung um 1930: Persönliche Erinnerungen," in Sven Papcke (ed.), *Ordnung und Theorie: Beiträge zur Geschichte der Soziologie in Deutschland* (Darmstadt: Wissenschaftliche Buchgesellschaft, 1986), p. 153. On the politics of the institute's students, see Wiggershaus, *The Frankfurt School,* p. 34.

202. Mattick's side of the correspondence has been deduced from Grossman's letters, the only ones that have survived. Letter from Grossman to Mattick, June 21, 1931, *Dynamik,* pp. 85–90.

203. Ibid., p. 92.

204. Ibid., p. 96.

205. Ilse Mattick interview.

206. On Gumbel, see Karin Buselmeier, "Vorwort," in Emil Julius Gumbel, *Verschwörer: Zur Geschichte und Soziologie der deutschen nationalsozialisten Geheimbünde 1918–1924, mit einem Vorwort zur Neuauflage von Karin Buselmeier und zwei Dokumenten zum Fall Gumbel* (Heidelberg: Verlag Das Wunderhorn, 1979), pp. 7–31, this volume includes the petition in support of Gumbel, "Protesterklärung republikanischer und sozialistischer Hochschullehrer," pp. 286–87; and Arthur D. Brenner, *Emil J. Gumbel: Weimar German Pacifist and Professor* (Boston: Brill, 2001).

207. For Grossman's leadership of the study group, see letter from Grossman to Mattick, September 16, 1933, IISG. On Arplan, see Karl Schlögel, *Berlin, Ostbahnhof Europas: Russen und Deutsche in ihrem Jahrhundert* (Berlin: Siedler, 1998), pp. 127–28; Gerd Voigt, *Russland in der deutschen Geschichtsschreibung 1843–1945* (Berlin: Akademie Verlag, 1994), pp. 216, 382; Reichsicherheitshauptamt Abteilung IV, R58 3443a, Bundesarchiv, Berlin.

208. Extract from a report on a visit to Gosplan in Kharkov by a group of members of the Arbeitsgemeinschaft zum Studium der sowjet-russiche Planwirtschaft touring the Soviet Union, Reichsicherheitshauptamt Abteilung IV, R58 3443a, Bundesarchiv Berlin, for Grossman's comment, pp. 18–19.

209. Stead, notes, Box 6, Folder 45, Stead Collection.

210. Grossmann, "Die Wert-Preis-Transformation bei Marx," p. 82.

211. Naum Jasny, *Soviet Economists of the Twenties: Names to be Remembered* (Cambridge: Cambridge University Press, 1972), pp. 188–89.

212. Letter from Grossman to Mattick, March 6, 1933, IISG; *Verzeichnis*, winter semester 1932–33, p. 56.

213. "Kurzer Lebenslauf," March 15, 1949, VdN-Akte von Henryk Grossman 13630, Sächsisches Staatsarchiv Leipzig; letter from Grossman to Mattick, March 6, 1933, IISG. Grossman's contribution, but not its content, is mentioned in Georg Hanselmann, "Aufhebung des Unterschieds? Bericht von einer Diskussion," *Frankfurter Zeitung und Handelsblatt* 77 (55–56), evening edition/first morning edition, January 21, 1933, p. 1. The KPD's *Arbeiter-Zeitung* and the social democratic *Volksstimme* also apparently carried reports of his intervention.

214. F. Jaspert, "Streiflichter von der Front des russischen Aufbaus. Aus den Aufzeichnungen eines deutschen Spezialisten," *Frankfurter Zeitung und Handelsblatt* 77 (821), second morning edition, Wednesday, November 2, 1932, p. 2.

215. Carl Grünberg, "Socialismus, Kommunismus, Anarchismus," in Ludwig Elster (ed.), *Wörterbuch der Volkswirtschaft*, vol. 2 (Jena: Fischer, 1898, first edition), pp. 527–76.

216. Ludwig Elster (ed.), *Wörterbuch der Volkswirtschaft*, 4th ed., in 3 vols. (Jena: Fischer, Jena 1931, 1932, and 1933).

217. Letters from Grossman to Mattick, June 21, 1931, *Dynamik*, p. 85; and November 16, 1931, ibid., p. 96.

218. Many of Grossman's and Grünberg's contributions to the *Dictionary* were republished together in Henryk Grossmann and Carl Grünberg, *Anarchismus, Bolschewismus,*

Sozialismus: Aufsätze aus dem Wörterbuch der Volkswirtschaft (Frankfurt am Main: Europäische Verlagsanstalt, 1971). The volume does not include any of their biographies or bibliographies.

219. Letter from Grossman to Mattick, June 21, 1931, *Dynamik* p. 85; letter from Grossman to Horkheimer, January 4, 1935, MHGS15 p. 294; *Verzeichnis*, summer semester 1931, p. 55; *Verzeichnis*, winter semester, 1931–32, p. 56; *Verzeichnis*, winter semester 1932–33, p. 56; *Verzeichnis*, summer semester 1933, p. 55.

220. Henryk Grossmann and Carl Grünberg, "Sozialdemokratischen und kommunistischen Parteien," in Elster *Wörterbuch*, vol. 3 (1933), p. 248.

221. Grossmann, "Bolshewismus," in Grossmann and Grünberg, *Anarchismus, Bolschewismus, Sozialismus*, (originally published in Elster *Wörterbuch*, vol. 1 [1931], pp. 421–44), p. 44.

222. Henryk Grossmann, "Debs, Eugene," in Elster *Wörterbuch*, vol. 1 (1931), p. 564; Henryk Grossmann, "Jaurés, Jean," in Elster *Wörterbuch*, vol. 2 (1932), pp. 382–83; Henryk Grossmann, "Sorel, Georges," in Elster *Wörterbuch*, vol. 3 (1933), pp. 236–37; Vladimir Ilych Lenin, "The Revolutionary-democratic Dictatorship of the Proletariat and the Peasantry," *Collected Works*, vol. 8, 4th ed. (Moscow: Progress Publishers, 1977 [1905]), pp. 297–98; *State and Revolution, Collected Works*, vol. 25, 4th ed. (Moscow: Progress Publishers, 1980 [1918, written 1917]), pp. 482, 495.

223. Henryk Grossmann, "Lenin, Wladimir Iljitsch," in Elster *Wörterbuch*, vol. 2 (1932), p. 830.

224. Grossmann, "Bolschewismus," p. 61. For a favorable mention of Trotsky's 1914 essay, "War and the International," see Grossmann, "Die Fortentwicklung des Marxismus," p. 323.

225. Grossmann, "Bolschewismus," p. 77.

226. Letter from Henryk Grossman to Walter Braeuer, January 13, 1948, Braeuer Collection. Also see Grossman, "Lebenslauf" UAL, pp. 64–66. Elster, despite his conservatism, was happy with the essay too: he "wrote me a letter in which he says that my essay on Bolshevism will always be a pièce de résistance in his dictionary (of political economy)," Henryk Grossman, "Recensionen [sic] der Pressarbeiten (Prof. Dr. Henryk Großman)," UAL, p. 69.

227. Henryk Grossmann, "Die dritte, Kommunistische Internationale (Komintern): 'Die Internationale der Tat,'" Elster *Wörterbuch*, vol. 2 (1932), p. 187.

228. Grossmann, "Die Fortentwicklung des Marxismus," pp. 281–328; letter from Grossman to Mattick, March 6, 1933, IISG; Henryk Grossmann, "Przycznek do historji socjalizmu w Polsce przed laty czterdziestu," in Karol Marks, *Niewydane Pisma* (Warsaw: Książka, 1923), pp. iii–xxvii; Henryk Grossmann, "Ekonomiczny system Karola Marksa," *Kultura Robotnicza* 2 (10), no. 32 (March 17, 1923): 295–99; Henryk Grossman, *Maruki shizumu notameno toso gojunen*, published by the journal *Chuo Koron*, 1933.

229. Grossmann, "Die Fortentwicklung des Marxismus," pp. 296–305.

230. Ibid., pp. 316–17; Arato and Breines, *The Young Lukács*, p. 180. Many years later, after two major shifts in his political outlook, Grossman explained that the absence of an entry on Stalin in Elster's dictionary was due to a policy of only including biogra-

phies of dead people; letter from Henryk Grossman to Albert Schreiner, April 14, 1948, Albert Schreiner Nachlaß, Ny 41 98/70, Bundesarchiv, Berlin. This convention had not prevented Grossman from dealing with other important, living figures such as Bauer, Kautsky, Hilferding, and Bukharin in non-biographical essays.

231. Grossmann, "Die Fortentwicklung des Marxismus bis zur Gegenwart," pp. 318–22.

232. Ibid., pp. 328–31.

233. Ibid., pp. 332–34.

234. Ibid., pp. 335–36.

Chapter 6: Exile and Political Reassessments

1. For example, see "Die gegenwärtige Lage in Deutschland und die Aufgaben der KPD: Resolution, beschlossen vom Politibüro des ZK der KPD am 10. Oktober 1933," *Die Kommunistische Internationale* 14 (19), November 15, 1933, pp. 1033, 1039.

2. Rolf Wiggershaus, *The Frankfurt School: Its History, Theories and Political Significance* (Cambridge: Polity, 1995), pp. 108, 127.

3. Bundesarchiv, Potsdam IV A 1 b 4764/42, Reichssicherheitshauptamt R59 St 3/443 I documents of the Arbeitsgemeinschaft zum Studium sowjet-russischer Planwirtschaft ("Arplan") for 1942–43, Berlin, December 30, 1942.

4. Wolfgang Schivelbusch, *Intellectuellendämmerung: zur Lage der Frankfurter Intelligenz in den zwanziger Jahren* (Frankfurt am Main: Suhrkamp, 1985), pp. 119, 127.

5. "Heinrich Grossman," Akten der WiSo Fakultät, Sig 45^2 Abt 150 Nr 376, p. 226, Archiv der Johann Wolfgang Goethe Universität, Frankfurt am Main (UFM).

6. UFM, pp. 231–32. The university's handbook for winter semester 1933–34 indicated three full professors were on leave, while seven remained; six junior professors, including Grossman were on leave, while only four remained to teach, Johann-Wolfgang-Goethe-Universität Frankfurt am Main *Verzeichnis der Vorlesungen Winter-Halbjahr 1933/34 und Personalverzeichnis* Verlag Universitätsbuchhandlung Blazek u. Bergmann Frankfurt am Main 1933 (*Verzeichnis*).

7. UFM, p. 235. See the text of article 3 of the "Law for the Reestablishment of the Professional Civil Service," which was referred to in the letter withdrawing Grossman's license to teach; Jeremy Noakes and Geoffrey Pridham, *Documents on Nazism 1918–1945* (New York: Viking Press, 1975), pp. 229–30.

8. Letter from Grossman to the dean, April 22, 1933, UFM, pp. 224–25.

9. UFM, p. 229.

10. Letter from Henryk Grossman to Max Beer, January 19, 1935, Box 1, Max Beer Nachlaß Archiv der sozialen Demokratie der Friedrich-Ebert-Stiftung (Beer Collection); letter from Henryk Grossman to Max Horkheimer, October 26, 1934, Max Horkheimer, *Gesammelte Schiften*, Band 15: *Briefwechsel 1913–1936* (Frankfurt am Main: Fischer, 1995) (MHGS15), p. 254; Stead, "29.II.45?" Box 5, Folder 32, Christina Stead Collection MS4967, National Library of Australia (Stead Collection). Grossman's 1665 edition of Bacon's works was published by J. B. Schönwetter in Frankfurt am Main.

11. Stead, "29.II.45?" Box 5, Folder 32, Stead Collection.

12. Postcard from M. Kisling to Grossman, January 12, 1950, VI 9, Max-Horkheimer-Archiv, Universitäts- und Stadtarchiv Frankfurt am Main (MHA), p. 225.

13. The day he moved out of his hotel, Henryk Grossman wrote to Leo Löwenthal on the Coupole's letterhead; February 12, 1934, A 325, Leo-Löwenthal-Archiv, Universitäts- und Stadtarchiv Frankfurt am Main (LLA), p. 81.

14. Henryk Grossmann, "Recensionen [sic] der Pressarbeiten (Prof. Dr. Henryk Großman)," UAL, p. 69.

15. Henryk Grossman, "Lebenslauf von Professor Dr. Henryk Grossman," August 3 1949, UAL, pp. 62–63.

16. Letter from Grossman to Beer, May 25, 1935, Beer Collection.

17. Letter from Walter Braeuer to Jürgen Scheele, May 5, 1991, Braeuer Nachlaß, Johann-Heinrich von Thünen Museum, Tellow; "Braeuer, Walter," in Werner Röder and Herbert Strauss (eds.), *Biographisches Handbuch der deutschsprachigen Emigration nach 1933* Band I: *Politik, Wirtschaft, öffentliches Leben* (München: K. G. Saur, 1980), p. 139; Georg Fülberth, "Widerstand und Gelehrsamkeit," in Frank Deppe, Georg Fülberth, and Rainer Rillling (eds.), *Antifaschismus* (Heilbronn: Distel Verlag, 1996), pp. 206–8.

18. Letters from Horkheimer to Grossman, May 30, 1935, MHGS15, p. 356; Grossman to Horkheimer, January 4, 1935, ibid., p. 296; October 30, 1935, quoted in ibid., note 8, p. 359; December 11, 1935, VI 9, MHA, p. 360; December 14, 1935, ibid., p. 359; Koyré's reviews included F. Lot, *La fin du monde antique et les débuts du moyen-age, Zeitschrift für Sozialforschung* (*ZfS*) 1 (1–2) (1932): 211; *Vocabulaire technique et critique de la philosophie, ZfS* 2 (2) (1933): 274; "La sociologie français contemporaine," *ZfS* 5 (2) (1936): 260–64.

19. On the friendship between Cornu and Grossman, see letter from Bill Blake to Christina Stead, March 24, 1950, Christina Stead and William J. Blake, *Dearest Munx: The letters of Christina Stead and William J. Blake* (Carlton: Miegunyah Press, 2005) p. 511. Jean Maitron, "Auguste Cornu," in Jean Maitron and Claude Pennetier (eds.), *Dictionaire biographique du mouvement ouvrier Français,* Tome 23: *Cler á Cy,* Quatrième parti: *1914–1939: De la première à la seconde guerre mondaile* (Paris: Les éditions ouvrieres, 1984), pp. 193–94; "Berlin 1900: Auguste Cornu raconte . . ." *L'Humanité,* September 29, 1980, p. 10; "Le philosophe Auguste Cornu est mort," *L'Humanité,* May 9, 1981, p. 7.

20. Letter from Grossman to Mattick, May 7, 1933, Henryk Grossmann, *Marx, die klassische Nationalökonomie und das Problem der Dynamik* (Frankfurt am Main: Europäische Verlagsanstalt, 1969) (*Dynamik*), p. 97; letter from Grossman to Mattick, June 17, 1933, *Dynamik,* p. 100.

21. Letter from Horkheimer to Grossman, July 30, 1934, MHGS15, p. 189.

22. Henryk Grossmann review of Elie Halévy's *Sismondi* (Paris, 1925), *ZfS* 3 (2) (1934): 291. This was Grossman's first review in the institute's journal since 1928.

23. Henryk Grossman, *Simonde de Sismondi et ses théories économiques. Une nouvelle interprétation de sa pensée* (Warsaw: Bibliotheca Universitatis Liberae Polniae, 1924), p. 50.

24. Henryk Grossman, "J. C. L. Simonde de Sismondi," in Edwin R. A. Seligman (ed.), *Encyclopaedia of the Social Sciences,* vol. 14: *Servitudes-Trade Associations* (New York: Macmillan, 1934), pp. 69–71. Grossman's bibliography included the 1926 Russian edi-

tion of Vladimir Ilych Lenin's "A Characterization of Economic Romanticism" (*Collected Works*, vol. 2, 4th ed. [Moscow: Progress Publishers, 1977, (1897)], pp. 129–265), which Grossman had not, apparently, been able to consult in 1923–24.

25. Henryk Grossmann review of Robert Bordaz's *La loi de Marx sur les capitaux à la lumière des événements contemporains*, *ZfS* 3 (2) (1934): 314–15.

26. Franz Borkenau, *Der Übergang vom feudalen zum bürgerlichen Weltbild: Studien zur Geschichte der Philosophie der Manufakturperiode* (Paris: Alcan, 1934); Henryk Grossmann, "Die gesellschaftlichen Grundlagen der mechanistischen Philosophie und die Manufaktur," *ZfS* 4(2) (1935): 161–231; English translation, "The Social Foundations of Mechanistic Philosophy and Manufacture," *Science in Context* 1 (1) (1987): 129–80. Letter from Grossman to Horkheimer, August 24, 1934, MHGS15, p. 223. Walter Benjamin had earlier been entrusted with the job of criticizing the book, but failed to produce a review; letters from Walter Benjamin to Gershom Scholem, January 15, 1933, Walter Benjamin, *Walter Benjamin Briefe 2 1929–1940* (Frankfurt am Main: Suhrkamp, 1978), p. 561; October 17, 1934, ibid., p. 624.

27. Birgit Lange-Enzmann, *Franz Borkenau als politischer Denker* (Berlin: Duncker & Humblot, 1994), p. 15.

28. Willy Strzelewicz, "Diskurse im Institut für Sozialforschung um 1930: Persönliche Erinnerungen," in Sven Papcke (ed.), *Ordnung und Theorie: Beiträge zur Geschichte der Soziologie in Deutschland* (Darmstadt: Wissenschaftliche Buchgesellschaft, 1986), p. 152.

29. Letter from Horkheimer to Grossman, May 30, 1935, MHGS15, pp. 356–57.

30. Richard Lowenthal, "Editor's introduction," in Franz Borkenau, *End and Beginning: On Generations of Cultures and the Origins of the West* (New York: Columbia University Press, 1981), p. 4; Valeria Russo, "Profilo di Franz Borkenau," *Rivista di filosofia* 72 (2) (1981): 297–98.

31. Letter from Grossman to Mattick, October 2, 1934, *Dynamik*, p. 107. The reference is to Nikolai Ivanovich Bukharin, *Historical Materialism* (New York: International Publishers, 1925 [1921]).

32. Letter from Grossman to Beer, January 19, 1935, Beer Collection.

33. The papers of the Soviet delegation were published shortly after the conference, in English, as N. Bukharin et al., *Science at the Cross Roads: Papers Presented to the International Congress of the History of Science and Technology held in London from June 29th to July 3rd, 1931 by the Delegates of the USSR* (London: Frank Cass, 1971 [1931]); Henryk Grossman review of G. N. Clark's *Science and Social Welfare in the Age of Newton* (New York and London, 1937) and G. Sarton's *The History of Science and the New Humanism* (London, 1937), *ZfS* 7 (1/2) (1938): 233–37. Gideon Freudenthal observes that neither Borkenau nor Grossman seems to have known about Boris Hessen's "The Social and Economic Roots of Newton's *Prinicipia*," in Bukharin, *Science at the Cross Roads*, pp. 147–212, "which is usually considered as representing the Marxist approach to the rise of early modern science," when they wrote their studies; "Introductory note" to translations of Borkenau's and Grossman's *ZfS* articles on the emergence of modern science out of the production process, *Science in Context* 1 (1) (March 1987): 105.

34. Letter from Grossman to Horkheimer, August 24, 1934, MHGS15, pp. 223–24.

35. Henryk Grossman, "Die Anfänge des Kapitalismus und die neue Massenmoral," original Folder 38, "Henryk Grossman," III-155, Archiwum Polskiej Akademii Nauk (APAN); translation "The Beginnings of the Capitalism and the New Mass Morality," in *Journal of Classical Sociology* 6 (2) (2006): 195–200.

36. Letters from Max Horkheimer to Grossman, September 25, 1934, MHGS15, p. 225; October 8, 1934, ibid., pp. 236–37.

37. Letter from Grossman to Horkheimer, January 4, 1935, MHGS15, pp. 294–95. Grossman also mentioned his tiring work routine in a letter to Beer, January 19, 1935, Beer Collection.

38. On the place of Grossman's article in the historiography of science, see Gideon Freudenthal, "The Hessen-Grossman Thesis: An Attempt at Rehabilitation," *Perspectives on Science* 13 (2) (Summer 2005): 166–93.

39. Grossmann, "The Social Foundations," p. 158.

40. Ibid., pp. 137, 152, 154–155, 168–70, 154–55; Freudenthal, "The Hessen-Grossman Thesis."

41. Grossmann, "Die gesellschaftlichen Grundlagen," p. 229. The translation of this passage in Grossmann, "The Social Foundations," p. 180, is not entirely satisfactory.

42. Ibid., p. 172; letter from Max Horkheimer to Grossman, May 30, 1935, MHGS15, pp. 356–57.

43. Letter from Horkheimer to Grossman, January 26, 1935, MHGS15, p. 301. The publication of Borkenau's book became an embarrassment and it is not mentioned alongside other institute monographs in Horkheimer's 1938 account of the IfS's activities; Max Horkheimer, "Idee, Aktivität und Program des Instituts für Sozialforschung," in Max Horkheimer, *Gesammelte Schriften,* Band 12: *Nachgelassene Schriften 1931–1949* (Frankfurt am Main: Fischer, 1985) (MHGS12), p. 154.

44. Letter from Grossman to Horkheimer and Friedrich Pollock, February 7, 1935, MHGS15, p. 316.

45. Letter from Grossman to Horkheimer, January 30, 1935, MHGS15, p. 311.

46. Stead, typescript notes, Box 6, Folder 45, Box 11, Folder 79, Stead Collection. In describing this idyll Grossman or Stead may have conflated events during Henryk's stay in Paris before World War I and that during the 1930s.

47. Letter from Grossman to Mattick, February 19, 1935, *Dynamik,* p. 111.

48. Letter from Grossman to Frau Favez (secretary of the institute's Geneva office), July 17, 1935, LLA, p. 94; letters from Grossman to Löwenthal, July 20, LLA, p. 96; July 29, 1935, ibid., p. 97–98; letter from Grossman to Pollock and Horkheimer, August 23, 1935, MHGS15, pp. 392–96. As Oskar Kurz had visited in May, Ramos-Sobrino's studies in Vienna may have established the initial link with Grossman; letter from Grossman to Beer, May 25, 1935, Beer Collection.

49. Letter from Grossman to Horkheimer and Pollock, August 23, 1935, MHGS15, pp. 392–95.

50. Trotsky's position shifted to a repudiation of the Third International in June 1933; see Tony Cliff, *Trotsky 1927–1940: The Darker the Night the Brighter the Star* (London:

Bookmarks, 1993), pp. 172–73, Leon Trotsky, *Writings of Leon Trotsky 1932–33* (New York: Pathfinder, 1972), p. 311.

51. Letter from Henryk Grossman to Paul Mattick, March 6, 1933, Mattick Collection, Internationaal Instituut voor Sociale Geschiedenis (IISG).

52. Letter from Grossman to Mattick, May 7, 1933, *Dynamik*, p. 98.

53. Letter from Grossman to Mattick, June 17, 1933, *Dynamik*, p. 100; Leon Trotsky, "Die deutsche Katastrophe," *Neue Weltbuhne* 2 (23), June 8, 1933, pp. 699–706; the English translation of the article is republished as "The German Catastrophe: The Responsibility of the Leadership," in Leon Trotsky, *The Struggle against Fascism in Germany* (Harmondsworth: Penguin, 1975), pp. 397–404.

54. Letter from Grossman to Mattick, November 1, 1933, *Dynamik*, p. 104.

55. Letter from Grossman to Mattick, January 31, 1935, IISG; Hanno Drechsler, *Die sozialistische Arbeiterpartei Deutschlands (SAPD): ein Beitrag zur Geschichte der deutschen Arbeiterbewegung am Ende der Weimarer Republik* (Meisenheim am Glan: Hain, 1965), p. 161; Leon Trotsky, *Writings of Leon Trotsky 1933–34* (New York: Pathfinder, 1975), pp. 49–52, note 31, p. 343.

56. For the background to and course of the Popular Front, see Julian Jackson, *The Popular Front in France: Defending Democracy, 1934–1938* (New York: Cambridge University Press, 1988).

57. Letter from Grossman to Mattick, October 2, 1934, *Dynamik*, pp. 107–8.

58. Letter from Grossman to Beer, January 19, 1935, Beer Collection; "Prologue: Trotsky and the French Section before July 1935," in Leon Trotsky, *The Crisis of the French Section* (New York: Pathfinder, 1977), pp. 21–23, 25.

59. Letter from Grossman to Horkheimer, January 30, 1935, MHGS15, p. 312.

60. Letter from Grossman to Mattick, February 19, 1935, *Dynamik*, pp. 109–10.

61. Letter from Grossman to Mattick, October 22, 1935, IISG.

62. Letter from Löwenthal to Grossman, January 12, 1937, LLA, p. 62.

63. For a discussion of the Communist International's Popular Front turn, see Duncan Hallas, *The Comintern* (London: Bookmarks, 1985), pp. 139–55.

64. See Jacques Danos and Marcel Gibelin, *June '36: Class Struggle and the Popular Front in France* (London: Bookmarks, 1986) for an excellent account of the French Popular Front.

65. See Pierre Broué and Emile Témime, *The Revolution and the Civil War in Spain* (London: Faber and Faber, 1972), pp. 123–71, 188–212.

66. Andy Durgan, "Freedom Fighters or Comintern Army? The International Brigades in Spain," *International Socialism* 84 (Autumn 1999): 122.

67. Ronald Fraser, *The Blood of Spain: The Experience of Civil War 1936–1939* (Harmondsworth: Penguin, 1981), pp. 166–67; Hugh Thomas, *The Spanish Civil War* (Harmondsworth: Penguin, 1971), pp. 203, 223.

68. Drechsler, *Die sozialistische Arbeiterpartei Deutschlands*, pp. 343–44.

69. Letter from Grossman to Horkheimer, November 6, 1936, MHGS15, pp. 714–15. Also see Horkheimer's reply, November 27, 1936, MHGS15, p. 748; and Franz Borkenau,

"State and Revolution in the Paris Commune, the Russian Revolution and the Spanish Civil War," *Sociological Review* 29 (1) (January 1937): 61, 64–65.

70. Franz Borkenau, *The Spanish Cockpit: An Eye-witness Account of the Political and Social Conflicts of the Spanish Civil War* (London: Faber and Faber, 1937).

71. Letter from Grossman to Horkheimer, December 19, 1936, MHGS15, pp. 797–98.

72. Gary L. Ulmen, *The Science of Society: Toward an Understanding of the Life and Work of Karl August Wittfogel* (The Hague: Mouton, 1978), p. 209; Ilse Mattick telephone interview on November 24, 1993, notes of which were confirmed by her in writing (Ilse Mattick interview).

73. Nikolai Dmitrievich Kondratiev, *Problemy ekonomicheskoi dinamiki* (Moscow: Ekonomika, 1989), p. 473.

74. Letter from Henryk Grossman to Paul Mattick, September 16, 1933, IISG; also letter from Grossman to Mattick, October 2, 1934, *Dynamik*, p. 107.

75. See the notes on Alfred Marshall's *Principles of Political Economy* and a quotation from the book, in English on the reverse of a letter to Grossman, September 22, 1917, APAN; letter from Blake to Stead, June 27, 1942, Stead and Blake, *Dearest Munx*, pp. 286–87; L. G. Healy, memorandum, "Re: Henryk Grossman; International Research Institute," October 15, 1940, Henryk Grossman file, Federal Bureau of Investigation (FBI file).

76. Letter from Chimen Abramsky to Rick Kuhn, January 12, 1996, in Rick Kuhn's possession.

77. VI 9 MHA pp. 357, 359; Fülberth, "Widerstand und Gelehrsamkeit," pp. 206–8. Letters from Grossman to Löwenthal, December 4, 1935, LLA, p. 100; February 26, 1936, ibid., p. 102.

78. Letter from Aliens Department of the Home Office to Mr. Adams, July 31, 1935, Society for the Protection of Science and Learning/Academic Assistance Council Files, Department of Western Manuscripts, Bodleian Library (SPSL); letter from Grossman to Max Beer, May 25, 1935, Beer Collection.

79. Letter from Grossman to Löwenthal, February 26, 1936, LLA, p. 102.

80. Letter from Aliens Department of the Home Office to Mr. Adams, July 31, 1935, SPSL.

81. Letter from Grossman to Löwenthal, February 26, 1936, LLA, p. 102.

82. Letter from Grossman to Horkheimer, January 28, 1936, VI 9 MHA, p. 357.

83. Letter from Grossman to Max Horkheimer, July 3, 1936, MHGS15, p. 583; letter from Grossman to Horkheimer, June 30, 1937, in Max Horkheimer, *Gesammelte Schriften,* Band 16: *Briefwechsel 1937–1940* (Frankfurt am Main: Fischer, 1995) (MHGS16), pp. 187–88.

84. There is a note at this point, separate from the rest of the text: "An interesting pointer on underconsumption theory already in Volume I [of *Capital*]. Marx cites the work of an industrialist, Ricardian, who finds it necessary to reduce the laborer's wages to a minimum 'to keep him industrious.' And, against underconsumption, he answers the argument, that was already being deployed 'and if it be said, that this [depressing wages to their minimum, G] begets glut, by lessening consumption' (on the part of the

workers), 'I can only reply that glut is synonymous with large profits.'" The quotation from Marx is in *Capital*, vol. 1 (Harmondsworth: Penguin, 1976), p. 743.

85. Quoted, with grammatical corrections, in Jürgen Scheele, *Zwischen Zusammenbruchsprognose und Positivismusverdikt: Studien zur politischen und intellektuellen Biographie Henryk Grossmanns (1881–1950)* (Frankfurt am Main: Lang, 1999), pp. 67–69. The fact that Grossman referred to aggregate wage statistics for Germany in 1935 but did not mention devaluation as a strategy pursued in France suggests that this manuscript was produced well after the start of 1936 and before Blum's devaluation of the franc on September 28, 1936.

86. Letter from Grossman to Horkheimer, November 6, 1936, MHGS15, pp. 713–14.

87. Letter from Grossman to Horkheimer, June 30, 1937, MHGS15, p. 188. Horkheimer preferred Grossman to present his views on this topic in a lecture, rather than an article; letter from Horkheimer to Grossman, July 18, 1937, ibid., p. 202.

88. Letter from Grossman to Mattick, October 22, 1936, IISG.

89. Letter from Horkheimer to Grossman, September 9, 1936, VI 9, MHA, p. 349.

90. "Dos 40 johrige jubeilium fun *Kapital*," *Sotsial-demokrat*, July 19, 1907, p. 1.

91. Letter from Grossman to Horkheimer, October 1, 1936, MHGS15, pp. 641–42.

92. Henryk Grossman, "Die Entwicklungstendenzen des 'reinen' und des empirischen Kapitalismus," original Folder 11, in 1997, Folders 40–45, APAN; "Uebungen zur Frage des Verhältnisses von Marx und Ricardo," *Verzeichnis*, summer semester 1928, p. 52. In 1930 Grossman taught a course on Marx as a historian of economics; "Marx als Historiker der Nationalökonomie," *Verzeichnis*, summer semester 1930, p. 54.

93. Letter from Horkheimer to Grossman, October 12, 1936, MHGS15, p. 660.

94. Max Horkheimer, "On the Problem of Truth," in Max Horkheimer, *Between Philosophy and Social Science: Selected Early Writings* (Cambridge, Mass.: MIT Press, 1993 [1935]), pp. 177–218.

95. Letter from Horkheimer to Grossman, October 1, 1935, MHGS15, p. 405. Also see the published article, Horkheimer, "On the Problem of Truth," p. 209.

96. For Grossman's influence on institute colleagues, also see Erich Fromm, Julian Gumperz, Max Horkheimer, Herbert Marcuse, Franz L. Neumann, and Friedrich Pollock, "Die Marxsche Methode und ihre Anwendbarkeit auf die Analyse der gegenwärtigen Krise. Seminardiskussion" MHGS12, (written in 1936), pp. 401–10.

97. Letter from Grossman to Horkheimer, August 1, 1937, MHGS16, p. 204; also see letter from Grossman to Horkheimer, January 30, 1935, MHGS15, pp. 311–12.

98. Karola Bloch, *Aus meinem Leben* (Pfullingen: Neske, 1981), p. 136. This was also Leo Lowenthal/Löwenthal's recollection; Martin Jay, *The Dialectical Imagination* (Berkeley: University of California Press, 1996 [1973]), p. 328. Also see Neil McLaughlin, "Origin Myths in the Social Sciences: Fromm, the Frankfurt School and the Emergence of Critical Theory," *Canadian Journal of Sociology* 24 (1) (1999): 116. Similarly Horkheimer censored Walter Benjamin's terminology in "L'Oeuvre d'art à l'époque de sa reproduction mécanisée," *ZfS* 5 (1) (1936): 40–68, according to Anthony Heilbut, *Exiled in Paradise: German Refugee Artists and Intellectuals in America from the 1930s to the Present* (Berkeley: University of California Press, 1997), p. 91.

99. Max Horkheimer, "The Latest Attack on Metaphysics," in *Critical Theory: Selected Essays* (New York: Continuum, 1992 [1937]), pp. 163, 181.

100. Letter from Grossman to Horkheimer, August 1, 1937, MHGS16, p. 205. Also see letter from Grossman to Mattick, March 6, 1933, IISG.

101. Letter from Grossman to Horkheimer, August 1, 1937, MHGS16, p. 206.

102. Letter from Grossman to Mattick, September 16, 1933, IISG.

103. Letters from Grossman to Horkheimer, July 20, 1935, MHGS15, p. 375; December 19, 1936, ibid., pp. 795–98. Letters from Grossman to Löwenthal, January 5, 1935, LLA, p. 91; from Grossman to Löwenthal, May 20, 1933, LLA, p. 67; Grossman to Löwenthal, June 22, 1933, LLA, p. 69; Löwenthal to Grossman, June 23, 1933, LLA, p. 6; Löwenthal to Grossman, July 11, 1933, LLA, p. 10; Löwenthal to Grossman, October 10, 1934, LLA, p. 32; Grossman to Löwenthal, December 4, 1935, LLA, p. 100, LLA. Grossman made a very serious effort to persuade Horkheimer and Löwenthal that the *ZfS* should publish an article by Beer; see letter from Grossman to Beer, January 19, 1935, Beer Collection. Letters from Löwenthal to Grossman, February 13, 1936, LLA, p. 57; from Grossman to Löwenthal, February 26, 1936, LLA, p. 102, Löwenthal to Grossman, March 14, 1936, LLA, p. 58; Löwenthal to Grossman, March 25, 1936, LLA, p. 59, and Löwenthal to Grossman, May 9, 1936, LLA, p. 61.

104. Letters from Grossman to Frau Favez, July 17, 1935, LLA, p. 94; Grossman to Dr Schachtel, July 11, 1935, LLA, p. 95.

105. Letter from Grossman to Löwenthal, December 10, 1933, LLA, pp. 75–76.

106. Letter from Grossman to Löwenthal, February 12, 1934, LLA, p. 81. Leo Löwenthal, "Zugtier und Sklaverei: Zum Buch Lefebvre des Noettes," *L'attelage. Le cheval de selle à travers les âges' ZfS* 2 (2) (1933): 198–212.

107. Hektor Rottweiler (Theodor W. Adorno), "Über Jazz," *ZfS* 5 (1937): 235–59. Letter from Grossman to Horkheimer, October 1, 1936, MHGS15, p. 641.

108. Letter from Grossman to Horkheimer, November 6, 1936, MHGS15, p. 715; from Horkheimer to Grossman, October 12, 1936, MHGS15, p. 660. Martin Jay notes Adorno's relationship with Seiber, *The Dialectical Imagination*, pp. 185–86. Grossman's spellings of Ernst *Schoen* and *Matyas* Seiber were a little astray.

109. Letter from Grossman to Horkheimer, May 25, 1937, MHGS16, pp. 162–63, ellipses in the original. As he referred to "Skarlett," Grossman probably read the German edition, published a year after the book appeared in the United States; Margaret Mitchell, *Vom Winde verweht* (Hamburg: Claassen, 1937).

110. Henryk Grossmann review of Karl Marx and Friedrich Engels' *The Civil War in the United States* (New York, 1937), *ZfS* 7 (1/2) (1938): 259–63.

111. Letter Grossman to Horkheimer, May 25, 1937, MHGS16, p. 161.

112. Letter from Grossman to Horkheimer in London, November 6, 1936, MHGS15, p. 715. In notes for a story, based on discussions with Grossman, Stead also wrote that London had not lived up to expectations; "The Exploits of Jan Callowjan," Box 11, Folder 79, Stead Collection.

113. Letter from Grossman to Horkheimer, June 30, 1937, MHGS16, pp. 188–89. Horkheimer was astonished by Grossman's admiration of Lloyd George; letter to Grossman, July 18, 1937, MHGS16, p. 202.

114. Letter Grossman to Horkheimer, May 25, 1937, MHGS16, p. 161. For Grossman's activities on behalf of the IfS, see, for example, letters from Grossman to Horkheimer, July 20, 1935, MHGS15, p. 376; from Löwenthal to Grossman, March 28, 1936, LLA, p. 60; from Herbert Marcuse to Grossman and members of the institute, May 6, 1936, MHGS15, p. 517; Grossman to Horkheimer, August 3, 1936, ibid., p. 583; Grossman to Horkheimer, December 19, 1936, ibid., pp. 796–97.

115. Letter from Horkheimer to Theodor Adorno, February 22, 1937, MHGS16, p. 46.

116. Alien Registration Form, Henryk Grossman file, Immigration and Naturalization Service, October 31, 1940; "Diskussion aus einem Seminar über Monopolkapitalismus (1937)," MHGS12, pp. 417–30.

117. Ibid., pp. 418–20.

118. Letter from Grossman to Horkheimer, April 14, 1938, VI 9, MHA, pp. 310–14.

119. Leon Kamin, *The Science and Politics of IQ* (New York: Halsted, 1974), pp. 20, 27. Also see Kenneth M. Ludmerer, *Genetics and American Society: A Historical Appraisal* (Baltimore: Johns Hopkins University Press, 1972).

120. Letters from Grossman to Löwenthal, February 12, 1934, LLA, p. 81; Grossman to Löwenthal, July 11, 1934, LLA, p. 27; Grossman to Löwenthal, February 26, 1936, LLA, p. 102; Grossman to Löwenthal, December 27, 1936, LLA, p. 105.

121. Letter from Horkheimer to Grossman, April 18, 1938, MHA, p. 306; Telegram from Pollock to Grossman VI 9, MHA, pp. 293–308.

122. Henryk Grossman, Alien Registration Form, Immigration and Naturalization Service, October 31, 1940.

123. R. W. Meadows report, October 15, 1941, FBI file; Wiggershaus, *The Frankfurt School*, p. 247; Alien Registration Form, Immigration and Naturalization Service.

124. Ilse Mattick interview.

125. Letter from Grossman to Löwenthal, August 4 [1938], LLA, p. 107.

126. "Oskar Kurz" V. A. 46466 Österreichische Staatsarchiv; "Kurz, Oskar," in Röder and Strauss, *Biographisches Handbuch*, p. 406; Stead, notes from a visit to "the Tyl," Box 5, Folder 32, Stead Collection.

127. Max Horkheimer, "Traditional and Critical Theory," in *Critical Theory: Selected Essays* (New York: Continuum, 1992 [1937]), pp. 213–14. Manfred Gangl has observed that "the whole essay should be read as an implicit critique of Lukács"; *Politische Ökonomie und Kritische Theorie: Ein Beitrag zur theoretischen Entwicklung der Frankfurt Schule* (Frankfurt: Campus Verlag, 1987), p. 151.

128. Apart from Horkheimer's essays from this period, see Barbara Brick and Moishe Postone, "Critical Pessimism and the Limits of Traditional Marxism," *Theory and Society* 11 (5) (September 1982): 652; Susan Buck-Morss, *The Origin of Negative Dialectics: Theodor W. Adorno, Walter Benjamin and the Frankfurt Institute* (Hassocks: Harvester Press, 1977), pp. xii, 24, 28, 42, 62; Phil Slater, *Origin and Significance of the Frankfurt School: A Marxist Perspective* (London: Routledge & Kegan Paul, 1977), p. 63.

129. Max Horkheimer, "Idee, Aktivität und Programm," pp. 158–59. See the draft outline of the project, Henrik [sic] Grossman, "The Nature of Economic Crisis," 1940 or 1941, IX 59.3, MHA. This indicated that it was an extension of *Simonde de Sismondi et ses théories,* and Henryk Grossmann, *Das Akkumulations- und Zusammenbruchsgetz*

des kapitalistischen Systems (zugleich eine Krisentheorie) (Frankfurt am Main: Verlag Neue Kritik, 1970 [1929]).

130. See the brief outlines of the project, 5b "Capitalism in the 13th Century," pp. 6.; 5c "Kapitalismus im 13. Jahrhundert," "Mitarbeiter 1939," IX 58 MHA. Also see Horkheimer, "Idee, Aktivität und Programm," pp. 158–59; Walter Braeuer, "Henryk Grossmann als Nationalökonom," *Arbeit und Wirtschaft* 8 (5) (1954): 149–51. Ilse Mattick reported that during the period of their friendship Grossman had immersed himself in work on the early middle ages. In 1942 he was still examining the way this period had influenced subsequent developments; Ilse Mattick interview.

131. The translations into Japanese were discussed in chapter 5. A modified version of the study of Marx's plan for *Capital* was published in Czech, "Plán Marxova: 'Kapitálu,'" *Dělnická Osvěta: Socialistická Revue* 23 (1937): 168–74. The essays that appeared in Serbo-Croatian were "Pedeset godina naučnog socijalizma" (a translation of "Further Developments in Marxism to the Present") with a German abstract, Grafički zavod "Rotacija," Zemun 1938 (reprinted from *Pravna misao: Časopis za pravo i sociologiju*); and "Plan i metod 'Kapitala'" (a translation of "The Alteration of the Original Plan of Marx's *Capital* and its Causes") Grafički zavod "Rotacija," Zemun 1938 (reprinted from *Pravna misao: Časopis za pravo i sociologiju*). Letter from Grossman to Mattick June 17, 1933, IISG.

132. Abram L. Harris, "Pure Capitalism and the Disappearance of the Middle Class," *Journal of Political Economy* 47 (3) (June 1939): 305–56.

133. William Blake, *Marxian Economic Theory and Its Criticism* (also published as *An American Looks at Karl Marx*) (New York: Cordon Company, 1939), pp. 513–14, 579; letter from Stead to Blake, June 25, 1942, Stead and Blake, *Dearest Munx*, p. 273.

134. Paul Sweezy, *The Theory of Capitalist Development* (New York: Monthly Review, 1970), pp. 18, 209–13, 303. The Oxford University Press edition was published in New York, in 1942; in London by Dennis Dobson in 1946. There was also a very brief and, again, critical mention of Grossman's crisis theory in Alexander Gourvitch, *Survey of Economic Theory on Technological Change and Employment* (New York: Augustus M. Kelley, 1966 [1940]), p. 242.

135. Ulmen, *The Science of Society*, p. 209.

136. Bloch, *Aus meinem Leben*, pp. 116, 139, 176–77.

137. Hans-Joachim Dahms, "Edgar Zilsels Projekt 'The Social Roots of Science' und seine Beziehungen zur Frankfurter Schule," in Friedrich Stadler (ed.), *Wien-Berlin-Prag: Der Aufstieg der wissenschaftlichen Philosophie. Zentenarien Rudolf Carnap-Hans Reichenbach-Edgar* (Wien: Zilsel Hölder-Pichler-Tempsky, 1993), pp. 476–77, 486–87. Zilsel did not even mention Grossman's contribution to the history of science in the bibliographic survey of the literature, which concludes his essay published under the auspices of the Institute of Social Research, "The Sociological Roots of Science," *American Journal of Sociology* 47 (4) (January 1942): 544–62. By this stage, relations between Grossman and the institute had broken down and Zilsel may have been concerned with the sensitivities of his benefactor, Horkheimer.

138. Letter from Grossman to Horkheimer, August 6, 1939, MHGS16, p. 624; letter from Grossman to Max Raphael, September 7, 1941, Max Raphael Nachlaß, NL Raphael I, C-210, Germanisches Nationalmuseum.

139. Letter from Grossman to Lotte Jacobi and Erich Reiss, May 7, 1938, Lotte Jacobi Papers, MC 58, Milne Special Collections and Archives, University of New Hampshire Library.

140. Letters from Grossman to Löwenthal, May 2, 1938, LLA, p. 106; July 28 [1939], LLA, p. 109; [August 1939], LLA, p. 110.

141. Letter from Stead to Blake, June 27, 1942, Stead and Blake, *Dearest Munx*, p. 286.

142. Henryk Grossman review of G. N. Clark's *Science and Social Welfare in the Age of Newton* (Oxford and London: Oxford University Press, 1937) and G. Sarton's *The History of Science and the New Humanism* (London, 1937), *ZfS* 7 (1/2) (1938): 233–37. The section on Hessen is translated in Gideon Freudenthal, "Introductory note" to "Controversy: The Emergence of Modern Science out of the Production Process," *Science in Context* 1 (1) (1987) 106–7. Henryk Grossman review of Lynn Thorndike's, *A History of Magic and Experimental Science Volumes 5 and 6* (New York, 1941), in *Studies in Philosophy and Social Science* (the successor of *ZfS*) 9 (3) (1942): 514–19. The reviews related to the theory of economic crisis were of F. Grandeau's *Theorie des Crises* (Paris, 1937), *ZfS* 8 (1/2) (1939): 300–301; Cleona Lewis's *America's Stake in International Investments* (London, 1938), *ZfS* 8 (1/2) (1939): 304–6; Jürgen Kuczynski's *Hunger and Work* (New York and London, 1938), *ZfS* 8 (1/2) (1939): 318–20; L. P. Ayres's *Turning Points in Business Cycles* (New York, 1939), *ZfS* (*Studies in Philosophy and Social Science*) 8 (3) (1939): 490–92; Joseph Schumpeter's *Business Cycles* (New York, 1939), *Studies in Philosophy and Social Science* 9 (1) (1941): 514–19; Salomon Fabricant and Julius Shirkin's *The Output of Manufacturing Industries 1899–1937* (New York, 1940), *Studies in Philosophy and Social Science* 9 (2) (1941): 352–54.

143. Letter from Grossman to Horkheimer, August 9, 1938, VI 9, MHA, p. 291.

144. Italicized *girls* in English in the original letter from Grossman to Horkheimer, August 6, 1939, MHGS16, pp. 624–25. Also see VI 9, MHA, p. 285.

145. Hazel Rowley, *Christina Stead: A Biography* (Melbourne: Minerva, 1993), p. 275.

146. Ilse Mattick interview; letter from Ilse Mattick to Rick Kuhn, January 31, 1994.

147. Dubiel, *Theory and Politics*, pp. 92–93. In this period "all belief in the possibility of revolutionary social change had been abandoned"; ibid., p. 95. Also see Horkheimer, "The Authoritarian State," in Andrew Arato and Eike Gebhardt (eds.), *The Essential Frankfurt School Reader* (New York: Continuum, 1993 [1942]), p. 102; "The End of Reason," *Studies in Philosophy and Social Science* 9 (3) (1942): 366–88; Theodor Adorno and Max Horkheimer, *Dialectic of Enlightenment* (London: Verso, 1979 [1944]), pp. 37, 41.

148. Leo Löwenthal, "Die Integrität des Intellektuellen: zum Andenken Walter Benjamins," *Merkur* 37 (2) no. 416 (March 1983): 226, quoted in Gangl, *Politische Ökonomie und Kritische Theorie*, p. 247.

149. Ilse Mattick interview.

150. "Horkheimer: Der Unversehrte," *Der Spiegel* (January 5, 1968): p. 103.

151. Letters from Grossman to Horkheimer and Pollock, January 4, 1935 MHGS15, p. 293; Horkheimer, December 19, 1936, ibid., p. 795.

152. Henryk Grossman taxation forms, IV 10.1–94, MHA; U.S. Bureau of the Census, *The Statistical History of the United States* (New York: Basic Books, 1976), p. 164. As Grossman only arrived in the United States as a migrant in April 1938, the income recorded is probably for only part of the year.

153. Letter from Felix Weil to Horkheimer, March 13, 1942, quoted in MHGS17, note 5, p. 279; also see Jay, *The Dialectical Imagination*, pp. 167–68.

154. Wiggershaus, *The Frankfurt School*, pp. 39, 161, 250, 262–65, 293.

155. Ibid., p. 263.

156. Horkheimer, "The Authoritarian State," p. 101.

157. See, for example, "Debatte über Methoden der Sozialwissenschaften, besonders die Auffassung der Methode der Sozialwissenschaften, welche das Institut vertritt," January 17, 1941, MHGS12, p. 547.

158. "Cultural Aspects of National Socialism," cited in Jay, *The Dialectical Imagination*, pp. 169–70; MHGS17, note 3, p. 33.

159. Grossman's taxation forms, IV 10.1–94, MHA.

160. Report by Löwenthal of a meeting with Grossman, April 9, 1941, VI 9, MHA, p. 281; report by Löwenthal on "60th Birthday incident (4/14/41)," April 16, 1941, VI 9, MHA, p. 280.

161. Letter from Horkheimer to Karl August Wittfogel, July 20, 1939, MHGS16, pp. 620–21; letter from Leo Löwenthal to Grossman, July 30, 1939, VI 9, MHA p. 286; MHGS17, note 2, p. 223.

162. Max Horkheimer and Theodor Adorno, "Diskussion über die Differenz zwischen Positivismus and materialistischer Dialektik," MHGS12 (written 1939), p. 438. Scheele draws attention to this passage; *Zwischen Zusammenbruchsprognose und Positivismusverdikt*, pp. 193–94.

163. Letter from Löwenthal to Horkheimer, November 26, 1941, MHGS17, p. 222.

164. Henryk Grossman, "Marx Classical National Economy and Problem of Dynamics," original Folder 27, in 1997 Folders 75–77, APAN. The translation includes material from a draft, Henryk Grossman, "Marx und die Klassische Oekonomie oder Die Lehre vom Wertfetisch," typescript, 1937, original Folder 18, in 1997 Folder 68, APAN. *Dynamik*, pp. 7–84. English translation of the published monograph, Henryk Grossman, "Marx, Classical Political Economy and the Problem of Dynamics," *Capital and Class* 2 (Summer 1977): 32–55 ("Dynamics" 1); ibid., 3 (Autumn 1977): 67–99 ("Dynamics" 2); Braeuer, "Henryk Grossmann als Nationalökonom," p. 150; MHGS17, notes 2 and 12, p. 252.

165. Letter from Löwenthal to Horkheimer, January 21, 1942, quoted in MHGS17, note 12, p. 252; letter from Löwenthal to Horkheimer, November 26, 1941, MHGS17, pp. 221–23. Löwenthal implausibly blamed Grossman's misquotations and hence the need to correct stencils for the delay. Also see letter from Löwenthal to Horkheimer, October 22, 1942, MHGS17, p. 356

166. Letter from Löwenthal to Horkheimer, March 3, 1942, MHGS17, p. 258.

167. Letter from Horkheimer to Weil, March 20, 1942, MHGS17, p. 280.

168. Letter from Grossman to Mattick, June 17, 1933, *Dynamik*, p. 102.

169. Grossman's courses in Frankfurt included "On the history of theories of value," *Verzeichnis*, winter semester 1927–28; "Critical and positive [observations] on the theory of wages," *Verzeichnis*, summer semester 1928; "History and critique of theories of interest, profit and rent," *Verzeichnis*, winter semester 1928–29, p. 55; "Marx as a historian of political economy" and "Changes in the concept of labor in economics (with particular attention to recent literature)," *Verzeichnis*, summer semester 1930. On the originality of Grossman's contribution on the importance of the dual nature of production, see Roman Rosdolsky, *The Making of Marx's "Capital"* (London: Pluto, 1980), p. 73. I. I. Rubin's 1930 *Marx's Theory of Production and Consumption* (London: Ink Links, 1979) was another exception to the neglect of the category of use-value by Marxists.

170. "Dynamics" 1, pp. 32–35.

171. Ibid., p. 37.

172. Karl Korsch, "Marxism and philosophy," in *Marxism and Philosophy* (London: NLB, 1970 [1923]), p. 64; Lukács, *History and Class Consciousness*, pp. xlvi–xlvii, 50, 164, 169; Grossman, *Simonde de Sismondi et ses théories*, pp. 30–31, 50.

173. "Dynamics" 1, p. 45; Henryk Grossman, "Marx und die Klassische Oekonomie oder Die Lehre vom Wertfetisch," pp. 26–30, 142–44.

174. "Dynamics" 1, pp. 37–40, 45; cf. Georg Lukács. *History and Class Consciousness*, pp. 169; also Grossman, "Marx und die Klassische Oekonomie oder Die Lehre vom Wertfetisch," pp. 26–30, 142–44.

175. "Dynamics" 1, pp. 39–41; letter from Grossman to Horkheimer, October 1, 1936, MHGS15, pp. 641–42.

176. "Dynamics" 1, pp. 44–45. Grossman made the same point and included a critique of Otto Bauer's misunderstanding, in 1907, of Marx's dialectical method as identical to Hegel's, in "Marx und die Klassische Oekonomie oder Die Lehre vom Wertfetisch," pp. 133–41.

177. Grossman, "Marx und die Klassische Oekonomie oder Die Lehre vom Wertfetisch," p. 111.

178. "Dynamics" 1, p. 41.

179. Ibid., also see pp. 47–48.

180. Ibid., pp. 42–43; The word *value-* is in Grossman's quotation from Marx but not the most recently published version of the original, Karl Marx note on excerpt from "D. Ricardo. Des principes de l'économie politique et de l'impôt traduit de Constancio etc. Paris 1835," *Karl Marx Friedrich Engels Gesamtausgabe*, part 4, vol. 2: *Exzerpte und Notizen 1843 bis Januar 1845* (Berlin: Dietz, 1981), p. 421.

181. "Dynamics" 1, pp. 43–44.

182. Henryk Grossmann, *The Law of Accumulation and Breakdown of the Capitalist System: Being also a Theory of Crises* (London: Pluto, 1992), p. 126.

183. Cf. Nikolai Bukharin's better known *Economic Theory of the Leisure Class* (New York: Monthly Review Press, 1972 [1919, written 1914]).

184. "Dynamics" 2, pp. 70–71, 74, 76, note 29 p. 90, note 57 p. 92, note 77 p. 94.

185. Ibid., p. 78.

186. Ibid., 85.

187. Ibid., pp. 78–82.

188. Ibid., pp. 79–82.

189. Ibid., p. 82; Grossman, "The Theory of Economic Crises," pp. 289–90.

190. "Dynamics" 2, p. 83.

191. Ibid., pp. 84–85.

192. Ibid., pp. 85–86.

193. Ibid., p. 87.

194. Ibid., p. 88.

195. Ibid., p. 88; Henryk Grossman manuscript starting "Die Entwertung sollen die Zusammenbruchstendenz aufheben . . . " in original Folder 45 "Stellungnahme zur Kritik am Hauptwerk," APAN.

196. "Dynamics" 2, p. 89.

197. The political differences were particularly apparent at an institute seminar in 1942, to which Paul Mattick presented a paper; Ilse Mattick interview.

198. Letter from Grossman to Horkheimer, April 30, 1943, MHGS17, pp. 443–44. On the project, see Wiggershaus, *The Frankfurt School*, pp. 353–56. Bertolt Brecht was, likewise, less than impressed by the project's lack of Marxist theoretical foundations; *Journals 1934–1955* (London: Methuen, 1993), p. 338.

199. This concern was raised by Pollock and Weil, MHGS17, note 6, p. 279.

200. See in particular, letter from Horkheimer to Pollock, June 9, 1943, MHGS17, pp. 453–54.

201. Grossman, "Marx und die Klassische Oekonomie oder Die Lehre vom Wertfetisch," pp. 31–33, 53–62.

202. Henryk Grossman, "The Evolutionist Revolt against Classical Economics. I. In France—Condorcet, Saint-Simon, Simonde de Sismondi," *Journal of Political Economy* 51 (5) (October 1943): 381–96 ("Evolutionist Revolt" 1); and "The Evolutionist Revolt against Classical Economics. II. In England—James Steuart, Richard Jones, Karl Marx," *Journal of Political Economy* 51 (6) (December 1943): 506–22 ("Evolutionist Revolt" 2).

203. Letter from Horkheimer to Löwenthal, January 21, 1943, quoted in MHGS17, note 1, p. 413. To Grossman, Horkheimer wrote, "If one reads your text carefully, one finds that the enthusiastic degradation of the author of *Capital* into a social scientist, which you undertake, has an apologetic side opposed to history which is only reined in by the content of the thesis;" letter January 20, 1943, MHGS17, p. 411.

204. "Evolutionist Revolt" 1, p. 381.

205. Ibid., p. 385.

206. Ibid., pp. 385–86.

207. Grossman's taxation form for 1942, VI 10 MHA p. 52. The institute contributed $40 for the translation, which Pollock understood to have cost $80, letter from Pollock to Grossman, December 17, 1942, VI 9, MHA, p. 229.

208. "Evolutionist Revolt" 2, pp. 513–14.

209. Ibid., p. 509.

210. Ibid., pp. 514, 517.

211. Ibid., p. 515–16.

212. Ibid., p. 516.

213. Ibid., p. 518.

214. Ibid. p. 518, quoting from Karl Marx, "Preface" to *A Contribution to the Critique of Political Economy* (Moscow: Progress Publishers, 1977 [1859]), p. 21.

215. "Evolutionist Revolt" 2, p. 519.

216. Ibid., p. 519.

217. Grossmann, *Das Akkumulations- und Zusammenbruchsgetz*, pp. 602–3; Henryk Grossmann, "Die Fortentwicklung des Marxismus bis zur Gegenwart," in Henryk Grossmann and Carl Grünberg, *Anarchismus, Bolschevismus, Sozialismus: Aufsätze aus dem Wörterbuch der Volkswirtschaft* (Frankfurt am Main: Europäische Verlaganstalt, 1971 [1933]), pp. 335–36.

218. "Evolutionist Revolt" 2, pp. 520–21.

219. Ibid.

220. Horkheimer's comments have only survived in substantial extracts sent by him to other members of the institute for comment; extract from a letter from Horkheimer to Grossman, January 20, 1943, MHGS17, ("Extract"), pp. 398–415. Grossman's reply was not kept, to be included in the Horkheimer Archive and Horkheimer decided not to respond to it, letter from Horkheimer to Löwenthal, February 19, 1943, cited in MHGS17, note 1, p. 413.

221. *Politics,* April 1944, p. 92. It is possible that the reviewer was Paul Mattick, who wrote for *Politics.* Morton G. White, "The Attack on the Historical Method," *Journal of Philosophy* 42 (13) (June 7, 1945): 326.

222. Henryk Grossman, "The Evolutionist Revolt against Classical Economics," in Bob Jessop (ed.), *Karl Marx's Social and Political Thought: Critical Assessments,* vol. 1 (London and New York: Routledge, 1990), pp. 253–74; and Mark Blaug (ed.), *Thomas Tooke (1774–1858), Mountifort Longfield (1802–1884), Richard Jones (1790–1855)* (Aldershot: Elgar, 1991), pp. 1–16.

223. Frederick Wild, memorandum on a meeting between Max Horkheimer and Henryk Grossman, March 6, 1944, quoted in MHGS17, note 2, p. 547.

224. "Memorandum on H. Grossman," VI 9, MHA, p. 245; letter from Grossman to Horkheimer and Pollock, April 3, 1944, VI 9, MHA, p. 244.

225. Letter from Pollock to Grossman, April 21, 1944, VI 17, MHA, p. 87.

226. See Grossman's letters to the Taxation Department in 1946, VI 10, MHA, pp. 82–92.

Chapter 7: From Independent Scholar to East German Professor

1. Martin Jay, *The Dialectical Imagination* (Berkeley: University of California Press, 1973).

2. Letter from Christina Stead to Bill Blake, June 28, 1942, Christina Stead and William J. Blake, *Dearest Munx: The letters of Christina Stead and William J. Blake* (Carlton: Miegunyah Press, 2005), pp. 288–89.

3. William Blake's FBI File 100–236179, Series 6, Folder 24, copy in Heather Rowley Collection MS 9244, National Library of Australia (Rowley Collection); Henryk Grossman, "Lebenslauf von Professor Dr. Henryk Grossman," August 3, 1949, Henryk Grossmann File, PA 40, Universitätsarchiv Leipzig (UAL), p. 63.

4. William J. Blake, *Imperialism, The Last Phase,* unpublished manuscript, 1948, Christina Stead Collection MS4967, National Library of Australia (Stead Collection).

5. Letter from Stead to Blake, June 28, 1942, Stead and Blake, *Dearest Munx,* p. 290, elipsis in the original.

6. Letter from Stead to Blake, May 7, 1942, Stead and Blake, *Dearest Munx,* p. 81. Ruth was Blake's daughter in a previous relationship. The book was Christina Stead, *House of All Nations* (New York: Simon and Schuster, 1938).

7. Letter from Stead to Blake, September 12, 1946, Box 16, Folder 120, Stead Collection.

8. Letter from Grossman to Stead and Blake, n.d. [March or April 1947], Box 17, Folder 125, Stead Collection.

9. Letter from Grossman to Stead and Blake, July 10, 1947, Box 17, Folder 125, Stead Collection.

10. Letter from Grossman to Stead and Blake, April 20, 1947, Box 17, Folder 125, Stead Collection.

11. Letter from Grossman to Blake, March 3, 1947, Box 17, Folder 125, Stead Collection.

12. Hazel Rowley, *Christina Stead: A Biography* (Melbourne: Minerva, 1993), pp. 275, 305. Rowley's excellent biography is the main source of information on Stead and Blake.

13. Adolf Berger, "Rafal Taubenschlag," *Polish Review* 3 (3) (Summer 1958): 4; Józef Modrzejewski, "Rafał Taubenschlag: 1881–1958," *Altertum* 4 (4) (1958): 248–56.

14. Stead, "QUESTIONS to ask the Tyl," undated, Box 5, Folder 32, Stead Collection; letter from Grossman to Stead and Blake, April 20, 1947, Box 17, Folder 125, ibid.; letters from Grossman to Rafał Taubenschlag, March 31, 1948, Rafał Taubenschlag, III-98 j. 80, Archiwum Polskiej Akademii Nauk (Taubenschlag Collection), p. 62; January 10, 1949, ibid., p. 63. The letter of March 31, 1948, mentions common friends—a priest and the "Stanleys"—whom I have not been able to identify.

15. Stead, notes, Box 6, Folder 45, Stead Collection; postcard from M. Kisling to Grossman, January 12, 1950, Max-Horkheimer-Archiv, VI 9, Max-Horkheimer-Archiv, Universitäts- und Stadtarchiv Frankfurt am Main (MHA), p. 225.

16. Letter from Grossman to Max Raphael, September 7, 1941, Max Raphael Nachlaß, NL Raphael I, C-210, Germanisches Nationalmuseum. Grossman and Raphael moved in some overlapping circles. For example, Raphael's *Prehistoric Pottery and Civilization in Egypt* (New York: Pantheon Books, 1947) and Grossman's "William Playfair, the Earliest Theorist of Capitalist Development," *Economic History Review* 18 (1–2) (1948): 65–83 were both translated into English by Norbert Guterman around 1947.

17. For Grossman's social life, see, for example, letter from Stead to Blake, December 7, 1946, Box 16, Folder 120, Stead Collection.

18. Letter from Stead to Blake, June 27, 1942, Stead and Blake, *Dearest Munx,* p. 286.

19. Letter from Stead to Blake, April 10, 1944, Stead and Blake, *Dearest Munx*, p. 296.

20. Letter from Grossman to Stead and Blake, May 4 and 5, 1947, Box 17, Folder 25, Stead Collection.

21. Letter from Alice and Joe [Maier] to Grossman, June 28, 1949; the content suggests the author was Alice Maier, VI 9 MHA p. 228; Grossman to Alice and Joe [Maier], May 30, 1949, VI 9, MHA, p. 229.

22. A letter from Stead to Blake, June 27, 1942, Stead and Blake, *Dearest Munx*, p. 287, mentioned that Grossman had received a letter from "Roces"; also see letter from Grossman to Walter Braeuer, May 21, 1948, Braeuer Nachlaß, Johann-Heinrich von Thünen Museum, Tellow (Braeuer Collection). Grossman's correspondence with Braeuer is published in Jürgen Scheele, *Zwischen Zusammenbruchsprognose und Positivismusverdikt: Studien zur politischen und intellektuellen Biographie Henryk Grossmanns (1881–1950)* (Frankfurt am Main: Lang, 1999), pp. 244–65. Roces Suárez had also translated communist workers' educational material by Wittfogel into Spanish during the 1930s. Henryk Grossmann, "Co vlastně učí Marx o dějinách a hospodářství," *CÍL: Socialistický Týdeník pro Kulturu a Politiku* 2 (23), June 14, 1946, pp. 356–58.

23. Letter from Grossman to Braeuer, May 21, 1948, Braeuer Collection.

24. Stead, notes, Box 5, Folder 32, Stead Collection.

25. For Grossman's kidney and stomach problems, see his letter to the Tax Department 1942, VI 10, MHA, p. 68. For the stroke, see Jay *The Dialectical Imagination*, p. 151. There is some evidence of a stroke in photos of Grossman from this period; *Täglicher Rundschau*, Berliner Ausgabe, March 10, 1949; also *Landes-Zeitung*, Ausgabe Rostock, March 16, 1949, reproduced in Gunzelin Schmid Noerr and Willem van Reijen (eds.), *Grand Hotel Abgrund: eine Photobiographie der kritischen Theorie* (Hamburg: Junius, 1988), p. 49; Fragebogen, March 15, 1949, VdN-Akte von Henryk Grossman 13630, Bezirksrat Leipzig 20237, Sächsisches Staatsarchiv Leipzig (Fragebogen SSAL).

26. Letters from Stead to Blake, June 27, 1942, Stead and Blake, *Dearest Munx*, p. 287; June 28, 1942, ibid., p. 289.

27. Letter from Stead to Blake, September 12, 1946, Stead and Blake, *Dearest Munx*, p. 356.

28. Letter from Grossman to Braeuer, August 25, 1947, Braeuer Collection.

29. Letter from Grossman to Stead and Blake, April 20, 1947, Box 17, Folder 125, Stead Collection.

30. Letter from Grossman to Stead and Blake, n.d. (between March 3, 1947, and April 20, 1947), Box 17, Folder 125, Stead Collection.

31. Stead, typescript notes, Box 5, Folder 32, Stead Collection.

32. Letter from Grossman to Alice and Joe [Maier], May 30, 1949, VI 9, MHA, p. 229; Fragebogen SSAL; W. Czernic Żalińska, *Salon sztuki "Skarbiec" in Warszawie* (Rocznik Muzeum Narodowego w Warszawie 1966), pp. 476, 493; letter from Grossman to Braeuer, n.d. (June 1947), Braeuer Collection. Christina Stead noted that Grossman's brother died in a Nazi gas truck; pencil annotation on typescript notes, Box 6, Folder 45, Stead Collection.

33. Stanisław was apparently alive in 1940, according to Grossman's application for first citizenship papers; cited by R. W. Meadows report, October 15, 1941, Henryk Grossman's file, Federal Bureau of Investigation (FBI file).

34. Letter from Grossman to Braeuer, May 12, 1948, Braeuer Collection.

35. Letter from Blake to Stead, March 4?, 1950, Stead and Blake, *Dearest Munx*, p. 489.

36. Letter from Grossman to the Tax Department 1942, VI 10, MHA, p. 68.

37. Letter from Stead to Blake, December 7, 1946, Stead and Blake, *Dearest Munx*, pp. 383–84.

38. Letter from Stead to Blake, June 27, 1942, Stead and Blake, *Dearest Munx*, p. 286.

39. Letter from Stead to Blake, September 12, 1946, Stead and Blake, *Dearest Munx*, p. 356.

40. Letter from Stead to Blake, September 12, 1946, Stead and Blake, *Dearest Munx*, p. 355, ellipsis in the original.

41. Georg Lukács, *History and Class Consciousness* (London: Merlin, 1971 [1923]), p. 70. Also see Walter Benjamin, "Theses on the Philosophy of History," in Stephen Bronner and Douglas Kellner, *Critical Theory and Society* (New York: Routledge, 1989 [duplicated 1942, written 1940]), pp. 260–61.

42. A letter from Grossman to Blake, March 3, 1947, Box 17, Folder 125, Stead Collection, refers to articles in four different newspapers; R. W. Meadows report, October 15, 1941, FBI file.

43. Charles Sadler, "'Pro-Soviet Polish-Americans': Oskar Lange and Russia's Friends in the Polonia, 1941–1945," *Polish Review* 22 (4) (1977): 26.

44. Don Binkowski, *Leo Krzycki and the Detroit Left* (Philadelphia: Xlibris, 2001), p. 149.

45. Tadeusz Kowalik, interview with Rick Kuhn, July 12, 1995 (Kowalik interview), in Rick Kuhn's possession.

46. Letter from Stead to Blake, September 12, 1946, Stead and Blake, *Dearest Munx*, p. 355; letter from Grossman to Stead and Blake, June 1, 1947, Box 17, Folder 125, Stead Collection.

47. Letter from Grossman to Rafał Taubenschlag, March 31, 1948, Taubenschlag Collection, pp. 62–63.

48. Christina Stead, "The Azhdnov Tailors," in *The Ocean of Story* (Ringwood: Penguin, 1986 [1971]). In notes and drafts, Stead identifies Grossman with the character in this story; Box 5, Folder 32, Stead Collection.

49. Grossmann, "Lebenslauf von Professor Dr. Henryk Grossman," UAL, pp. 62–63; letter from Grossman, no addressee, but apparently to Albert Schreiner, April 14, 1948, UAL, p. 5; Fragebogen, August 2, 1949, UAL, p. 100.

50. On Eisler's background, see "Eisler, Gerhart," in Werner Röder and Herbert Strauss (eds.), *Biographisches Handbuch der deutschsprachigen Emigration nach 1933* Band I: *Politik, Wirtschaft, öffentliches Leben* (München: K. G. Saur, 1980), p. 151; Jürgen Schebera, "The Lesson of Germany: Gerhart Eisler im Exil: Kommunist, Publizist, Galionsfigur der HUAC-Hexenjäger," *Exilforschung: Ein Internationales Jahrbuch* 7 (1989): 85–97; David Caute, *The Great Fear: The anti-Communist purge under Truman*

and Eisenhower (London: Secker & Warburg, 1978), p. 582. On Schreiner, see "Schreiner, Albert," in Röder and Strauss, *Biographisches Handbuch,* p. 668; Klaus Hermsdorf, Hugo Fetting, and Silvia Schlenstedt, *Kunst und Literatur im antifaschistischen Exil 1933–1945* Band 6: *Exil in Niederlanden und Spanien* (Frankfurt am Main: Röderberg, 1981), p. 277; Patrik von Zur Muhlen, *Spanien war ihre Hoffnung: Die deutsche Linke im Spanischen Bürgerkrieg 1936 bis 1939* (Bonn: Neue Gesellschaft, 1983), pp. 146, 242, 269, 370. Letter from Professor Gerhart Eisler to Rat der Stadt Leipzig, Amt für Opfer des Faschismus (VdN), November 10, 1950, SSAL.

51. Letter from Grossman to Schreiner, November 26, 1948, Albert Schreiner Nachlaß, NY 4198/70, Stiftung Archiv der Parteien und Massenorganisationen der DDR, Bundesarchiv Berlin (Schreiner Collection), p. 124. After leaving New York on August 14, 1948, Hanna wrote several letters to Grossman even before she and her husband had reached Leipzig.

52. Note to determination form, September 12, 1950, SSAL; letter from Blake to Stead, March 7, 1950, Stead and Blake, *Dearest Munx,* p. 489. On Alexan, Bloch, Boenheim, Budzislawski, Norden, and Herzfelde, see Bernd-Rainer Barth et al. (eds.), *Wer war wer in der DDR* (Frankfurt am Main: Fischer, 1996); Herbert A. Strauss and Werner Röder (eds.), *International Biographical Dictionary of Central European Emigres 1933–1945,* vol. 2, part 1: *The Arts, Sciences and Literature* (New York: K. G. Saur, 1980–83); Röder and Strauss, *Biographisches Handbuch;* Thomas M. Ruprecht, *Felix Boenheim: Arzt, Politiker, Historiker* (Hildesheim: Georg Olms, 1992).

53. Alexander Stephan, *"Communazis": FBI Surveillance of German Emigré Writers* (New Haven: Yale University Press, 1995), pp. 6, 7, 178; Eike Middell et al., *Kunst und Literatur im antifaschistischen Exil 1933–1945* Band 3: *Exil in den USA* (Leipzig: Reclam, 1983), pp. 111–12, 629; letter from Grossman to Stead and Blake, June 1, 1947, Box 17, Folder 125, Stead Collection.

54. Program "Die Tribuene fuer freie deutsche Literatur und Kunst, Feier fuer Thomas Mann zu seinem siebzigsten Geburtstag," New York Times Hall 240 West 44th St, Saturday 9 June 1945," Series 4, Folder 5, Rowley Collection.

55. Letter from Grossman to Braeuer, n.d. (June 1947), Braeuer Collection.

56. Letters from Stead to Blake, June 27, 1942, Stead and Blake, *Dearest Munx,* p. 287; April 10, 1944, ibid., p. 296.

57. See the handwriting in letters from Grossman to Stead and Blake, March 3, 1947, Box 17, Folder 125 Stead Collection; June 1, 1947, ibid.; letter from Grossman to Braeuer, June 15, 1948, Braeuer Collection.

58. "Henryk Grossman," III-155 Archiwum Polskiej Akademii Nauk (APAN), includes large numbers of completed request slips from the New York Public and Columbia University Libraries. "Marx, classical national economy and the problem of dynamics," original Folder 77, APAN; this is also mentioned in an editorial note in Max Horkheimer, *Gesammelte Schriften,* 17: *Briefwechsel 1941–1948* (Frankfurt am Main: Fischer, 1996), p. 279. Grossman wrote of the experience of trying to get a book published in the United States to Blake, July 10, 1947, Box 17, Folder 125, Stead Collection. The Polish essay is Henryk Grossman, "Położonie amerykańskiej burżuaziji i amerykańskiego

kapitaliszmu," 1945, original Folder 78, APAN. In 1948, Grossman believed that his pessimistic assessments in the essay had been confirmed by events; letter from Grossman to Taubenschlag, March 31, 1948, Taubenschlag Collection, pp. 62–63.

59. Letter from Grossman to Social Studies Association Inc., May 9, 1946, VI 9, MHA, p. 241. A year later he wrote to Stead and Blake that "I am not decided what to do now: finish Descartes? or the book on Marx simple reproduction (which I regard as my chief contribution to Marxist theory)"; May 4 and 5, 1947, Box 17, Folder 125, Stead Collection.

60. Henryk Grossman, report to the institute, May 9, 1946, A 325, Leo-Löwenthal-Archiv Universitäts- und Stadtarchiv Frankfurt am Main (LLA), p. 197; also at VI 9, MHA, p. 240.

61. Henryk Grossman, "Der Einfluss der Maschinen auf die Struktur der cartesianischen 'science universelle,'" p. 23, originally in Folder 24, APAN. Another version was in Folder 30. The texts in quotation marks are paraphrases from Vladimir Ilych Lenin, *State and Revolution, Collected Works*, vol. 25, 4th ed. (Moscow: Progress Publishers, 1980 [1918, written 1917]), pp. 385–497.

62. Grossman report to the institute, May 9, 1946, A 325, LLA, p. 197.

63. Henryk Grossman, "Descartes' new ideal of science. Universal science vs. science of an elite," originally in Folder 31, pp. 68–69, APAN, published as Henryk Grossman, "Universal Science vs. Science of an Elite: Descartes' New Ideal of Science," in Gideon Freudenthal and Peter McLaughlin (eds.), *Marxist Historiography of Science: The Hessen-Grossman Thesis,* forthcoming.

64. Henryk Grossman, "William Playfair, the Earliest Theorist of Capitalist Development," *Economic History Review* 18 (1–2) (1948): 65–83.

65. Letter from Grossman to Blake, March 3, 1947, Box 17, Folder 125, Stead Collection.

66. Letter from Grossman to Taubenschlag, March 31, 1948, Taubenschlag Collection, pp. 62–63.

67. Letter from Grossman to Stead and Blake, May 4 and 5, 1947, Box 17, Folder 125, Stead Collection.

68. Grossman, "William Playfair," pp. 67–68.

69. Ibid., pp. 70–74.

70. Ibid., pp. 79–81.

71. Ibid., pp. 75–76.

72. Letter from Grossman to Braeuer, June 25, 1948, Braeuer Collection.

73. Letter from Grossman to Blake, July 10, 1947, Box 17, Folder 125, Stead Collection.

74. Earle Micajah Winslow, *The Pattern of Imperialism: A Study in the Theories of Power* (New York: Columbia University Press, 1948), pp. 182–83.

75. Letter from Grossman to Blake, July 10, 1947, Box 17, Folder 125, Stead Collection. In 1947, Philip Vaudrin of Oxford University Press, who had published Sweezy's *The Theory of Capitalist Development,* invited Grossman to lunch and asked for a book proposal; ibid.

76. Letters from Stead to Blake, June 27, 1942, Stead and Blake, *Dearest Munx,* p. 286; June 28, 1942, ibid., p. 288.

77. Letters from Louis F. Costuma to J. E. Hoover, July 31, 1940, FBI file; from Costuma to the Chief of Police in Provincetown, July 31, 1940, ibid.

78. L. G. Healy, memorandum "Re: Henryk Grossman; International Research Institute," October 15, 1940, FBI file.

79. Henryk Grossman's taxation forms, IV 10.1–94, MHA; U.S. Bureau of the Census, *The Statistical History of the United States* (New York: Basic Books, 1976), p. 164.

80. Stead Collection Stead to Blake, September 12, 1946, Stead and Blake, *Dearest Munx*, p. 356.

81. For the anticommunist campaigns of the 1940s and 1950s, see Caute, *The Great Fear*, on Eisler, pp. 233–34.

82. Letter from Grossman to Stead and Blake, n.d. (between March 3, 1947, and April 20, 1947), Box 17, Folder 125, Stead Collection.

83. Letter from Grossman to Braeuer, August 25, 1947, Braeuer Collection. Also see letters from Grossman to Braeuer, January 13, 1948, Braeuer Collection; October 10, 1948, ibid.; and letter from Grossman to Taubenschlag, March 31, 1948, Taubenschlag Collection, p. 63.

84. Mario Keßler, *Exilerfahrung in Wissenschaft und Politik: Remigrierte Historiker in der frühen DDR* (Köln: Böhlau, 2001), p. 183.

85. Letter from Grossman to Stead and Blake, June 1, 1947, Box 17, Folder 125, Stead Collection.

86. Letter from Grossman to Braeuer, August 25, 1947, Braeuer Collection; letter from Grossman to Schreiner, April 14, 1948, UAL, p. 5.

87. Letters from Grossman to Braeuer, October 10, 1948, Braeuer Collection; August 25, 1947, ibid.

88. Letter from Grossman to Taubenschlag, March 31, 1948 Taubenschlag Collection, pp. 62–63.

89. Letter from Grossman to Braeuer, May 21, 1948, Braeuer Collection.

90. Letters from Grossman to Braeuer, August 25, 1947, Braeuer Collection; June 25, 1948, ibid.

91. Letters from Grossman to Leni Braeuer, May 12, 1948, Braeuer Collection; and to Braeuer, June 15, 1948, ibid. The communist control of the police and Russian backing was crucial to the success of the coup in Czechoslovakia; see Chris Harman, *Bureaucracy and Revolution in Eastern Europe* (London: Pluto, 1974), pp. 46–48.

92. Letter from Schreiner to Hermann Budzislawski, April 16, 1947, Schreiner Collection p. 58; Budzislawski to Schreiner, March 20, 1948, Schreiner Collection, p. 66; Schreiner to Wieland Herzfelde, August 28, 1948, Schreiner Collection, p. 164.

93. Letter from Grossman to Albert Schreiner, April 14, 1948, Schreiner Collection, p. 103.

94. Letter from Grossman to Schreiner, July 20, 1948, Schreiner Collection, p. 107.

95. Helga Welsh, *Revolutionärer Wandel auf Befehl: Entnazifizierungspolitik in Thüringen und Sachsen (1945–1949)* (München: Oldenbourg Verlag, 1989), p. 82.

96. Norman Naimark, *The Russians in Germany: A History of the Soviet Zone of Occupation, 1945–1949* (Cambridge, Mass.: Belknap Press of Harvard University Press, 1995), pp. 442–43.

97. Walter Markov, *Zwiesprache mit dem Jahrhundert* (Berlin: Aufbau, 1989), p. 181.

98. Keßler, *Exilerfahrung*, pp. 183–84.

99. Thomas Kuczynski, "Leipzig—Stern unter den deutschen Nachkriegsuniversitäten," in Manfred Neuhaus and Helmut Seidel (eds.), *Universität im Aufbruch. Leipzig 1945–1956. Beiträge des siebten Walter-Markov-Kolloquiums* (Leipzig: Rosa-Luxemburg-Stiftung Sachsen, 2002), p. 36.

100. Letters from Grossman to Braeuer, January 13, 1948, Braeuer Collection; May 12, 1948, ibid.; May 21, 1948, ibid.; June 15, 1948, ibid.; June 25, 1948, ibid.; July 26, 1948, ibid.

101. Fritz Behrens, *Alte und die neue Probleme der politischen Ökonomie: Eine theoretische und statistische Studie über die produktive Arbeit im Kapitalismus* (Berlin: Dietz, 1948), p. 43, cited by Scheele, *Zwischen Zusammenbruchsprognose und Positivismusverdikt*, p. 225.

102. Letter from Gerhard Menz, dean of the Faculty of Economics and Social Science to Friedrich Behrens, dean of the Faculty of Social Science, May 4, 1948, UAL, p. 5; letter from Gerhard Menz to the Universities and Science Section of the Ministry of Education, July 27, 1949 UAL, pp. 116–17; letter from Behrens to Heinz Rocholl, senior government advisor to the State Government of Saxony, August 3, 1948, UAL, p. 16.

103. Letter from Grossman to Braeuer, July 28, 1948, Braeuer Collection.

104. Letter from Grossman to Braeuer, September 7, 1948, Braeuer Collection.

105. *Universität Leipzig Personal- und Vorlesungsverzeichnis Wintersemester 1948–49* (Leipzig, 1948), pp. 58, 59.

106. Markov, *Zwiesprache*, p. 184; Keßler, *Exilerfahrung*, p. 184.

107. Kowalik interview.

108. He had made a similar inquiry ten months earlier, but there had been no reply; letters from Grossman to Taubenschlag, March 31, 1948, Taubenschlag Collection, p. 62; January 10, 1949, ibid., p. 63.

109. This was Tadeusz Kowalik's supposition; Kowalik interview.

110. Letter from Grossman to Stead and Blake, May 4 and 5, 1947, Box 17, Folder 125, Stead Collection. Hundreds of Jews returning to Poland from the Soviet Union were also murdered in 1945 and 1946. On July 4, 1946, there was a pogrom in Kielce during which forty-two Jews were killed and at least eighty wounded. The international press reported the event; Leo Cooper, *In the Shadow of the Polish Eagle: The Poles, the Holocaust and Beyond* (Houndsmills: Palgrave, 2000), pp. 185–96.

111. Letter from Grossman to Alice and Joe [Maier], May 30, 1949, VI 9, MHA, p. 229.

112. Memo by Pollock, April 13, 1948, VI 9, MHA, p. 239.

113. Communications between Pollock and Dr Frederick Wild (the institute's lawyer), September 1948, MHA, VI 9 17, p. 237; October 11, 1948, ibid., p. 236; November 14, 1948, ibid., p. 233; November 15, 1948, ibid., p. 233; January 12, 1949, ibid., pp. 231, 236–37. Letter from Grossman to Braeuer, December 24, 1948, Braeuer Collection; Schmid Noerr and van Reijen, *Grand Hotel Abgrund*, p. 50; Rolf Wiggershaus, *The Frankfurt School* (Cambridge: Polity, 1995), p. 271.

114. Letter from Chimen Abramsky to Rick Kuhn, January 12, 1996, in Rick Kuhn's possession.

115. Letter from Grossman to Braeuer, December 24, 1948, Braeuer Collection.

116. Letter to Grossman, June 28, 1949; the content suggests the author was Alice Maier, VI 9, MHA, p. 228.

117. Letter from Grossman to Braeuer, March 19, 1949, Braeuer Collection. In contemplating his departure from New York, Grossman had discussed the pros and cons of taking ready-made clothing for Braeuer and his wife or just cloth; letter from Grossman to Braeuer, July 26, 1948, Braeuer Collection.

118. The photograph taken in Berlin is in *Täglicher Rundschau,* March 10, 1949 and is reproduced in Schmid Noerr and van Reijen, *Grand Hotel Abgrund,* p. 49, from *Landes-Zeitung* (Rostock), March 16, 1949. The other photograph, possibly taken in New York, is in Fragebogen SSAL.

119. For Grossman's directorship of the Economic Planning Institute, see Fragebogen, August 3, 1949, UAL, p. 100; *Universität Leipzig Personal- und Vorlesungsverzeichnis Somersemester 1949* (Leipzig, 1949), p. 24.

120. Letters from Blake to Stead, (presumably) February 28, 1950, Stead and Blake, *Dearest Munx,* p. 487; March 21, 1950, ibid., p. 507.

121. Letter from Blake to Stead, March 10, 1950, Stead and Blake, *Dearest Munx,* p. 496.

122. Letter from the Rat des Stadtkreises Leipzig, Dezernat Sozial- u. Wohnungswesen, Abteilung VdN, to Ministerium für Wirtschaft u. Arbeit des Landes Sachsen, November 13, 1951, SSAL.

123. Letter from Grossman to Braeuer, March 19, 1949, Braeuer Collection; letters from Albert Schreiner to Grossman, June 3, 1948, Schreiner Collection, p. 105; September 2, 1948, ibid., p. 109. Schreiner was personally involved in organizing the apartment during his "vacation."

124. Letter from Dr. Dyck of the university administration to Henryk Grossmann, May 4, 1949 UAL, p. 28; letter from Dr. Dyck to the Universities and Science Section, Ministry for Education, Saxony, to the University Administrative Director, December 16, 1949, UAL, p. 92; letter from Ernst Eichler of the University of Leipzig to the Universities and Science Section of the Ministry for Education, May 24, 1949, UAL, p. 47.

125. Letter from Schreiner to the rector of the University of Leipzig, June 8, 1949, UAL, p. 33.

126. Karl Heinz Lange, "Versuch einer Erinnerung an Henryk Grossman," October 15 2002, handwritten manuscript, in Rick Kuhn's possession ("Versuch").

127. Letter from Grossman to Braeuer, June 8, 1949, Braeuer Collection.

128. Letter from Grossman to Braeuer, May 12, 1949, Braeuer Collection.

129. Ibid.; letter from Grossman to Braeuer, June 6, 1949, Braeuer Collection.

130. Letter from Grossman to Braeuer, May 12, 1949, Braeuer Collection.

131. Letter from Grossman to Braeuer, June 8, 1949, Braeuer Collection.

132. File note, March 15, 1949, SSAL; Ergänzungsblatt zum Personalfragebogen, July 4, 1950, UAL, p. 88; Persönlicher Fragebogen eines Wissenschaftlers, August 3, 1949, UAL, p. 70.

133. Fragebogen, August 3, 1949, UAL, pp. 100–101. Shortly after his arrival in East Germany he still described himself as being of the Mosaic faith; Fragebogen SSAL.

134. Eugen Varga, "Akkumulation und Zusammenbruch des Kapitalismus," *Unter dem Banner des Marxismus* 4 (1) (1930): 60–95; letter from Grossman to Braeuer, June 8, 1949, Braeuer Collection.

135. Grossman, "Lebenslauf von Professor Dr. Henryk Grossman" and "Lebenslauf" UAL, pp. 62–66; "Kurzer Lebenslauf" SSAL.

136. *Universität Leipzig Personal- und Vorlesungsverzeichnis Somersemester 1949*, pp. 62, 65. He had initially proposed to teach all four of his contact hours on the history of political economy; Henryk Grossman memo, March 23, 1949, UAL, p. 25.

137. Letters from Eva Müller to Rick Kuhn, August 29, 2002, in Rick Kuhn's possession; October 15, 2002, ibid.

138. Lange, "Versuch."

139. Letter from Eva Müller to Rick Kuhn, October 15, 2002, in Rick Kuhn's possession.

140. Letter from Schreiner to Paul Wandel, September 5, 1949, also letter, September 7, 1949, Schreiner Collection, pp. 86–87, cited in Keßler, *Exilerfahrung*, p. 184.

141. Lange, "Versuch."

142. Letter from Henryk Grossman to Heinz Lange, November 17, 1949, in Lange's possession, copy held by Rick Kuhn.

143. Course form, UAL, p. 38.

144. Letter from Grossman to Stead and Blake, May 4 and 5, 1947, Box 17, Folder 125, Stead Collection.

145. Letters from Blake to Stead, March 4, 1950, Stead and Blake, *Dearest Munx*, p. 488; March 7, 1950, ibid., p. 89.

146. Letter from Stead to Blake, April 10, 1944, ibid., p. 296.

147. Letters from Blake to Stead, March 7?, 1950, ibid., p. 489; March 21, 1950, ibid. p. 508.

148. Letters from Blake to Stead, March 4?, 1950, ibid., p. 488; March 7, 1950, ibid., p. 489.

149. Note, apparently from Rat der Stadt Leipzig, Amt für Opfer des Faschismus (VdN) to Volkssolidarität, Wirtschaftsabteilung, Leipzig, December 28, 1949, SSAL.

150. Letter from Blake to Stead, March 7, 1950, Box 16, Folder 120, Stead Collection A newspaper clipping, n.d., about the Leipzig's nomination of Grossman and others is attached.

151. Rowley, *Christina Stead*, p. 365.

152. Letters from Blake to Stead, March 21, 1950, Stead and Blake, *Dearest Munx*, p. 508; March 24, 1950, ibid., p. 511.

153. In the original the quotations are in German; letter from Blake to Stead, March 14, 1950, Box 16, Folder 120, Stead Collection.

154. Letter from Blake to Stead, March 21, 1950, ibid., p. 508.

155. Letter from Blake to Stead, March 11, 1950, ibid., p. 498; Ruprecht, *Felix Boenheim*, pp. 341–42.

156. Letter from Blake to Stead, March 24, 1950, Stead and Blake, *Dearest Munx*, p. 511.

157. Letter from Blake to Stead, March 23, 1950, ibid., pp. 509–10. There is no other evidence to support Alice Maier's recollection, twenty years later, that he was disappointed with Leipzig; Jay *The Dialectical Imagination*, p. 151.

158. Henryk Grossmann, "W. Playfair, der frueheste Theoretiker der Kapitalistischen Entwicklungstendenzen," August 4, 1950 typescript, original Folder 44, in 1997 Folder 27, APAN; letter from Grossman to Schreiner, May 26, 1950, Schreiner Collection, p. 126. On Dietz and Schälike, see Siegfried Lokatis, "Dietz: Probleme der Ideologiewirtschaft im zentralen Parteiverlag der SED," in Christian Jansen, Lutz Niethammer, and Bernd Weisbrod, *Von der Aufgabe der Freiheit: Politische Verantwortung und bürgerliche Gesellschaft im 19. und 20. Jahrhundert. Festschrift für Hans Mommsen zum 5. November 1995* (Berlin: Akademie, 1995), pp. 533–48.

159. Letter from Grossman to Schreiner, May 26, 1950, Schreiner Collection, pp. 126–27; Henryk Grossmann, "Probleme der methodologischen Grundlagen beim Aufbau des Marxschen *Kapital*," original Folder 12, in 1997 Folder 64, APAN.

160. Henryk Grossmann, "Probleme der methodologischen Grundlagen beim Aufbau des marxchen Kapital," original Folder 12, in 1997 Folder 64, APAN, p. 43.

161. G. Mayer, "Beurteilung," UAL, p. 58.

162. Report on visit to Grossmann on August 23, 1950, SSAL.

163. Ruprecht, *Felix Boenheim*, pp. 341–42.

164. Death Notice, November 27, 1950, UAL, p. 78.

165. Stead, notes, "The Traveller's Bed and Breakfast," Box 15, Folder 111, Stead Collection. Rowley identifies Gerardus as Grossman; *Christina Stead*, p. 372.

166. Gareth Pritchard, *The Making of the GDR 1943–1953: From Antifascism to Stalinism* (Manchester: Manchester University Press, 2000), pp. 166–67; Dietrich Starit, *Die Gründung der DDR: Von der sowjetischen Besatzungsherrschaft zum sozialistischen Staat*, 3rd ed. (München: Deutscher Taschenbuch, 1995), pp. 179–81.

167. Helmut Steiner, "Notizen zu einer 'Gesellschaftsbiographie' des Fritz Behrens," in Eva Müller, Manfred Neuhaus, and Joachim Tesch (eds.), *"Ich habe einige Dogmen angetastet..." Werk und Wirken von Fritz Behrens: Beiträge des vierten Walter-Markov-Kolloquiums* (Leipzig: Rosa-Luxemburg-Stiftung Sachsen, 1999), p. 22; Keßler *Exilerfahrung*, p. 185.

168. Hans-Uwe Feige, "Ketzer und Kampfgenosse—der Leipziger Ordinarius für Philosophie Ernst Bloch," *Deutschland Archiv* 25 (7) (July 1992): 698.

169. Manfred Heinemann et al. (eds.), *Hochschuloffiziere und der Wiederaufbau des Hochschulwesens in Deutschland: Die sowjetische Besatzungszone* (Edition Bildung und Wissenschaft, Akademie-Verlag, 1998), p. 266; Staritz, *Die Gründung der DDR*, p. 198.

170. Georg Fülberth, "Widerstand und Gelehrsamkeit," in Frank Deppe, Georg Fülberth, and Rainer Rillling (eds.), *Antifaschismus* (Heilbronn: Distel Verlag, 1996), pp. 206–17.

171. On the end of the period of lively debate, see Wolfgang Abendroth, *Ein Leben in der Arbeiterbewegung Gespräche* (Frankfurt am Main: Suhrkamp, 1976), pp. 222–23.

172. Ruprecht, *Felix Boenheim*, pp. 341–42.

173. "Beurteilung," August 14, 1950, UAL, p. 58; "Aufzählung der nicht veröffentlichten und nicht registrierten Arbeiten von Prof. Dr. Henryk Grossman," UAL, p. 68; letter from Grossman to Schreiner, April 14, 1948, Schreiner Collection, p. 103.

174. Fritz Behrens, *Zur Methode der politischen Ökonomie* (Berlin: Akademie Verlag, 1952), p. 46 et seq.; and Werner Krause and Günther Rudolph, *Grundlinien des ökonomischen Denkens in Deutschland 1848 bis 1945*, pp. 320–21, 565.

175. While the German new left republished Grossman's work, his positions were more widely adopted in the English-speaking world; for example, see Paul Mattick, who had been expounding Grossman's crisis theory since the 1930s and now found a wider audience, *Marx and Keynes* (London: Merlin, 1974 [1969]); Paul Mattick, *Economic Crisis and Crisis Theory* (London: Merlin, 1981 [1974]); David Yaffe, "The Marxian Theory of Crisis, Capital and the State," *Economy and Society* 2 (1973): 186–232; Anwar Shaikh, "An Introduction to the History of Crisis Theories," in Bruce Steinberg et al., *U. S. Capitalism in Crisis* (New York: Union for Radical Political Economics, 1978), pp. 219–41; Chris Harman, *Explaining the Crisis* (London: Bookmarks, 1984).

Bibliography

Note: This bibliography includes only Grossman's work, archival sources, interviews and personal communications. A full bibliography of all sources used in this book can be found in "Henryk Grossman bibliography" on the web in HTML and PDF formats at http://eprints.anu.edu.au/archive/00003453, http://www.marxists.org/archive/gross man/moreinfo.htm and http://www.anu.edu.au/polsci/rick/pub.htm#bibliography.

Items are listed by their dates of publication. The author's name is that given in the item.

Books and Articles

Grossman, Henryk. *Proletariat wobec kwestii żydowskiej z powodu niedyskutowanej dyskusyi w Krytyce* (The Proletariat and the Jewish Question, Arising from the Undiscussed Discussion in Krytyka). Kraków: Drukani Wladysława Teodorczuka, January 1905, pp. 45. Also published in a modified Yiddish version: "Dem proletariat benegeye tsu der yidenfrage." *Yidisher sotsial-demokrat* 1 (April 1905): pp. 6–13, and 3 (June 1905): 7–11.

"Od redakcyi" (From the editor). *Zjednoczenie* 1 (February 1905): 1–3. Grossman edited this issue of *Zjednoczenie.*

Komitet organizacyjny żydowskiej partyi socyalno-demokraticyczney w Galicyi Czego chcemy? (What Do We Want?). Kraków, April 30, 1905, pp. 8. Also published in Yiddish: "Vos Viln Mir?" (What Do We Want?). *Yidisher sotsial-demokrat* 2 (May 1905): 1–9. Grossman wrote this manifesto, according to Leon Feyner "Di bundishe presse in Krake fun 1905 bis 1930," *Historisher samlbuch: materialn un dokumentn tsushtayer tsu der geshikhte fun algemainer yidishn arbeter-bund,* (Warsaw: Farlag "Ringen," 1948), p. 18. Solomon Reyzen indicated Grossman "published" the manifesto, *Leksikon fun der yidisher literatur, prese un filologie,* vol. 1, 2nd ed. (Vilno: Vilner Farlag fun B. Kletskin, 1926), column 616.

"Odpowiedzi Polskiej Partyi Soc.-Dem. Galicyi" (Reply to the Polish Social Democratic Party of Galicia). In Żydowska Partya Socyalno-Demokratyczna Galicyi, *Przed Kongresem*, Kraków: June, 2 1905, pp. 1–6. Probably written by Grossman, according to Henryk Piasecki, *Sekcja Żydowska PPSD i Żydowska Partia Socjalno-Demokratyczna* (Wrocław : Zakład Narodowy imienia Ossolińskich, 1982), p. 126.

Jüdische sozial-demokratische Partei in Galizien. *Bericht zum Gesamt-Parteitage der Oesterreichischen Sozialdemokratie in Wien 1905 (1 Mai-23–Oktober 1905)* (Report to the Congress of the General Austrian Social Democratic Party in Vienna 1905 [May, 1–October 23, 1905]). Krakau: "Der Sozialdemokrat," 1905, pp. 2.

Jüdische sozial-demokratische Partei in Galizien, *An die Sozialdemokraten in Oesterreich!* (To the Social Democrats of Austria). Krakau: "Der Sozialdemokrat," 1905, pp. 2. Grossmann wrote this appeal, according to Leon Feyner, "Di bundishe presse in Krake fun 1905 bis 1930," Historisher samlbuch: materialn un dockumentn tsushtayer tsu der geshikhte fun algemainer yidishn arbeter-bund, (Warsaw: Farlag "Ringen," 1948), p. 19.

Grossmann, Jindřich. "Židovská Strana Sociálně Demokratická v Haliči" (The Jewish Social Democratic Party of Galicia). *Akademie: Socialistická Revue* (1906). German translation: "Die Jüdische Sozialdemokratische Partei in Galizien. In Raimund Löw. *Der Zerfall der "Kleinen Internationale": Nationalitätenkonflikte in der Arbeiterbewegung des alten Österreich (1889–1914)*. Wien: Europaverlag, 1984, pp. 220–27.

Grossman, Henryk. *Der Bundizm in galitsien* (Bundism in Galicia). Kraków: Ferlag der *Sotsial-democrat*, 1907 (cover indicates 1908, title page 1907) pp. 48. Dedicated to the tenth anniversary of the Bund in Russia. Also published in *Der sotsial-demokrat* between September 13, 1907, and November 29, 1907.

Grossmann, Henryk. "Eine Wiener Volkszählung im Jahre 1777" (A Viennese Census in the Year 1777). *Statistische Monatschrift*, new series 16 (1911): 56–58.

Grossman, Henryk. "Rozległość Galicyi po zajęciu jej przez Austrę" (The Size of Galicia after its Occupation by Austria). *Kwartalnik Historyczny* 15 (1911): 472–78.

Grossman, Henryk. "Polityka przemysłowa i handlowa rządu Terezynansko-"Józefińskiego w Galicyi 1772–1790: Referat na V. Zjazd prawnikow i ekonomistow polskich" (The Industrial and Commercial Policy of the Theresian-Josephine Regime in Galicia 1772–1790: Thesis for the V. Congress of Polish Economists). (Till's) *Przeglad prawa i administracyi*, (1912): pp. 1–43.

Grossmann, Henryk. "Die amtliche Statistik des galizischen Aussenhandels 1772–1792" (The Official Statistics of Galician Foreign Trade 1772–1792). *Statistische Monatschrift*, new series 18 (1913): 222–33.

Grossmann, Henryk. *Österreichs Handelspolitik mit Bezug auf Galizien in der Reformperiode 1772–1790* (Austria's Trade Policy with Regard to Galicia in the Reform Period 1772–1790). *Studien zur Soziale-, Wirtschafts- und Verwaltungsgeschichte*, edited by Carl Grünberg, vol. 10 Wien: Konegen, 1914, pp. xvii + 510.

Grossmann, Henryk. "Die Anfänge und geschichtlich Entwicklung der amtlichen Statistik in Österreich" (The Beginnings and Historical Development of Official Statistics in Austria). *Statistische Monatschrift*, new series 21 (1916): 331–423. Also appeared as "Sonderdruck aus dem Juni-Juli-Heft der *Statistichen Monatschrift*".

Grossmann, Henryk. "Erwiderung" (Reply). *Statistichen Monatschrift* 21 (1916): 676–77.

Grossmann, Henryk. "Die Kreditorganisation des Königreiches Polen vor dem Kriege" (The Organization of Credit in the Kindom of Poland before the War). In Ludwig Ćwikliński (ed.), *Das Königreich Polen vor dem Kriege (1815–1914): Zehn Vorträge, gehalten in Wien im März 1917*. Leipzig and Wien: Deuticke, 1917, pp. 180–209.

Grossman, Henryk. "Znaczenie i zadania pierwszego proszechnego ludności w Polsce" (Significance and Tasks of the First General Census in Poland). *Miesięcznik Statystyczny* 1 (1920): 88–106.

Grossman, Henryk. "Statystyka ruchu towaronego na kolejach zelaznych. (The Statistics of Railway Freight and Goods Transport). *Miesięcznik Statystyczny* 3 (1921): 1–28.

Grossman, Henryk. "Majątek społeczny Królestwa Polskiego" (The Social Wealth of the Kingdom of Poland). *Miesięcznik Statystyczny* 5 (1922): 255–77.

Grossman, Henryk. "Teorja kryzysów gospodarczych (The Theory of Economic Crises)." *Bulletin International de l Académie Polonaise des Sciences et des Lettres. Classe de Philologie. Classe d'Histoire et de Philosophie. Les Années 1919, 1920* (1922 [presented June 16, 1919]): 285–90. Reprinted, with a preface by Rick Kuhn, as "The Theory of Economic Crises." in Paul Zarembka and Susanne Soederberg (eds), *Value, capitalist dynamics, and money Research in political economy* 18, New York: Elsevir Science, 2000, pp. 171–80.

Grossman, Henryk. "Przycznek do historji socjalizmu w Polsce przed laty czterdziestu" (Some Historical Notes on Socialism in Poland Forty Years Ago). Introduction to Karol Marks, *Karol Marks: Pisma niewydane, 1 Listy Marksa do Kugelmana, 2 Przyczynek do Krytyki socjal-demokratycznego programu partyjnego. Przełożył, wstępem i uwagami zaopatrzył Prof. Dr. H. Grossman* (Karl Marx: Unpublished Works, 1 Letter to Kugelmann, 2 Introduction to the Critique of the Social Democratic Party Program. Translated, introduced and annotated by Prof. Dr. H. Grossman). Warsaw: Książka, 1923, pp. iii–xxvii.

Grossman, Henryk. "Ekonomiczny system Karola Marksa" (The Economic System of Karl Marx). *Kultura Robotnicza* 2 (10), no. 32 (March 17, 1923): 295–99.

Grossman, Henryk. *Simonde de Sismondi et ses théories économiques. Une nouvelle interprétation de sa pensée* (Simonde de Sismondi and His Economic Theories: A New Interpretation of His Thought). Bibliotheca Universitatis Liberae Polonae fasc. 11, Warszawa: 1924, pp. 77. Italian translation: "Sismondi e la critica del capitalismo" as an appendix to Aldo G. Ricci (ed.), *Chiarimenti sull'equilibrio tra produzione e consumo, di Simonde de Sismondi*. Bari: Laterza, 1972.

Grossman, Henryk. "Struktura spo eczna i gospodarcza Księstwa Warszawskiego na podstawie spisów ludności 1808–1810 roku" (The Social and Economic Structure of the Duchy of Warsaw on the Basis of the Results of the Census of 1808 and 1810). *Kwartalnik Statystyczny* 2 (1925): pp. 1–108. (With a French abstract, Henri Grossman, "La structure social et économique du Duché de Varsovie," under the title *Revue trimenstrielle de statistique* 2 [1] [1925]).

Grossmann, Henryk. "Eine neue Theorie über Imperialismus und die soziale Revolution" (A New Theory of Imperialism and the Social Revolution). *Archiv für die Geschichte des Sozialismus und der Arbeiterbewegung* 13 (1928): 141–92.

Grossmann, Henryk. *Das Akkumulations- und Zusammenbruchsgetz des kapitalistis-chen Systems (zugleich eine Krisentheorie)* (The Law of Accumulation and Collapse of the Capitalist System [also a Theory of Crisis]). Schriften des Instituts für Sozial-forschung an der Universitität Frankfurt am Main, edited by Carl Grünberg, vol. 1. Leipzig: C. L. Hirschfeld Verlag, 1929, pp. xvi + 628. Republished in 1967 (with an introduction by Wolf Rosenbaum and a biographical note by Klaus H. Hennings) and 1970 (without Rosenbaum's introduction) by Verlag Neue Kritik, Frankfurt am Main. Japanese edition with a preface by Grossman *Shihon no chikuseki narabi ni hokai no riron,* translated by Hiromi Arisawa and Katsumi Moritani. Tokyo: Kaizosha, 1932, p. 832. Italian edition: *Il crollo del capitalismo: La legge dell'accumu-lazione e del crollo del sistema capitalista,* translated by L. Gianninazzi, preface by Rocco Buttiglione. Milan: Jaca Book, 1977. Spanish edition: *La ley de la acumulación y del derrumbe del sistema capitalista: una teoría de la crisis,* introduced and edited by Jorge Tula. México: Siglo Veintiuno Editores, 1979. Serbo-Croat edition: *Zakon aku-mulacije i sloma kapitalistickog sistema (ujedno i teorija kriza).* Beograd: Prosveta, 1983, translated by Mara Fran with an appendix by Mara Fran "Beleska o piscu i delu" (A Comment on the Writer and His Work), pp. 477–481. English edition: *The Law of Accumulation and Breakdown of the Capitalist System: Being also a theory of Crises,* translated and abridged by Jairus Banaji, introduced by Tony Kennedy. Lon-don: Pluto, 1992. This lacks the final part of the German editions. A section of this part, on wages and class struggle, can be found in Kenneth Lapides, "Henryk Gross-mann on Marx's Wage Theory and the 'Increasing Misery' Controversy," *History of Political Economy* 26 (2) (Summer 1994): 247–66.

Grossmann, Henryk. "Die Änderung des ursprunglichen Aufbauplans des Marxschen 'Kapital' und ihre Ursachen" (The Change to the Original Plan of Marx's *Capital* and its Causes). *Archiv für die Geschichte des Sozialismus und der Arbeiterbewegung* 14 (1929): 305–38. Czech translation (with some changes): "Plán Marxova: 'Kapitálu.'" *Dělnická Osvěta: Socialistická Revue* 23 (1937): 168–74. Serbo-Croatian translation by Mara Fran: "Plan i metod 'Kapitala.'" Beograd: Graficki zavod "Rotacija", Zemun, 1938 (reprinted from *Pravna misao: Časopis za pravo i sociologiju* [1938]). A section of the article is translated into English in Kenneth Lapides, "Henryk Grossmann and the Debate on the Theoretical Status of Marx's *Capital,*" *Science & Society* 56 (2) (Summer 1992): 144–50.

Grossmann, Henryk. Items in Ludwig Elster (ed.), *Wörterbuch der Volkswirtschaft,* Erster Band. 4th ed. Jena: Fischer, 1931.

"Adler, Victor," pp. 21–22.

* "Anarchismus" (Anarchism), pp. 97–109.

"Bebel, August," pp. 301–2.

* "Bolschewismus" (Bolshevism), pp. 421–44.

* "Christlicher und religiöser Sozialismus" (Christian and Religious Socialism), with Carl Grünberg, pp. 538–59.

"Debs, Eugene," p. 564.

"Leon, Daniel de," pp. 564–65.

Grossman, Henryk. Items in Ludwig Elster (ed.), *Wörterbuch der Volkswirtschaft*, Zweiter Band. 4th ed. Jena: Fischer, 1932.
"Guesde, Jules," pp. 256–58.
"Herzen, Alexander," pp. 350–61.
"Hydman, Henry Mayers," pp. 369–70.
* "Internationale: Die Zweite Internationale" (International: The Second International), with Carl Grünberg, pp. 432–39.
* "Internationale: Die dritte Internationale" (International: The Third International), pp. 439–49.
"Jaurès, Jean," pp. 382–83.
"Kropotkin, Peter," pp. 696–97.
"Lenin, Wladimir Iljitsch" (Lenin, Vladimir Ilyich), pp. 828–31.
"Plechanow, Georg" (Plekhanov, Georgii), pp. 1149–42.
Grossmann, Henryk. "Die Wert-Preis-Transformation bei Marx und das Krisenproblem" (The Value-Price Transformation in Marx and the Problem of Crises). *Zeitschrift für Sozialforschung* 1 (1932): 55–84.
Grossmann, Henryk. "Die Goldproduktion im Reproduktionsschema von Marx und Rosa Luxemburg" (Gold Production in the Reproduction Schemes of Marx and Luxemburg). In *Festschrift für Carl Grünberg zum 70. Geburtstag*. Leipzig: Hirschfeld, 1932, pp. 152–84.
Grossman, Henryk. Items in Ludwig Elster (ed.), *Wörterbuch der Volkswirtschaft*, Dritte Band. 4th ed. Jena: Fischer, 1933.
"Olinde Rodrigues," p. 99.
"Georges Sorel," pp. 236–38.
* "Sozialistische und kommunistische Parteien" (Socialist and Communist Parties), with Carl Grünberg, pp. 238–57.
* "Die Fortentwicklung des Marxismus bis zur Gegenwart" (Further Developments in Marxism to the Present), pp. 313–41. Appeared as a separate publication: *Fünfzig Jahre Kampf um den Marxismus 1883–1932* (Fifty Years of Struggle over Marxism 1883–1932), (Jena: Fischer, 1932); as a Japanese translation by Yoshitaro Hirano of Tokyo, "Maruki shizumu notameno toso gojunen." *Chuo Koron* 48 (543), 1933; and as a pamphlet. Serbo-Croatian translation by Mara Fran: "Pedeset godina naucnog socijalizma," with a German abstract, Beograd: Graficki zavod "Rotacija," Zemun, 1938 (reprinted from *Pravna misao: Časopis za pravo i sociologiju* 1938), p. 56.
Grossman, Henryk. "Die Anfänge des Kapitalismus und die neue Massenmoral" original Folder 38, "Henryk Grossman", III-155, Archiwum Polskiej Akademii Nauk, written 1934. English translation "The beginnings of the capitalism and the new mass morality" *Journal of Classical Sociology* 6 (3) (2006): 201–213.
Grossman, Henryk. "Sismondi, Jean Charles Léonard Simonde de." In Edwin R. A. Seligman (ed.), *Encyclopaedia of the Social Sciences*, vol 14: *Servitudes-Trade Associations*. New York: Macmillan, 1934, pp. 69–71.
Grossmann, Henryk. "Die gesellschaftlichen Grundlagen der mechanistischen Philosophie und die Manufaktur" (The Social Foundations of Mechanical Philosophy and

Manufacture). *Zeitschrift für Sozialforschung* 4 (2) (1935): 161–231. Also as an appendix to Franz Borkenau, *Der Übergang vom feudalen zum bürgerlichen Weltbild*. Gelsenkirchen: Junius, 1970. Italian translation: Franz Borkenau, Henryk Grossmann, and Antonio Negri. *Manifattura, societa borghese, ideologia*. Rome: Savelli, 1978. English translation by Gabriella Shalit: "The Social Foundations of Mechanistic Philosophy and Manufacture" *Science in Context* 1 (1) (1987): 129–80.

Grossmann, Henryk. "Diskussionen aus einem Seminar über Monopkapitalismus (1937)" (Discussions at a Seminar on Monopoly Capitalism). In Max Horkheimer, *Gesammelte Schriften*, Band 12: *Nachgelassene Schriften 1931–1949*. Edited by Gunzelin Schmid Noerr. Frankfurt am Main: S. Fischer Verlag, 1985, pp. 418–20.

Grossman, Henryk. *Marx, die klassische Nationalökonomie und das Problem der Dynamik* (Marx, Classical Political Economy and the Problem of Dynamics). Institut für Sozialforschung mimeographed, New York: 1941; then Frankfurt am Main: Europäische Verlagsanstalt, 1969, p. 133, with appendix "Briefe Henryk Grossmanns an Paul Mattick über Akkumulation" (Henryk Grossmann's Letters to Paul Mattick on Accumulation) and afterword by Paul Mattick. Italian translation: Giogio Backhaus, *Marx, l'economia politica classica e il problema della dinamica*. Bari: Laterza, 1971. French translation: *Marx, l'économie politique classique et le probleme de la dynamique*. Paris: Champ Libre, 1975. English translation by Pete Burgess: "Marx, Classical Political Economy and the Problem of Dynamics." *Capital and Class* 2 (Summer 1977): 32–55 and 3 (Autumn 1977): 67–99.

Grossman, Henryk. "The Evolutionist Revolt against Classical Economics. I. In France—Condorcet, Saint-Simon, Simonde de Sismondi." *Journal of Political Economy* 51 (5) (October 1943): 381–396. "The Evolutionist Revolt against Classical Economics. II In England—James Steuart, Richard Jones, Karl Marx." *Journal of Political Economy* 51 (6) (December 1943): 506–22. Part of these essays appeared in an authorized translation into Czech by Jiří Stolz, "Co vlastně učí Marx o dějinách a hospodářství" (What Marx Really Taught about History and Political Economy). *CÍL: Socialistický Týdeník pro Kulturu a Politiku* 2 (23) (June 14, 1946): 356–58. Reprinted in Mark Blaug (ed.), *Thomas Tooke (1774–1858), Mountifort Longfield (1802–1884), Richard Jones (1790–1855)* (Aldershot: Elgar, 1991), pp. 1–16; and Bob Jessop (ed.), *Karl Marx's Social and Political Thought: Critical Assessments*, vol. 1 (London and New York: Routledge, 1990), pp. 253–74.

Grossman, Henryk. "Descartes' new ideal of science: universal science vs. science of an elite." Originally in Folder 31, "Henryk Grossman", III-155, Archiwum Polskiej Akademii Nauk written 194?, published as "Universal science vs. science of an elite: Descartes' new ideal of science" in Gideon Freudenthal and Peter McLaughlin (eds), *Marxist historiography of science: the Hessen-Grossman thesis*, forthcoming.

Grossman, Henryk. "William Playfair, the Earliest Theorist of Capitalist Development." *Economic History Review* 18 (1–2) (1948): 65–83.

Grossmann, Henryk. *Aufsätze zur Krisentheorie* (Essays on Crisis Theory). Frankfurt am Main: Verlag Neue Kritik, 1971. Includes "Eine neue Theorie über Imperialismus...," pp. 113–64; "Die Änderung des ursprünglichen Aufbauplans...," pp. 9–42; "Die Wert-Preis-Transformation ...," pp. 45–74; "Die Goldproduktion im Reproduktionsschema von Marx und Rosa Luxemburg," pp. 77–109; and "The Evolutionist Revolt . . . ," pp. 167–213. Spanish edition: *Ensayos sobre la teoría de la crisis: Dialéctica y metodología en "El capital"* translated by Alfonso García Ruiz. México: Pasado y Presente, 1979; also includes the correspondence in "Briefe Henryk Grossmans an Paul Mattick über die Akkumulation".

Grossmann, Henryk. *Anarchismus, Bolschevismus, Sozialismus: Aufsätze aus dem Wörterbuch der Volkswirtschaft* (Anarchism, Bolshevism, Socialism: Essays from the Dictionary of Economics) (with Carl Grünberg). Edited by Claudio Pozzoli, Frankfurt am Main: Europäische Verlagsanstalt, 1971. Includes Grossmann's and Grünberg's contributions to *Wörterbuch der Volkswirtschaft* (asterisked [*] above).

Several of Grossman's important publications are available on-line in English at the Henryk Grossman Internet Archive, http://*www.marxists.org/archive/grossman*.

Reviews

Grossmann, Henryk. Review of Othmar Spann's *Die Haupttheorien der Volkswirtschaftslehre* 12. bis 15. Auflage (Principle theories of political economy) (Leipzig, 1923), *Archiv für die Geschichte des Sozialismus und der Arbeiterbewegung* 13 (1928): 341–44.

Grossmann, Henryk. Review of Maurice Bourgin's *Les systemes socialistes et l'évolution économique* (Socialist Systems and Economic Evolution), 3rd ed. (Paris, 1925), *Archiv für die Geschichte des Sozialismus und der Arbeiterbewegung* 13 (1928): 344–45.

Grossmann, Henryk. Review of Elie Halevy's *Sismondi* (Paris, 1925), *Zeitschrift für Sozialforschung* 3 (2) (1934): 291.

Grossmann, Henryk. Review of Robert Bordaz's *La loi de Marx sur les capitaux a la lumiere des événements contemporains* (Marx's Law of Capital in the Light of Contemporary Events) (Paris, 1933), *Zeitschrift für Sozialforschung* 3 (2) (1934): 314–15.

Grossmann, Henryk. Review of G. N. Clark's *Science and Social Welfare in the Age of Newton* (New York and London, 1937); and G. Sarton's *The History of Science and the New Humanism* (London, 1937), *Zeitschrift für Sozialforschung* 7 (1/2) (1938): 233–37. A section of this review, dealing with Boris Hessen, is translated in Gideon Freudenthal, "Introductory note" to "Controversy: The Emergence of Modern Science out of the Production Process," *Science in Context* 1 (1) (1987): 106–7.

Grossmann, Henryk. Review of Karl Marx and Friedrich Engels' *The Civil War in the United States* (New York, 1937), *Zeitschrift für Sozialforschung* 7 (1/2) (1938): 259–63.

Grossmann, Henryk. Review of F. Grandeau's *Theorie des Crises* (Crisis Theory) (Paris, 1937), *Zeitschrift für Sozialforschung* 8 (1/2) (1939): 300–301.

Grossmann, Henryk. Review of Cleona Lewis's *America's Stake in International Investments* (London, 1938), *Zeitschrift für Sozialforschung* 8 (1/2) (1939): 304–6.

Grossmann, Henryk. Review of Jürgen Kuczynski's *Hunger and Work* (New York and London, 1938), *Zeitschrift für Sozialforschung* 8 (1/2) (1939): 318–20.

Grossmann, Henryk. Review of L. P. Ayres' *Turning Points in Business Cycles* (New York, 1939), *Zeitschrift für Sozialforschung* (Studies in Philosophy and Social Science) 8 (3) (1939): 490–92.

Grossman, Henryk. Review of Joseph Schumpeter's *Business Cycles* (New York, 1939), *Studies in Philosophy and Social Science* 9 (1) (1941): 514–19.

Grossman, Henryk. Review of Salomon Fabricant and Julius Shirkin's *The Output of Manufacturing Industries 1899–1937* (New York, 1940), *Studies in Philosophy and Social Science* 9 (2) (1941): 352–54.

Grossman, Henryk. Review of Lynn Thorndike's *A History of Magic and Experimental Science* vols. 5 and 6 (New York, 1941), *Studies in Philosophy and Social Science* 9 (3) (1942): 514–19.

Published Correspondence

"Briefe Henryk Grossmans an Paul Mattick über die Akkumulation" (1931–1937). In Henryk Grossman. *Marx, die klassische Nationalökonomie und das Problem der Dynamik.* Frankfurt am Main: Europäische Verlagsanstalt, 1969, pp. 85–113.

"Briefe Henryk Grossmanns an Walter und Leni Braeuer (1947–1949)." In Jürgen Scheele. *Zwischen Zusammenbruchsprognose und Positivismusverdikt: Studien zur politischen und intellektuellen Biographie Henryk Grossmanns (1881–1950).* Frankfurt am Main: Lang, 1999, pp. 244–65.

Letters to and from Max Horkheimer and others. In Max Horkheimer. *Gesammelte Schiften,* Band 15: *Briefwechsel 1913–1936.* Frankfurt am Main: Fischer, 1995.

Letters to and from Max Horkheimer in Max Horkheimer. *Gesammelte Schiften,* Band 15: *Briefwechsel 1937–1940.* Frankfurt am Main: Fischer, 1995.

Letters to and from Max Horkheimer and others. In Max Horkheimer. *Gesammelte Schiften,* Band 16: *Briefwechsel 1941–1948.* Frankfurt am Main: Fischer, 1996.

Translations

"Die Internationale und der Weltkrieg: 6. Die polnische Sozialdemokratie." Translations from Polish into German of three reports from *Naprzód* of August 2, 1914, August 7, 1914, and August 17, 1914, in *Archiv für die Geschichte des Sozialismus und der Arbeiterbewegung* 6 (1916): 479–87.

Journals which Grossman edited

Promień (The Ray). Grossman headed the sub-branch of the editorial board in Kraków, established December 16, 1903, until late 1904.

Der sotsial-demokrat (The Social-democrat), Kraków. Grossman was the responsible editor and and publisher from October 1905 until October 1906.

Zjednoczenie (Unification). In 1905 Grossman was the editor and publisher of the initial double number, 1–2, of this magazine, which was the organ of the Związek Młodzieży Socjalistycnej (Union of Socialist Youth).

Archives

Australia

National Library of Australia, Canberra
Christina Stead Collection MS 4967.
Heather Rowley Collection MS 9244.

Austria

Archiv der Bundespolizeidirektion, Wien
    Jahrbuch der Sozialdemokratischen und Anarchistischen Bewegung des Jahres 1901 to 1918 C 1021.
Israelitische Kultusgemeinde Wien, Matrikelamt
    Kurz Birth certificate, 385/1885.
    Grossmann Marriage certificate, 341/I/1908.
    Stanislaus Eugen Grossmann Birth certificate, 691/1914.
Österreichisches Staatsarchiv, Kriegsarchiv, Wien (ÖSK)
    Dr. Heinrich Grossmann
        Vermerkblatt für die Qualifikationsbeschreibung, Quall. Kart. 874.
        Abt 10KW: Personalblatt, k. u. k. Kreigsministerium.
        1916 1. Abt. 45–1/468, k. u. k. Kreigsministerium.
        1917 1. Abt. 92–1026, k. u. k. Kreigsministerium.
        Präsidialbüro 1918 5–16/12–2, k. u. k. Kreigsministerium.
    Dr. Oskar Kurz
        Landsturmevidenzblatt (mit Beilage), Grundbuchsblätter Wien 1885.
        Personalnachweis, Grundbuchsblätter Wien 1885.
    Verein für Geschichte der Arbeiterbewegung, Wien
        Letter from Grossman in Kraków to Viktor Adler, October 23, 1905, Adler-Archiv, Mappe 176.
        Alte partei Archiv, Sitzungsprotokolle, Parteivertretung, Exekutive Handprotokolle 12.1.1905 bis 16.8.1905 Heft 3.

Germany

Archiv der sozialen Demokratie der Friedrich-Ebert-Stiftung, Bonn
    Alfred Henke Nachlaß, Declaration by Henryk Grossmann on the Radek Affair, September 17, 1912.
    Max Beer Nachlaß, Box 1, letters from Henryk Grossman to Max Beer, January 19, 1935 and May 25, 1935 (Beer Collection).
Bundesarchiv Berlin
    Albert Schreiner Nachlaß, NY 4198/70, Stiftung Archiv der Parteien und Massenorganisationen der DDR (Schreiner Collection).
    Reichsicherheitshauptamt Abteilung IV, R58, 3443a.

Reichssicherheitshauptamt Abteilung IV, R59, 3443 I.
Germanisches Nationalmuseum, Nürnberg
  Letter from Henryk Grossman to Max Raphael, September 7, 1941, Max Raphael Nachlaß I, C-210.
Institut für Zeitgeschichte, Archiv, München
  "The collapse of German democracy and the expansion of National Socialism: a research project of the Institute of Social Research," September 15, 1940, pp. 38, 43, 66, MS 175.
Johann-Heinrich von Thünen Museum, Tellow, Mecklenburg-Vorpommern
  Braeuer Nachlaß (Braeuer Collection).
Johann Wolfgang Goethe Universität, Frankfurt am Main, Archiv.
  "Grossmann, Heinrich 1927–1967," Akten des Rektors Abt 1 Nr 15.
  "Grossmann, Heinrich," Akten der WiSo Fakultät," Sig 452 Abt 150 Nr 376 (UFM).
  "Grünberg, Carl," Akten der WiSo FAK, Sig 452 Abt.150 Nr 376.
Lange, Karl Heinz, Leipzig, private possession
  Letter from Henryk Grossman to Heinz Lange November 17, 1949, copy held by Rick Kuhn.
Leo-Löwenthal-Archiv, Universitäts- und Stadtarchiv Frankfurt am Main (LLA)
  A 325.
Max-Horkheimer-Archiv, Universitäts- und Stadtarchiv Frankfurt am Main (MHA)
  IV 10.1–94, VI 9, VI 10, IX 58, IX 59.3.
Sächsisches Staatsarchiv Leipzig (SSAL)
  VdN-Akte von Henryk Großmann 13630, Bezirksrat Leipzig, 20237.
Universitätsarchiv Leipzig (UAL)
  "Henryk Grossmann," PA 40.

Netherlands

Internationaal Instituut voor Sociale Geschiedenis, Amsterdam
  Mattick Collection, (IISG)

Poland

Archiwum Akt Nowych, Warszawa
  "Sprawa Grossmana" sygn 305/V/11 podt. 3, Archiwum Londyńskie Polskiej Partii Socjalistycznej (Sprawa Grossmana).
Archiwum Państwowe w Krakowie, Kraków (APK)
  Spisy Ludnosci Miasta Krakowa, r. 1900: Grossman; Kurz, Oskar and Markus.
  Akta metrykalne Izraelitow w Krakowie.
  Księgę protokolow z zebran PPS-D.
  Starostwo Grodzkie Krakowskie, Dyrekcja Policji, akta dot. ruchu rob. 1908–1918, m. in. Sprawozdanie Kom. Wykon. ZPSD za czs od 1 VI 1908 do 30 IX 1911 r. na VI Kongres ZPSD w X 1911 r., 27.
  Starostwo Grodzkie Krakowskie, Zalozenie i dzialalnsc zydowskiej partii socjalno-demokratiycznej 'separatystów' in Galicji w 1905 r., 80.

Starostwo Grodzkie Krakowskie, Relacja z zebrani mlodziezy akademicki, 283.
Glowny Urzad Statystyczny, Centralna Biblioteka Statystyczna, Warszawa (GUS)
   Akta Osobowe Henryka Grossman.a
Polskiej Akademii Nauk, Archiwum, Warszawa
   Henryk Grossman, III-155, due to ongoing reorganization and recataloguing, refer-
   ences to this collection may have been superseded (APAN)
   Rafał Taubenschlag, III-98 (Taubenschlag Collection)
Uniwersytetu Jagiellońskiego, Archiwum, Kraków (AUJ)
   Chaskel Grossman(n) Winter Semester 1900/1901 to Summer Semester 1903/1904,
   503 to 510, S II.
   J. Rotter and K. Subecki "Protokol r wiecu ogólno-akadem. odbytego dniu 28
   November 1901 w Coll. Novum w Krakowie," Wiece opolakademickie, SII 738.
   Liber Promotionum Universitas Jagellonicae Ab Anno 1893, Nr 3407, S II 520.
   Liber Rigorosum C. R. Facultatis Juridico Politicae, WP II 524
Urzad Stanu Cywilnego, Kraków

United Kingdom

Bodleian Library, Department of Western Manuscripts, Oxford
   Society for the Protection of Science and Learning/Academic Asistance Council
   Files, (SPSL)

United States of America

Federal Bureau of Investigations, Washington
   Henryk Grossman file, (FBI file).
Immigration and Naturalization Service, Washington
   Henryk Grossman, Alien Registration Form, October 31, 1941.
   Henryk Grossman, Report of Departure of Alien, 1949.
YIVO Institute for Jewish Research Archive, New York
   Bund Archive (Bund Archive)
      MG2 F107, MG2 F130, MG7 F29.

Interviews and personal communications

Abramsky, Chimen letter to Rick Kuhn January 12, 1996, met Grossman in New York in
   December 1948.
Bajkowski, Eugene personal communication to Rick Kuhn, February 29, 2000 in
   Canberra, a friend of Grossman's Warsaw lawyer Janusz Buki, in Shanghai in
   1948–1952.
Kowalik, Tadeusz interview, with Rick Kuhn, July 12, 1995, in Warsaw, had discussions
   with Oscar Lange and Oskar Kurz.
Lange, Karl-Heinz "Versuch einer Erinnerung an Henryk Grossmann" October 2002, a
   former student of Grossman in Leipzig, held by Rick Kuhn.

Mattick, Ilse telephone interview, with Rick Kuhn November 24, 1993, Boston/Vermont, knew Grossman in the late 1930s and early 1940s.

Scheele, Jürgen personal communication to Rick Kuhn, December 7, 1993 in Frankfurt am Main, had discussions with Walter Braeuer.

Photographs

Landes-Zeitung. Rostock, March 16, 1949.

Tägliche Rundschau. Berlin, Deutschland Ausgabe, March, 10 1949.

Henryk Großmann, VdN-Akte 13630, Bezirksrat Leipzig 20237, Sächsisches Staatsarchiv Leipzig.

PO 2195, YIVO Institute for Jewish Research Archive, New York.

Index

RICK KUHN, both an academic and a political activist, is a reader in political science at the Australian National University. His publications include *Class and Struggle in Australia*, articles on contemporary Australian, German and Austrian political economy and Australian labour history. Since the mid-1970s, Rick Kuhn has been an activist in his union, Socialist Alternative and its predecessors, and a range of social movements. He was the convenor of the anti-war coalition in Canberra before and during the 2003 invasion of Iraq. His web site is www.anu.edu.au/polsci/rick.

The University of Illinois Press
is a founding member of the
Association of American University Presses.

Composed in 10.5/13 Minion
with Meta display
by BookComp, Inc.
Manufactured by Thomson-Shore, Inc.

University of Illinois Press
1325 South Oak Street
Champaign, IL 61820-6903
www.press.uillinois.edu